ARCTIC LAW AND GOVERNANCE

The objective of this book is to identify similarities and differences between the positions of Finland (as an EU Member State) and China, on Arctic law and governance. The book compares Finnish and Chinese legal and policy stances in specific policy areas of relevance for the Arctic, including maritime sovereignty, scientific research, marine protected areas, the Svalbard Treaty and Arctic Council co-operation. Building on these findings, the book offers general conclusions on Finnish and Chinese approaches to Arctic governance and international law, as well as new theoretical insights on Arctic governance.

The book is the result of a collaboration between The Northern Institute for Environmental and Minority Law (Arctic Centre, University of Lapland) and researchers from Wuhan University.

Arctic Law and Governance

The role of China, Finland and the EU

Edited by
Timo Koivurova, QIN Tianbao, Tapio Nykänen
and Sébastien Duyck

•HART•
OXFORD • LONDON • NEW YORK • NEW DELHI • SYDNEY

HART PUBLISHING
Bloomsbury Publishing Plc
Kemp House, Chawley Park, Cumnor Hill, Oxford, OX2 9PH, UK

HART PUBLISHING, the Hart/Stag logo, BLOOMSBURY and the Diana logo are trademarks of Bloomsbury Publishing Plc

First published in hardback, 2017
Paperback edition, 2019

A catalogue record for this book is available from the British Library.

Library of Congress Cataloging-in-Publication Data

Names: Koivurova, Timo.

Title: Arctic law and governance : the role of China, Finland, and the EU / edited by Timo Koivurova [and three others].

Description: Oxford [UK] ; Portland, Oregon : Hart Publishing, 2017. | Includes bibliographical references and index.

Identifiers: LCCN 2016045784 (print) | LCCN 2016046049 (ebook) | ISBN 9781849467025 (hardback) | ISBN 9781509911493 (Epub)

Subjects: LCSH: Jurisdiction, Territorial—Arctic regions. | Territorial waters—China. | China—Relations—Arctic regions. | Arctic regions—Relations—China. | Arctic regions—International status. | Arctic Council. | Territorial waters—Finland. | Finland—Relations—Arctic regions. | Arctic regions—Relations—Finland.

Classification: LCC KZ4110.C45 A73 2017 (print) | LCC KZ4110.C45 (ebook) | DDC 341.4/4091632—dc23

LC record available at https://lccn.loc.gov/2016045784

ISBN: HB: 978-1-84946-702-5
PB: 978-1-50993-009-8
ePDF: 978-1-50991-150-9
ePub: 978-1-50991-149-3

Typeset by Compuscript Ltd, Shannon

Foreword - China

The melting of the sea ice makes the Arctic more accessible, and enhances both its special geospatial attributes and its global value in terms of natural resources. On the other hand, economic globalisation is always a process of social development with historical significance that is closely connected to production and consumption in different parts of the world. As the Arctic plays a major role in the global environment and is the subject of conflicting interests, both inside and outside the region, the Arctic began to gain a more intimate connection with the other parts of the world, including economic, political, security and social connections, that promoted the Arctic's regional urbanisation, and attracted the attention of external countries as well.

The Arctic is a vast territory that has immense stretches of true wilderness and cities with long histories. Its land and water includes the territories of eight Arctic nations and millions of kilometres of global commons. The region could serve as an energy source in the future (or, from the perspective of climate change, could be considered as the northern hemisphere's green lung). It was also the theatre of competition between the US and Russia during the Cold War. It is such a complicated place that its regional affairs are mixed with global concerns.

China came across the Arctic on our way to the global market. With the influence of climate change and environmental protection, the exploration of new trade routes, the multiple sources of resources together with technology creation and international co-operation, the Arctic shows its potential necessity for China's sustainable development. And due to its rapid economic development, China also offers a wealth of accessible external resources to the Arctic for its regional development and environmental protection.

As a huge external country, China's presence in the Arctic has its own specificity, which could be defined as having four aspects. The first is China's adjacent character. China is the closest external country to the Arctic by land. China, as the world's largest market, has a strong connection with the Arctic, which is a resource-rich region. Even on the climatology side, China and the Arctic are strongly connected with each other through climate change and extreme weather. The second aspect is legitimacy, that is, China's activities in the Arctic will obey the international rules such as the United Nations Convention on the Law of the Sea. The third aspect is constructive activities, which means that China is willing and able to offer traffic infrastructure construction products and services to the Arctic society, and avoid environmental pollution as well. The fourth aspect concerns multilateral and bilateral co-operation. China is also willing to show our co-operative character in Arctic activities.

China has not published an Arctic Policy until now. The lack of knowledge about the Arctic may be one of the reasons. To China, the Arctic is an unfamiliar space with a special environment. Although we joined the Spitsbergen Treaty in the 1920s, we began to carry out scientific research in the area only 80 years later. Our first scientific investigation of the Arctic Ocean began in 1999, later than Germany and Japan, to name two other external countries. In addition to our own Arctic scientific efforts, we are also trying to catch up by strengthening scientific and technology cooperation. Promoting the communication of knowledge and experience is another way for China to gain a better understanding of the Arctic. To increase awareness, understanding and knowledge of the Arctic and its global impacts, the Polar Research Institute of China (PRIC) established the China-Nordic Arctic Research Center (CNARC) in Shanghai in 2013, together with institutes from five Nordic countries. Finland is one of the original sponsors of the Arctic Council and also plays a role as the promoter of regional governance, having an advantage in Arctic research and teleology in particular. Increasing our communications with each other will be a win-win situation for both China and Finland.

Zhang Xia
Head of Polar Strategic Studies Division, Polar Research Institute of China (PRIC)

Foreword - Finland

Finland is an Arctic country. A large proportion of its area lies above the Polar Circle, and it is the home country of one of the Arctic indigenous peoples, the Saami. Finland has no permanently ice-free ports, and consequently our Arctic marine technologies are highly developed. The same applies to many other skills and techniques needed for running a modern society in harsh climatic conditions. The vulnerability of the Arctic environment is well understood in Finland, and Finland is a leading nation in the development of energy saving and environmentally friendly solutions in industry, infrastructure and housing alike.

Finland has not been an Arctic littoral state since World War II. Nevertheless, Finland pays great attention to advancing sustainable development of the Arctic Ocean. Finland has played an active part in promoting Arctic cross-border co-operation, and was instrumental in the birth of the Arctic Council. The Arctic Council is the only international body directly involved in Arctic management. It has a unique organisational structure that enables representatives of the indigenous nations to sit at the same table with representatives of the Arctic states as permanent participants. Since the founding of the Arctic Council, Finland has contributed extensively to scientific research on various aspects of the Arctic, from flora and fauna to shipping.

Finland welcomes China to join Arctic co-operation. From the outset, Finland has supported China's inclusion as an observer to the Arctic Council. The Arctic Council benefits greatly from observers with resources for Arctic research that are ready to promote the Council's goals in co-operation with all the member states and permanent participants. This publication is a perfect example of the fruitful co-operation between Finland and China, and serves to highlight the Arctic expertise available in both countries.

China is understandably interested in the economic resources that the Arctic regions have to offer both now and in the future. Prospects for the opening of new shipping lanes as well as the exploitation of fisheries and hydrocarbon reserves in the Arctic are all-important for a large nation from the viewpoint of the security of supply. While oil and gas remain in the focus of public attention in regard to the natural resources of the Arctic, it is to be hoped that China will seek to develop more forward-looking economic co-operation in the Arctic, and join the efforts to reduce the world's hydrocarbon dependency.

It is also the common hope of the Arctic inhabitants that China will show genuine dedication to the protection of the Arctic environment. The effects of climate change are amplified in the polar regions, and one additional factor contributing to the warming of the Arctic is soot fallout, which decreases the albedo of snow and ice, causing them to melt faster. Soot fallout originates from coal-burning factories and power plants, as well as biomass burning and diesel engines, situated much further south, including China. China is already making great advances in increasing renewable energy production, which is a most welcome development from both a global and Arctic perspective.

The Arctic is neither a cornucopia of natural resources nor a nature preserve. It is the home of the Arctic peoples, including the indigenous populations whose livelihoods are directly dependent on the wellbeing of the Arctic ecosystem. The Arctic needs development, but that development must be sustainable and conditioned by scientific research. China's involvement in efforts to promote sustainable development and protection of the nature in the Arctic holds great promise to all the inhabitants of the region.

Jyrki Kallio
Senior Research Fellow at the Finnish Institute of International Affairs
Formerly Finland's Senior Arctic Official (2008–09)

Preface

This volume is the final outcome of a bi-national project conducted throughout 2014 to compare Finnish (or EU, where relevant) and Chinese perspectives on specific aspects of Arctic governance. The project, which was enabled by a grant provided by the Academy of Finland, brought together a diverse team of researchers from the Northern Institute for Environmental and Minority Law (Arctic Centre/University of Lapland, Finland) and from the Research Institute for Environmental Law (RIEL), Wuhan University (China).

The main objective of the project was to identify similarities, differences and divergences between the positions of China and Finland (and the European Union due to Finland's membership) on current and future Arctic law and governance. As non-coastal states are expected to take a greater interest in the Arctic and increase their activities in the region as a result of globalisation and climate change, understanding the positions and expectations of such actors is crucial to better anticipate trends likely to contribute to the future of Arctic governance.

During the course of the project, the authors of the contributions included in this book took part in academic events gathering both Chinese and Finnish groups of researchers. First, a joint workshop was hosted by the Arctic Centre in spring 2014 to explore some of the points of convergence or divergence between the perspectives of Finnish and Chinese scholars on the role and status of Finland (or the EU) and China in the Arctic. A seminar was then organised by RIEL/Wuhan University in autumn 2014 in order to provide the authors with the opportunity to present the first versions of their chapters and benefit from the feedback of their peers. A peer-review process was organised to ensure that the revised versions of the contributions to this volume could benefit from the feedback of researchers representing a different academic perspective.

Additionally, the project also benefited from further interactions on these issues during Dr Tapio Nykänen's and Sébastien Duyck's research visits at Wuhan University's Research Institute for Environmental Law, Prof Koivurova's visiting professorship at Beijing University and Dr Hasanat's post-doctoral fellowship at the China-Nordic Arctic Research Centre of the School of Law and Political Science at the Ocean University of China.

This volume is not intended as a textbook exploring all legal and political issues relevant to the study of the presence of China in the Arctic region. Instead, it is somewhat of a kaleidoscope, offering different perspectives on several specific aspects that underline this broader question. Rather than seeking comprehensiveness and coherence between the articles included in this volume, we have preferred to give each of our authors the freedom to reflect on her or his own research findings and to contribute to the rich academic conversation on Arctic governance with a unique approach to highlighting the linkages between the perspectives of two players that are expected to continue to play important roles in the Arctic.

We are grateful to the Academy of Finland for having enabled our institutes to study this captivating topic in more depth as well as for having enabled our institutions to grow closer academic links with each other. We are also thankful to all the authors of this volume for setting some time aside from their own research agendas in order to engage in this academic conversation and share their analysis in this book. Our gratitude also extends to our colleagues at the University of Lapland and Wuhan University who supported us with various aspects of the project. The editors are thankful to Zhang Xia, Head of Polar Strategic Studies Division, Polar Research Institute of China, and to Jyrki Kallio, Senior Research Fellow at the Finnish Institute of International Affairs and former Senior Arctic Official to the Arctic Council of Finland, for their opening words introducing the subject matter covered by this book. Finally, our appreciation goes to our language reviewer Zoë Chandler, of Inkling Oy, who provided us with valuable support during the final stage of this project.

Bern, Rovaniemi, Wuhan, June 2015

Contents

Biographies

Sébastien Duyck is a visiting researcher at the Northern Institute for Environmental and Minority Law, University of Lapland (Finland) and a research fellow at the World Trade Institute, University of Bern (Switzerland). Sébastien's research focuses on the integration of human rights in international environmental governance and on issues related to Arctic marine governance. Sébastien has written academic papers and book chapters on Arctic governance including in relation to the role of non-state actors in polar governance, the relevance of the UN Framework Convention on Climate Change in the region and the relevance of some principles of the Antarctic Treaty System to the Arctic. Sébastien has conducted research consultancies on Arctic governance for the European Parliament and for the Nature Resources Defense Council (NRDC) and on climate governance for the Mary Robinson Foundation for Climate Justice, the CGIAR Research Program on Climate Change, Adaptation and Food Security (CCAFS) and for Carbon Market Watch.

Piotr Graczyk is a PhD Candidate and Research Fellow at the UiT The Arctic University of Norway in Tromsø, Norway. His research interests include roles of the Arctic Council in Arctic governance, Norwegian foreign policy in the region and engagement of non-Arctic actors in the Arctic. Piotr's doctoral project focuses on the institutional impact on member states' policies and interests, where he looks at the Arctic Council's role in shaping an Arctic shipping regime. Piotr has gained experience and expertise in Arctic affairs, among others, during his work as a policy assistant (internship) at the Arctic Council Secretariat in Tromsø (2008–09) and frequent membership of Polish observer delegations to the Arctic Council's meetings as an adviser to the Polish Ministry of Foreign Affairs. He is a member of the Flagship Arctic Ocean at the Fram Centre in Tromsø and NRF-UArctic Thematic Network on Geopolitics and Security. He authored and co-authored several peer-reviewed journal articles that were published, among others, in *Polar Record* and *the Yearbook of Polar Law*, as well as book chapters. Piotr is also involved in the development of the Model Arctic Council course under the auspices of the University of the Arctic. He holds an MA in international relations with a major in security and strategic studies from the University of Warsaw.

Waliul Hasanat, LLD, is an Associate Professor of Law at the University of Rajshahi where he has been teaching since 1996 (on leave of absence); he is presently working as a researcher at the Northern Institute for Environmental and Minority Law at the Arctic Centre of the University of Lapland since 2005. He did his Doctor of Laws at the Faculty of Law at the University of Lapland on the subject of the Arctic Council. He has published a number of articles on various Arctic issues in well-known international peer reviewed journals, and several books with an emphasis on governance. He is a co-editor of *Current Developments in Arctic Law*, and served as special editor of the fourth volume of the Yearbook of Polar Law. His main research interests include public international law, international soft law, soft law forms of co-operation, the Arctic Council, the Barents co-operation, the Northern Forum, climate change in the Arctic, Arctic law and governance, environmental protection, regional climate policy, changes in the Circumpolar North and sustainable development and the protection of minorities. He is a postdoctorate fellow of the China-Nordic Arctic Research Centre to the School of Law and Political Science at the Ocean University of China.

Dr **Lassi Heininen** is a Professor of Arctic Politics at the Faculty of Social Sciences, University of Lapland, and Adjunct Professor (Docent) of Northern Geopolitics at University of Oulu, Finland. He is also Visiting Professor at the University of Akureyri, Iceland, and Trent University, Canada, and serves as the Leader of the UArctic-NRF Thematic Network on Geopolitics and Security Studies. Professor Heininen teaches and lectures regularly abroad and supervises PhD students from Finland and other Arctic countries. His research fields include International Relations, Geopolitics, Security Studies, Environmental Politics, Russian Studies, Northern and Arctic Studies and Political History. He is the author of more than 200 scientific publications, and the Editor of *the Arctic Yearbook*, a peer-reviewed online international publication (see: www.arcticyearbook.com). His recent publications include *Security and Sovereignty in the North Atlantic* (ed) from Palgrave Pivot (2014); 'Northern Geopolitics: Actors, Interests and Processes in the Circumpolar Arctic' in *Polar Geopolitics* (2014); 'Finland as an Arctic and European State' in *International Relations and the Arctic* (Cambria Press, 2014); 'Arctic Security—New Challenges and Global Problems' in *The Yearbook of Polar Law* 2013, Volume 5; 'Arctic Strategies and Policies—Inventory and Comparative Study' (Northern Research Forum, 2011). Prof Heininen is actively involved in speaking at international scientific conferences, seminars and workshops, as well as at gatherings implementing the interplay between science and politics.

Dr **Kamrul Hossain** is an Adjunct Professor of International Law at the University of Lapland and the Director of the Northern Institute for Environmental and Minority Law (NIEM) of the Arctic Centre at the University of Lapland. Dr Hossain has played key roles in the preparation of a number of research projects, and has co-ordinated a number of research projects including the EU-funded project, 'Understanding and

Strengthening European Union-Canada Relations in Law of the Sea and Ocean Governance'. Dr Hossain has published a good number of scholarly articles in high-quality international journals. He served as the Special Editor for Volume 3 of *the Yearbook of Polar Law* published in 2011. He regularly teaches at the University of Lapland, and periodically at other foreign universities. He completed visiting fellowships at a number of foreign universities including the University of Toronto in Canada, Scott Polar Research Institute of the University of Cambridge in the UK and Muroran Institute of Technology in Japan. He has received a number of prestigious awards including the SYLFF Fellowship at the University of Helsinki. In 2012, Dr Hossain was awarded a Faculty Research Fellowship by the Canadian Department of Foreign Affairs and International Trade (DFAIT).

Ms **Julia Jalo,** Master of Law, graduated in 2014 from Renmin University of China Contemporary China Studies Program. Her scientific background is in Political Science and she has had a China focus in her studies since the 1990s. She has attended Fudan University's Doing Business in China course, pursued two years of language studies at Beijing Foreign Studies University as well as attended Renmin University's Summer School's course Understanding Energy in China. She has worked in the European Union 7th framework project Integrating and Developing European Asia Studies and recently in a semi-governmental Finnish project 'Pure Finland' in Beijing, bringing together China-related private and public sector actors. Julia has lived in China for five years and speaks fluent Mandarin. Julia's thesis contributed to the project 'Arctic Law and Governance in People's Republic of China and in Finland'. Currently she is working in China.

Dr **Xiaoyi Jiang** is currently an Associate Professor of Environmental Law at the Wuhan University China Institute of Boundary and Ocean Studies (CIBOS), China. She holds a PhD on the topic of legal issues for implementing the Clean Development Mechanism from the University of Western Sydney Australia. Her research and publications emphasise climate change issues and maritime sovereignty and rights issues. Her doctoral research was published by Springer in 2012. In addition, Xiaoyi has successfully been awarded funding for over 10 competitive research projects since completing her PhD thesis and has published over 20 journal articles, book chapters and reports. Since joining the CIBOS in 2010, which is supported by Ministry of Foreign Affairs of the People's Republic of China, she has also given her time to teach the course of International Environmental Law for graduate students.

Research Professor **Timo Koivurova** is the Director of the Arctic Centre, University of Lapland. Professor Koivurova is also a Docent at two Finnish universities. He worked as a Visiting Professor of International Law at the University of New South Wales, Australia (2011). He had a Visiting

Professorship at Beijing University, China (2014), which was connected to a project on Arctic law and governance in China and Finland funded by the Finnish Academy. Increasingly, his research addresses the interplay between environmental law, legal status of indigenous peoples, law of the sea in the Arctic waters, the role of law in adapting to climate change and the function and role of the Arctic Council. He has published on the above-mentioned topics extensively. Professor Koivurova is the International Law expert for an official publication on Finnish law and an editor-in-chief in *the Yearbook of Polar Law* (Brill) together with Professor Gudmundur Alfredsson and an editor of *the Nordic Journal of International Law*, *Nordic Journal of Environmental Law* as well as *the Arctic Review of Law and Politics*. He contributed to the legal chapter in the Arctic Council's Arctic Human Development Report. Professor Koivurova is the chair of the University of the Arctic's Arctic Law Thematic Network and a board member in the Arctic Research Consortium of the United States (ARCUS) and in the Arctic Circle initiated by Iceland's President. Professor Koivurova is a member of the Nordic Research Network for Sami and Environmental Law (NORSEL) and the IUCN's Commission on Environmental Law (CEL). He was nominated for co-chair of the International Law Association ILA Committee on indigenous peoples' land rights in 2014.

Tuuli Kuusama is a Master's student at the University of Lapland. She will graduate from the University of Lapland majoring in International Relations. In her Master's thesis she will focus on China's involvement in the Arctic Council's work. The topic of her Bachelor's thesis dealt with the evolving Arctic policies of the European Union. Prior to moving to Lapland Mrs Tanninen studied Nordic and German languages and political science at the University of Helsinki. Mrs Tanninen has been active in many organisations including the 'Social Science Professionals' and its Student Board.

LI MiaoMiao obtained the Master's degree in Environmental law in Wuhan University in 2016. Currently, she is a practising lawyer in Dentons Law Office (Shenzhen Branch) focusing on foreign investment and corporate compliance. In 2011, she worked at the Intermediate People's Court in Kunming as an intern and voluntarily helped at the Street Children Relief Center in Chongqing. Furthermore, she attended a seven-month training programme at Mekong School of Earthrights International in Thailand. Currently, her research concentrates on the environmental and social responsibility of Chinese overseas investment in Cambodian dams.

Dr **Nengye Liu** is a Senior Lecturer, School of Law, University of New England, Australia. He has a Doctor of Law from the Department of Public International Law, Ghent University, Belgium. Prior to moving to Dundee, he was a 'Future Ocean' Research Associate at the Walther-Schücking-Institute for International Law, University of Kiel, Germany. He also has a bachelor and a master of law from Wuhan University, China. Dr Nengye Liu has published widely in the fields of international law of the sea and international environmental law (eg *Ocean Development and International Law*, *Journal of Maritime Law and Commerce*, *Heidelberg Journal of International Law*, *International Journal of Marine and Coastal Law*, *Ocean Yearbook*, *Journal of International Maritime Law*, *Yearbook of Polar Law* and *Asia Pacific Journal of Environmental Law*). He serves as Associate Editor of *the Yearbook of International Environmental Law* (Oxford) and reviewer for various journals. Dr Liu has been invited to present his research results in nearly 20 countries across five continents.

Tapio Nykänen is a doctor in social sciences and University Lecturer in Political Science at the University of Lapland. He specialises in political theory, religion and politics, politics of the Arctic region and culture of the indigenous Saami people.

Dr **QIN Tianbao** is a Luojia Professor of Law, Associate Dean for the School of Law and Director of the Research Institute of Environmental Law (RIEL), Professor of the National Center for Collaborative Innovation on Territorial Sovereignty and Maritime Rights, the China Institute of Boundary and Ocean Studies, Wuhan University. He is a Legislative Expert for China's Ministry of Environmental Protection and Ministry of Agriculture, and Hubei Provincial Parliament, an Adviser to the Chinese Delegation on negotiations on biodiversity, climate change and law of the sea issues, and an environmental law expert for several projects of International Financial Institutions in China. Dr Qin is the Secretary-General of the Chinese Society of Environment and Resources Law (CSERL), a member of the Commission on Environmental Law and Commission on Ecosystem Management of the IUCN, a member of the Governing Board of the IUCN Academy of Environmental Law and a member of the Committee on the Legal Principles relating to Climate Change of the International Law Association. Currently, his research focuses on the areas of laws and policies concerning climate change, energy security, biotechnology and biodiversity, water and ocean and trans-boundary environmental issues. Professor Qin is the author of several books and more than 60 articles in these fields.

Ren Shidan has held the position of associate professor at Southwest University of Political Science & Law in China since 1 July 2011. She defended her PhD on environmental law at Wuhan University in China in 2011. Ren Shidan focuses on different topics of environmental law, with an emphasis on the relationship between the environment and poverty from a law perspective. Since 2013, her research has had a specific focus on legal issues in China's activities in the Arctic region.

Adam Stepien is a researcher at the Arctic Centre at the University of Lapland, Finland. He is generally interested in how external actors and global discourses affect the Arctic region. As a doctoral candidate at the Faculty of Social Sciences at the University of Lapland, Adam Stepien works on interconnections between the Arctic and the realm of development assistance, with emphasis on the role of identity and experiential knowledge. As a researcher at the Arctic Centre, he focuses on Arctic governance, sociocultural changes and Arctic indigenous politics. He has dedicated much attention to the EU-Arctic nexus in the light of these diverse perspectives. He has taken part in a number of projects dealing with the EU's role in the Arctic, including most recently working on the 'Strategic Environmental Impact Assessment of development of the Arctic' report. Adam Stepien is a member of the ARKTIS Doctoral Programme and teaches a course in 'Arctic Politics and Law' at the University of Lapland.

Xiaoguang Zhou is currently a PhD. candidate at Law School of Wuhan University. He is awarded a Chinese Postgraduate Award to pursue his higher degree research. He got his LLB and LLM from Wuhan University. He is a member of the Chinese Environmental Law Research Association. His research focuses on national and international climate change law and international dispute settlement. Since 2012, he has published on issues of climate change and international dispute settlement in Chinese journals.

1

Introduction

TIMO KOIVUROVA, QIN TIANBAO,
SÉBASTIEN DUYCK AND TAPIO NYKÄNEN

THE AIM OF this book is to contribute to a better and deeper understanding of China's current and potential role in the Arctic and its approach to Arctic affairs. Furthermore, the authors examine the national and international context of Chinese legal and political stances relevant for the developments currently taking place in the region. The focus here is on the participation in Arctic governance from the perspective of relevant legal instruments and policy forums.

These overarching objectives are discussed by comparing China's multifaceted presence in the Arctic to Finland and the European Union, as both polities are highly appropriate points of reference. China is a relative newcomer to Arctic affairs and its interests are largely focused on maritime issues. Finland also does not belong to the exclusive club of Arctic Ocean coastal states, but at the same time it is a seasoned Arctic actor equipped with experience and sensitivity in the realm of Arctic regional politics. In contrast to Finland, but similarly to China, the EU is a relative novice as regards Arctic affairs and acts as an observer in the Arctic Council—the primary intergovernmental forum for discussing circumpolar questions. However, due to resistance from some Arctic actors and problems in acquiring official observer status in the Arctic Council, the EU has more than any other 'external actor' attempted to highlight and enhance its responsible approach, engagement and contribution to Arctic governance. It is hoped that such a comparative approach founded on the identification of similarities, differences and divergences supports a more balanced and substance-based analysis of China's Arctic engagement. This is especially important as the public discourse on the topic is often based on stereotypes and unsubstantiated simplifications. The comparison highlights opportunities for external actors to participate productively in Arctic governance, and reveals constraints, challenges and possibilities faced by these international players. The following chapters examine how China's Arctic activities, policies and relevant laws are currently developing.

This book is an exercise in bridging disciplines—law, political science, international relations and policy research. It is also a dialogue between Chinese and Nordic academic cultures. The authors believe that the transdisciplinary and culturally diverse character of this publication (and of the project, of which it is a result) sheds new light on Arctic issues, making it particularly interesting for readers interested both in the role of China in international relations and international law and in the developments within Arctic governance.

I. WHY THE ARCTIC?

Considerable attention has been dedicated to the consequences of climate change in the Arctic. As numerous scientific studies have shown, the region has been warming approximately twice as fast as the global average.[1] This will have overwhelming repercussions for the region's ecosystems and render its economic potential more accessible. The retreat of the sea ice in the Arctic Ocean and other changes open up the region to economic development, including the utilisation of navigational waterways, primarily the Northern Sea Route,[2] new fishing grounds (which involves numerous uncertainties) and—in a more limited and indirect manner—the exploitation of oil, gas and minerals.[3]

It is therefore no surprise that research on Arctic governance has increased a great deal after the year 2007, which was marked by dramatic sea ice loss and the planting of the Russian flag at the North Pole on Lomonosov ridge, triggering concerns over possible tensions or a scramble between

[1] Arctic Climate Impact Assessment (ACIA), *Scientific Report* (Cambridge, Cambridge University Press, 2005) available at www.acia.uaf.edu; Intergovernmental Panel on Climate Change, TF Stocker et al (eds), *Climate Change 2013: The Physical Science Basis.* Contribution of Working Group I to the Fifth Assessment Report of the Intergovernmental Panel on Climate Change (Cambridge, Cambridge University Press, 2013).

[2] T Scovazzi, 'Legal Issues Relating to Navigation Through Arctic Waters' (2009) 1(1) *The Yearbook of Polar Law* 371; OR Young, 'Whither the Arctic? Conflict or Cooperation in the Circumpolar North' (2009) 45(1) *Polar Record* 73; M Blunden, 'Geopolitics and the Northern Sea Route' (2012) 88(1) *International Affairs* 115; M Liu and J Kronbak, 'The Potential Economic Viability of Using the Northern Sea Route (NSR) as an Alternative Route between Asia and Europe' (2010) 18(3) *Journal of Transport Geography* 434; DL Gautier et al, 'Assessment of Undiscovered Oil and Gas in the Arctic' (2009) 324 *Science* 1175; Arctic Monitoring and Assessment Programme (AMAP), *Arctic Oil and Gas 2007* (Oslo, AMAP, 2008); J Dittmer, S Moisio, A Ingram and K Dodds, 'Have you Heard the one about the Disappearing Ice? Recasting Arctic Geopolitics' (2012) 30(4) *Political Geography* 202.

[3] The Arctic holds up to 13% and 30% of world oil and gas reserves respectively, according to statistical probability data compiled by the US Geological Survey, DL Gautier et al, 'Circum-Arctic Resource Appraisal: Estimates of Undiscovered Oil and Gas North of the Arctic Circle' (2008) 3049 *US Geological Survey Fact Sheet.*

Arctic states or among business actors and northern communities.[4] For instance, a number of studies focuses on the role and functioning of the Arctic Council[5] or the Barents Euro-Arctic Council.[6] Recently, research on the role and activities of the new Arctic actors—both governmental (the EU, China, India, Brazil, Japan, Korea) and non-governmental (NGOs and multinational companies) has also been growing.[7]

From the viewpoint of governance—both legal and political—the changing Arctic is a very complex setting. The security situation in the region has significantly altered since the Cold War, when it served as a strategic theatre of two superpowers.[8] Nowadays, five Arctic coastal states—which are partly composed of autonomous and self-governing entities, like Greenland, Nunavut, Sahka Republic or Alaska—together with three further states with territories located above the Arctic Circle (Finland, Iceland and Sweden) constitute the membership of the Arctic Council. This high-level intergovernmental forum—to which much attention is given in this volume (primarily in Chapter 2 by Qin and Li, and Chapter 6 by Koivurova et al)—is a soft law body, in which Arctic indigenous peoples' organisations are also permanent participants. The work of the Council has been focused on producing scientific assessments and developing recommendations. Only recently have the Arctic states started to develop Arctic-specific legally binding agreements under the auspices of the Council: the Search and Rescue Agreement was signed by the eight states in 2011 and an agreement on marine oil pollution response was adopted during the Kiruna ministerial meeting in May 2013.[9] At its 2011 ministerial meeting, the Council's institutional organisation was also strengthened with the establishment of a permanent secretariat.

[4] T Koivurova, 'Power Politics or Orderly Development? Why Are States "Claiming" Large Areas of the Arctic Seabed?' in SR Silverburg (ed), *International Law Contemporary Issues and Future Developments* (Boulder, Westview Press, 2011); Young, 'Whither the Arctic' (n 2).

[5] See eg T Koivurova and DL VanderZwaag, 'The Arctic Council at 10 Years: Retrospect and Prospects' (2007) 40(1) *University of British Columbia Law Review* 121–94.

[6] W Hasanat, 'Cooperation in the Barents Euro-Arctic Region in the Light of International Law' (2010) 2 *Yearbook of Polar Law* 279, N Sellheim, 'Problem-Solving Capabilities, Goal-Attainment and Effectiveness of the Barents Environmental Cooperation' (2012) 4 *The Yearbook of Polar Law* 519.

[7] Y Kim and S Blank, 'The Arctic: A New Issue on Asia's Security Agenda' (2011) 23(3) *The Korean Journal of Defense Analysis* 303. A great deal of academic effort has been directed towards clarifying the EU's Arctic ambitions, including the legal research on EU's legal competences relevant to the Arctic; see eg T Koivurova, K Kokko, S Duyck, N Sellheim and A Stepien, 'The Present and Future Competence of the European Union in the Arctic' (2012) 48(4) *Polar Record* 361; A Stępień, T Koivurova and P Kankaanpää (eds), *The Changing Arctic and the European Union* (Leiden, Brill/Nijhoff, 2016).

[8] L Heininen and C Southcott (eds), *Globalization and the Circumpolar North* (Fairbanks, University of Alaska Press, 2010).

[9] SM Kao, NS Pearre and J Firestone, 'Adoption of the Arctic Search and Rescue Agreement: A Shift of the Arctic Regime Toward a Hard Law Basis?' (2012) 36 *Marine Policy* 832.

Moreover, the Council has attracted an increasing number of states and other actors interested in becoming observers to the Council. While observership provides only limited opportunities to participate in the work of the Council, many see this status as a symbolic acknowledgement of justified Arctic interests.[10] Responding to this growing interest, the Arctic states and the permanent participants have recently adopted more elaborated criteria and requirements applying to the current and prospective observers.[11] During the 2013 ministerial meeting, several countries were accepted as observers, opening for the first time this status to Asian countries (besides Italy, China, India, Japan, Singapore and South Korea were also accepted).[12] The European Union's application for observer status was not formally approved in 2013, mainly because of Canadian and Inuit criticism of the EU's ban on seal products, but the EU has become a so-called 'observer in principle', enjoying all the privileges of observers apart from official status (for more information, see Stepien and Koivurova et al in this volume).

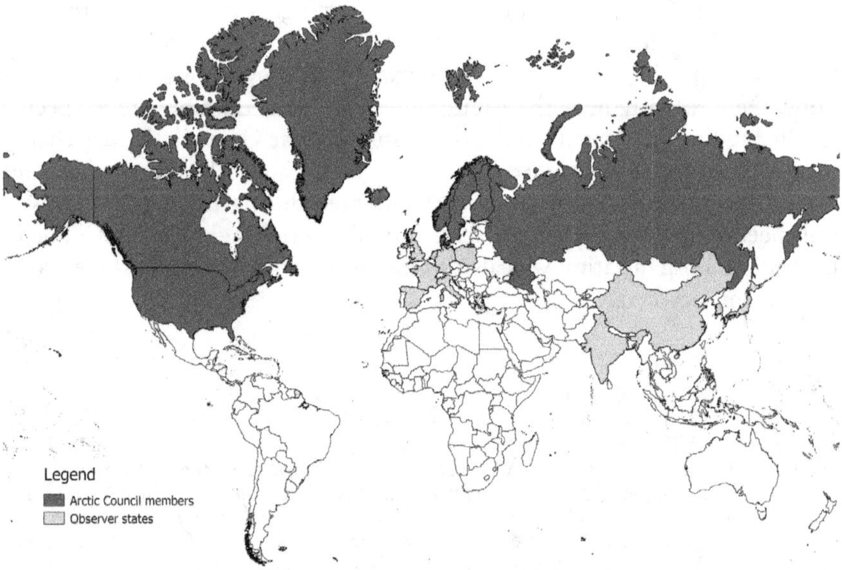

Figure 1.1: Member and observer states of the Arctic Council

[10] T Koivurova, 'Limits and Possibilities of the Arctic Council in a Rapidly Changing Scene of Arctic Governance' (2011) 46(2) *Polar Record* 146; Koivurova and VanderZwaag, 'The Arctic Council at 10 Years' (n 5).

[11] Arctic Council. *Senior Arctic Officials Report to Ministers* (Nuuk, Greenland, May 2011).

[12] Germany, Poland and the United Kingdom were present as observers already during the Rovaniemi AEPS founding meeting in 1991. Later on, the Netherlands also contributed to the work of AEPS. France became an observer in 2000 and Spain in 2006. Interestingly, Japan attended the 1996 Ottawa meeting but did not at that time apply for the status of observer.

II. WHY CHINA IN THE ARCTIC? WHY FOCUS ON 'EXTERNAL ACTORS'?

There is an extensive body of research arguing that the global power balance is gradually tilting—in the planes of geopolitics, economic as well as international governance and law—towards the rising powers of Asia, in particular China.[13] An argument has been made that Asian states—in an analogical way to how the decolonised states challenged international law during the 1960s and 1970s—will likely view many traditional areas of international law with suspicion, given their origin in European practice.[14] For example, Chinese officials have argued that Arctic states need to ensure that the Arctic remains a global commons.[15] According to this view, 'the Arctic occupies a unique position for all of us as humankind who live on the blue planet'.[16]

Currently, there is growing interest in China's possible role in the region, both from the side of policymakers[17] and the research community.[18] Among the topical issues are: Chinese interests in Arctic shipping and resources; China's role as origin and destination for cargo; opportunities for Chinese extractive companies in the Arctic (eg regarding iron ore or rare earths extraction in Greenland); Chinese relations with Arctic actors such as Norway, Iceland, Canada, Greenland and Finland, or Chinese research interests in the Arctic.[19] We suggest that there is still space in the landscape of current scholarship for developing a better understanding of China's perspectives

[13] Kim and Blank, 'The Arctic: A New Issue on Asia's Security Agenda' (n 7).

[14] O Yasuaki, *A Transcivilizational Perspective on International Law* (Leiden/Boston, Martinus Nijhoff Publishers, 2010).

[15] E Rosenthal, 'Race is On as Ice Reveals Arctic Treasures' *New York Times* (18 September 2012) www.nytimes.com/2012/09/19/science/earth/arctic-resources-exposed-by-warming-set-off-competition.html?emc=eta1&_r=0; C Campbell, 'China and the Arctic: Objectives and Obstacles—Staff Research Report' (Washington DC, US-China Economic and Security Review Commission, 2012).

[16] Minister Hu Zhengye, as cited in DC Wright, *The Dragon Eyes the Top of the World: Arctic Policy Debate and Discussion in China* (Newport, Rhode Island, China Maritime Studies Institute—Naval War College, 2011) 28. See also F Yu, 'Increasingly Fierce Disputes in Arctic Council' (2012) *World Affairs* 6; T Nykänen in this volume.

[17] F Lasserre, 'China and the Arctic: Threat or Cooperation Potential for Canada?' (2010) 11 *China Papers*. Centre for International Relations—The University of British Columbia and Canadian International Council; Campbell, 'China and the Arctic: Objectives and Obstacles' (n 15).

[18] Wright, *The Dragon Eyes the Top of the World* (n 16); L Jakobson 'China Prepares for an Ice-Free Arctic' (2010) 2 *SIPRI Insights on Peace and Security*.

[19] L Jakobson, 'China Prepares for an Ice-Free Arctic' (n 18); F Perreault, 'Can China Become a Major Arctic Player' (2012) 73 *S Rajaratnam School of International Studies Commentaries*; D Degeorges, 'The Role of Greenland in the Arctic' (2012) 7 *Laboratoire de l'IRSEM*; Lasserre, 'China and the Arctic: Threat or Cooperation' (n 17); Finnish Institute for International Affairs, Seminar on 'Changing Climate of Arctic Governance—a Finnish and Chinese Perspective' (20 April 2012) www.fiia.fi/en/event/453/changing_climate_of_arctic_governance_-_a_finnish_and_chinese_perspective.

on international politics and legal topics, in particular those directly within the frameworks of Arctic governance or otherwise relevant in the Arctic context.

As China, contrary to the Arctic states and actors such as the European Union,[20] has not produced a comprehensive strategic document on its Arctic policy, Chinese expectations and proposals for the region often need to be derived from political statements and Chinese approaches to international law and governance, including those promoted in other relevant international forums.

While the Arctic Council contributes greatly to political regional governance within the scope of its mandate, various international and national regulatory regimes constitute the core of the legal framework for Arctic governance. The Law of the Sea Convention (LOS Convention) together with International Maritime Organization (IMO) instruments and national law-based regulations are the most relevant instruments shaping the response to various regional maritime challenges, in particular those related to the use and navigation of the Arctic sea routes.[21] In addition, international law provides a framework for the protection of Arctic indigenous peoples' rights—ILO Convention 169 or the UN Declaration on the Rights of Indigenous Peoples[22]—as well as norms relevant for the protection of the Arctic environment, including its terrestrial dimension, eg through the Convention on Biological Diversity or the Convention on International Trade in Endangered Species.[23] The primary role played by China and the EU in these global venues may be contrasted with their back row position in the framework of Arctic regional co-operation.

Many sources of risks for the Arctic environment are located south of the Arctic Circle, primarily in the industrialised regions of Asia, Europe and North America. That is particularly true for climate change and long-range pollutants. Consequently, these risks have been the focus of Arctic circumpolar co-operation since its early stages. The Arctic Council (and earlier

[20] L Heininen, *Arctic Strategies and Policies: Inventory and Comparative Study* (Rovaniemi, Northern Research Forum, 2011).

[21] T Koivurova and EJ Molenaar, *International Governance of the Marine Arctic. Overview and Gap Analysis* (Oslo, WWF International Arctic Programme, 2009); EJ Molenaar, 'Arctic Marine Shipping: Overview of the International Legal Framework, Gaps and Options' (2009) 18(2) *Journal of Transnational Law and Policy* 289; Koivurova, 'Power Politics or Orderly Development?' (n 4).

[22] United Nations Declaration on the Rights of Indigenous Peoples, GA Res 61/295, UN Doc A/RES/61/295 (14 September 2007), 46 *International Legal Materials* 1013 (2007); Indigenous and Tribal Peoples Convention, International Labour Organization (ILO) Convention 169, in force 5 September 1991, 28 *International Legal Materials* 1382 (1989).

[23] 1992 Convention on Biological Diversity, in force 29 December 1993, 31 *International Legal Materials* 818 (1992); 1973 Convention on International Trade in Endangered Species of Wild Fauna and Flora, in force 1 July 1975, 993 UNTS 243.

the Arctic Environmental Protection Strategy, AEPS) has notably delivered some of its most significant scientific assessments in relation to these global environmental threats, including reports related to persistent organic pollutants,[24] its 2005 Arctic Climate Impact Assessment[25] and the 2011 mercury assessment.[26] (To read more about the work of the Council in this area, see Chapter 6 by Koivurova et al.)

A few examples of such environmental footprints may prove illustrative here. Climate change is considered the critical factor of change for the Arctic environment and its peoples.[27] Although some Arctic states are among the main global emitters of greenhouse gases, the Arctic region itself—being affected to such a great extent—does not produce significant amounts of CO2. Meanwhile, 29 per cent of global emissions of greenhouse gases originate from China and 11 per cent from the EU.[28] 13 per cent of black carbon—both a threat for health and an important short-term climate forcer in the Arctic—coming to the Arctic from sources outside of the region originates in East Asia, while the whole of Europe is responsible for 59 per cent due to its proximity to the Circumpolar North. The Arctic environment is a place where various pollutants are deposited due to wind patterns and ocean currents. For instance, 12 per cent of hexachlorobenzene—one of the main persistent organic pollutants—arrives in the Arctic from South-East Asia while 35 per cent of it comes from Europe. More than half of Arctic deposition of mercury comes from long-range sources, including 33 per cent from Asia and 22 per cent from Europe. For nitrogen oxides—which are important acidifying pollutants, chiefly for the Arctic marine environment—the East Asian impact amounts to roughly 21 per cent compared to Europe's 24 per cent.[29] It is clear therefore that the state of the Arctic environment

[24] Arctic Monitoring and Assessment Programme (AMAP) 2009. Arctic Pollution 2009: Persistent Organic Pollutants, Radioactivity, Human Health.

[25] ACIA 2005 (n 1); as well as the follow-up assessments, including Arctic Monitoring and Assessment Programme, *Arctic Climate Issues 2011: Changes in Arctic Snow, Water, Ice and Permafrost. SWIPA—Overview Report* (Oslo, Arctic Monitoring and Assessment Programme, 2011) available at www.amap.no/swipa.

[26] Arctic Monitoring and Assessment Programme (Assessment Leads: P Outridge and R Dietz), *AMAP Assessment 2011: Mercury in the Arctic* (Oslo, Arctic Monitoring and Assessment Programme, 2011) available at www.amap.no/documents/doc/amap-assessment-2011-mercury-in-the-arctic/90.

[27] ACIA 2005 (n 1) www.acia.uaf.edu; CAFF (Conservation of Arctic Flora and Fauna), Arctic Biodiversity Assessment: *Status and Trends in Arctic Biodiversity; Report for Policy Makers; Synthesis* (2013) www.arcticbiodiversity.is.

[28] Data for 2013; JGJ Olivier et al, 'Trends in Global CO2 Emissions: 2014' (2014) PBL Netherlands Environmental Assessment Agency and the Institute for Environment and Sustainability (IES) of the European Commission's Joint Research Centre (JRC) www.pbl.nl/sites/default/files/cms/publicaties/PBL_2014_Trends_in_global_CO2_emisions_2014_1490_0.pdf.

[29] All data from Ecologic Institute and others (S Cavalieri et al), *EU Arctic Footprint and Policy Assessment, Final Report*, European Commission (2010) arctic-footprint.eu.

depends largely on the developments and policies of so-called 'actors external to the Arctic'.[30]

Important external economic actors, such as China and the EU, also influence developments in the Arctic through their consumption of Arctic resources. The demand generated by these markets—which is also influenced by the domestic regulations and policies of these countries—plays a key role in shaping global prices and consequently the prospects (and profitability) for the extraction of these resources in the future. For example, iron and nickel are commonly extracted in the Arctic regions, and much of these materials are exported. China imported more than 60 per cent of iron ore available in international trade (2013), while the EU around 10–11 per cent.[31] China accounts also for 44 per cent of global demand for nickel (2011).[32] Much attention has been recently given to Arctic hydrocarbons. Rough estimates suggest that the EU market constituted 24 per cent of final demand for Arctic oil and gas production, while the Chinese market only accounted for 1 per cent (data from 2005), but this last figure is set to increase due to recently approved plans for delivering gas from Western Siberia to Chinese clients.[33] Chinese economic growth, environmental policies and strategic decisions made by Chinese leaders are therefore of key relevance for the future trends of Arctic change.

III. WHY COMPARE CHINA WITH FINLAND AND THE EU?

This book focuses on China's role and interests in the Arctic as well as, correspondingly, the Chinese legal and political approaches to issues of relevance for the changes taking place in the region. However, discussing the presence of China in the Arctic requires points of reference in order to avoid turning into an abstract and notional undertaking or building on established prejudices.[34] What influence does China have in the Arctic?

[30] Adam Stepien refers in his chapter of this volume to detailed data on the Chinese environmental footprint more directly relevant for Arctic peoples.

[31] Organization for Economic Cooperation and Development (OECD), 'The Iron Ore Market in 2011' (2012) www.oecd.org/sti/ind/OECD%20May12%20Summary%20%20Iron%20ore%20doc%20%283%29.pdf. Number for Europe without CIS is 12%, with EU countries accounting for above 10%.

[32] Compared to 8% in 2001, which is a good example of the rise in economic leverage of the Chinese market for Arctic resource developments.

[33] L Hornby, 'Putin Snubs Europe with Siberian Gas Deal that Bolsters China Ties' *Financial Times online* (10 November 2014) www.ft.com/intl/cms/s/0/79eeabb0-6888-11e4-acc0-00144feabdc0.html#axzz3Q8Ry0spM.

[34] See discussions on comparative politics and comparative law in M Irving Lichbach and AS Zuckerman (eds), *Comparative Politics: Rationality, Culture, and Structure* (Cambridge, Cambridge University Press, 1997); D Kennedy, 'New Approaches to Comparative Law: Comparativism and International Governance' (1997) 2 *Utah Law Review* 545. There is previous

What does it mean to participate in developments in the region as a responsible actor? What could be considered appropriate behaviour in the region for an external actor? What is the discourse on the Arctic in China and to what extent is it different from that of other actors? Comparing China's policy statements, ongoing activities in the circumpolar world and the positions that its government supports in intergovernmental forums to that of other non-Arctic states helps contextualise some aspects of the Chinese presence and interest in the Arctic.

Finland and the European Union have been chosen here as the points of reference. Finland—an Arctic state but without an Arctic Ocean coastline and one of the initiators of Arctic regional co-operation—is an example of an approach typical of a seasoned and experienced Arctic actor. Finland still advocates new developments (such as creating a treaty basis for regional co-operation or establishing a protection regime for the waters surrounding the North Pole),[35] but operates within prevalent Arctic discourses and possesses a great sensitivity to the specificities prevailing in the region. Comparisons with Finland prove the most fruitful in areas involving experience, sensitivity and direct access to region decision-making (for instance in comparing discourses and interests). Owing to the importance of Arctic shipping for Finland's shipbuilding industry, the country has clear interests in regional development to tap into the opportunities that its northernmost regions might benefit from in the context of increased shipping[36] and to the access that such development could provide for its mineral resources. Yet, the country is also geographically somewhat of an 'outsider' to the mainstream discourse within the realms of Arctic shipping and offshore resource extraction as it does not possess any coast on the Arctic Ocean itself.

However, Finland might not provide an appropriate basis for such a comparative study in other contexts, for instance where the differences in the status of Arctic states and external actors are particularly pronounced. As an Arctic state, Finland has greater influence on regionally-specific decision-making than China or the EU, particularly in the venues of Arctic regional co-operation. Moreover, Finland is limited in its policymaking by

research also on comparing policy entities as to their Arctic policies and laws. eg this research includes a number of studies such as 'Transatlantic Policy Options for Supporting Adaptation in Marine Arctic' (Arctic Transform) (where the Arctic policies and laws of the EU and the United States were compared) and an EU-funded project comparing the ocean governance and law of the sea positions of Canada and the EU.

[35] 'Finland's Strategy for the Arctic Region 2013'. Government resolution on 23 August 2013. Prime Minister's Office, Finland, vnk.fi/documents/10616/334509/Arktinen+strategia+2013+en.pdf.

[36] See 'Raportti: Jäämeren rautatie: Rovaniemi—Kirkkoniemi' ('Report: The Arctic Ocean Railway: Rovaniemi,—Kirkkoniemi'—translation by the editor) Lapin Liitto 2012, www.arcticcorridor.fi/assets/Logoja-ja-muuta/JAAMERENRAPORTTIVALMISvedos.pdf. See also T Nykänen's contribution to this volume.

its obligations towards the EU and the competences reserved for decision-making within the Union.[37] In many international organisations, Finland has only very limited capacity to contribute directly to the development of new norms as the country is represented through the EU. Consequently, the EU has been chosen as the second point of reference for analysing the Chinese presence in the region. Despite a significant legacy through various forms of engagement of European Communities and then the EU in the Arctic, the EU institutions—once they decided to develop a more conscious Arctic policy—have been welcomed in the region with suspicion and resistance. As in the case of China, the EU cannot build the legitimacy of its regional involvement on the basis of its geographical location. The EU and China therefore face similar constraints and challenges in their willingness to display a greater interest for regional developments.

In addition to the value that the Finnish and European experiences can provide in contextualising the presence and interests of China in the Arctic, the inclusion of these two perspectives in relevant chapters of this book provides additional insights on the diversity of priorities and interests that different states might have with regard to future Arctic developments. Finland has traditionally been a supporter of international law, in much the same way as other smaller powers in international relations, perceiving international law as crucial and generally beneficial to smaller states (ie owing to the equality of states principle). The EU institutions have taken more radical stances on Arctic governance, advocating (via a resolution by the European Parliament) at some point for an Arctic treaty modelled on the Antarctic Treaty to govern the region (European Parliament, 2008).[38] As described in several chapters of this volume, China's presence in the Arctic has up to now relied mainly on a rather pragmatic approach, primarily through involvement in scientific activities and the participation by some of its economic actors in regional developments. In this context, it has been our presumption that by comparing these three policy actors it is possible to enhance our understanding also of the current legal dynamics in the Arctic.

IV. STRUCTURE OF THE BOOK

The contributions to this book have adopted three main approaches in order to review the role and position of China in the Arctic. Analyses focusing on the country are followed by comparative studies using Finland and the European Union as points of reference in order to better understand singularities and opportunities related to the presence of China in the Arctic.

[37] Koivurova et al, 'The Present and Future Competence of the EU' (n 7).
[38] The idea was abandoned after 2008.

The contributions to the first part of the book provide several studies of the status of China in the Arctic, of its domestic discussion related to how the country could be involved in the region as well as of its past experience engaging with the most important forum for regional co-operation.

The volume opens with a chapter by QIN Tianbao and Li Miaomiao exploring legal arguments that would support a stronger position for China in the Arctic. The recent approval of China's observer status at the Arctic Council offers the point of departure for Qin and Li's contribution. This status provides only very limited opportunities for observers to play an active role in the region. The authors thus seek to identify in international law arguments that would support a stronger involvement in the region. Both the Law of the Sea Convention and the Svalbard Treaty contain provisions that define some rights for China in the region. The authors also note that a proactive regional policy, for instance through stronger bilateral ties, internal capacity building and a better defined Arctic strategy, could contribute greatly to placing China in a better position with regard to Arctic states.

In the third chapter, Ren Shidan addresses the right to conduct peaceful scientific research in the Arctic, providing a Chinese perspective on some of the key legal and practical issues impeding the ability of third states to fully enjoy this right. Having sponsored several research expeditions since 1999, China is not a newcomer when it comes to Arctic research. Building on its experience in the Antarctic, the country has gradually increased its research programme with the establishment of a research station on Svalbard and the commissioning of a polar research vessel. International law—most notably the UN Convention on the Law of the Sea and the Svalbard Treaty—does indeed provide a right for the country to conduct research in many areas of the Arctic. The author notes however that coastal states have laid obstacles to the full exercise of this right. To counter these difficulties, REN offers several concrete suggestions, for instance arguing for a more proactive participation by China in the various international organisations co-ordinating and facilitating research across the circumpolar world.

Julia Jalo and Tapio Nykänen then analyse nine Chinese articles published in the semi-governmental magazine *World Affairs* (世界知识, *Shijie zhishi*) between 2004 and 2014. The authors' aim is to reconstruct the Chinese political discourse on the Arctic as it is produced in these materials. The chapter highlights some of the most influential attitudes and opinions in Chinese discussion over Arctic questions, even though they do not include all possible stances or nuanced arguments. Jalo and Nykänen suggest that while China has been watching closely the discursive battle between the Arctic states, it has not as yet created a clear plan for its own actions in the North—in other words, the plan is to wait and see and act behind the public scenes. Furthermore, the articles that Jalo and Nykänen analyse construct a world where categories of classical realism play a significant role. States with actual physical power matter the most: others play a lesser role as 'co-operators'. This does not imply that small states would be insignificant. China has for example developed its bilateral relations with the Nordic countries and does want to build a win-win relationship with these countries in joint projects.

In the fifth chapter, Jiang Xiaoyi and Xiaoguang Zhou deliver an overall assessment of the legal position of China with regard to the Arctic. Having identified the aspects of Arctic development with the most relevance for the country, the authors discuss the scope of the rights that it enjoys in the region under the international law of the sea. Accordingly, China, as a non-Arctic state, benefits from a legal regime that is much less favourable than that of the five coastal states. Jiang and Xiaoguang complement this review with a discussion of the main statements by Chinese civil servants with regard to the region and of the regional presence of the country.

The second part of the book seeks to compare the Arctic discourses used in China and in Finland in order to shed light on how the position and rhetorics of China differ from those of small Arctic nations, Finland serving as an example.

In Chapter 6, Lassi Heininen considers whether, despite the important asymmetry characterising the two countries, China and Finland share some common traits with regard to the Arctic. Describing the differences prevailing between the positions of both countries, the chapter indicates that China and Finland come from extremely different perspectives when considering Arctic affairs. However, and despite this asymmetry, the two countries share some common features with regard to some of the key elements shaping their Arctic policies. First, in recent years both countries have strengthened the prominence of references to the Arctic when defining their national identity. Additionally, in relation to some of the most important areas for polar co-operation, China and Finland also share a strong interest in further economic development in the Arctic—especially in shipping, an industry that remains particularly important for both countries. As the two nations are impacted by climate changes in the Arctic, although these impacts manifest themselves differently, the importance of increasing the understanding of regional environmental trends remains at the core of the interest that Beijing and Helsinki have in the Arctic. Both countries also strongly emphasise in a relatively similar manner the importance of their national Arctic (or polar) expertise and ongoing research projects. Finally, Heininen points at the convergence of agendas between China and Finland with regard to the importance of international co-operation to address circumpolar issues.

In Chapter 7, Tapio Nykänen analyses the political rhetoric on the Arctic in China and Finland. In both countries there are two hegemonic discourses: (1) the Arctic has huge economic possibilities in transportation and natural resources; and (2) the Arctic is a vulnerable place of indispensable environmental importance. Both discourses locate the Arctic much closer to the centre of the geopolitical and geoeconomic maps than it used to be. There are also some differences. China emphasises the 'common' nature of the Arctic, at least outside the Exclusive Economic Zones (EEZ), which means that resources in these areas should be free for everybody to utilise. This message is dressed up in the clothes of environmental worries about 'common' nature. Finland also recognises the 'common' nature of the Arctic. However, it strongly emphasises the role of the Arctic countries and their expertise in Arctic operations and policy. Another way of seeing Finland's geopolitical and geoeconomic location is in terms of discourse about the world of streams and mobility, where Finland could serve as a hub.

The third part of the volume seeks to better understand the current and future role of China in Arctic governance by comparing its positions and activities in specific areas of regional relevance with those of the European Union.

The Arctic Council is in the international limelight since states and political entities from outside the region express a growing interest in participating in the Arctic Council's work as the premier intergovernmental institution. Timo Koivurova et al examine how China has performed as an observer in the Arctic Council. The only way currently for the non-Arctic states and the European Union to get involved is to obtain observer status at the Council. Therefore, admission of new observers has become one of the more pertinent issues in the debate on the shape and role the Arctic Council should play in regional governance structure. The chapter starts with an overview of the evolution of the observer status. This chapter studies what China has been able to do with its observer status. It will be asked whether China has been able to live up to the requirements established for observers at the Nuuk ministerial meeting. In addition to that, China's concrete actions in the Arctic Council and its Working Groups will be analysed.

The following three chapters consider thematic issues at the core of Arctic governance. Sébastien Duyck discusses in Chapter 9 various opportunities for the conservation of marine living resources in areas of the high seas in the Arctic. The chapter first introduces the global legal regime applicable to biodiversity beyond national jurisdiction as well as relevant ongoing processes meant to further define this regulatory framework. The initiatives undertaken by the Arctic states to protect the Arctic marine environment are then reviewed. The chapter concludes by considering the positions on this issue of two major non-Arctic actors that have expressed strong interest in the region: China and the European Union. Indeed, the international legal regime applicable to the high seas provides very limited prerogatives for coastal states to restrain the rights of third states for the sake of marine conservation. This study highlights that China and the EU are likely to have different positions on the conservation of marine biodiversity in the High Arctic. The Arctic states will thus need to accommodate the diverging perspectives of non-Arctic states if they decide to establish a regional arrangement to conserve high seas living resources in the Arctic.

In the penultimate chapter of this volume, Adam Stepien discusses the ways in which China and the EU have engaged Arctic indigenous organisations and how these major global actors have approached these comparatively small Arctic groups. The need for engagement stems from the influence external actors exert on the Arctic region and the role of indigenous groups in the multilayered frameworks of Arctic governance. However, the interests and activities of the major external players are primarily a result of the requirements put on the observers in the Arctic Council—engraved in the Nuuk Observer Rules—concerning respect and support for Arctic indigenous peoples. As the attempts to engage indigenous organisations by the EU and especially China have been so far limited in scope and content, the author also investigates the general approach of these major global actors to indigenous issues and rights in a broader international context. The dynamics examined in this chapter are a testament to the specificity of the Arctic and the globally unique position indigenous groups have gained in the regional governance structures.

In the final chapter, Nengye Liu and Kamrul Hossain examine China's role in the development of an international legal regime for Arctic shipping. China, as the world's third largest shipping power, is interested in the potential opportunities of Arctic shipping. The chapter first looks into the development of an international legal regime for Arctic shipping and discusses more specifically China's interest in Arctic shipping. The authors then analyse challenges and opportunities for China in relation to Arctic shipping. Article 234 of the United Nations Convention on the Law of the Sea, which relates to the particular case of ice-covered waters, might affect Chinese shipping. The authors thus present the position of the country in relation to this provision. The negotiation of the Polar Code within the International Maritime Organization constituted the most important recent development that will shape maritime transport in the Arctic. China, the authors note, has however not played any active role in this particular process. The chapter concludes with a reference to the relevance in relation of this issue of the Arctic Council and of China's recent status as an observer.

The volume concludes with a chapter that builds on the main findings contained in the previous contributions to discuss the path followed by external entities seeking to play a role in the Arctic and the response that this interest has triggered among regional actors. The chapter begins by providing a short summary of the legal status of non-Arctic or non-coastal states in relation to Arctic governance. While the vast majority of resources found in the Arctic Ocean fall within the jurisdiction of one of the five Arctic coastal states, third states do enjoy under international law several rights that are relevant to Arctic developments. The extent to which these rights can be enjoyed in practice nevertheless depends to a large extent on the response of local actors. In order to strengthen its engagement in Arctic affairs, the three entities reviewed in the present book have each adopted their own strategies. The chapter then briefly reviews the reaction of Arctic actors to this increasing global interest towards the region. This assessment enables the identification of good practices and challenges among the approaches followed by the three entities. On the basis of the literature reviewed and on the discussions generated throughout this project, these conclusions also highlight four specific issues in relation to which additional research would be beneficial in order to further the understanding of the present and future role of non-Arctic states in the Arctic.

Part I

Chinese Perspectives

2

Strengthening China's Role in the Arctic Council

QIN TIANBAO AND LI MIAOMIAO

I. INTRODUCTION

ARCTIC[1] ISSUES CONTINUE to heat up. Developments in the Arctic are not only relevant for regional actors, but have also become important in the governance of global climate change. As an intergovernmental high-level forum, the Arctic Council has been regarded as the main symbolic way for non-Arctic countries to participate in Arctic governance, and therefore it plays an increasingly important role or even the leading role in Arctic governance. China's Arctic interests have become increasingly apparent because of climate change. However, China's observer status provides the country with only limited influence on developments in the region. Given that the Arctic Council plays an increasingly significant role in the Arctic governance of globalisation, China should actively strengthen its role in the Arctic Council to safeguard its Arctic interests. In fact, there is nothing exceptional about China's advocacy to strengthen its role in the Arctic Council. In recent years, strengthening the role of observers in the Arctic Council has become an issue of interest for actors such as member states, observers, non-governmental organisations and academics. For example, Norway believes that in order to maintain the influence of the Arctic Council and sustainable co-operation to prevent problems with divergence, observers should be given a greater role in the Council.[2] According

[1] The Arctic region includes the Arctic waters, islands and north continent of Europe, northern Asia and North America, with a total area of 21 million square kilometres. Its land area is 8,000,000 square kilometres and it belongs to the United States, Canada, Russia, Denmark, Iceland, Norway, Finland and Sweden. Arctic waters cover 13 million square kilometres, including the waters under the jurisdiction of coastal states, and the high seas and international seabed area recognised by many countries.

[2] Transcript of the Debate on High North/Arctic strategies, Stortinget (Norwegian Parliament), Oslo, 2 February 2010, available at www.regjeringen.no/en/aktuelt/highnorth_debate/id592606/.

to a joint statement released in November 2008 at the Senior Arctic Officials (SAO) meeting in Kautokeino, Norway, some observers to the meeting stated that observers hope to co-operate not only in scientific research but also in decision-making.[3] At the Wilton Park conference exploring Arctic issues, declarations were also made that the Arctic Council needs to be strengthened; one way to achieve this goal is to improve the openness of the Council and enhance its representativeness.[4] In addition, some non-Arctic countries are also expressing their willingness to become member states of the Council.[5]

This chapter attempts to combine China's Arctic interests and the limitations of its status as an observer in the Arctic Council, and focuses on China's possibilities and ways of strengthening its current observer role in the Arctic Council.

II. ARCTIC COUNCIL AND CHINA

In 1987, Mikhail Gorbachev delivered his speech on 'strengthening co-operation in the Arctic region' in Murmansk, and presented the initially extensive plans on co-operation in Arctic affairs.[6] As a result, in 1991, under the initiative of Finland, eight Arctic states, Finland, Sweden, Norway, Denmark, Iceland, Canada, the United States and Russia, signed the Rovaniemi Declaration and adopted the Arctic Environmental Protection Strategy (AEPS).[7] In the AEPS, the eight countries committed to protecting the environment in the Arctic and to co-operate: 'the purpose is to identify, reduce and ultimately eliminate pollution'.[8] But the AEPS did not specify the decision-making process; it also set the stage for the

[3] Joint Statement of the observer states presented at the SAO Meeting in Kautokeino, Norway, 19–20 November 2008, available at oaarchive.arctic-council.org/handle/11374/889.

[4] Report on Wilton Park Conference, 'The High North: Challenge And Opportunities', 18–21 February 2010, available at www.wiltonpark.org.uk/wp-content/uploads/wp1017-report.pdf, 6.

[5] See: T Nilsen, 'Non-Arctic Countries Want Membership in Arctic Council' *Barents Observer* (Kirkeness, 3 October 2008) barentsobserver.com/en/node/21258.

[6] Gorbachev proposed that: a nuclear weapon-free zone be declared in northern Europe; naval activity be limited in the seas adjacent to northern Europe; peaceful co-operation be the basis for utilising the resources of the Arctic; scientific study of the Arctic be given great significance for all mankind; the countries of the North co-operate in matters of environmental protection; and the Northern Sea Route be opened by the Soviet Union to icebreaker escorted passage. For an analysis, see DR Rothwell, *The Polar Regions and the Development of International Law* (Cambridge, University Press, 1996) 229–31.

[7] Arctic Environmental Protection Strategy, Canada, Denmark, Finland, Iceland, Norway, Sweden, Union of Soviet Socialist Republics, and United States, 14 January 1991, 30 *International Legal Materials* 1624, 2.1(v) at 1631 [AEPS].

[8] Ibid, 1631.

following ministerial meeting.[9] In 1993, affected by the 1992 Rio Conference on Environment and Development, the Nuuk Declaration adopted by the Nuuk ministerial meeting recognised the importance of environmental information disclosure and public participation in the decision-making process;[10] the second meeting on AEPS co-operation occurred in 1996 in Inuvik, Canada, and adopted the Inuvik Declaration. The process of negotiating the establishment of the Arctic Council had thus begun.[11] The main reasons for shifting to the Arctic Council from AEPS were that the AEPS was limited to scientific research, decisions made at the ministerial meetings were weakened by the lack of binding obligations, and expectations for robust response mechanisms and obligatory instruments were not met.[12] In September 1996, eight countries signed the Ottawa Declaration in Ottawa, Canada, declaring the establishment of the Arctic Council. The Ottawa Declaration modifies the rules of participation[13] during AEPS and elaborated new rules. It clearly defined the participants of the Arctic Council as being of three types: member states, permanent participants[14] and observers.[15] Indigenous peoples, which had observer status at the beginning of AEPS, were now raised to permanent participants. Before member states make a decision the permanent participants should be fully consulted (Ottawa Declaration 1996, paragraph 2). In addition, in fact, AEPS is fully integrated into the Arctic Council. The mandate of the Arctic

[9] T Koivurova and D vanderZwaag, 'The Arctic Council at 10 Years: Retrospect and Prospects' (2007) 40(1) *UBC Law Review* 121, 126.

[10] ibid, 127.

[11] See eg the Inuvik Declaration's emphasising that '[the Arctic states] are fully committed to the earliest possible establishment of the Arctic Council', 21 March 1996, available at library.arcticportal.org/1272/1/The_Inuvik_Declaration.pdf.

[12] W Hasanat, 'Towards Model Arctic-Wide Environmental Cooperation Combating Climate Change' (2009) 20 *Yearbook of International Environmental Law* 122, 125.

[13] See the reference to the rationale described in the AEPS for the participation of the observers: 'The decision to invite observers should be based on a pragmatic and functional evaluation of their involvement in and contribution to Arctic environmental questions'; AEPS (n 7) 1668; see also the list of organisations invited as observers: 'In order to facilitate the participation of Arctic indigenous peoples the following organizations will be invited as AEPS observers: the Inuit Circumpolar Conference, the Nordic Saami Council and the U.S.S.R. Association of Small Peoples of the North'; ibid.

[14] There are 6 permanent seats of the local community representatives in the Arctic Council. These representatives include the Aleut International Association, Arctic Athabasca Parliament, Ge Wei Xun International Parliament, Inuit Circumpolar Conference, Russian Association of Northern indigenous peoples and the Saami Council.

[15] The Arctic Council has permanent observers, including 6 non-Arctic countries: France, Germany, the Netherlands, Poland, Spain and the United Kingdom; international organisations: the World Conservation Union (IUCN), the International Red Cross, the Nordic Council, United Nations Environment Programme, United Nations Development Programme; NGO: Association of World Reindeer, Arctic University and WWF Arctic Planning Group. On 15 May 2013, the eighth ministerial meeting of the Arctic Council held in the northern city of Kiruna, Sweden approved China, Italy, Japan, Korea, India and Singapore as official observers of the Arctic Council. The Arctic Council also has special observers, including the EU.

Council includes both Arctic sustainable development and environmental protection, unlike AEPS, which had been mainly limited to environmental protection. To this end, the Arctic Council established a new working group, the Sustainable Development Working Group (SDWG), to address sustainable development issues based on the four working groups of AEPS. In terms of its organisational structure, the Arctic Council has SAOs who are responsible for preparing ministerial meetings and co-ordinating the work of the Council (compared to Senior Arctic Affairs Officials in AEPS; only the name changed, as they still hold the same responsibilities). Moreover, there are also ministerial meetings, which are held at the end of two-year periods of chairmanship,[16] biannual Deputy Ministers' meetings, a permanent secretariat[17] and subsidiary bodies.[18] The Arctic Council has become increasingly significant in Arctic governance since its establishment. The most notable successes of the Arctic Council include identifying issues, conducting scientific assessments to highlight these issues, and raising awareness of trans-boundary pollution and climate change issues facing the Arctic, and then formulating assessment reports[19] which result into policy, thereby promoting regional and international co-operation in the Arctic.[20]

In 1925, the Duan Qirui interim government signed the Svalbard Treaty, which is China's first official contact with the Arctic. Then, as part of the Ninth Five-Year Plan[21] (2006–10), a polar expedition programme was approved by the Chinese Academy of Science, thereby officially involving China in Arctic affairs through scientific expeditions.[22]

[16] The 8 member states assume chairmanship in turn: (1996–98) Canada; (1998–2000) the United States; (2000–02) Finland; (2002-04) Iceland; (2004–06) Russia; (2006–08) Norway; (2009–11) Denmark; (2011–13) Sweden; (2013–15) Canada and (2015–17) United States.

[17] The chair country used to be responsible for the establishment of the Secretariat. This changed in May 2011 when the seventh ministerial meeting of the Arctic Council in Greenland's capital, Nuuk decided to organise the Permanent Secretariat in Tromsø, Norway. In 2013, the Permanent Secretariat was officially established.

[18] See Arctic Council Observer Manual for Subsidiary Bodies, art 4.4. The subsidiary bodies of the Arctic Council are: (1) working groups; (2) task forces; (3) expert groups; and (4) such other subsidiary bodies as the Arctic Council may create.

[19] 'The Arctic Climate Impact Assessment Report', 'Arctic Human Development Report', 'Arctic Biodiversity Assessment', 'Arctic Energy Report' and 'Arctic Marine Shipping Assessment Report' etc. 'Arctic Climate Impact Assessment Report' and 'Arctic Marine Shipping Assessment Report' greatly promoted the Arctic governance processes. The Arctic Council ministerial meeting held in Kiruna on 15 May 2013 discussed the written assessment of biological diversity in the Arctic, the Arctic Review Report and the Arctic Ocean acidification assessment reports by the working groups.

[20] See P Kankaanpaa and OR Young, 'The Effectiveness of the Arctic Council' (2012) 31 *Polar Research* 1–3.

[21] 'Report of the ninth five year plan of National Economic and Social Development and 2010 vision plan and outline', passed by the Fourth Session of the Eighth National People's Congress on 5 March 1996.

[22] Since 1990 China has conducted 4 scientific Arctic expeditions and established its first Arctic scientific research station, 'Yellow River Station', in 2004.

But due to a shortage of funds (80 per cent of the funds were allocated to the Antarctic expedition), the Arctic expedition was originally developed slowly, but has improved steadily since the turn of the century. During the past two decades, the main ways whereby China has participated in Arctic affairs have been to carry out scientific expeditions, and the 'core of China's Arctic expedition [revolved] mainly around climate change and the ecological environment',[23] and there was no intersection with the Arctic Council. Until 2006, based on the background of global climate change, both in traditional security areas such as national sovereignty and in non-traditional security areas, such as resources, international shipping and biodiversity, the Arctic is increasingly becoming the focus of international politics. China therefore applied to become an observer of the Arctic Council, but due to obstruction from some member states, China did not initially achieve its goal. In 2007, China was approved as an ad hoc observer, and based on this status could participate in the Council's activities. In 2009, China again applied for observer status. However, due to disputes on the seal trade between Canada and the EU, Canada retaliated by preventing the EU's access to the status of observer, which also resulted in the shelving of China's application. On 15 May 2013, the eighth ministerial meeting of the Arctic Council held in the northern city of Kiruna, Sweden approved six countries, including China, as observers to the Arctic Council. So far, China has raised its status in the Arctic Council from a bystander to an ad hoc observer to an observer. The difference between an ad hoc observer and observer is that an observer is automatically invited to attend all meetings open to observers, while ad hoc observers should get approval before attending each meeting (that said, approval has been routinely granted).

III. THE NECESSITY TO STRENGTHEN CHINA'S ROLE IN THE ARCTIC COUNCIL

National interests determine a country's decision to participate in the Arctic Council. China enjoys important strategic interests in the Arctic, including the environment, resources and shipping, as a result of which China should actively participate in the Arctic Council. But, the limited role of an observer does not provide China with enough influence to further effectively its interests in the Arctic. Therefore, China should take vigorous action under the framework of international law, and then strengthen its role in the Arctic

[23] Zhang Jiansong, 'Interview: Arctic Sea Ice Expedition Integrated into a Wide Range of Focus', http://news.xinhuanet.com/tech/2010-07/02/c_12289461.htm.

Council in order to overcome the existing shortcomings of observer status and maintain a growing interest in the Arctic.

A. China Enjoys Important Strategic Interests in the Arctic

China's Arctic interests include environmental safety, energy security, economic interests and scientific benefits. With respect to environmental security, Arctic cold air activities and changes in atmospheric circulation at high latitudes have a direct bearing on China's weather and climate, significantly impacting China's ecological environment and agricultural production systems and other socioeconomic activities.[24] Furthermore, the rising sea level also poses a potential threat to the eastern coast of China.[25] In terms of energy security and economic interests, on the one hand, given that China is the world's largest importer of iron ore and copper, as well as the second largest importer of hydrocarbons, China is certainly interested in the Arctic's mineral and hydrocarbon resources. Moreover, in the era of globalisation, the resource benefits of producing countries are flowing to peripheral countries through the chain of industry. As a result, even though China is a non-Arctic country, it may share profits from the exploitation of oil and gas resources with the resource-producing countries. Therefore through feasible diplomatic strategy and industry links, China enjoys considerable resource interests in the Arctic. On the other hand, due to global warming and the acceleration of the melting of Arctic sea ice, China is hopeful that the Arctic will open to shipping in the near future. Currently, China's foreign trade mostly depends on the Strait of Malacca and the Suez Canal, where the safety coefficient is very low, and the shipping cost is also high due to power control and rampant piracy. Besides, the traffic capacity of the Suez Canal is saturated. Although Arctic shipping would provide the shortest route between Asia, Europe and America, a number of scholars question its cost-effectiveness. Nevertheless, it is still an opportunity for China to promote economic benefits in shipping costs and ensure China's energy security. With respect to research interests, Arctic scientific expeditions can help China resolve research questions in fields such as the marine environment, atmosphere, space physics and space environment detection. They can also serve to promote the development of related technologies and the use of high-tech. In addition, China can share its research achievements with the international community.

It is important to note, however, that China has not yet officially released an Arctic strategy to explicitly declare its Arctic interests. Unclear interests

[24] T Guoqiang, 'Arctic Issue and China's Policy' (2013) 38 *China International Studies* 29.

[25] H Zhengyue, 'China's Views on Arctic Affairs—The Report of Assistant Foreign Minister Hu Zhengyue in the Activities on Arctic Research Trip' (2009) *World Knowledge* 55.

may lead to vigilance from the Arctic countries and other countries as well as Arctic non-state actors concerning China's participation in Arctic affairs. To some extent, this has limited China's ability to participate effectively in the Arctic Council.

B. China's Role is Limited in the Arctic Council

The status of observers originates from the practice of the United Nations.[26] International organisations did not originally enable other parties to have observer status. But with the development of international organisations and demands to perfect ways of participating in international affairs, more and more international organisations have realised the advantages of the observer system and established the status of observer in a succession of documents.

So far, the Arctic Council's regulations about the observer system are scattered in the Ottawa Declaration (1996), Rules of Procedure of the Arctic Council (2013), the Arctic Officials Report (Senior Arctic Officials Report to Ministers, Nuuk, Greenland, 12 May 2011) and the Arctic Council Observer Manual for Subsidiary Bodies (2013). In accordance with these documents, the primary duty of the observers is to observe the work of the Arctic Council. A permanent observer can automatically participate in meetings of the subsidiary bodies of the Arctic Council and ministerial meetings and get involved in the work of the working groups, apart from the SAOs' closed-door meetings and member states' heads of delegations, especially in the meetings of the subsidiary bodies. Observers have the right to attend meetings, make statements, present written statements, submit relevant documents and state their views on the issues under discussion. Observers also have the right to propose projects through an Arctic state or a permanent participant.[27]

China's role in the Arctic Council has been limited. On the one hand, this is due to the general restrictions applied on the participation of observers, and on the other hand, partly due to China's lack of capacity to participate. The following three aspects are particularly relevant. First, the scope of privileges of observers has been limited. China has no substantial decision-making power. Decision-making authority at all levels in the Arctic Council is the exclusive right of the eight member states with the involvement of the

[26] After the First World War, the Allies formed the League of Nations, but the United States refused to join. In order to cope with this situation, an 'observer' system was specially arranged for League of Nations conferences. 1921 US President Harding sent an observer to attend the International Alliance of Women and Juveniles' trading restrictions meetings.

[27] Rules of Procedure of the Arctic Council, adopted by the Arctic Council at the First Arctic Council Ministerial Meeting in Iqaluit (1998) paras 37–38.

permanent participants.[28] In fact, as an observer, China is just a bystander, whose manner and level of participation are subject to the rules of the eight member states; although China has been approved as an observer, it is still limited by the 'criteria for admitting observers'[29] of the Rules of Procedure, in particular the provision stating that observers must admit the sovereignty, sovereign rights and jurisdiction of Arctic states. The criterion is likely to be used by Arctic states in the future on the grounds that specific items should belong to their sovereignty, sovereign rights and jurisdiction, thus limiting the scope of China's and other observers' participation in Arctic affairs. Secondly, regulations on the procedure for exercising observers' privileges are ambiguous and thus limit the latitude for influence. The Arctic Council's Observer Manual for Subsidiary Bodies provides specific access to the privileges of observers for the first time compared with previous soft law documents, which simply listed the observers' privileges. However, the Manual still does not make it clear how observers should obtain documents and information and in what time frame, the order and time when they can make statements, and how they should present project proposals.[30] The fuzziness of procedure on exercising privileges is not conducive for China to exercise its privilege as an observer. Thirdly, China's own lack of capability for participation constrains its role in the Arctic Council. On the one hand, as a crucial scientific research participant, China still needs to improve its capabilities in terms of management and scientific research, in spite of the great improvements made in Chinese expedition equipment during the past 20 years. Moreover, China's research mostly focuses on natural science and the country lacks the capability to explore Arctic resources. Furthermore, as a newcomer, China does not yet have enough experience about the procedures for the operation of the Arctic Council, including lack of access to information and ability of agenda setting. All of these factors greatly limit China's participation in Arctic Council meetings and working groups.

IV. THE POSSIBILITY OF STRENGTHENING CHINA'S ROLE IN THE ARCTIC COUNCIL

China shall strengthen its role in the Arctic Council for the purpose of gaining benefits in the Arctic. Is it possible for China to strengthen its current observer status and then act more effectively in the Arctic Council? In fact, the answer is yes according to existing prerequisites based on the legal foundation, the organisational foundation of the Arctic Council and the geopolitical situation in the Arctic.

[28] See Ottawa Declaration on the establishment of the Arctic Council (1996) para 7.

[29] Rules of Procedure (1998) Annex 2, art 6.

[30] Arctic Council Observer Manual for Subsidiary Bodies (2013) paras 7.2–7.5.

A. The UNCLOS and Svalbard Treaty are International Law Grounds for China to Strengthen its Role in the Arctic Council

The position of China in the Arctic Council should be strengthened due to the legal positioning of China. Arctic states in the Arctic Council develop soft law documents and scientific assessments that are of relevance for the areas of the Arctic where China has legal standing, and thus affect Chinese rights and obligations towards the areas that were recognised by the United Nations Convention on the Law of the Sea (UNCLOS) and Svalbard Treaty, including the high seas, international seabed, exclusive economic zone, continental shelf and Svalbard Archipelago. Thus, China should have a stronger position in the Council.

As an indirect but very important foundation, the UNCLOS and Svalbard Treaty vested China with a wide range of rights in the Arctic. China has signed and approved the UNCLOS, whose provisions on Arctic rights could be cited with particular reference to activities such as innocent passage on territorial waters, freedom of navigation and over-flight in exclusive economic zones, freedom of laying submarine cables and pipelines in exclusive economic zones and on the continental shelf, and freedom on the high seas.[31] Furthermore, the international seabed is the common heritage of mankind and managed by the International Seabed Authority. China acceded to the Svalbard Treaty on 1 July 1925. Pursuant to the treaty, citizens of the High Contracting Parties may enter archipelago waters and its territorial waters and engage in valid manufacturing and commercial activities under Norwegian law. Specifically, these include passing rights, resource rights, scientific research rights, right of calling and right to use wireless telegraphy stations.[32]

In conclusion, China is entitled to a wide range of rights in the Arctic under the UNCLOS and the Svalbard Treaty, which thereby provide a basis for China to strengthen its role in the Arctic Council given that documents adopted by the Council are usually related to the areas where China enjoys legal rights. China's demand to enhance its role in the Arctic Council is legitimate and rational.

B. The Proposition of Strengthening the Arctic Council Establishes a Favourable Organisational Foundation

The Arctic Climate Impact Assessment Report released in 2004 by the Arctic Council evaluated that climate change led to ice melting in the

[31] See United Nations Convention on the Law of the Sea, 10 December 1982, in force 16 November 1994, 21 *International Legal Materials 1261* (1982) (UNCLOS) arts 17, 58, 87, 136, 137.

[32] Spitsbergen (Svalbard) Treaty, 9 February 1920, in force 14 August 1925, 2 *League of Nations Treaties Series* 8, arts 2–8.

Arctic, greatly increasing possibilities for exploiting oil, natural gas and other energies and resources in the Arctic area. Besides, a number of problems exist in the Arctic Council, the most important intergovernmental co-operation regime: for instance, the Council is a high-level forum established in accordance with a declaration, rather than a treaty (unlike typical international organisations), the allocation and work assignment between working groups, especially SDWG, is not as effective as it could be, lacking effective systematic methods to co-ordinate the interests of the region and indigenous people with the interests of non-Arctic States, and the Council lacks a funding mechanism, etc.[33] Therefore, for the purpose of improving the effectiveness of management in the Arctic, the Arctic states unanimously proposed to strengthen the Arctic Council by enabling it to exercise more controlling power over multiple issues. Such propositions were submitted to conferences of the Council repeatedly from 2004.[34] The proposition was finally accepted at the seventh Arctic Council ministerial meeting in Nuuk, Greenland in May 2011. Foreign Ministers of member states signed the first binding agreement, the Arctic Search and Rescue Agreement, 15 years after the Council was established.[35] The agreement divides search and rescue areas among the member states and sets responsibilities, changing the long-lasting situation in which the Arctic Council governed by soft laws. The Council was also strengthened with the establishment of a permanent secretariat in Tromsø, Norway, which started operating formally in 2013. The expenditure of the secretariat is apportioned evenly among eight member states, each contributing no more than one million dollars, relieving the funding problem of the Council. The meeting also set criteria for admitting observer states. The measures taken by the Arctic States to strengthen the Arctic Council show that the Council is turning gradually from an intergovernmental high-level forum to an organisation with a political decision-making function, also indicating that the soft legislation format is changing to a hard legislation format in Arctic governance.

As the Arctic Council shifts its focus to address climate change, the observer states of the Council, including China, have greater opportunities to push for more open decision-making in the Council and the introduction of an agenda that supports the common interests of humankind.

[33] T Koivurova, 'Limits and Possibilities of the Arctic Council in a Rapidly Changing Scene of Arctic Governance' (2010) 46(2) *Polar Record* 146.

[34] The 2007 Senior Officials' Meeting discussed the 'future of the Arctic Council', and formally included the strengthening of the Arctic Council on the agenda of the Council. The 2009 ministerial conference issued the Tromsø Declaration, which further emphasises the need for reform of the Arctic Council.

[35] In addition, the Arctic Council's ministerial meeting at Kiruna, Sweden, in 2013, adopted the second binding legal text, the 'Agreement on Cooperation on Marine Oil Pollution Preparedness and Response in the Arctic'.

Furthermore, the observer states can see to it that legal documents incorporate their demands.

C. The Complex Geopolitical Structure of the Arctic Region Fosters a Favourable Political Environment

The complex geopolitical structure is helpful for China to co-operate with the Arctic states, other observer states and associations of indigenous peoples that share common interests, bilaterally or multilaterally, indirectly promoting the role of China in the Arctic Council. The oppositional dual structure of the Cold War is a thing of the past while the emerging trend in the Arctic is geopolitical integration. However, the Arctic states still differ in their views over the waters surrounding Svalbard and maritime delimitation. Besides, there are also inter-states organisations such as the European Union and the Arctic Ocean Sciences Board, and non-governmental organisations, such as the International Arctic Science Committee. Others to be taken into consideration are indigenous peoples and their associations, including the Saami Council and five other representatives from local communities, which have been granted the status of permanent participants in the Arctic Council. Indigenous people value their own cultures, identities and livelihood, and function as an important force in the area. The indigenous peoples hold their own interpretation of sovereignty, especially with regard to utilising land and resources.[36] With such interpretation, indigenous peoples claim rights to land and water, self-determination and self-management. They also consider that sovereignty does not merely involve relations between states and propose that the concept of sovereignty be overhauled; they have worked to that end and have in fact made progress. As stated above, the coming issue is how to reinforce co-operation relationships with the Arctic States, observer states and the indigenous peoples. The present bewildering geopolitical circumstances and complex relationships between subjects provide China with favourable conditions to use diplomatic wisdom and expand co-operative mechanisms.

V. THE WAYS TO STRENGTHEN CHINA'S ROLE IN THE ARCTIC COUNCIL

Before discussing the ways whereby China can strengthen its role in the Arctic Council, China should first clarify its special status in the Arctic and be aware of its advantages and disadvantages. First, thanks to its research

[36] See 'A Circumpolar Inuit Declaration on Sovereignty in the Arctic' (2009) available at www.inuitcircumpolar.com/sovereignty-in-the-arctic.html.

on climate change, China plays an important role in the climate change governance of the Arctic. Secondly, as a result of China's strong economic growth, the country's demand for energy resources and shipping makes it the top national energy purchaser and user of shipping. Thirdly, as a near Arctic state, China has a relative geographical advantage in the Arctic. Meanwhile, China should also clarify the barriers that hinder efforts to strengthen its role in the Arctic Council, including the lack of international and domestic legal basis as well as inadequate research structure and soft power. To this end, China should take advantage of opportunities to mitigate these weaknesses, in order to strengthen its role in the Arctic Council.

First, China should stress the implementation and development of the current international legal framework of the law of the sea,[37] and seek to ensure that the interpretation and application of international law are favourable to China in order to make explicit the interests of non-Arctic countries in the Arctic, including China, and then provide legitimacy for strengthening the role of China in the Arctic Council. Secondly, China should actively participate in multilateral co-operation and expand bilateral co-operation in order to indirectly strengthen its role in the Arctic Council. Thirdly, China should divide the areas of co-operation into low sensitivity co-operation such as scientific research and climate change and high sensitivity areas such as marine energy and resources development, and then start co-operation from the low sensitivity areas, and gradually engage in high sensitivity issues. Finally, China should focus on capacity building, including research capacity and 'soft power', to directly enhance its role in the Arctic Council. In addition, through the development of China's Arctic strategies and legislation, China should declare its Arctic interests and establish legal guidelines for China to strengthen its role in the Arctic Council.

A. To Seek the Most Favourable Interpretation and Application of International Law from China's Perspective

As analysed in section IV.B, soft law documents and scientific assessments adopted by the Arctic Council are of relevance for the areas where China has legal standing according to the UNCLOS and Svalbard Treaty. However, the scope of the areas where China enjoys legislative rights is not as clear as it could be due to the dispute on the scope of application of the

[37] 'For the focus disputes of the Arctic, such as the demarcation and the waterway issues, the Chinese government believes that it should be under the current system of international law, based on scientific data, which means that the development of international law should be addressed through the negotiation of new arrangements'. 'China supports the existing legal order, including UNCLOS, but believes that this legal framework requires coping with the situation and the implementation of refinements and progressive development'. See Zhengyue, 'Arctic Research Trip: China's Arctic affairs of view' (n 25).

Svalbard Treaty coupled with the ambitious provisions and insufficiency of the UNCLOS. Thus, in order to strengthen the legitimacy basis for China to enhance its role in the Council, China should seek favourable interpretation and application of the UNCLOS and the Svalbard Treaty to make the scope of rights explicit.

First, in the Svalbard archipelago, the scope of application of the Svalbard Treaty should be broadly interpreted in accordance with the purpose of the treaty, which is to promote the fair and free use of islands and waters. Norway's sovereignty was restricted when the treaty was entered into; therefore Norway's sovereign rights should not be exclusive in the exclusive economic zone and the continental shelf. Therefore, the scope of application of the treaty should include islands and territorial waters, exclusive economic zone and continental shelf.

Secondly, in recent years, the disputes on the Arctic have become progressively more focused on how to divide the 'outer continental shelf', which is related to the understanding and application of Article 76[38] of the Convention. Based on this article, in order to access the outer continental shelf, the coastal states should submit an application to the UN Commission on the Limits of the Continental Shelf, along with the relevant information regarding hydrology, location, seabed topography, reefs, biological and non-biological resource distribution to prove their claims. However, because of the technological requirements contained in the rule itself, though some applications have been submitted to the Commission, only the Norwegian application has been approved.[39] To this end, China should insist on the applicability of Article 76 with respect to the review mechanism of the Commission, requesting that the states concerned can delineate the outer limits of their outer continental shelf only with support from sufficient scientific evidence. It would contain the delimitation claims by the Arctic nations for a longer period. However, to further address this issue, a special Arctic agreement and Arctic regional treaty are needed.[40]

Thirdly, Article 234 of the UNCLOS is related to marine environmental protection in the Arctic, in particular to the prevention of ship source pollution. At the time of formulation, it was brought up as a supplementary provision during international negotiations. When Arctic navigation becomes possible, international control of the shipping lanes and marine

[38] The article specified the continental shelf system. Paras 1–3 specify the definition of the continental shelf; paras 4–7 provide specific methods and limitations of the outer continental shelf delimitation; paras 8–9 specify the procedures to apply for confirmation of the outer continental shelf.

[39] In 2001 the Russian government made a submission to the Commission to claim Arctic outer continental shelf waters. The Commission refused the application as a result of its investigation of the materials and data deficiencies. Thereafter, Iceland and Denmark in 2009 also submitted applications, but these have not been approved.

[40] L Huirong and D Yue, *Legal Issues on Arctic From the Perspective of Law of Sea* (Beijing, China University of Political Science Publishing, 2012).

environmental protection will become real problems. This raises an important question, namely what are the Arctic coastal states' administrative rights regarding waters pollution caused by ships. How should the interests of the flag states and the coastal states be balanced? An enforcement mechanism is required for the aforesaid provision. Absent an enforcement mechanism, the provision alone will not solve the governance problem of the Arctic marine environment. Therefore, it is imperative to develop a set of supplementary rules of navigation applicable to the international community in light of Article 234.

B. Actively Participate in Multilateral Co-operation and Expand Bilateral Co-operation

International co-operation on Arctic affairs has been carried out along two different paths. The first is dominated by the eight Arctic states within the Arctic region; the Arctic Council is a key example. The second is large-scale group co-operation involving the participation of actors within and without the Arctic region or led by the UN.[41] Moreover, bilateral co-operation aiming at enhancing practical interests is also playing an increasingly important role. The overall strategy in promoting co-operation to strengthen China's role in the Arctic Council is to 'act positively',[42] consolidating the multilateral and bilateral co-operation mechanisms according to the different nature of Arctic issues and co-operation areas, thereby eventually enhancing Chinese discourse and initiative in the Arctic Council. Participation in multilateral co-operation mainly refers to participation in multilateral co-operation mechanisms, such as the International Arctic Science Committee and the United Nations, to strengthen China's role in the Arctic Council indirectly. Expanding bilateral co-operation, in turn, means that China should emphasise co-operation with Arctic countries, the observer states and non-state actors.

i. Multilateral Co-operation

The *National Strategy for the Arctic Region* of the United States, which was released on 13 May 2013, stresses, in the section entitled 'Strengthen

[41] Z Xia and T Jingfang, 'International Cooperation Research under Arctic Economic Rediscovery' in Ding Huang (ed), *Polar National Policy Research Report* (Beijing, Science Publishing, 2013).

[42] In August 2011, the Chinese Foreign Ministry in Nanning City issued a 'White Paper on China's Diplomacy' that first used 'positive action' instead of 'keeping a low profile, to make a difference', the concept identified by Deng Xiaoping, indicating that the diplomatic guidelines had changed.

International Co-operation', that the 'remote and complex operating conditions in the Arctic environment make the region well-suited for collaborative efforts by nations seeking to explore emerging opportunities while emphasizing ecological awareness and preservation'. In fact, the Chinese government actively responded: 'Arctic affairs are regional, but also cross-regional, such as climate change and shipping and therefore [there is a] need to strengthen co-operation at both regional and international levels'.[43] Therefore, China has participated in several multilateral co-operation mechanisms. China is a member of the International Arctic Science Committee, member of the Arctic Science Committee and member of the Management Committee of the Arctic Ny-Ålesund Science Laboratory Advisory Committee. China also hosts the China-Nordic Arctic Research Center, and is also the first Asian country to participate in the Arctic Science Summit Week (ASSW). In addition, China is a member of the Intergovernmental Panel on Climate Change (IPCC) and International Maritime Organization (IMO). The above are organisational resources that can be used by China to strengthen its role in the Arctic Council. For instance, China sent a delegation to attend the 1996 meeting of the International Arctic Science Committee (IASC), in which only state-level scientific institutions are allowed to participate, and was accepted as a member.[44] Since then, China has participated in various scientific research co-operation activities organised by IASC. In fact, there are many environmental, social and cultural organisations in the Arctic regions, such as the Barents Euro-Arctic Council, the International Polar Foundation (IPF), the International Arctic Social Sciences Association (IASSA), the Northern Arctic Research Forum (NARF) and the University of the Arctic (UA). Chinese institutions may consider applying for participation in these organisations and their activities to expand multilateral co-operation.

ii. Bilateral Co-operation

International bilateral co-operation is guided by practical interests. Identifying the common points of view with potential co-operation partners is the key issue for China in developing bilateral co-operation to strengthen its role in the Arctic Council.

First, in co-operation with Arctic states, China shares the same interest in shipping with the United States, interest in energy and strategy security with Russia, interest in research with Canada and interest in enhancing the role of observers and promoting economic and trade co-operation with five European Arctic Council members. However, to date, the fields of

[43] See Foreign Ministry spokesman Tang Guoqiang's statements at the 2010 meeting of the Arctic Frontier Forum.

[44] See Chinese Antarctic Center of Surveying and Mapping, International Arctic Science Committee, pole.whu.edu.cn/cacsm/gb_article.php?modid=04001.

co-operation between China and member states have been mostly restricted to scientific research and environmental protection, with virtually no co-operation in ocean energy resources exploration and utilisation, shipping utilisation, strategic security and other fields. For instance, in 2010, China made agreements on Arctic research with Norway and Canada. In 2013, China and Iceland signed a Free Trade Agreement that expanded their co-operation from environmental protection and climate change—which are stressed in the Arctic Cooperation Framework Agreement (2012)—to trade co-operation as well. In 2013, the five Nordic countries took an important role when China was approved as an observer in order to enhance the openness of the Arctic Council. Besides, there are some good signals too. In particular, in 2013, Chinese delegates attended a number of important international conferences and expanded the topics to issues of laws and policies, marine resources and shipping in the Arctic: these conferences included the 4th Sino-US consultation on law of the sea and polar affairs, the 2nd Sino-Russia Marine Science Seminar and the Sino-Canada Arctic academic exchange conference.[45] However, China should keep focusing on assessing the possibility of co-operation and developing its co-operation with member states in the areas where it shares common points of view with these states but has not yet developed bilateral co-operation.

Secondly, when co-operating with observers, especially observer states and the EU,[46] it should be noted that although the EU and observer states have different priorities in Arctic scientific research, environmental protection, exploration and utilisation of resources, and shipping utilisation, they all have common points of view with China. The European observers became involved in the Arctic Council much earlier during its initial stages (except for Italy) and their interests focus on exploration and utilisation of offshore oil and gas resources.[47] On the other hand, Asian observers,

[45] From 10 to 13 October2012, the second Sino-Russia Marine Science Seminar was held in Vladivostok, Russia. The theme of the meeting was the marine environment and resources in the 21st century; 4 aspects were developed and discussed around the marine geological process and its effect, physical oceanography and global climate change, ocean mineral resources and its mineralisation, and marine ecosystem evolution. From 8 to 9 April 2013, the fourth Sino-US consultation on law of the sea and polar affairs was held in San Francisco, USA. Both sides exchanged views on common concerns about the law of the sea and polar affairs such as Arctic Council observers, Antarctic search and rescue, and Antarctic tourism. The 5th meeting was decided to be held in Beijing to deepen co-operation on international maritime law and policy, and co-operation in the Arctic and Antarctic areas. On 12 March 2013, the Sino-Canada Arctic academic exchange conference was held in Shanghai. Both sides discussed issues such as Arctic passage, China joining the Arctic Council and the role of the Arctic regional communities in Arctic governance. See 2013 National Annual Report on Polar Program of China, www.chinare.gov.cn/caa/gb_news.php?modid=05001&id=1443.

[46] The EU was approved as an ad hoc observer, but the Kiruna meeting in 2013 abolished the status of 'ad hoc observers'.

[47] T Koivurova and E J Molenaar, 'Canada, the EU, and Arctic Ocean Governance: A Tangled and Shifting Seascape and Future Directions' (2009) 18(2) *Transnational Law & Policy* 247.

including China, are newcomers in the Arctic Council and have different points of view. India's current priority in its Arctic strategy is scientific research, although it pays attention to scientific, environmental and commercial interests as well.[48] Business and industry play a critical role in the development of Japan's Arctic policy, which often raises the development of the Northern Sea Route as a priority. Singapore sees an opportunity in the Arctic to use its expertise in the running of major port facilities and two industries of vital importance to Singapore's economy: offshore and marine engineering.[49] Unlike some other Asian countries, South Korea is not hesitant to express its interest in exploring new energy sources in the Arctic in its National Basic Energy Plan 2008–30. Furthermore, strengthening their role in the Arctic Council and safeguarding their own interests in the Arctic region are the common points of view of all observer states (even though many counties have not stated these aims clearly). In fact, China and observer states and the EU have developed co-operation measures. For instance, in 2010, the Warsaw format meeting was organised under a Polish proposal to organise a working level meeting of the representatives of the observer states with the chair of the Arctic Council to exchange views.[50] In 2013, China and the EU signed the China-EU 2020 Strategic Agenda for Co-operation, with an emphasis on strengthening bilateral exchanges and co-operation in integrated ocean management, marine science and technology research and development, development of marine economy and utilisation of marine energy. China signed joint declarations with South Korea and India in 2008 and 2013, respectively, with an emphasis on strengthening co-operation in joint research and investigation in fields such as polar science and technology. In conclusion, it is obvious that the observer states and the EU all seek to strengthen their own role in the Arctic Council, but China has not developed any kind of co-operation in this area with other observers; China, the observer states and the EU also share common views in the fields of scientific research, environmental protection, shipping and offshore energy and resources, and have carried out co-operation for scientific research and environmental protection. However, in the field of shipping and marine energy resources, they have not yet carried out any substantial co-operation. Therefore, the main areas of co-operation in future bilateral co-operation between China and other observer states and the EU are exploration and utilisation of offshore energy and resources, as well as shipping utilisation.

[48] See India and the Arctic (2013) mea.gov.in/in-focus-article.htm?21812/India+and+the+Arctic.

[49] A Tonami, 'Arctic Newcomers: Japan, South Korea and Singapore' (2014) available at www.eastasiaforum.org/2014/02/15/arctic-newcomers-japan-south-korea-and-singapore/.

[50] P Paszkowski, 'Warsaw Meeting of Arctic Council Observer States' (2010) available at www.mfa.gov.pl/en/news/aktualnosc_34660.

Lastly, it is important to strengthen co-operation with non-state actors, particularly indigenous peoples' organisations, that are permanent participants of the Arctic Council. On the one hand, permanent participants have expressed concern that strengthening the role of the observers would threaten their own status.[51] Therefore, China should actively take action to dispel the doubts of indigenous peoples' organisations. On the other hand, indigenous peoples' organisations play a significant role in Arctic governance. They advocated for redefinition of sovereignty based on human security, which changed traditional national sovereignty to some extent, especially the Arctic nation-led model, to enhance their role in any intergovernmental co-operation in Arctic governance. In fact, although China has neither ratified ILO Convention 169 nor applied it to human security in the country, China voted in favour of the UN Declaration on the Rights of Indigenous Peoples and has also expressed concerns about the situation of indigenous people in the Arctic. A good example is in the draft Arctic Expedition Management Regulation,[52] which stresses the obligation to respect the rights and customs of indigenous people when carrying out expeditions. Thus, the Chinese government should focus on how to actually express concern about indigenous peoples, for instance, providing financial support or ratifying ILO Convention 169, and deepening China's co-operation with them.

In short, China should make full use of existing multilateral co-operation organisations and is actively involved in other multilateral co-operation organisations, based on the common points of view as a starting point to expand bilateral co-operation with member states, observers and indigenous peoples' organisations.

C. Areas of Co-operation

China's current participation in Arctic affairs is mainly limited to scientific and environmental issues,[53] as the country is rarely involved in the fields of marine energy and resources development and shipping utilisation. In fact, according to the sensitivity of the different issues, the Arctic issues include the low sensitivity areas of scientific research and climate change, and other more sensitive issues such as marine energy and resources development and

[51] Inuit Circumpolar Council, 'The Role and Application Process of Observers in the Arctic Council, Views from the Inuit Circumpolar Council' (2010) a–f.

[52] Legislative project of 'Arctic Expedition Management Regulation', which was conducted by the State Oceanic Administration, began around 2006, had not been formally adopted until now.

[53] In 2010, Norway and Canada signed an agreement on Arctic research; in 2012, China and Iceland signed an Arctic co-operation framework agreement; China signed joint declarations with South Korea and India in 2008 and 2013, respectively, with an emphasis on strengthening co-operation in joint research and investigation in the field of polar science and technology.

Arctic governance, as well as highly sensitive issues such as the dispute over Arctic shipping. In order to strengthen China's role in the Arctic Council, China should expand its areas of co-operation in a clear and timely manner. These efforts should start from low sensitivity areas, and gradually expand to tackle problems in high sensitivity areas.

Low sensitivity areas include climate change and scientific research. Actually, this is the priority of China's participation in Arctic co-operation. China should continue to promote Arctic ecology and environmental protection-related legal issues in global climate change negotiations, making them a key part of the governance of global climate. Moreover, China should continue to co-operate in scientific research, in order to save expedition funds and share data. Medium sensitivity areas include exploration and utilisation of offshore energy and resources, as well as the improvement of Arctic governance. First, the melting of the Arctic ice is opening plentiful oil, gas and gas hydrate resources to competition, which is the focus of international contention.[54] One of these resources, gas hydrate, is considered a potential energy of the twenty-first century because of its high energy density, wide distribution and accumulation in shallow sediments.[55] The world's only commercial gas hydrate company, the Messoyakha Gas Field of Russia, also confirmed that commercial development has become possible. So far, Arctic countries have made breakthroughs in technologies related to gas hydrate accumulation, exploration technology and production test equipment. China, as a non-Arctic country that emphasises scientific investigation and ignores the exploration and utilisation of offshore energy and resources, can learn from the South Korean experience[56] in co-operation and acquisition of holdings as means of becoming involved in the exploration and utilisation of offshore energy and resources. Secondly, with regard to the Arctic governance model, China should actively advocate to change the traditional nation-led model of governance in the Arctic, emphasising the important role of indigenous peoples, non-Arctic countries and international organisations in the Arctic Council. The high sensitivity areas mainly refer to the disputes concerning Arctic shipping. Sovereignty disputes between Arctic states can usually be solved by bilateral agreement,[57] but other disputes including Arctic shipping ownership and outer continental shelf division remain

[54] T Koivurova, 'Dialectic of Understanding Progress in Arctic Governance' (2013) 22(1) *Michigan State International Law Review* 7–8.

[55] YF Makogon and SA Holditch, 'Natural Gas-hydrates: a Potential Energy Source for the 21 Century' (2007) *Journal of Petroleum Science and Engineering* 14.

[56] In February 2011, for the first time, South Korea achieved the right to develop Arctic resources. South Korea decided to buy a 20% holding in the Umiak field, which was owned by the Canadian energy company MGM, as a chance to participate in Arctic resource development.

[57] Such as the agreement between Greenland and Canada on the division of the continental shelf, 17 December 1973, in force 13 March 1974, 950 United Nations Treaties Series 152; the agreement between Iceland and Norway on fisheries and the continental shelf questions, 28 May 1980, in force 13 June 1980, 32705 UN Delimitation Treaties Infobase; Agreement on

unsolved, leaving room for China to co-operate with other countries. For example, Russia and Canada have made claims that they have jurisdiction over Arctic shipping. Although China's shipping interests are consistent with those of the United States, the European Union and Japan, China should assess the situation cautiously. China should either clearly defend the principles of innocent passage and freedom of navigation through new shipping, like the United States and the European Union, or depart from its user interests and co-operate with Russia and Canada as soon as possible in order to promote the expected shipping interests.

In short, China should focus on co-operation in higher sensitivity areas, including utilisation of shipping and offshore resources and energy, as well as the improvement of the openness of the Arctic Council, on the basis of enhancing co-operation in low sensitivity areas including Arctic environmental protection and research.

D. Capacity Building

Capacity building plays an important role in strengthening China's role in the Arctic Council. China, on the one hand, should continue to strengthen Arctic research capacity to respond to future utilisation of resources and shipping, and, on the other hand, should focus on 'soft power' building in the Arctic Council and finally, supported by scientific data, seek to maximise its role in decision-making.

i. Research Capacity

Since China started its Arctic scientific expeditions in 1990, the greatest concern of the Chinese government in the Arctic has been on low political issues, which mainly include scientific expeditions, Arctic climate and ecological environment.[58] So far, China has established a preliminary observation system to observe physical altitude, climate change, ecology,

the Continental Shelf between Iceland and Jan Mayen, 22 October 1981 in force 2 June 1982, 21 *International Legal Materials* 1222; Delimitation Agreement Between The United States And The Soviet Union Concerning The Bering And Chukchi Sea, 1 June 1990, not in force; the Agreement between the Kingdom of Denmark and the Kingdom of Norway concerning the Delimitation of the Continental Shelf in the Area between Jan Mayen and Greenland and concerning the Boundary between the Fishery Zones in the Area, 18 December 1995, in force 18 December 1995; Maritime Delimitation And Co-Operation Treaty Between Russia And Norway In The Barents Sea And The Arctic Ocean, 15 September 2010, in force 7 July 2011, UN Treaties Series Reg No 49095; and Arctic Co-Operation Agreement Between Canada And The United States, 11 January 1998, Consolidated Treaty Series 1988/29.

[58] The former Vice Premier Li Keqiang on a polar expedition to commemorate the fifth anniversary of China, forum statement: 'Polar expedition is of importance to explore earth science

marine and other aspects in the Arctic, and assembled a high-quality team of experts. Furthermore, China has greatly enhanced its marine science and climate change research capabilities. China has established reliable Arctic expedition capabilities.[59] In the context of climate change, the feasibility of resource exploitation and utilisation of waterways has increased. The Ocean Career Development Twelfth Five-Year Plan (2011–15)[60] continues to focus on strengthening scientific capabilities based on the Eleventh Five-Year Plan on Marine Science and Technology Development (2006–10); for the first time, it also proposes to 'strengthen polar research and utilisation of biological resources, to carry out the collection and application assessment of microbial genetic resources [and to] strengthen survey and research on Arctic waterway utilisation, and actively participate in international co-operation in related fields'. This shows that China has the intention to expand the scope of its Arctic expeditions to the utilisation of resources and waterways. This poses new demands and challenges for China's expedition capacity in terms of how to improve the expedition equipment and harness its Arctic exploration to enhance its use of resources and shipping in the Arctic.

ii. Soft Power

In order to leverage its Arctic scientific ability in the Arctic Council, China must improve its soft power in the Council, which includes the ability to develop the agenda, draft proposals, resolve disputes and guide public opinion. If a country can shape international rules, so that they are aligned with its own interests and values, its behaviour seems more likely to have legitimacy to others.[61] The Arctic is now in a preparatory phase to enter the global market, and dominance in establishing rules and institutions is becoming the main focal point in the competition. According to the Arctic Council Observer Manual for Subsidiary Bodies, an observer can propose a project though member states and permanent participants, which could offer China a breakthrough to strengthen its soft power in the Arctic Council. China should work within the power structure of international politics and comply with the norms of international laws, and then develop global and friendly projects supported by data obtained in its expeditions. Once

and recognise the mysteries of nature. It is closely related to long-term interests of China's development, and also has practical significance to research and response to global climate change'; see L Keqiang, 'Polar Expedition and Long-term Interest of China', news.xinhuanet.com/politics/2009-11/20/content_12508072.htm.

[59] See A Chircop, 'The Emergence of China as a Polar-Capable State' (2011) 7 *Canada Naval Review* 9.

[60] See www.soa.gov.cn/zwgk/fwjgwywj/shxzfg/201304/t20130411_24765.html.

[61] JS Nye, 'Soft Power, The Means to Success in World Politics' (2014) 10 *Public Affairs* 10–11.

the agenda has been fixed, China should begin to reserve its expertise, and construct the framework of the agenda. Another important way for China to strengthen its soft power is to express its views and opinions effectively in the Arctic Council based on the rights to make written and oral statements and put forward views.

E. Strengthening China's Domestic Arctic Strategy and Legislation

Strengthening China's Arctic strategy and legislation can, first, serve to identify and clarify China's Arctic strategic interests, which will help to dispel the doubts of the Arctic states and permanent participants concerning China and reduce public opinion resistance to China's stronger role in the Arctic Council. Secondly, strategy formulation and expedition legislation could provide a path for China to strengthen its role in the Arctic Council.

So far, all of the Arctic states have adopted a national strategy or policy for the Arctic, and some of them are constantly updating their strategies; some non-Arctic countries have also introduced Arctic strategies.[62] The strategies and policies of all the countries and the EU, although they have different priorities, serve mainly to protect their sovereign interests, national security interests, economic interests as well as the political stability of the Arctic and institutionalised co-operation. China's Twelfth five-year plan stressed that it must

> improve the ocean legislative framework .... accelerate to enact Antarctic activities management regulations [and] strengthen the marine economy, the Bohai Sea region, marine disaster prevention and mitigation, ocean cruising law enforcement,

[62] Canada: Government of Canada, *Canada's Northern Strategy Our North, Our Heritage, Our Future* (Ottawa, Ministry of Indian Affairs and Northern Development and Federal Interlocutor for Métis and Non-Status Indians, 2009); Denmark: Kingdom of Denmark Ministry of Foreign Affairs, *Denmark, Greenland and the Faroe Islands: Kingdom of Denmark Strategy for the Arctic 2011–2020* (Copenhagen, Ministry of Foreign Affairs, 2011); Finland: Prime Minister's Office, *Finland's Strategy for the Arctic Region* (Helsinki, Prime Minister's Office Publication. 2009); Iceland: Althingi, *A Parliamentary Resolution on Iceland's Arctic Policy* (Reykjavik, Ministry of Foreign Affairs, 2011); Norway: Norwegian Government, *The Norwegian Government's High North Strategy* (Oslo, Norwegian Ministry of Foreign Affairs, 2006); Russia: President of the Russian Federation D Medvedev, *The Fundamentals of State Policy of the Russian Federation in the Arctic in the Period till 2020 and beyond* (Moscow, Rossiyskaya Gazeta, 2009); Sweden: Government Offices of Sweden, *Sweden's Strategy for the Arctic Region* (Stockholm, XGSGrafics Service, 2011); US: The White House. *National Security Presidential Directive and Homeland Security Presidential Directive* (Washington, DC, The White House, 2009); see also concerning the observer states Germany's Arctic policy guidelines: Assume responsibility, seize opportunities, Federal Foreign Office, November 2013; UK Polar Regions Department Foreign and Commonwealth Office (2013), Adapting To Change: UK Policy towards the Arctic; European Commission (2008) 'The European Union and the Arctic Region' COM(2008) 763 final, 20 November 2008; Council of the European Union, 'Conclusions on Arctic issues', 2985th Foreign Affairs Council meeting (2009); European Parliament, 'Resolution on a sustainable EU policy for the High North' (2011) 2009/2214(INI).

> ocean exploration, military legislative study, sea and ocean management and other aspects of the Basic Law.

However, it did not propose to strengthen the legislation concerning the Arctic. Obviously, China has no legislation on Arctic affairs to claim its Arctic interests. The absence of an Arctic strategy has not only raised doubts about China's motivation for participating in Arctic affairs, but has also severely restricted China's ability to participate effectively in the Arctic Council. To this end, China should actively develop an Arctic strategy that is consistent with China's diplomatic strategy and ocean strategy and make sense of strategic objectives, strategic interests and ways to achieve objectives. The priorities of the Chinese Arctic strategy, first of all, should highlight the importance of environmental and climate change in Arctic governance, and China's role in Arctic climate governance; secondly, it should emphasise the improvement of the Arctic governance model, advocating that the traditional Arctic states-led model should be amended into a new model that emphasises the special status of indigenous peoples and the important role of international organisations and non-Arctic countries; thirdly, China should insist that substantive disputes in the Arctic should be solved under the framework of the UNCLOS and relevant international co-operation mechanisms. In addition, China should actively implement relevant Arctic-specific legislation to provide legal guidelines for specific ways to strengthen China's role in the Arctic Council.

VI. CONCLUSIONS

The Arctic Council, as the most important policy-shaping international organisation dealing with the Arctic, combined with a series of practices under the proposal to strengthen the Arctic Council, will play an increasingly important role or even the leading role in Arctic governance. For this reason, the debate on the role of indigenous peoples organisations, non-Arctic states and NGOs in the Arctic Council is becoming increasingly heated, especially for observer states that have a crucial role in responding to the challenges of climate change in Arctic governance. However, existing observers have no decision-making power on issues related to climate change in the Arctic Council.

Based on the UNCLOS and Svalbard Treaty, China has many legitimate rights and interests in the Arctic. As the most important co-operation mechanism focusing on environmental protection and sustainable development of the Arctic, the Arctic Council should provide access to non-Arctic countries, including China, rather than be monopolised by the Arctic states. To this end, China should adhere to developing the current international sea framework and promoting favourable interpretation and application of the existing international law. In addition to strengthening international co-operation and capacity building, there is a need to actively strengthen Arctic strategies and legislation, which are all effective ways for strengthening China's role in the Arctic Council.

In addition, it is worth noting that this chapter sought to explore the role of China, as an observer state, in the Arctic Council. Considering the limitations of the Arctic Council in Arctic governance in the context of climate change, as well as the strong calls to increase the openness of the Arctic Council, especially from non-Arctic countries, it would also be worthwhile to explore how China seeks a breakthrough by becoming a member state of the Arctic Council.

3

Legal Issues in Arctic Scientific Research: A Chinese Perspective

REN SHIDAN

I. INTRODUCTION

THE ARCTIC, A region centred on the Arctic Ocean and surrounded by the Eurasian and North American mainland as well as several islands, is a crucial area for the development of marine environmental and ecological research. In addition, the Arctic is one of the most sensitive areas impacted by global environmental changes. Climate change has become a serious environmental threat and dealing with it must be a priority all around the world. Carrying out the relevant scientific research in the Arctic is essential for forecasting the future trends in global climate and environmental changes. As a result, the Arctic has become the key area for scientific research concerning the Earth. In addition, non-Arctic countries are now actively involved in the region through their scientific research activities.

China possesses neither Arctic territory nor the ability to take part actively in regional decision-making through the Arctic Council. In spite of China being a non-Arctic state, its government pays great attention to the research value of the Arctic and its significant impact on climate change, focusing particularly on the latter. In a speech at the Arctic Frontiers Conference held on 21 January 2013, Chinese Ambassador Zhao Jun called China a 'near-Arctic state'. This was the first reference to China as a 'near-Arctic state'. In the speech, he explained the reason behind this as being that 'the northeast part of China is close to 50 degrees north latitude'. He further proposed that as a 'near-Arctic state', China is significantly influenced by the natural changes and economic developments in the Arctic region through impacts—induced by climate change—to activities including agricultural production, shipping, trade, as well as social and economic development. As a result, he thought that carrying out scientific research in the Arctic will help China to gain a better understanding of many major issues, such as the evolution of the environment and ecosystem of the Arctic, and its implications for the global environment. He also argued that such research would enhance China's capacity to deal with climate change, natural disaster mitigation and prevention, etc.[1] This statement reflects how China views Arctic scientific research.

China's governmental Arctic scientific expedition began in the late 1990s, which is not only later than other Arctic scientific expedition powers, but also later than the Chinese Antarctic scientific expedition, which began in the early 1980s. China organised its first and second Arctic expeditions in 1999 and 2003, respectively. In 2004, it established its first Arctic scientific station, 'Yellow River', to carry out scientific research work. With its research in fields such as oceanography, atmospheric physics, biology, high latitude physics and glaciology, the station has obtained data, information and samples. In 2008 and 2010, China organised its third and fourth Chinese Arctic expeditions. The fourth expedition expanded the scope of research into the Bering and Arctic Ocean off the coast of Canada, extending China's marine research to the North Pole. In 2012, China organised its fifth Arctic expedition, during which the 'Snow Dragon' research ship travelled from the Pacific Ocean to the Atlantic Ocean through the Northern Sea Route and returned to China sailing a straight line from Iceland to the Bering Strait via the North Pole. This was the first trip by a Chinese ship to reach such high latitude. On 11 July 2014, China's sixth Arctic scientific expedition set sail from Shanghai to the North Pole to perform scientific research tasks over a period of 76 days and covered a total distance of about 11,000 nautical miles. In addition to these official activities, Chinese researchers engaged in international co-operation, or carried out some Arctic expeditions sponsored by non-governmental organisations. In the Arctic area, Chinese expeditions are mainly concentrated in US Alaska, northern Canada and the Svalbard archipelago. As part of its marine scientific research, China has inspected the waters of the Chukchi Sea. The core objectives of the Chinese Arctic research focused on two themes: climate change and the environment.[2]

However, in recent years, researchers in the Arctic coastal countries have questioned China's frequent Arctic expeditions. For example, Shiloh Rainwater proposed that China has maintained a vast, well-funded Arctic research apparatus since the mid-1990s and that the country is preparing to exploit a seasonally ice-free Arctic.[3] In fact, it is China's identity as a rising

[1] Zhao Jun, 'China and the High North' (2013), speech by Chinese Ambassador Zhao Jun at the Arctic Frontiers Conference on 21 January 2013.

[2] Zhang Jiansong, 'Exclusive Interview: A Wide Range of Melting of Arctic Sea Ice Become the Scientific Focus', available at http://news.xinhuanet.com/politics/2010-07/01/c_12287178.htm.

[3] S Rainwater, 'Race to the North: China's Arctic Strategy and Its Implications' (2013) 66(2) *Naval War College Review* 61–62.

superpower that creates suspicions, as the country is becoming involved in Arctic affairs (including through scientific research).[4] Some foreign scholars have thought that China actively participates in Arctic affairs mainly in order to meet its rapidly rising energy demand. For example, Shiloh Rainwater proposed that Arctic resources and sea-lanes present a welcome strategic remedy for China's energy import-dependent economy.[5] This analysis is countered by Canadian scholar Frederic Lasserre. Lasserre proposes that, although Arctic research has certainly received renewed impetus recently, Chinese polar science is by far more focused on Antarctic research than on Arctic research.[6] Through his analysis, he considered how to interpret China's scientific interest in the Arctic: as China becomes a major power in the twenty-first century, its science must match its overall ambitions and be aligned with the quality of the science produced by other developed countries.[7] An 'ice-free' Arctic might contribute to meet China's rapidly rising energy demand, but there is no guarantee that this will be the case. The Chinese government is not unaware that non-Arctic states do not have any privileged access to resources located in the Arctic. But would China suddenly abandon or reduce its Arctic scientific research if it cannot access natural resources in the region? The obvious answer is no. The viewpoint of Frederic Lasserre may therefore be more pertinent.

This chapter examines legal issues related to China's Arctic scientific research. The main research question is the following: does China have the legal right to carry out scientific research in the Arctic? If the answer is affirmative, then what is the extent of this right? Are there legal obstacles for China to carry out scientific research in the Arctic? And if so, what are the solutions proposed to address these challenges? The following sections (II, III and IV) will analyse each of these questions one after another.

II. LEGITIMACY OF CHINA'S ARCTIC SCIENTIFIC RESEARCH

China is a contracting party to the United Nations Convention on the Law of the Sea (UNCLOS), the Svalbard Treaty and other relevant international treaties. Consequently, the country has obligations under these treaties,

[4] D Huang, *Annual Report on National Polar Policy Research 2012–2013* (Beijing, Science Press, 2013) 50.

[5] ibid, 62. Dd—d

[6] This assessment is confirmed by the comparison of the missions taking place in both regions. The length of the Chinese Antarctic expedition is 180 days per year, while the longest Arctic expedition is only 3 months, and the personnel size that China invests in Arctic expeditions is only half of the personnel of its Antarctic expeditions.

[7] F Lasserre, 'China and the Arctic: Threat or Cooperation Potential for Canada?' (2013) 11 *China Papers of Canadian International Council* 1–16.

but is also given specific rights as a party to these instruments. The freedom to carry out scientific research in the Arctic area is among the rights guaranteed to China by these treaties.

A. The United Nations Convention on the Law of the Sea (UNCLOS)

The UNCLOS was adopted on 10 December 1982 at the last meeting of the third UN Conference on the Law of the Sea in Montego Bay, Jamaica, and entered into force in 1994. It has now secured the ratification of more than 150 countries. The UNCLOS is the cornerstone of the current international law of the sea. It applies to the marine environment of the entire globe, and therefore includes the entire marine environment of the Arctic, however it is defined.[8] All Arctic states, except for the United States, are parties to the UNCLOS. In May 2008, the United States and the other four Arctic coastal states jointly signed the Ilulissat Declaration. According to the Ilulissat Declaration, the five coastal states regard the framework defined under UNCLOS as providing a solid foundation for responsible management by themselves and other users of the Arctic Ocean through the national implementation and application of the relevant provisions of the Convention.[9] Thus, although the United States is not a contracting party of the UNCLOS, it has also expressed that it is committed to following its provisions in the region.

There are more detailed rules in part XIII of the UNCLOS about the purpose of scientific research that is covered by the Convention, the procedure for examination and approvals of such activities, and the rights that the coastal states can claim.[10] According to Article 238 of the UNCLOS, 'all states, irrespective of their geographical location, and competent international organizations have the right to conduct marine scientific research subject to the rights and duties of other States as provided for in the convention'.[11] These provisions apply to all states parties engaged in Arctic scientific research.

China is a signatory party to the UNCLOS. On 15 May 1996, the Standing Committee of the National People's Congress of the People's Republic of China approved the United Nations Convention on the Law of the Sea. In July of the same year, the convention came into effect in China. As a signatory and ratifying state of the convention, China can refer to the rights

[8] T Koivurova and E Molenaar, *International Governance and Regulation of the Marine Arctic: Overview and Gap Analysis* (Oslo, WWF International Arctic Programme, 2009).

[9] The Ilulissat Declaration (2008) available at http://www.oceanlaw.org/downloads/arctic/Ilulissat_Declaration.pdf.

[10] United Nations Convention on the Law of the Sea, 10 December 1982, in force 16 November 1994, 21 *International Legal Materials* 1261 (1982) (UNCLOS).

[11] ibid, art 240.

provided by the convention to safeguard China's national rights and interests in the Arctic region. According to the UNCLOS, China shall have the right to enter the high seas in the Arctic to conduct research activities. Additionally, China also has the right to conduct scientific research in the exclusive economic zone (EEZ) or on the continental shelves of the coastal states subject to the rights and duties of these states as provided for in the convention.

B. The Svalbard Treaty

The Svalbard archipelago is located between 10° to 35° east longitude and 74° to 81° northern latitude, 657 kilometres north of the coast of Norway, and is composed of nine main islands (Spitsbergen, North East Land, Edge Island, Barents Island, King Charles Land, Prince Charles Foreland, Kvit Island, Hopen and Bear Island) and numerous small islands. The archipelago covers an area of 61,020 square kilometres and nearly 60 per cent of the area is covered by glaciers. The biggest among its islands is the Spitsbergen Island, covering an area of 39,044 square kilometres.

The Svalbard archipelago is a good place to study the advance and retreat of glaciers, and other impacts of global climate change. The sediments extracted from the numerous mountain lakes of the archipelago are good carriers of information to analyse the environmental consequences of the evolution of the Arctic climate. The Svalbard archipelago is located on the path of the North Atlantic Current. It is consequently called 'the oasis in the Arctic', being affected by the warm waters carried by the current. In summer, a variety of plant species grow in the area, so it is among the best places to research Arctic flora. Therefore, the Svalbard archipelago has always served as a hub in the history of Arctic scientific expeditions. In Ny-Ålesund, there are now field observation and research bases from Norway, France, Germany, Britain, Italy, Japan, South Korea and other countries. China's first Arctic station—'the Yellow River station'—is also located in Ny-Ålesund.

On 9 February 1920, 18 countries, including the United Kingdom, the United States, Denmark, Norway, Sweden, France, Italy, the Netherlands, Japan and others, signed the Svalbard Treaty (also called Spitsbergen Treaty) in Paris. By 1925, 33 countries, including China, the former Soviet Union, Germany, Finland, Spain and others, had joined the treaty. The treaty has a total of 51 contracting states at present. The Svalbard Treaty acknowledged 'the full and absolute sovereignty of Norway over the Svalbard archipelago'.[12] But citizens of states parties are free to enter the archipelago,

[12] Spitsbergen (Svalbard) Treaty, 9 February 1920, in force 14 August 1925, 2 *League of Nations Treaties Series* 8, art 1.

on the premise of abiding by Norwegian law, and enjoy the rights to fish and hunt, conduct legitimate productive or commercial activities in the Svalbard archipelago region and its territorial sea, and also have the right to carry out scientific research under certain conditions. Article 5 of the Svalbard Treaty points out that specific conventions may also be subsequently concluded to lay down the conditions under which scientific investigations may be conducted in the Svalbard archipelago.[13] However, the states parties to the Svalbard Treaty have thus far not concluded a new treaty related to scientific research in the Svalbard archipelago. Therefore, one cannot deny the legitimacy that the contracting states including China have to establish a logistics base for an Arctic expedition and to implement scientific research in the Svalbard archipelago.

III. RIGHTS OF CHINA'S ARCTIC SCIENTIFIC RESEARCH

Overall, China's scientific research rights in the Arctic include the rights to carry out scientific expeditions, engage in scientific research co-operation and share information concerning the Arctic. China has always attached great importance to Arctic scientific research co-operation. China is involved in many international scientific committees and bodies, such as the International Arctic Science Committee (IASC) and the Arctic Ocean Science Committee (AOSC). Already in the 1990s, before the country had established a permanent Arctic facility, Chinese scientists were working together with scientists from Canada, Finland, Germany, Norway, Russia, and the USA.[14] However, some foreign analysts, such as Roger W Robinson, Jr, think that Beijing's Arctic strategy is underpinned by the initial use of soft power to attain its regional objectives and that science and resource diplomacy and active engagement in multilateral institutions are already playing a large role in this 'long con' in the so-called High North.[15] In fact, the Arctic environment is extremely complex, and it is difficult to complete research in related areas when relying only on national capacity; close co-operation between several countries is thus necessary. Although research collaboration could be seen as a way of engaging in diplomacy, it is also a legal right of China endowed by relevant international treaties and 'soft laws'.

[13] ibid, art 5.

[14] Chinese Arctic and Antarctic Administration (CAA), 'International Cooperation and Exchange' (21 July 2015) available at www.chinare.gov.cn/caa/gb_article.php?modid=06001.

[15] RW Robinson Jr , 'China's Long-term Arctic Strategy' (13 October 2013) www.troymedia.com/2013/10/13/chinas-long-term-arctic-strategy/.

A. The Implementation Rights of Arctic Scientific Expeditions

On the basis of the UNCLOS, the Svalbard Treaty and other international treaties, China has the right to conduct scientific research and studies in the high seas over the Arctic region and the territorial sea, EEZ and continental shelves of Arctic coastal states, as well as the Svalbard archipelago region. Of course, the freedom to conduct scientific research is subject to obligations.

In general, marine scientific research shall be conducted exclusively for peaceful purposes, with appropriate scientific methods; shall not unjustifiably interfere with other legitimate use of the sea; and shall be in conformity with international law and the preservation of the marine environment.[16] The UNCLOS has also made special provisions on the marine environmental protection of ice-covered areas. According to Article 234 of the convention,

> coastal States have the right to adopt and enforce non-discriminatory laws and regulations for the prevention, reduction and control of marine pollution from vessels in ice-covered areas within the limits of the EEZ, where particularly severe climatic conditions and the presence of ice covering such areas for most of the year create obstructions or exceptional hazards to navigation, and pollution of the marine environment could cause major harm to or irreversible disturbance of the ecological balance, and such laws and regulations shall have due regard to navigation and the protection and preservation of the marine environment based on the best available scientific evidence.[17]

While conducting scientific research in the Svalbard archipelago, parties also need to abide by the relevant Norwegian laws and regulations on the environment and resources protection and management, for example, the Svalbard Environmental Protection Act (2002).

In view of scientific research conducted in different sea areas, the UNCLOS includes specific provisions. First, within the scope of the high seas, the contracting states shall have the freedom to conduct scientific research; secondly, marine scientific research within the territorial waters shall be subject to being conducted only with the express consent of and under the conditions set forth by the coastal state;[18] thirdly, the convention lays down detailed regulations on marine scientific research carried out in the EEZ and continental shelf.

The first of these provisions relates to programme requirements. Marine scientific research carried out in the EEZ and continental shelf shall be subject to consent by the coastal state. Countries and international organisations interested in related marine scientific research should submit a

[16] UNCLOS, art 240.
[17] ibid, art 234.
[18] ibid, art 245.

scientific research plan at least six months in advance, through official channels, to provide the coastal state with information, including a description of the nature, goals, time, region, methods and tools, as well as indicating information related to the sponsoring institutions and the extent to which the coastal state should be able to participate or be represented in the project.[19] Under normal circumstances, the coastal countries shall grant approval for scientific research that is carried out in accordance with the UNCLOS and that is undertaken 'exclusively for peaceful purposes'. The coastal countries can refuse a scientific research project in any of the following circumstances: the scientific research plan is directly related to the exploration and development of the natural resources; it involves the drilling of the continental shelf, the use of explosives, or the introduction of harmful materials into the marine environment; or it involves the construction, operation or use, etc of artificial islands and facilities.[20]

Secondly, the convention stipulates the rights of the coastal countries and the obligations of the countries conducting research. The coastal states have the right to participate in the relevant scientific research projects. If the coastal state so requires, research countries should provide it with a preliminary report, the final results and conclusions, data that can be copied and samples that can be separated without damaging their scientific value, and provide the corresponding evaluation and interpretation. If there is any major change in the research programme, immediate notice must be given to the coastal countries by the research countries. Unless otherwise agreed, the equipment should be removed immediately after research is completed. If the research country fails to conduct its research in accordance with the conditions of the prior notice or does not comply with the obligations in the convention under study, the coastal state is entitled to pause or stop the related scientific research activities in the EEZ or continental shelf.[21]

In fact, the five Arctic coastal states generally have legislated to establish management systems on the Arctic scientific research. The scopes of application of these legislations cover not only domestic scientific research institutions and individuals, but also foreign scientific research institutions and individuals. The United States, for example, promulgated the Arctic Expedition and Policy Act in 1984, which is a specialised legislation managing the behaviour of Arctic expeditions. In addition, Approval Rules for the Foreign Ships Carrying out Marine Scientific Research in the United States and the Alaska National Interest Lands Conservation Act adopted in 1980 also contain special provisions about regulating the activities of Arctic expeditions. As another example, the Russian approved the federal law 'on the Exclusive

[19] ibid, art 248.
[20] ibid, art 246.
[21] ibid, art 249.

economic zone of the Russian Federation' in 1998, which provides the main rules through which Russia regulates related scientific research.

B. Scientific Research Co-operation and Information Sharing

Scientific research co-operation and information sharing are crucial for the good conduct and dissemination of marine scientific research. Part XIII of the UNCLOS on 'Marine scientific research' contains a specific session (section 2) that provides additional rules on international co-operation. According to Article 242:

> (1): States and competent international organizations shall, in accordance with the principle of respect for sovereignty and jurisdiction and on the basis of mutual benefit, promote international cooperation in marine scientific research for peaceful purposes.

In terms of information sharing, Article 244(2) stipulates that:

> States, both individually and in cooperation with other States and with competent international organizations, shall actively promote the flow of scientific data and information and the transfer of knowledge resulting from marine scientific research, especially to developing States, as well as the strengthening of the autonomous marine scientific research capabilities of developing States through, inter alia, programs to provide adequate education and training of their technical and scientific personnel.

In addition to the provisions of the UNCLOS, the IASC, the Arctic Ocean Sciences Board (AOSB) and Ny-Ålesund Science Managers Committee (NySMAC) further define the conditions for the engagement of China in international scientific research communication and for the co-operation with other countries and other actors. The regulations on how to standardise the behaviour of Arctic scientific expeditions introduced by these international organisations also provide a legitimate foundation for China to engage in scientific research co-operation.

IASC is a non-governmental international scientific organisation. Under the International Arctic Science Committee Founding Articles that were co-signed on 28 August 1990 by the representatives of the eight Arctic states in Resolute Bay, Canada, only scientific institutions' representatives with national-level authority are eligible to participate in the organisation's activities on behalf of its countries. China joined IASC in 1996. Since its foundation, IASC has conducted fruitful work. On the basis of the principle of 'peaceful scientific co-operation', IASC actively co-ordinates and guides the Arctic expeditions from different countries and organises large international co-operation programmes to address important scientific problems. The committee provides a platform for scientists in different countries and regions to communicate.

The Ny-Ålesund Science Managers Committee is an international research institution engaging in Arctic research that was set up to co-ordinate the scientific research of each country in the Ny-Ålesund region. NySMAC was established in 1994, with the purpose of strengthening co-operation and co-ordination between countries engaging in Arctic scientific research in Ny-Ålesund, Norway. In 2005, China hosted the Arctic Scientific Summit Week and was successfully elected as a member of the Ny-Ålesund Science Managers Committee. NySMAC holds meetings regularly for the experts of each country in order to enable them to communicate research achievements. In this context, NySMAC also serves as a platform enabling Chinese scientists to engage in co-operation and communication.

IV. LEGAL OBSTACLES TO CHINA'S ARCTIC SCIENTIFIC RESEARCH

On the basis of the UNCLOS, the contracting states conducting scientific research in the territorial sea, EEZ and continental shelves of Arctic coastal countries face more restrictions than when engaging in scientific research in the high seas. Indeed, they need to follow: (1) the compulsory provisions of by the UNCLOS related to scientific research countries (described in section III of this chapter); (2) the provisions contained in other international conventions and which relate to maritime and environmental aspects of marine scientific research; (3) the domestic legislation of Arctic coastal states regulating scientific expeditions, including procedural and substantive norms and (4) environmental regulations related to the rights and interests of indigenous peoples in the domestic legislation of the Arctic coastal countries. Additionally, coastal states have the right to prohibit scientific research activities by the nationals of other states. Coastal states cannot bluntly prohibit research, but they may do so if any of the criteria highlighted above are not met.

Through the analysis of previous Chinese scientific research activities, foreign scholars acknowledge that there is no reason to believe that China does not abide by these rules.[22] However, the above restrictions have in fact caused challenges for China in scientific research activity in the Arctic. From a legal point of view, the obstacles that China has faced in Arctic scientific research have mainly resulted from the restrictions imposed by the scientific research application system established by the Arctic coastal states. In recent Arctic expeditions, China has once again encountered these types of problems.[23]

[22] Lasserre, 'China and the Arctic' (n 7) 4.

[23] L Huirong and D Yue, *Legal Issues in the Arctic: from the Perspectives of the Law of the Sea* (Beijing, China University of Political Science and Law Press, 2012) 247–50.

China organised a second Arctic expedition in 2003, with the main aim of investigating and studying the Arctic Ocean, atmosphere, changes of sea ice and the interactions between these physical systems. According to the research plan, some of the sites selected to conduct this research were located in the Russian EEZ. Based on the Russian law adopted in 1998, the applicant for the marine scientific investigation shall fill in the request according to the format set out in the regulation and send it to the Russian Federation's administrative authority of science and technology. Foreign applicants shall submit a request through diplomatic channels six months before starting their marine science research. Furthermore, if within four months from the date that the Russian Federation administrative authority in charge of science and technology received the written request, the applicant has not received any formal response from the authority, the applicant might begin to conduct marine science research six months from the date of the request according to the legislation of the Russian Federation, international treaties and accepted principles of international law. The Chinese research team filled in its application form for the second expedition and sent it to the Chinese embassy in Moscow on 30 January 2003. The embassy submitted the form to the administrative authority of the Russian Federation in charge of science and technology. However, Russia did not give an answer. On 10 July 2003, the Russian embassy delivered a note to the Chinese Foreign Ministry, stating that Russia did not agree to permit Chinese research vessels to enter the Russian EEZ for the purposes of marine research. Russia did not explain the reasons for this refusal. At this point, it was beyond the four-month time limit stipulated in the rules. In desperation, China revised the inspection plan on the one hand and no longer entered the Russian EEZ, on the other hand. China addressed these issues with Russia through diplomatic channels. After the Chinese team completed the related research, on 11 August 2003, China received a reply from the Russian administration. Russia had finally granted China's request to enter the Russian EEZ, but this decision had no practical significance. At this point, the Chinese team had completed the scientific research in the Arctic and had set out to return home.

The question of the partition of the outer continental shelf is currently one of the most controversial issues in the Arctic region. In addition, Norway and other contracting states diverge in their views about the applicable scope of the Svalbard Treaty. Considering the above analysis, we can see that those disputes have implications for China's right to enjoy free access and engage in scientific research. These disputes do create problems for researchers, as they limit access to certain areas or cause additional administrative burdens.

A. The Dispute of the Arctic Coastal States on the Outer Continental Shelf

The UNCLOS lays down provisions enabling coastal states to claim an EEZ as well as a continental shelf, including possibly an outer continental shelf. According to Article 76 of the UNCLOS coastal states can claim the continental shelf beyond 200 nautical miles, referred to as the 'outer continental shelf'. If the coastal states want to obtain the recognition of their outer continental shelf, they must submit an application to the Commission on the Limits of the Continental Shelf (CLCS) and provide detailed evidence. The CLCS shall then provide suggestions related to the continental shelf outside the boundaries. According to UNCLOS, any limits of the outer continental shelf established in accordance with these recommendations shall be final and binding.[24]

Russia, Canada and Denmark argue that the Lomonosov Ridge on the Arctic Ocean floor is a natural extension of their continental shelves, and accordingly claim sovereign rights to the continental shelf beyond 200 miles into the Arctic Ocean. On 20 December 2001, the Russian government submitted its claim to the Secretary General of the United Nations, including claims related to the Arctic continental shelf external boundary. The CLCS considered and subsequently rejected the Russian submission in June 2002. The most important reason for refusal was that the Russian survey materials and data were not enough to prove that there is a natural connection between the land and the part that is 200 nautical miles off. In other words, Russia was not yet able to fully prove that the continental shelf beyond 200 nautical miles is a natural extension of its coastal land territory.[25] In addition, the United States and Canada conducted a joint geography survey in the Arctic Ocean. The United States claimed that its outer continental shelf extends far into the Arctic north, covering at least an area twice the size of California, and may overlap with the claim submitted by Russia.[26]

In 2006, Norway delivered its submission to the CLCS concerning the Norwegian Sea, the Barents Sea and other waters. In 2009 April, the CLCS delivered its conclusions on the external boundary of the Norwegian outer continental shelf. Norway became the first country that delimited its continental shelf. The submissions that other Arctic coastal states proposed overlapped. In the harsh natural conditions of the Arctic seas, it is difficult to provide the full information required by the UNCLOS in a short period.

[24] UNCLOS, art 76(8).

[25] Y Shuanywu and L Mo, 'The Knots of the Arctic Dispute and Their Solution' (2009) 62(6) *Wuhan University Journal of Philosophy & Social Sciences* 831.

[26] T Guoqiang, 'Arctic Issues and China's Countermeasures' (2013) 1 *International Studies* 18.

Additionally, the CLCS cannot make a ruling in the case of overlapping claims, in which case the countries involved have to resolve their territorial disputes through mutual consultation.

B. The Dispute on the Application Scope of the Svalbard Treaty

It had been said earlier that the Svalbard Treaty, which entered into force in 1925, gave Norway sovereignty, while at the same time it also made it clear that a national of the contracting states has rights to free access to the archipelago and to conduct legitimate productive or commercial activities when the international sea law had not yet determined the EEZ and continental shelf system. With the development of the law of the sea under the UNCLOS, all countries began to review the geographic scope of application of the Svalbard Treaty in relation to the new areas defined in the UNCLOS. States parties to the Svalbard Treaty claimed that, although its original scope is limited to the Svalbard archipelago land and its territorial sea, the treaty shall also apply in relation to the EEZ and continental shelf.

Norway believes that the Svalbard Treaty should be literally and restrictively interpreted despite the adoption of the UNCLOS. Specifically, the Svalbard Treaty should only be applicable to the islands and territorial waters and other states' free access to hunting and fishing rights should therefore be limited to this geographic scope. According to the Norwegian interpretation, the UNCLOS shall apply to areas of the archipelago that are not covered explicitly in the Svalbard Treaty, such as the EEZ and continental shelf. Norway claims that, as a coastal state, it enjoys sovereign rights over these two regions and that the treaty does not provide additional rights to other contracting states either in the EEZ or in the outer continental shelf related to the archipelago.

Other states parties claim that the continental shelf of the Svalbard archipelago belongs to the applicable scope of the Svalbard Treaty. The states parties should thus have the right of exploration and development of natural resources on the continental shelf. Consequently, they argue that Norway must, in relation to the use of the archipelago continental shelf, not only comply with the provisions of the UNCLOS, but also be bound by the principles of the Svalbard Treaty. Consequently, the sovereign rights of Norway as a coastal state are limited with regards to the archipelago.[27]

[27] T Pedersen and T Henriksen, 'Svalbard's Maritime Zones: The End of Legal Uncertainty' (2009) 24 *The International Journal of Maritime and Coastal Law* 141–61.

As a matter of fact, different rules of international law may conflict with each other. In this context, treaty interpretation has an important role to play. The Vienna Convention on the Law of Treaties provides rules guiding the interpretation of international treaties. Article 31 of the convention stipulates that:

> A treaty shall be interpreted in good faith in accordance with the ordinary meaning to be given to the terms of the treaty in their context and in the light of its object and purpose.

Norway is thus too rigid in its adoption of the literal interpretation and ignores the objective and original purpose of the Svalbard treaty.

Ida Caracciolo, an Italian professor of international law, argues that to resolve the dispute on the application scope of the Svalbard Treaty it is necessary to interpret the relevant provisions of the Svalbard Treaty following Article 31 of the Vienna Convention on the Law of Treaties. According to his analysis, the scope of application of the Svalbard Treaty should include the Svalbard archipelago and its territorial sea, EEZ and continental shelf. And his explanations are as follows:[28]

First, according to the Svalbard Treaty, the exercise of Norwegian sovereignty on the Svalbard archipelago is based on its 'terra nullius' legal regime. This recognition is accompanied by the revocation of the territorial claims of other contracting states. This agreement resulted in the implementation of a principle of 'sovereignty and common use' in order to maintain the freedoms of the contracting states associated with the regime of 'terra nullius'. Norway's sovereignty over the islands was therefore defined originally with specific limits attached to its exercise. Consequently, the sovereignty of Norway in the EEZ and continental shelf of the archipelago is not exclusive.

Secondly, the Svalbard Treaty aims to protect the interests enjoyed by its contracting parties in the archipelago by establishing an equitable legal regime that ensures peaceful development. The law of the sea codified since the adoption of the Svalbard treaty provides broader rights to the coastal state, including sovereign rights to the seabed and subsoil, as well as in relation to the exploitation of living and non-living resources. In this context, if the unilateral extension by Norway of its sovereignty over the archipelago's waters and continental shelf is accepted, this situation would severally affect the equitability of the regime established by the Svalbard Treaty. In order to avoid such outcome, any extension must be agreed upon by consensus among all contracting parties.

[28] I Caracciolo, 'Unresolved Controversy: the Legal Situation of the Svalbard Islands Maritime Areas: An Interpretation of the Paris Treaty in Light of United Nations Convention on the Law of the Sea' (presentation at the International Boundaries Research Unit Conference, Durham University, 2 April 2009).

In my opinion, Professor Caracciolo's argument is applicable to resolve the dispute on the application scope of the Svalbard Treaty. Thus, as a party to the Svalbard Treaty, China must have free access to the Svalbard archipelago, its territorial sea, EEZ and continental shelf for the purpose of scientific research.

Even so, China must still comply with the relevant legislation in Norway when conducting scientific research activities in the Svalbard archipelago area. 60 per cent of the archipelago is currently designated as nature conservation areas—national parks or nature reserves—and Norway is planning to expand the conservation areas or create new ones. Strict environmental protection rules also impose certain limits on China in its scientific research activities on the islands. For example, at present 'the Yellow River station'—located in Ny-Ålesund, Norway—is the only fixed Chinese research station in the Arctic. However, because the area is protected under Norwegian laws related to nature conservation, the activities of the station personnel are strictly limited and the Chinese research team must restrict its exploration to the station and nearby areas. Of course, even if China is a state party to the Svalbard Treaty, it must respect Norway's sovereignty and abide by the laws of Norway in order to carry out scientific research in the Svalbard archipelago area. More importantly, it is each state's duty to protect the environment of the globe. Norway's environmental protection laws do have an impact on the research activities of China. But these laws cannot be defined as substantial legal obstacles. Therefore, not all legal issues which might adversely reflect on China's Arctic scientific research are legal obstacles.

V. APPROACHES TO SAFEGUARDING CHINA'S RIGHTS TO CONDUCT ARCTIC SCIENTIFIC RESEARCH

In section IV, this chapter analyses the legal obstacles that China met when carrying out scientific research in the Arctic, but these obstacles are not unsolvable. Take the scientific research application problems that China met in the second Arctic expedition, for example. Russia has adopted complete management procedures for marine scientific research and has also recognised a time limit for approval authority. Overall, these management rules are reasonable and there is no provision that discriminates against foreigners. But in practice, Russia has strong wariness towards foreigners' scientific research applications; some foreign scientific researchers, such as Larry Mayer, a marine geologist at the University of New Hampshire in Durham, even consider that Russia has a history of impeding access to scientists from other nations seeking to work in its waters. For example, the Integrated Ocean Drilling Program could not obtain permission to drill in Russian parts of the Bering Sea in 2009.[29] Therefore, more political and diplomatic means are required to solve such problems. To further strengthen Arctic research co-operation, carrying out 'scientific diplomacy' may be a direct and effective countermeasure. The Arctic coastal countries' competition over the limits of their outer continental shelves and the dispute over the scope of application of the Svalbard Treaty will have negative impacts on China's Arctic scientific research. The resolution of these disputes depends on negotiation between the countries involved and the improvement of the regional rules and regulations related to this issue. As a non-Arctic state and an observer of the Arctic Council, China has only very limited direct influence on the establishment of rules and institutions in the Arctic region. But China can enhance the strength of its message in the Arctic in many ways. The country can participate more actively in the decision-making process related to the Arctic Council as well as to other relevant intergovernmental organisations and entities promoting cooperation including IASC and NySMAC, thereby indirectly safeguarding the rights of China's Arctic scientific research.

A. Strengthening Arctic Scientific Research Co-operation

Is there a need to strengthen China's Arctic scientific research co-operation with other countries and actors inside and outside the Arctic region? How can co-operation be strengthened?

Strengthening China's Arctic scientific research co-operation with other countries and actors inside and outside the Arctic region is not only necessary for China, but is also in the interest of other countries and actors inside and outside the Arctic region. China needs to strengthen its scientific research co-operation with other countries and actors inside and outside the Arctic domain.

First, China needs to strengthen its scientific research co-operation with the Arctic. With an early start and high level of Arctic research, the Arctic countries have played an important and unique role in Arctic issues. China's Arctic research could not have been done without co-operation with other Arctic States. Co-operating with scientists from the Arctic states can provide China Arctic scientific research with not only technology and experience, but also legal information about the scientific management of its countries in order to ensure the smooth implementation of scientific research. This is also the experience gained by China in previous Arctic scientific research practice.[30] One of the partners of China's second Arctic scientific research

[29] D Cressey, 'Open Water' (2011) 478 *Nature* 177.
[30] Huirong and Yue, *Legal Issues in the Arctic* (n 23) 248.

is the Fairbanks University of Alaska, the United States. In April 2003, before China started its investigations, the university's International Arctic Research Centre faxed some information about scientific research to China. In addition to graphical representations and roadmaps related to the inspection area, this information also included files on obligations that China had to comply with while engaged in local research, including related environmental protection, species protection and respecting indigenous people's rights. The main content was a series of obligations that the companies related to the Alaskan oil and gas industry need to follow when securing access to mining rights by renting the Beaufort Sea continental shelf. The lease included requests from Alaska Outer Continental Shelf Office, National Resource Center and National Marine Fisheries Service that the mining shall not damage the environment, species and aboriginal livelihood; the lease also requested that the companies related to the Alaskan oil and gas industry should sign an agreement with the Alaska Eskimo Whaling Commission in order to ensure that the company's behaviour complies with the Commission's relevant protection requirements and does not conflict with agreements concluded in relation to the development of the continental shelf. The university also provided China with the protocol signed by companies related to the oil and gas industry and Alaskan Eskimo Whaling Commission to avoid conflict and alleviate oil leaks, including work instructions and consultation procedures, solutions for avoiding conflicts, dispute resolution, urgent items and other related help, goods policy, etc.

Secondly, China needs to strengthen its scientific research co-operation with other countries and actors outside the Arctic region. China is not the only non-coastal state that carries out scientific expeditions in the Arctic. The European Union, Japan, South Korea and other countries and actors outside the Arctic region have expressed their interest in Arctic scientific research. In terms of Arctic scientific expeditions, the problems that China met are similar to those of countries or actors outside the Arctic region. Therefore, it is necessary to strengthen co-operation to enhance the opportunities for countries or actors from outside the Arctic region to contribute to regional (scientific) governance. The European Union has very close links with the Arctic region. From the perspective of geographical location, three Arctic countries are members of the European Union—Denmark (Greenland), Finland and Sweden. Additionally, the European Union has established very close relationships with two other Arctic states—Iceland and Norway—through the European Economic Area. In the field of scientific research co-operation, the European Union and the Arctic countries have a very strong regional alliance. By contrast, China, Japan, South Korea and other Asian countries have found it more difficult to engage in international research collaboration. Therefore, China should pay more attention to co-operation with Japan, South Korea and other Asian countries.

Other countries or actors both inside and outside the Arctic domain also need to strengthen co-operation with China. First of all, even for the Arctic sovereignty countries, strengthening scientific research co-operation is also important. The five Arctic coastal states signed the Ilulissat Declaration to highlight the importance of scientific research co-operation in 2008. According to the Ilulissat Declaration, the five coastal states will work to strengthen their co-operation with each other and other interested parties. The co-operation includes the collection of scientific data concerning the continental shelf, the protection of the marine environment and other scientific research.[31] In addition, in their Arctic policy, the Arctic countries explicitly put forward that co-operation must be strengthened in terms of Arctic expeditions and sharing research achievements to promote knowledge and understanding of the Arctic. On 10 May 2013, the Obama administration released a document entitled National Strategy for the Arctic Region.[32] Strengthening international co-operation is one of the three major 'lines of efforts' identified by the strategy. Secondly, due to China's rise, the country plays an important role that must not be ignored in Arctic scientific research development. On 24 July 2014, in the Beijing-Moscow video seminar on 'Arctic research and development prospects for co-operation between China and Russia', that was held by the Russian news agency in Beijing, *Владимир славянских Кориа золото*, expressed that when it comes to Arctic scientific research, Russia and China can play to their respective advantages: 'Russia's experience is richer than that of China. China can provide money that scientific research needs'.[33]

Scientific research co-operation and information sharing is one of China's legal rights endowed by the UNCLOS and other international treaties and related scientific cooperation entities. Making full use of the rights is a basic way for China to strengthen scientific research co-operation with other countries and actors inside and outside the Arctic domain. These measures could include but are not limited to the following. First, China should invite more foreign scientists in its Arctic scientific expeditions and make greater use of the scientific research platforms provided by the International Arctic Science Committee, the Ny-Ålesund Science Managers Committee and other international scientific organisations to increase communication. Up to now, China has carried out a co-operation study, communicated with researchers and established a good international co-operation relationship with the United States, Norway, South Korea, Japan, Finland, Russia and other

[31] The Ilulissat Declaration (2008).

[32] Available at www.whitehouse.gov/sites/default/files/docs/nat_arctic_strategy.pdf.

[33] C Jing, 'China and Russian Expand Scientific Expedition Cooperation in Arctic Pole is Possible and Necessary' *Chinese Youth Daily* (27 July 2014).

countries on issues related to the Arctic Ocean, sea ice, the upper atmosphere physics, biology and ecology, as well as other fields of polar research. Secondly, as a member of the International Arctic Science Committee, and Ny-Ålesund Science Managers Committee and other international scientific organisations, China should actively participate in the international scientific research projects of the international scientific organisations. Thirdly, in the framework of the International Arctic Science Committee, China not only has the right to carry out international co-operation, but also has the possibility of setting up a regional coalition organisation. From the reports of the meetings of the International Arctic Science Committee, we can see that South Korea and Japan are quite active and involved in many projects in the IASC. China, South Korea and Japan are all Asian countries and thus share similarities and commonalities in terms of the Arctic. Therefore, China could cooperate with other regional actors and jointly seek to set up the Asian Regional Committee in the framework of the International Arctic Science Committee Organization with South Korea and Japan, and put more emphasis on carrying out Arctic scientific research projects together.

B. Making China's Voice Heard in Arctic Affairs

The competition for establishing the relevant norms and institutions has become the main competition area among the goals set in the Arctic policies of actors involved in the region.[34] Both the Arctic countries and extraterritorial countries and actors paying attention to the Arctic are hoping to ensure that Arctic norms and governance are aligned with their own best interests. However, in the current stage, China must actively participate in the process of establishing Arctic rules and regulations through a variety of ways.

As the current Arctic area's most important international scientific organisation, the IASC has set and will continue to adopt 'Agreed Measures', 'Resolution' and other similar decisions, which will play a great role in regulating the behaviour of Arctic scientific expeditions and aspects of international research co-operation. China is a full member of the IASC, having the right to participate in the establishment of these 'soft law' norms. Making full use of IASC membership to actively participate in 'soft law' decisions about standardising the behaviour of Arctic expeditions is one effective way to safeguard the rights of China's Arctic research.

The Arctic Council is a very important platform helping to magnify China's 'voice' in the Arctic. The Arctic Council was set up as a high-level

[34] Huang, *Annual Report on National Polar Policy Research 2012–2013* (n 4) 111.

forum based on the Ministerial Declaration published in Ottawa, 19 September 1996. The Arctic Council's fundamental purpose is to maintain the sustainable development of the Arctic, focusing mainly on the three fields of Arctic environment, society and economy, as well as exploring co-operation measures and problems in Arctic development and environmental protection. The Arctic Council comprises three categories, respectively the members (eight Arctic sovereign states), permanent participants and observers. The Arctic Council does not handle affairs concerning military security; decisions are adopted by consensus among all of its members. In addition, the Arctic Council has also established six expert working groups: the Arctic Contaminants Action Program (ACAP), Arctic Monitoring and Assessment Program (AMAP), Conservation of Arctic Flora and Fauna (CAFF), Emergency Prevention, Preparedness and Response (EPPR), Protection of the Arctic Marine Environment (PAME) and Sustainable Development Working Group (SDWG). Most of the substantive work of the Council takes place within these six working groups. The strongest role that the Arctic Council has traditionally played is in the domain of scientific research, in particular through monitoring and assessment.

In 2013, China was approved as an observer of the Arctic Council. As an observer, although China does not have voting rights, it can participate in the subsidiary institution meetings and ministerial meetings of the Arctic Council, as well as each group's work. At meetings of subsidiary institutions, in particular, it can become involved in the discussion of relevant problems through written and oral presentations. Being involved in the relevant discussion and offering to carry out related projects help to improve China's voice in the establishment of relevant international rules, enhance China's influence in Arctic-related affairs, as well as establish a more extensive and solid foundation to maintain China's rights with respects to Arctic research.

VI. CONCLUSIONS

China's northeast border is close to 50 degrees north latitude. Changes in the Arctic climate and environment profoundly affect China's climate and environment, with a direct influence on China's industrial and agricultural production as well as the life of its people.[35] Therefore, the Chinese government pays great attention to Arctic climate change and environmental

[35] Speech by C Lianzeng, deputy director of China's state oceanic administration, at the initiative meeting of the Fourth Chinese Arctic Scientific Exploration: 'Arctic scientific research is of great significance for attainable development', www.gov.cn/jrzg/2010-06/25/content_1637741.htm.

problems, as well as the value of scientific research on these issues.[36] As of October 2014, China has organised six Arctic scientific expeditions. The focus of Chinese Arctic scientific research mainly revolves around two themes: climate change and the environment.

As the melting of Arctic sea ice has intensified, both China's identity as a rising superpower and the growth in energy demand have caused the Arctic countries to be suspicious to a certain extent about the motivations behind the increase of Chinese Arctic activities in recent years.[37] In fact, the right to carry out scientific research in the Arctic area is guaranteed in the UNCLOS and other international conventions. The UNCLOS gives China the rights to carry out scientific research in Arctic high seas. With the consent of the Arctic coastal states China can conduct scientific research in their EEZ and on their continental shelf. And China can conduct marine scientific research in the territorial sea of the Arctic coastal states only with their express consent and under the conditions that they set forth. According to the Svalbard Treaty, China has also the right to freely enter the Svalbard archipelago to conduct scientific research and to establish a fixed scientific station. In addition, scientific research co-operation and information sharing are important aspects of the right of China to conduct scientific research in the Arctic. Section 2 of part XIII of the UNCLOS lays down the special provisions on this particular issue. The international scientific organisations in the Arctic, such as the IASC, which establish the 'soft laws' norms regulating the actions of Arctic scientific expeditions, also provide a legal basis for China's scientific research co-operation and sharing of scientific research benefits in the Arctic.

According to the UNCLOS, China's scientific research in the EEZ and on the continental shelves of the Arctic coastal states must follow the following sources of law: provisions of the UNCLOS related to the scientific research, provisions related to maritime and environmental issues contained in other relevant international conventions, national legislation adopted by the Arctic coastal states and regulating scientific expeditions, and domestic environmental legislations and regulations of these coastal states as well as norms protecting the rights of indigenous peoples. China has complied with the above regulations when carrying out Arctic scientific research. But the above regulations sometimes create obstacles in China's Arctic scientific

[36] L Keqiang. 'Polar Exploration Concerns China's Long-term Interests', news.xinhuanet.com/politics/2009-11/20/content_12508072.htm (20 November 2009).

[37] S Rainwater, 'Race to the North' (n 3); Lasserre (n 7).

research. During China's past Arctic expeditions, China once failed to carry out its original plan because of Russia's refusal without reason. The legal obstacles to China's Arctic scientific research are also derived from the competition over the delimitation of the outer continental shelves of Arctic coastal countries states and the dispute over the geographic scope of the Svalbard Treaty, which have implications on the ability of China to freely conduct scientific research in the Arctic. On the former, as a non-Arctic state, China has no right to interfere with the delimitation of the outer continental shelves of Arctic coastal countries states. On the latter, it seems more reasonable to interpret the relevant provisions of the Svalbard Treaty following Article 31 of the Vienna Convention on the Law of Treaties and is more conducive to China's Arctic scientific research.

These legal obstacles to developing scientific research in the Arctic area are however not unsolvable. China could take two types of actions to maintain China's Arctic scientific research rights. The first type of measures could be called 'direct response measures', which involve strengthening Arctic scientific research co-operation between China and other countries or actors both inside and outside the Arctic. In Arctic scientific research affairs, China needs to work with other countries or actors both inside and outside the Arctic, as much as these actors also need China for the success of their scientific work. The second type of action could be called 'indirect measures'. Promoting China's right to have a say in the establishment of relevant international and regional rules and ensuring that Arctic regulations and governance are aligned with the interests of China would lay a solid foundation for maintaining China's rights to Arctic scientific research. In order to achieve this purpose, China should make full use of the IASC and its membership of other international scientific organisations, as well as its observer status in the Arctic Council, and actively participate in the establishment of 'soft laws' and activities influencing Arctic governance, thereby magnifying China's 'voice' in Arctic affairs.

4

Chinese Arctic Discussion—a Micro Reading of World Affairs

JULIA JALO AND TAPIO NYKÄNEN

I. INTRODUCTION

IN THIS CHAPTER we take a close look at Chinese discussion of Arctic politics. We will analyse nine Chinese articles published in the semi-governmental magazine *World Affairs* (世界知识, *Shijie zhishi*) between 2004 and 2014. Our aim is to reconstruct the Chinese political discourse on the Arctic as it is produced in our material. We seek to develop a nuanced understanding of some dimensions of Chinese political talk on Arctic politics and China's role in it. However, our results can be generalised in certain respects: they illustrate important attitudes and opinions in Chinese discussion over Arctic questions, even though they do not include all possible stances or nuanced arguments.

World Affairs magazine is published by World Affairs Press (*Shijie zhishi chubanshe*) in Beijing, China. The World Affairs Press is a state-owned publishing house, under the direct leadership of the Ministry of Foreign Affairs. The house specialises in publishing books on politics and international affairs (primarily translated from other languages) as well as magazines. Publishing houses, like other forms of media in China, are viewed as a means for political propaganda, and thus have always been firmly controlled by the government. There has been a strong culture of economic and other kinds of interdependency between the Ministry of Foreign Affairs and World Affairs Press that includes partially or fully subsidising publishing projects, especially those on politics and foreign affairs. Meanwhile, the Ministry has held the right to appoint the president and editor-in-chief of the house. Many of the appointees have been ambassadors returning from overseas stints for whom the Ministry has found it difficult to find a suitable job. The employees between the Ministry and the Foreign Affairs Press have been to some degree interchangeable. It has been common practice for the Ministry to borrow editors from the publishing house whenever there are difficult-to-fill vacancies in Chinese embassies. In addition, the publishing house has also enabled certain powerful officials at the Ministry to resolve job problems for their spouses or relatives, most of whom have been given support staff positions.[1]

World Affairs is a semi-monthly magazine that was founded in 1934 from a 'rising need for Chinese to understand the world and the interrelationship between China and the rest of the world'. Because of its close connection with PRC's Foreign Ministry, *World Affairs* magazine is regarded as representing to some extent the opinions of the government. The magazine has been characterised as one of the most influential Chinese current affairs magazines. The magazine features in-depth coverage and reviews of topics in international affairs, trends in hotspots of the world economy, major news events and figures, as well as China's diplomatic achievements and trends. The magazine is published in Mandarin and its articles are broadly cited by the Chinese news media. The main task of the magazine is to promote the Communist Party's and the government's foreign policy line and analyse the changes in the international situation from a Marxist point of view.[2]

The research data for the analysis was selected by entering the keyword 'Arctic' in the search field of the *World Affairs* website. The search result yielded a total of 10 articles. One article was removed from the research as its topic appeared to be Syria, not Arctic politics. All the other articles dealt with Arctic affairs. The number of articles found was very small in light of the fact that in the period between 2004 and 2014 general interest in Arctic issues has risen significantly in China. A search with the word 'Arctic' (北极,'beiji') with all available resources on the China Knowledge Resource Integrated Database (中国知网,'zhongguo zhiwang'), which stores all Chinese scholarly journals, news articles, etc. gives the result indicated in the table below.

Table 4.1: Articles on the Arctic in the *Zhongguo Zhiwang* database

Year	Number of Articles on the Arctic
2004	590
2005	651
2006	783
2007	983
2008	1014
2009	1262
2010	1591
2011	1650
2012	1830
2013	1872

[1] L Zhao, 'The Publishing of Youth-Literature in China' (Thesis, University of British Columbia, 2014).

[2] See the introduction provided on *World Affairs* on the magazine's website: sjzs.qikan.com/Introduce.aspx.

This search does not reveal the nature of the articles: for example, journalist articles and articles that fall in the category of natural sciences are included here. It is not possible to say whether the number of articles in the fields of political science/international relations has increased correspondingly in China. In spite of this, the fact is that the number of articles considering the Arctic in *World Affairs* is small compared to the general interest in the subject. This may indicate the cautious attitude of the Chinese government or simply the consideration that the Arctic has not been politically very important until recently. An interesting rise in the number of the articles in *World Affairs* was also seen in 2013, when the Arctic Council prepared to decide whether to accept China as its observer. Three of our nine articles were published in 2013.

We analyse our material with both qualitative and simple quantitative methods. We start by counting some keywords to see what topics seem to be important for the authors. Keywords were chosen after a tentative reading of the material: we chose themes that seemed to be considered often or constantly. This approach makes our study content-based. However, our initial reading was in turn based on previous literature on Chinese discussion, so the keywords also illuminate the existing scientific discussion on the topic.[3]

Theoretically speaking, our text represents the constructivist/interpretist theory of international relations.[4] Our starting point is the idea that political desires, interests and identities evolve through social interaction.[5] In other words, the social and political world we face is constructed in speech acts that are to have an effect on the behaviour of others. Speech acts, in turn, are based in *discourses*—the general ways of understanding—but they also challenge these discourses and aim to create new hegemonic ways of seeing things (see also Nykänen in this volume).

In practice, political speech often has both domestic and international goals, and the dimension that is examined or seen as most important depends on the research objects. The texts we study in this chapter are written for the Chinese audience, so they have at least some domestic political goals. However, they also shape possible Chinese foreign policy, so in the longer term they have an international horizon as well. In our chapter we are interested

[3] See eg DC Wright, *The Dragon Eyes the Top of the World: Arctic Policy Debate and Discussion in China* (Newport, Rhode Island, China Maritime Studies Institute—Naval War College, 2011) 28; L Jakobson and J Peng, 'China's Arctic Aspirations' (2012) 34 *SIPRI Policy Paper*; L Jakobson 'China Prepares for an Ice-Free Arctic' (2010) 2 *SIPRI Insights on Peace and Security*; S Kopra, 'China's Arctic Interests' (2013) 2 *Arctic Yearbook* 107–24; L Xing and R Gjedssø Bertelsen, 'The Drivers of Chinese Arctic Interests: Political Stability and Energy and Transportation Security' (2013) 2 *Arctic Yearbook* 53–68.

[4] See eg M Bevir and RAW Rhodes, 'Interpretive theory' in D Marsh and G Stoker (eds), *Theory and Methods in Political Science* (London, Palgrave Macmillan, 2002).

[5] CS Browning, *Constructivism, Narrative and Foreign Policy Analysis. A Case Study of Finland* (Bern, Peter Lang, 2008) 23.

mainly in this dimension, ie what kind of mindset do the articles create for the purposes of Chinese foreign policy?

It should be emphasised that international political discourses are shaped in interaction, and thus are counterproductive. In a nutshell (a very small one), this means that if you speak enough about your friends, you will create friends. Likewise: if you draw enough pictures about your enemy, it is likely that he will start to take them seriously at some point. We examine the articles also from this point of view. What countries/actors seem to be important for China—according to the authors—and in what light are these actors represented? Are there clear pictures of enemies and, on the other side of the coin, of friends that are seen to have greater potential as co-operators than some other parties?

II. CHINA, USA AND RUSSIA

We start our analysis by simply counting the number of times the United States, Russia, Canada, Norway, Denmark, Iceland, Sweden and Finland as the Arctic Countries (A8) are mentioned. Additionally, we note how many times other Asian countries actively participating in Arctic issues, namely China, India, Japan, Korea and Singapore, are mentioned. This simple analysis reveals the importance of the country from the Chinese perspective and gives a starting horizon for more detailed analysis.

From the group of A8, Russia is mentioned the most, a total of 181 times, the United States 97 times and Canada 88 times. After these three countries, there is a clear difference in how many times the rest of the A8 countries are mentioned; Denmark is mentioned 40 times, Norway 32 times, Iceland 20 times, Sweden and Finland both 6 times. From the second group of Asian countries, Korea is mentioned 18 times, Japan 10, Singapore 3 and India 3 times. China is mentioned 77 times.

This simple method reveals the significance of Russia, the US and Canada in the Arctic context and possibly also in the global perspective. In the Arctic, China seems to be most concerned about Russia's moves, as Russia is mentioned 1.8 times more often than the second most mentioned country, the United States. This already reveals the importance of Russia for China, but on its own this fact does not tell why China is interested in its northern neighbour this much.

III. MILITARY, STRATEGY AND NATURAL RESOURCES

To examine the importance of the more detailed topics of interest we also counted words that refer to substantial political issues in the Arctic. The chosen words (originally in Chinese) are translated as 'natural resources', 'energy', 'oil', 'natural gas', 'fishery', 'minerals', 'shipping lane', 'ship route', 'shipping', 'sailing', 'economic benefit', 'benefit', 'science', 'research', 'climate', 'contradiction', 'global', 'co-operation', 'fight', 'dispute', 'strategy', 'sovereignty', 'sovereign rights', 'security' and 'military'. As stated, the words were chosen based on our preliminary understanding of common topics in discussions related to the future of the Arctic.

The word 'military' gets the most hits (82). However, the articles do not actually analyse or introduce *Chinese* military interests in the Arctic. The word count result is based on reporting Arctic militarisation by Arctic states, which seems to have woken the interest of the Chinese. The articles devote quite a bit of space to the military moves of the Arctic states and some of them deal mainly with recent military and strategic development of the big Arctic states, namely Russia, the US and Canada.

The words 'strategy' and 'dispute' get the next most hits, both 78 times. China seems to be well aware and perhaps also concerned about the struggle of the Arctic states over Arctic governance. However, the authors do not seem to offer any solutions to the disputes.

Based on our experience of Chinese official talk about the Arctic, which places a great deal of emphasis on scientific research in the area, we had expectations about the frequent appearance of words related to scientific research. It was thus somewhat surprising to find that the words 'science'/'scientific' and 'research' are mentioned only 27 and 23 times respectively.

Almost all of the articles include a section that describes the resources found in the Arctic, some in lesser and some in greater detail. Therefore, 'natural resources' are mentioned 73 times. The word comes up in all articles except in the speech given by Chinese assistant Foreign Minister Hu Zhengyue about China's views on the Arctic. However, the authors are content to merely describe the amounts and quality of the natural resources: they do not actually discuss in what ways China could get its hands on them.

The words 'co-operation' (mentioned 26 times) and 'global' (41 times) imply that the Arctic has growing importance in China's sight: it is not just a remote area with natural resources but also a battlefield for global political actors, China amongst them. The word 'benefit' gets 40 hits and belongs to this category too, as many of the articles explain that the disputes, efforts and interests of the different actors in the Arctic all have the same origin, namely, the benefits to be gained in the region.

Based on the word count analysis it seems that China is most interested in the military and strategic moves of the Arctic states, and is paying special attention to the big Arctic states, especially Russia. In other words, Chinese scholars see the political horizon in the Arctic in terms of classical realism of international relations.[6] In this perspective, international politics is ultimately a playing field of rivals or enemies and what matters the most is the physical power they are able to use.

IV. CHINESE SELF-VIEW IN THE ARCTIC CONTEXT

In this section we will analyse how the position of China itself is represented in the chosen articles. To briefly describe the articles for the reader, one could say that the articles are written for the Chinese public and are non-scientific in nature. The articles are typically 3000–4000 characters in length and feature pictures, such as of an icebreaker, a polar bear or an international conference. The authors of the articles represent several different backgrounds. A large proportion of the authors, four in total, come from the China Institutes of Contemporary International Relations (CICIR), different institutes such as the Institute of American Studies, Institute of Russian Studies, Institute of World Political Studies and Center for Marine Strategy Studies, where the authors often hold posts such as Deputy Director or Associate Professor. CICIR belongs to one of China's largest and oldest civilian research institutions for international studies. It is a government-affiliated foreign policy think-tank. The Institute is also affiliated with China's top intelligence agency, the Ministry of State Security, and overseen by the Central Committee of the Communist Party.[7] Two of the authors come from the Ocean University of China's Research Institute of Polar Politics and Law. Other organisations associated with the authors are the Liaoning Academy of Social Sciences, People's Liberation Army (PLA), Foreign Language Institute and Shanghai International Studies University's Center for Russian Studies. One of the articles is a speech given by China's Assistant Minister of Foreign Affairs, but the author remains unknown.

The first article from 2004, 'Běijí jiāng shàngyǎn zhēngduó zhàn?', is written by Wang Honggang, the Deputy Director at China Institutes of Contemporary International Relations (CICIR) Institute of American Studies.[8] The article does not mention China at all. It is very neutral in tone and describes the slowly developing race for the Arctic from an outsider perspective. The second article, 'É běijí "chā qí" yǐn rán "bīng dìrè zhàn"' by Li Dong, was written in 2009,[9] thus after the August 2007 event of Russia

[6] See also D Shambaugh, 'Chinese Thinking about World Order' in X Huang and R Patman (eds), *China and the International System* (London, Routledge, 2013).

[7] D Shambaugh, 'China's International Relations Think Tanks: Evolving Structure and Process' (2002) 171 *The China Quarterly* 575–96.

[8] H Wang, 'Běijí jiāng shàngyǎn zhēngduó zhàn?' (2004) 22 *World Affairs*.

[9] D Li, 'É běijí "chā qí" yǐn rán "bīng dìrè zhàn"' (2007) 17 *World Affairs*.

planting their flag on the seabed under the North Pole. Even though the Arctic discussion is turning into an increasingly hot topic globally, the second article is very similar to the first one in terms of structure and style. It describes the political battle over the Arctic, though placing a greater emphasis on Russia and how its perceptions conflict with those of the other Arctic states. Putting emphasis on Russia is very natural since the author comes from the CICIR Institute of Russian Studies.

The second article refers to China only twice, doing so very concisely yet expressively in two important contexts. The first time China is referred to is after a sentence stating that the Arctic land areas belong to the A8 countries, but the Arctic Ocean areas belong to the international seas in which all the countries in the world can freely conduct scientific investigations. China is mentioned in the next sentence as currently having the Yellow River station, one of hundreds of international research stations in the Arctic.[10] The second reference to China is in the context of the country becoming the 16th signatory of the International Arctic Science Committee, which was founded by the representatives of national scientific organisations of the eight Arctic countries on 28 August 1990.[11] With these two references the author tells the reader that China is currently pursuing active research in the Arctic and has been engaged in Arctic affairs since as early as 1990.

The third article from 2009 is not credited to an author in the original source, but is a speech delivered by China's Assistant Minister of Foreign Affairs Hu Zhengyue.[12] The article is the first one to have an active view of China, describing China's engagement in the Arctic in the present tense. In the article China is referred to as a 'country in the Northern Hemisphere', and thus a country that is affected by the changes in the Arctic. The article positions China as a territory that is impacted by the melting of the Arctic Ocean, which gives a reason for China to attach great importance and learn more about Arctic climate change in order to understand the impact of such changes on China.[13] Further in the article, China is viewed as contributing important scientific research on climate change to both the world and itself. The article sees China as a country that is concerned about environmental protection and that is actively participating in and contributing internationally to global environment protection. At the end of the article, China is described as being in the role of giving strong support to the existing legal framework within the Arctic. China is supporting the United Nations Law of the Seas as the basic framework that should be applied for all the actions taken in the Arctic. In this context there is a grouping between the littoral states and other countries, China being a member of the latter. However,

[10] ibid.
[11] ibid.
[12] H Zhengyue, 'Zhōngguó duì běijí shìwù de kànfǎ' (2009) 5 *World Affairs*.
[13] ibid.

the author suggests that both of these groups should be able to play by the same rules.[14]

The fourth article was written by Shi Chunyang in 2010,[15] when China had been denied observer status for the second time by the Arctic Council ministerial meeting in 2009. The country was adopting a subtle attitude towards the Arctic so as to not provoke negative responses from the Arctic states. The structure of the article is almost identical with the two first articles, but includes updated information. It is totally neutral in its views and does not mention China at all. A third article of the same type leads us to wonder about whether this is the picture China wants to paint of itself in the Arctic context? Or is it merely the circumstances that had forced Chinese voices to become so neutral? The emphasis in the article is very much on the A5 countries' struggle for influence and control over the Arctic. Only in the last sentence does the author's wish for peace become evident,[16] yet it does not have any obvious connections with China. 'Let the Arctic become a land of peace, stability and co-operation as was the general consensus reached by the participators', the author says.

The fifth article by Fu Yu was written in 2012[17] before the Arctic Council 2013 ministerial meeting, where China's observership was finally granted. It maintains a very neutral tone when describing the situation of the Arctic Council and its considerations with regard to adopting new observers. Yet, the latter part of the article has a strong political agenda. The author assertively reflects a self-view of China that wants to assure everyone of the rights China has in the Arctic and how it should be included in decision-making and development concerning the area. Partly, the author also speaks to the government, giving the suggestion that greater attention should be paid to the Arctic area.

The article starts using a very confident voice with a section entitled 'China cannot be left out from commonly developing the Arctic'.[18] The author describes how China's continuing economic development and active participation in Arctic affairs has led Norway to start explicitly supporting China's participation in the Arctic Council. The section continues in a similar vein by echoing the famous statement often repeated in the Chinese debates—'the Arctic is the common heritage of mankind'—by saying 'the Arctic is the common property of the whole world'.[19] The author is positioning China closer to the Arctic by defining it as a non-Arctic country, but a signatory of the Svalbard Treaty; this means that China has responsibilities it cannot

[14] ibid.
[15] C Shi, '"Běijí wŭ guó" zhēng běijí' (2010) 22 *World Affairs*.
[16] ibid.
[17] F Yu, 'Rìyì jīliè de běijí lǐshì huì zhī zhēng' (2012) 6 *World Affairs*.
[18] ibid.
[19] ibid.

shirk in the fields of Arctic environmental protection, scientific research, joint development and other such topics. The author continues giving reasons for China's participation by stating that China is located in the Northern Hemisphere and the ongoing changes in the Arctic will have a great impact on the natural environment and ecosystem in China. He addresses his words to the Chinese government by saying that it should certainly be highly concerned about Arctic governance.

Further, the author assures the readers of China's right to participate.

> China as a signatory state of the 1982 United Nations Law of the Sea Convention thus enjoys rights to participate in development and scientific expeditions in the international marine area of the Arctic. It can be said that active participation in Arctic Council affairs is the legitimate right of the Government of China.[20] [translation from original]

In the last part of the article China is considered against the other applicants for observer status; at that point, the article once again takes on a more neutral tone. An interesting contrast is made with Japan, pointing out that while the Japanese are planning to build a research centre in the Arctic, China has already started to equip an 8000-tonne heavy icebreaker suitable for Arctic navigation, expected to be operational in 2014.[21] The comparison gives the reader a picture of China as an active participant in Arctic developments, ahead of Japan.

The sixth article, written by Sun Kai and Guo Peiqing in 2013,[22] takes a kind of humorous outsider view of the political battle of the Arctic countries, describing them as ancient warlords wrestling over the white pole. The article identifies Russia, the US and Canada as the warlords who have made the most active moves. After the humorous title the authors neutrally describe the developments of these three countries in their Arctic sphere from 2006 onwards. While describing the opportunities ushered in by the melting of Arctic ice, the authors say that the Arctic countries are not the only interested parties—countries located outside the Arctic are also eager to join. Later, China is mentioned as belonging to the group of 'countries outside the Arctic' that have developed a strong interest in the Arctic in recent years. The other such countries according to the article are Japan, South Korea, Singapore and Italy. In this article Japan is described as the 'country outside the Arctic' that is at the forefront of Arctic research. It is interesting to note that different authors refer to Japan totally differently.[23] China is referred for the second time in this article together with the other observer status applicants—Japan, South Korea, Italy, India and Singapore—as desiring to

[20] ibid.
[21] ibid.
[22] K Sun and P Guo, 'Běijí: Àncháo yǒng dòng dì dìqiú jìntóu' (2013) 5 *World Affairs*.
[23] For a reference to Japan, see Yu 'Rìyì jīliè de běijí lǐshì huì zhī zhēng' (n 17).

become observer members of the Arctic Council. The authors see China, as a country without an Arctic strategy, as being essentially no different from other countries outside the Arctic actively participating in Arctic affairs.[24] Further, China is reported to have attended the international North Pacific Arctic Conference together with other countries in a neutral tone.

Later, the article no longer mentions China but implicitly refers to China as an 'outside-Arctic country'. In the article 'outside-Arctic countries' are described as having shared views about the Arctic, whereas the Arctic countries are described as each having their own unique view of the matters. These unique views are described as confrontational. China is thus seen to belong to a group that shares a common view, unlike the group of Arctic countries with their disputing views. An example of the above-described rhetoric in the article is found when the authors talk about foreign vessels' right to use Canada's Northwest Passage and the Northern Sea Route near Russia. The rights to use the waters depend on how these areas are seen in the international law. The article describes two different approaches to the question taken by the different 'groups' of actors. The 'outside-Arctic country' group supports the idea that those areas should be regarded as international waters, while individual countries such as Canada and Russia would see the same areas as their internal waters. Different attitudes towards questions concerning Arctic governance among the Arctic countries and between the 'outside-Arctic countries' are said to be of great concern to 'outside Arctic countries' in the article. Further, the authors describe the Arctic countries' attitudes towards 'outside-Arctic countries' to fall into two different groups: big countries, which are not enthusiastic about having outside Arctic countries join Arctic co-operation, and small Arctic countries, which warmly welcome these countries to join in.[25]

The seventh article written by Zhang Xinbo and Li Zheng[26] does not mention China at all. It states that melting ice has three consequences: the opening up of new sea routes, access to resource development and increase in natural catastrophes. It describes actions taken by the US, Russia and South Korea in detail, but in a neutral tone. When starting their analysis of South Korea, the authors say that South Korea's moves this year have also been very conspicuous.[27] The attitude of the authors becomes clearer towards the end of the article. They write about Denmark, Norway and Iceland as well as Japan as other countries that have also taken measures to actively expand their own benefits in the battle for the Arctic. In the last paragraph the authors call these unidentified countries actively involved in the Arctic as 'eight immortals crossing the sea, each showing their magical

[24] Sun and Guo '*Běijí: Ànchháo yǒng dòng dì dìqiú jìntóu*' (n 22).
[25] ibid.
[26] X Zhang and Z Li, 'Zuì rè běijí jiājù dàguó zhēngduó zhàn' (2013) 17 *World Affairs*.
[27] ibid.

powers'.[28] The authors' explanation for the metaphor is that all the involved parties have no other purpose for their actions than economic benefits and the associated security interests.[29] The authors end the article by predicting more tensions to come in the Arctic.

> And as the Arctic waterways are opening up, all the parties will move forward to realise their national strategies or specific policies concerning the Arctic, and the 'battle for the Arctic' will definitely become more intense.[30] [translation from original]

The eighth article was written by Guo Peiqing[31] after China gained observer status in the Arctic Council in 2013. The author analyses the role of the Arctic Circle Forum in the process whereby China and the other applicant countries succeeded in gaining observer status in the Arctic Council.[32] In the article China is referred to as a 'non-Arctic country',[33] East Asian country or as itself. The author places himself as an outsider when analysing the relationships within Arctic states, between the Arctic Council and the Arctic Circle Forum, and between non-Arctic states and Arctic states as well as the relationship between China and North European countries.

He describes the sceptical and rejecting attitude of the Arctic states towards non-Arctic countries. It is interesting that at the beginning of the article he generalises this to apply to all the Arctic countries, but later separates the big countries' attitudes towards the 'non-Arctic countries' from those of the small countries. He points out that non-Arctic countries have only the right to become observers, and that China's application was rejected twice. He also points out that the requirements for the observers were altered, making their position clearly subordinate in relation to the permanent members. The author remarks that the A5 have been marginalising the three Northern European countries and the indigenous peoples' representatives in the important questions. He then explains that these worries about being excluded from the Arctic Council are shared with the non-Arctic countries and the three Northern European countries.

The Arctic Council's dilemma concerning the new observers is discussed in the article by citing western scholars and public opinion about China's behaviour and how to best control it. In this paragraph China is described as an object that the Arctic Council needs to control by accepting it as an observer member. The consequence of leaving China outside the Arctic Council is expressed by quoting Scott Highleyman, the director of the International Arctic of the Pew Charitable Trust.

[28] ibid.
[29] ibid.
[30] ibid.
[31] P Guo, 'Běijí quān lùntán: Běijí lǐshì huì de "tà páng zhī hǔ"'? (2013) 21 *World Affairs*.
[32] ibid.
[33] ibid.

> If China is excluded, the countries concerned might need to pay a higher price in confronting China's Arctic presence.[34] [translation from original]

The author keeps the same approach when grouping China together with South Korea and Japan as objects that have the potential to realise their common goals in the international arena if excluded from the Arctic Council. In this way, the author again gives an example of how western scholars view China as a threat that has to be controlled by absorbing it into the Arctic Council.

> Excluding the Asian countries from joining will undermine the Arctic Council's legitimacy in Arctic affairs.[35] [translation from original]

Later in the article, China is referred to with the other six applicants for observer membership. They are seen as ingredients that contribute to recognising and strengthening the legitimacy, authority and effectiveness of the Arctic Council.[36] In the same context, China is mentioned especially as a big country that had been left outside the system, and now that it has been brought within, it will act as a factor that will benefit the Arctic Council in developing and maintaining the Arctic states' leadership in Arctic affairs.[37]

The author is expressing his own view when he points out that the Arctic states have not fundamentally changed their attitudes towards the non-Arctic countries, which include China. In his opinion, there is a need 'to establish mutual respect and understanding between Arctic and non-Arctic countries'.[38]

The author is grouping China with the EU and other non-Arctic states by describing them as great vibrant countries and areas that cannot be excluded from Arctic affairs just because they are not located inside the Arctic Circle.

In the last part of the article the author states that the Nordic countries differ from the rest of the Arctic states in that they do not perceive China as a threat. The author objectifies China by stating that the Nordic countries will lead China in the Arctic Council and use China's Arctic presence to balance the other big Arctic states' strength. To describe the situation in more vivid terms, the author uses the idiom 'throw out a sprat to catch a mackerel',[39] where China is the sprat, the Nordic countries fishermen and the mackerel is the big Arctic countries: Russia, the US and Canada. The last part of the article is developed around this idea. It describes how Iceland has benefited from becoming friends with China, and how the other Nordic countries are also expected to hold out olive branches to China. The author questions

[34] ibid.
[35] ibid.
[36] ibid.
[37] ibid.
[38] ibid.
[39] ibid.

whether China can get corresponding benefits or returns. He throws the ball to the Chinese government in his last statement:

> In this game using and being used is a dialectical relationship. Determining the nature of tactical and strategic gains and losses is confusing. It is an intelligence test for Chinese Foreign Affairs. The principle of checks and balances applies not only between the Arctic Council and the Arctic Circle Forum, but also to China and the Nordic countries.[40] [translation from original]

The author is suggesting that the Chinese foreign policy actors should pay more attention to ensuring that China will not be exploited and the government should make sure it gets some rewards from the co-operation.

The last article is by Russian studies expert Na Chuanlin,[41] and it concentrates on reporting Russia's moves in the Arctic. China is mentioned only when referring to US pivot towards Asia giving some leeway for developing Russia's Arctic military strategy. The author gives credit to Russia for its successful moves in the Arctic. The author says:

> Russia's implementation of Arctic military strategy to expand its military presence in the Arctic is really a good move.[42] [translation from original]

The article continues by pointing out various problems in the strategy and stating that the other littoral states will not be turning a blind eye to Russia's moves.

V. COMPARISON WITH THE PREVIOUS STUDIES

Our analysis of the articles shows relatively few similarities with the previous studies that have analysed Chinese debate on the Arctic. The articles do not follow the pattern that Jakobson & Peng and Wright described in their studies.[43] The discussion in *World Affairs* (*Shijie zhishi*) magazine has

[40] ibid.

[41] C Na, 'Èluósī chóngxīn kāishǐ běijí jūnshì cúnzài' (2014) 1 *World Affairs*.

[42] ibid.

[43] See L Jakobson and J Peng, 'China's Arctic Aspirations' (n 3): 'Over the past few years an evolution has taken place in public analysis by Chinese scholars of China's interests and rights in the Arctic. Before 2011 it was commonplace for Chinese analysts to air assertive, even hawkish views. Since late 2011, following the Arctic Council's second deferral of decisions on permanent observership applications, Chinese Arctic scholars have become more subdued in public. The concern that overly proactive statements run the risk of offending Arctic states and consequently undermining China's position in the Arctic today shapes the public face of Chinese analysis. Several scholars advocate that China should try to avoid sensitive issues such as resource exploration and focus instead on climate change considerations, which will allow China to constructively participate in global cooperation'; DC Wright, 'China's Growing Interest in the Arctic' (2013) 15(2) *Journal of Military and Strategic Studies* 54. Wright agrees with Jacobson and Peng's findings about the declining trend in the amount of articles and the tone becoming more subdued: 'Given these trends, one can only assume that Chinese academics interested in the Arctic in general, along with the more strident commentators among their number in particular, have been instructed to reduce their Arctic-related scholarship or at least to cool their rhetoric over it'.

not shown any traces of making strong arguments about China's rights to use the Arctic before 2009 and therefore the discussion has neither any following subdued trend after 2009. More descriptive would be to say that general style of suggestions and comments are rather cautious in the articles throughout the material and there is no clear change in the style or approach to the subject.

However, our material has some points in common with Martin Kossa's findings,[44] while some points differ from his analysis. Next, we will compare and comment on our results with some recurring phrases Kossa found in his material.

First, '*[A]ll the articles started in a similar fashion by claiming that the Arctic is undergoing huge changes that will impact not only the Arctic states, but the whole world.*'[45]

In the case of our material, this observation is partly true and partly not. Many of the articles in our sample have similarities in the first chapter, but not quite in the same way as Kossa describes. The topic of most of our articles is related to Arctic governance, so the starting paragraph usually refers to the heated discussion around the Arctic governance in the fashion of: 'Recently the cold Arctic is becoming very hot, but this is not because of the temperature, but because of the Arctic states' heated battle over the area'.[46] Content similar to Kossa's repeating paragraph is found in only two of the articles[47] in our sample, though the authors have not always placed them at the beginning of the article as Kossa mentioned.

Secondly, '*[A]rticles stressed the impact on China by pointing out that China is located in the Northern Hemisphere and that it is a near-Arctic state*'.[48]

Some of the articles we analysed point out that China is located in the Northern Hemisphere, but none of the articles refer to China as a near-Arctic state. Quite the opposite, many of the articles clearly say that China is not an Arctic state.

Thirdly, '*the Arctic belongs to all of the people on earth, not only to the littoral states*'.[49] This finding is quite the contrary to Kossa's material, where all of the articles included the sentence. When it comes to the articles we analysed, this kind of argument would be a great oversimplification or even clearly false. We made an analysis of the word 'belong' to trace what the

44 M Kossa, 'China and its Emerging Arctic Agenda' (Thesis, Zhejiang University, 2013).
45 ibid, 79.
46 cp Wang, 'Běijí jiāng shàngyǎn zhēngduó zhàn?' (n 8); Li, 'É běijí "chā qí" yǐn rán "bīng dìrè zhàn"' (n 9); Shi, '"Běijí wǔ guó" zhēng běijí' (n 15).
47 Such articles in our material are the political speech of Zhengyue, 'Zhōngguó duì běijí shìwù de kànfǎ' (n 12) and the article written by Yu (n 17).
48 Kossa, 'China and its Emerging Arctic Agenda' (n 44).
49 ibid.

authors in our sample have to say about the question. The word 'belong' can be found in four of the articles.[50] In the sample the word 'belong' was used three times in close connection with Arctic water areas. The authors were usually saying that the Arctic sea area does not belong to any country, because it is in international waters. When discussing the story of evolving national claims in the Arctic, Wang mentions that the Arctic belonged to international territory a long time ago. Zhang and Li make a comment in their article that the US, by auctioning rights to explore Arctic oil and gas, was suggesting that the Arctic belongs to them. We have to add that although Fu does not use the word belong at all, he makes the sharpest comments of the whole of our material in his article. He uses the sentence 'the Arctic is the common property of the whole world'[51] in his article, and thus comes closest to the meaning in Hossa's material. However, the concept of the 'common property' Fu uses has a milder connotation and does not necessarily mean that the Arctic would belong to all of the people on the earth. Rather it refers to the concept of the 'common heritage of mankind' from international law and is supposed to mean that the Arctic has value to all mankind and should be protected from (harmful) exploitation. Of course the statement can also mean that if the natural resources of the Arctic are exploited, they should be open to all the mankind.[52]

Fourthly, '*The Arctic is very important to China*'.[53] Here again we must take the same approach as in the previous comparisons with Kossa's findings. This is because most of our material is not very straightforward when it comes to Chinese views. Instead many of the articles in our sample take an outsider view on the Arctic. However, two of the articles have the same pattern: the political speech and Fu's article.[54]

In terms of topics, Kossa found that many of the articles dealt with issues of Arctic governance and Chinese participation. Similarly, most of our material also deals with Arctic governance and more specifically describes how it has evolved. However, different from Kossa's material, we found that Chinese participation in the Arctic is given quite little space. Usually the authors mention more generally non-Arctic countries' rights to participate, if at all.

Lastly, the authors emphasise the importance of China's right to participate actively ('canyuquan') in the sessions of the Arctic Council.[55] In Kossa's materials, China's right to participate was based on the Svalbard Treaty or on the country being a permanent member of the UN Security Council.

[50] Wang (n 8); Li (n 9); Shi (n 15); X Zhang and Z Li, 'Zuì rè běijí jiājù dàguó zhēngduó zhàn' (n 26).

[51] Yu (n 17).

[52] To read more about this dimension see Nykänen, Ch 7 in this volume.

[53] Kossa (n 44).

[54] Zhengyue (n 12); Fu (n 17).

[55] Kossa (n 44) 81–82.

In our material Fu, Sun & Guo and Guo discuss the participation of non-Arctic countries in their articles. Guo points out the restrictions on participation in the Arctic Council between the Arctic states and the non-Arctic states, as the latter can only be accepted as observers, never more.[56] Sun and Guo describe all kinds of different arenas for non-Arctic countries to participate in Arctic issues, the Arctic Council being only one of them.[57] While Guo and Sun keep their tone neutral when discussing the right to participate, Fu's article has the same tone as Kossa's material had, self-confidently claiming that '*participation in Arctic affairs is China's legitimate right*'.[58]

VI. CONCLUSIONS

Chinese interest in the Arctic has grown in the past years; it has also been noticed by the western media and scholars. As the debate on China's motivations and future aims is going strong in the West, there is also debate on the Arctic within China. Since China does not have an Arctic strategy, studying debates is seen as one way to shed some light on Chinese foreign policy in Arctic issues.

Our analysis illuminates the fact that while China has been watching closely the discursive battle between the Arctic states, it has not as yet created a clear plan for its own actions in the North—or, in other words, the plan is to wait and see and act behind the public scenes. The articles do not make any open policy recommendations or comments about China's participation in the Arctic.

The Chinese are aware that western scholars and politicians easily see them as a threat. China has been keeping the same attitude of quietly observing the situation and has refrained from taking sides throughout the whole studied material. The authors of the articles noticed some changes for the better in the attitudes of some of the Arctic countries, but it was indicated that there is still a basic view among the Arctic countries that China needs to be kept in control. The rare opinions put forward in the articles express the hope for more equality between the Arctic States and the non-Arctic countries for better future development and co-operation within the Arctic.

Importantly, the authors of our material divide the Arctic countries into two groups, the big countries (Russia, the US and Canada) and the rest. The world is seen through the categories of classical realism, where states with actual physical power matter the most: others play a minor role as 'co-operators'. This does not imply that small states would be totally

[56] Guo, 'Běijí quān lùntán: Běijí lǐshì huì de "tà páng zhī hǔ"?' (n 31).
[57] Sun and Guo (n 22).
[58] Yu (n 19).

insignificant. One should keep in mind that China has developed its bilateral relations with the Nordic countries and does want to build a win-win relationship with these countries in joint projects.[59]

It should probably be emphasised once more that Russia has a very important place in Chinese political discussion on the Arctic. This is, of course, not surprising at all. In the conventional geopolitical imagination, the Northern Hemisphere is divided into the West and East, and in this structure Russia has been seen as the most important strategic companion for China in its challenge to the West.[60] On the other hand, Russia is China's neighbour and thus the capacity of its military is always a matter of interest for China.

[59] There are several examples of joint projects and co-operation at different levels. In scientific work a meaningful step was the founding of the China-Nordic Arctic Research Center in Shanghai. See eg Arctic Centre: China-Nordic Arctic Research Center inaugurated: www.ulapland.fi/news/China-Nordic-Arctic-Research-Center-inaugurated/tligk1sq/63c5d540-dedc-4697-b6e5-11f620c5f600.

[60] eg P Andrew-Speed and R Dannreuther, *China, Oil and Global Politics* (London, Routledge, 2011) 83.

5

China and Maritime Sovereignty and Rights Issues in the Arctic

Chinese Legal Perspectives on Arctic Governance

XIAOYI JIANG AND XIAOGUANG ZHOU

I. INTRODUCTION

THE ARCTIC REGION is now one of the hottest topics worldwide due to the consequences of ice melting in the Arctic Ocean as a result of climate change. Retreating Arctic Ocean sea ice and other changes open the region to economic development—the exploitation of oil, gas and minerals and utilisation of navigational waterways, primarily the Northern Sea Route and Northwest Passage.

As a result, Arctic issues are attracting worldwide attention. The membership of the Arctic Council comprises the eight Arctic States, which are the five Arctic coastal states of the Arctic Ocean—the US, Canada, Denmark (Greenland), Norway and Russia—together with three further states, Finland, Sweden and Iceland. They make efforts to develop Arctic-specific legally binding agreements under the auspices of the Council in spite of unsettled disputes over Arctic maritime sovereignty and rights among these states.

As a non-Arctic State, China is also paying increasing attention to Arctic maritime sovereignty and sovereign rights issues. For decades, the main activity of China in the Arctic has been scientific exploration. As early as the 1990s, China began to prepare for scientific exploration in the Arctic. However, this situation may change as the melting Arctic is bound to bring various benefits for China. At the same time, the rising role of China in the global economy, international relations and international law has engendered questions about Chinese Arctic interests and the effects that Chinese involvement may have on regional governance. In spite of its interests,

China is being cautious in Arctic issues and has not produced a comprehensive strategic document on its Arctic policy.

Against this background, it is necessary to explore Chinese ideas about the Arctic through analysing the relevant political statements and general Chinese approaches to international law and governance. In addition, it is timely to compare Chinese legal perspectives on Arctic governance with those espoused by traditional Arctic players. In particular, there are similarities and differences between the positions of Finland and China on Arctic law and governance. By comparing these two policy actors, neither of which is a littoral state to the Arctic Ocean, it is possible to obtain an enhanced understanding of the current policy and legal dynamics in general and in the region in particular.

With the increasingly dramatic sea ice loss and since the planting of the Russian flag at the North Pole on Lomonosov ridge,[1] research on Arctic governance has increased a great deal. Recently, research on the role and activities of the new Arctic actors, China included, has been growing.[2] Currently, there is increasing interest in China's possible role in the region. However, there is a dearth of literature that seriously or thoroughly compares Chinese legal perspectives on Arctic governance with other countries, particularly the Nordics.

As there is no authoritative statement of policy from the Chinese government on the Arctic, most overseas studies deal with this topic through analysing the relevant political statements and exploring the research in China. Consequently, there is an extensive body of research arguing that there is a 'Chinese threat'. On the one hand, the global power balance is gradually tilting towards the rising powers of Asia—in particular China.[3] On the other hand, there are, for example, arguments from Chinese officials that the Arctic should be treated as 'the inherited wealth of all humankind' or that Arctic states need to ensure that the Arctic remains a global commons.[4] Moreover,

[1] Under the UN Convention on the Law of the Sea, the 5 states with territory inside the Arctic Circle—Canada, Norway, Russia, the US, and Denmark, through its control of Greenland—have economic rights over a 200-mile zone around the north of their coastline. However, the convention is open to appeal, and several countries are disputing the limits of this zone. Russia believes that its Siberian shelf is directly linked to the Lomonosov ridge, an underwater mountain crest that runs 1,240 miles across the polar region. Russia symbolically staked its claim to its continental shelf on 2 August 2007 when 2 mini submarines reached the seabed more than 2 1/2 miles beneath the North Pole and planted a 1-meter-high titanium Russian flag on the underwater Lomonosov ridge.

[2] Y Kim and S Blank, 'The Arctic: A New Issue on Asia's Security Agenda' (2011) 23(3) *The Korean Journal of Defense Analysis* 303–20.

[3] ibid.

[4] E Rosenthal, 'Race is On as Ice Melt Reveals Arctic Treasures' *New York Times* (18 September 2012) www.nytimes.com/2012/09/19/science/earth/arctic-resources-exposed-by-warming-set-off-competition.html?emc=eta1&_r=0; C Campbell, 'China and the Arctic: Objectives and Obstacles' US-China Economic and Security Review Commission Staff Research Report (13 April 2012).

most studies on the topic of maritime sovereignty and maritime rights issues in China focus on trying to clarify the situation in the South China Sea,[5] and the Arctic is relatively neglected. Thus, it is necessary to examine whether that has any consequences for Arctic governance. In spite of many overseas studies, it is difficult to get the whole picture of the Chinese perspectives on Arctic issues due to the language barrier.

On the other hand, academics in China are increasingly showing interest in the region, and suggesting policies and actions for the state. The aim of the present work is to discuss how to safeguard and enhance China's Arctic maritime rights. Some of these academics consistently hold the view that China should see the Arctic international water area as the treasure of mankind, suggesting that it could oppose some of the Arctic states' sovereignty claims and that China has a legitimate right to play a part in Arctic resource exploration. However, the main limitation of this discussion is that it lacks consideration for traditional Arctic players. There are no results in the literature comparing in a meaningful way the general stances of China and Finland on the changing Arctic governance. Accordingly, a contribution can be made to the gap in the current knowledge base of this field through discussing and comparing Chinese and Finnish approaches to Arctic governance.

This chapter intends to take a close look at Arctic maritime sovereignty and maritime rights issues from a Chinese legal perspective and then conduct a legal comparison between the Chinese and Finnish approaches. To this end, the chapter is divided into six parts. The second part discusses China's Arctic interests. Part III focuses on the legal basis for China's Arctic activities. Part IV explores China's application of the international law in the Arctic. Part V discusses what China can do to safeguard and expand its Arctic maritime rights. Part VI offers some concluding remarks on Chinese and Finnish approaches to Arctic governance and international law.

II. CHINA'S ARCTIC INTERESTS

Climate change brings about a changing Arctic. Even though China is a non-Arctic state, the melting Arctic is also bound to bring both opportunities and challenges for the country in the environmental, economic, political, scientific and other spheres.

A. Environmental Aspect

There is strong scientific evidence that climate change is occurring and mostly human-induced. At the same time, considerable attention has been

[5] See eg L Buszynski, 'Rising Tensions in the South China Sea: Prospects for a Resolution of the Issue' (2010) 6(2) *Security Challenges* 85–104.

drawn to the consequences of climate change in the Arctic. In the Arctic, climate change occurs faster and more severely than in most other parts of the Earth.[6] As the Arctic plays an essential role in the whole earth system, Arctic climate change will have tremendous impacts globally.

China is one of the countries most vulnerable to the adverse impact of climate change.[7] Compared to the eight Arctic states, China is a non-Arctic state. In spite of that, the northernmost county in China is only 1,300 kilometres from the Arctic Circle, and China is also adjacent to Russia—one of the eight Arctic states. Chinese Arctic specialists therefore currently refer to China as a 'near-Arctic state' and the term 'stakeholder' is also often used. As a state near the Arctic, China's continental and oceanic environment is relatively sensitive to Arctic climate change. First, China is vulnerable to the impacts of the rising sea level, because China has a long continental coastline, and most of the relatively developed cities in China, including Shanghai, are along the continental coastline. Secondly, despite its huge territory, China still has a vulnerable ecosystem due to the lack of arable land and forest, huge population and the expansion of deserts. Thus, climate change poses a serious risk to food security in China. Because of impacts on sea levels and agriculture, for example, China is greatly influenced by climate and environmental changes in the Arctic.[8] A number of Chinese scholars have recommended that Chinese research should remain primarily focused on how the melting Arctic will affect China's environment and how in turn such changes could affect domestic agriculture and economic development.[9]

B. Economic Aspect

The formerly ice-covered Arctic is undergoing an extraordinary transformation as a result of the unprecedented rate at which the ice is diminishing.[10]

[6] TF Stocker et al (eds) *Climate Change 2013: The Physical Science Basis*. Contribution of Working Group I to the Fifth Assessment Report of the Intergovernmental Panel on Climate Change (Cambridge, Cambridge University Press, 2013).

[7] 'China's Policies and Actions for Addressing Climate Change—2', the National Development and Reform Commission (2012) available at www.ccchina.gov.cn/WebSite/CCChina/UpFile/File1324.pdf.

[8] 'China Defends Arctic Research Missions' *China Daily* (1 February 2012) available at www.chinadaily.com.cn/china/2012-02/01/content_14514014.htm. See also S Kopra, 'China's Arctic Interests' (2013) 2 *Arctic Yearbook*.

[9] L Jakobson and J Peng, 'China's Arctic Aspirations' (2012) 34 SIPRI Policy Paper; see also H Liu, '中国可以在北极做什么' ['What Can China Do in the Arctic?'] Jingji Cankao Bao, 27 December 2011.

[10] According to 1 report, the annual average extent of Arctic Ocean ice has shrunk by 2.7% per decade, with a decrease of 7.4% per decade during the summer months; S Solomon et al (eds), *Climate Change 2007: The Physical Science Basis*, Contribution of Working Group I to the Fourth Assessment Report of the Intergovernmental Panel on Climate Change (Cambridge University Press: Cambridge, 2007) 7. See also L Jakobson, 'China Prepares for an Ice-Free Arctic' (2010) 2 *SIPRI Insights on Peace and Security*.

The prospect of the melting Arctic being regularly navigable during summer, leading to both shorter shipping routes and access to untapped natural resources, has impelled China to pursue its interests in the high north.

The Arctic Ocean is slowly opening up to navigation during the summer months. Estimates about when the Arctic Ocean could be consistently ice-free during the summer season vary greatly, from 2013 to 2060.[11] Nevertheless, China is motivated by the prospect of new and in some cases shorter shipping routes. Nearly half of China's GDP is thought to be dependent on shipping because China's economy is reliant on foreign trade. In 2009, China was the largest exporter and second-largest importer of globally shipped goods.[12] As the Arctic sea ice melts, two international shipping routes—the Northwest Passage and the Northeast Passage—become increasingly usable for commercial purposes. China's access to these alternate shipping routes has substantial commercial implications. For seaborne trade, China highly depends upon the Shanghai to Hamburg route via the Malacca Strait and the Suez Canal. The conventional routes have inevitable weaknesses—piracy and narrow thoroughfare. The use of the Northeast Passage would offer a 6,400 km shorter route to Europe and alleviate China's 'Malacca dilemma'.[13]

In spite of the benefits China might gain from a shortened Arctic passage, China needs to meet challenges. First, shippers would have to contend with unpredictable and often violent weather conditions, but they have limited expertise in polar navigation. Most vessels and related machinery used in Arctic waters are designed and constructed in Northern Europe, and China has little indigenous expertise in this field.[14] This impairs the logistics costs and timing of the shipping. Secondly, Russia has jurisdiction over much of the Northeast Passage and thus has the power to impose regulations on international vessels traversing its water.[15] The users would have to comply with Russian environmental and navigation regulations and might have to pay high passage fees. In addition, Canada considers that it is sovereign over

[11] For estimates of 2013, 2040 and 2060, see A Grupta 'Geopolitical implications of Arctic Melt-down' (2009) 33(2) *Strategic Analysis* 174; Arctic Council, *Arctic Marine Shipping Assessment 2009 Report* (Arctic Council, April 2009) 30; and US National Snow and Ice Data Center, 'Arctic Sea ice shrinks as temperatures rise' Press release (3 October 2006) nsidc.org/news/press/2006_seaiceminimum/20061003_pressrelease.html. See also Jakobson, 'China Prepares for an Ice-Free Arctic' (n 10). See also chapter by N Liu and K Hossain in this volume.

[12] World Shipping Council, 'Global Summary of Liner Trade' www.worldshipping.org/about-the-industry/global-trade/trade-statistics. See also Campbell, 'China and the Arctic: Objectives and Obstacles' (n 4).

[13] The 'Malacca dilemma' refers to China's high dependence on the Malacca Strait for seaborne trade. 78% of its energy imports pass through this narrow thoroughfare. The perceived threats of bottlenecks or blockades of Chinese trade via the Malacca Strait have driven analysts and policymakers to consider alternative routes to secure China's shipped exports and imports. See Campbell (n 4).

[14] ibid.

[15] ibid.

the waters of the Northwest Passage on the grounds that those waters are internal waters.[16] Considering the Northwest Passage as part of Canada's internal waters would enable Canada to regulate activities therein and to enforce its laws in the Passage—with foreign states and ships enjoying no maritime rights under international law.[17]

According to estimates, the Arctic contains up to 30 per cent of the world's undiscovered gas and 13 per cent of the world's undiscovered oil and 9 per cent of the world's coal.[18] These untapped resources will become more accessible as the Arctic melts. There will be attractive opportunities for both the Arctic and non-Arctic states. However, according to the US Geological Survey, close to 90 per cent of the resources are located within the territorial jurisdiction of Arctic states, and under the international law will thus be subject to the management and legal oversight of those countries.[19] Consequently, China with its territorial disadvantages and lack of cold water drilling expertise will have to partner with the littoral states to tap into the resources.

C. International Status

As a rising developing country, China is expected to participate broadly and have its voice better heard in global affairs. As the changing Arctic has attracted worldwide attention, China could improve its international status through playing a more active role in Arctic issues.

First, the future of the Arctic Ocean is closely related to climate change. Due to its rapid economic development, China has become one of the major developing countries and largest CO2 emitters. Thus, how China copes with climate change could influence its international status. As mentioned earlier, China is one of the countries which are most affected by climate change. Moreover, the Arctic Ocean plays a crucial role in the global climate system. China is thus greatly influenced by climate and environmental changes in the Arctic. Under these circumstances, getting involved in Arctic affairs not

[16] R Dufresne, 'Canada's Legal Claims over Arctic Territory and Waters' Parliamentary Information and Research Service (6 December 2007) available at www.parl.gc.ca/Content/LOP/ResearchPublications/prb0739-e.pdf, 15.

[17] ibid.

[18] US Geological Survey, 'Arctic Oil and Gas Report: Estimates of Undiscovered Oil and Gas North of the Arctic Circle' (2008) available at geology.com/usgs/arctic-oil-and-gas-report.shtml.

[19] K Offerdal, 'High North Energy: Myths and Realities' in SG Holtsmark and BA Smith-Windsor, *Security Prospects in the High North: Geostrategic Thaw or Freeze?* (Rome, Italy, NATO Defense College, 2009) 152–53. See also Campbell (n 4).

only demonstrates China's efforts and actions to deal with climate change, but also helps to address climate change issues in China.

Secondly, in spite of the fact that there are many pending issues surrounding the Arctic and unsettled disputes among the Arctic states, the environmental protection and governance of the High Arctic are global common issues, which the non-Arctic states and Arctic states need to co-operate on to deal with the various practical and potential problems in the Arctic region. In this regard, the changing Arctic provides an opportunity for China to improve its international status through actively participating in Arctic affairs and discussing the political framework and legal foundation for future Arctic activities.

On the other hand, as China is seeking the 'right to speak up' in Arctic affairs, its increasing international status brings about a negative phenomenon—the so-called Chinese threat. Actually, China applied for observer status of the Arctic Council many times before recently being granted permanent observer status. For this reason, the Chinese government faces the challenge of lessening global fear and improving its international image at the same time.

D. Other Aspects

The Arctic has significant military value. The increasing military importance of an ice-free Arctic is reflected in decisions taken during recent years by all five littoral states to strengthen their military capabilities in the Arctic. Some Chinese scholars also pointed out that the Arctic has significant military value.[20] Moreover, due to its unique physical characteristics, the Arctic also has scientific value for all countries, including China. Scientific expeditions to the Arctic provide opportunities for China to share relevant leading-edge scientific research.

The Chinese government now prioritises the pursuit of development and international status. The prospect of the melting Arctic would bring various benefits to China in the above-mentioned factors. Against this background, China's desire to become a major Arctic player might be motivated by interests related to the melting Arctic. However, there are various barriers due to its territorial disadvantage and lack of techniques and expertise. Facing this situation, international co-operation is the only effective way to alleviate the barriers.

[20] See eg X Han, '备受关注的北极主权之争' ['Closely Watched Dispute over Arctic Sovereignty'] (2008) 253(9B) *Bingqi Zhishi Fangwu Guancha Jia* 16–19; Z Li, '北极航线的中国战略分析' ['Analysis of China's Strategy on the Arctic Route'] (2009) 1 *Zhongguo Ruankexue* 1–7; see also Jakobson (n 10).

III. LEGAL BASIS FOR CHINA'S ARCTIC ACTIVITIES

A. China-related International Legal and Political Framework for the Arctic

China is a signatory to the United Nations Convention on the Law of the Sea (UNCLOS)[21] and to the Svalbard Treaty.[22] Thus, the UNCLOS and Svalbard Treaty provisions constitute the legal basis for China's activities in the Arctic. The UNCLOS, which entered into force in 1994, remains the most comprehensive international legal framework for governance of state activities over the world's oceans, including the Arctic Ocean. The Convention aims to regulate all aspects of the resources of the sea and uses of the ocean. In the case of the Arctic Ocean, the USA is the only Arctic state yet to ratify the Convention. For China, in spite of the fact that China is not a littoral state, the relevant provisions constitute the legal basis for its activities in the Arctic.

The Svalbard Treaty is considered as another legal foundation to safeguard China's Arctic interests. The Treaty establishes Norway's full and absolute sovereignty over the Svalbard archipelago but stipulates that it must remain demilitarised. China ratified the treaty in 1925. The treaty grants its 42 parties equal rights to undertake fishing, hunting, mining, trading and industrial activities in the area of the treaty.

In addition to the UNCLOS and the Svalbard Treaty, China has been admitted as an observer state to the Arctic Council, and thus must comply with the relevant provisions under the Arctic Council. The Arctic Council was formally established by the Ottawa Declaration in 1996. The Arctic Council is a high-level intergovernmental forum to provide a means for promoting co-operation, co-ordination and interaction among the Arctic States, in particular on issues of sustainable development and environmental protection in the Arctic. It is not an international organisation with a firm legal charter but rather an international forum. China looks on the Arctic Council as the most influential regional governmental organisation. However, the full member states are the eight Arctic states. China was only an ad hoc observer and applied to become a permanent observer state many times. China has now been admitted as an observer, among 12 non-Arctic countries. Although China no longer needs to apply to be admitted to each Arctic Council meeting, it has virtually no influence on the decision-making process at ministerial meetings.[23] Only Arctic Council member states have voting rights.

[21] United Nations Convention on the Law of the Sea, 10 December 1982, in force 16 November 1994, 21 *International Legal Materials* 1261 (1982) (UNCLOS).

[22] Spitsbergen (Svalbard) Treaty, 9 February 1920, in force 14 August 1925, 2 *League of Nations Treaties Series* 8, art 1.

[23] For more details, see www.arctic-council.org/index.php/en/about-us/arctic-council/observers.

B. China's Arctic Sovereignty and Maritime Rights under International Law

According to the international law and regulations, China has no legal basis to make any Arctic sovereignty claims of its own and no legal basis to contest existing sovereignty claims. In spite of that, China has limited maritime rights in the Arctic.

First, according to the Convention, China has the following kinds of rights:

China has the right of navigation. China enjoys the freedom of navigation in a coastal state's exclusive economic zone (EEZ) and the high seas and the right of innocent passage through the territorial sea.[24]

China has the right of fishing and enjoys the freedom of fishing in the high seas.[25]

China has the right of natural resource exploitation. China may exploit the resources of the international seabed under a parallel system established to ensure equitable participation by developing countries.[26]

China has the right of marine scientific exploration. China may carry out marine scientific research in the Area,[27] enjoy the freedom of scientific exploration in the high seas[28] and conduct marine scientific exploration in territorial sea, EEZ and on the continental shelf with the consent of the state.[29]

Secondly, according to the Svalbard Treaty, China enjoys the freedom of undertaking fishing, hunting, mining, trading and industrial activities in the Svalbard archipelago. In addition, Chinese citizens enjoy the same right of access to and residence in Svalbard as citizens of all states party to the treaty.

[24] UNCLOS, arts 3 and 57 on the sovereignty rights related to territorial sea and EEZ; art 17 in relation to the right of innocent passage through the territorial sea; arts 58 and 87 concerning the freedom of navigation respectively in the EEZ and in the high seas.

[25] UNCLOS, art 87 regulates the freedom of fishing in high seas.

[26] UNCLOS, art 136 provides that the area of the ocean beyond national jurisdiction (international seabed), and its resources are 'the common heritage of mankind'. No state may claim sovereign rights over any part of this area or its resources. The mineral resources of the Common Heritage are administered by the International Seabed Authority. Part of the area proposed for exploitation is to be allocated to the applicant and the other is to become the reserved area. The reserved areas are set aside for activities by developing states or by the Authority through its Enterprise.

[27] UNCLOS, art 143 provides that states parties may carry out marine scientific research in the Area.

[28] UNCLOS, art 87.

[29] UNCLOS, art 76 defines a process through which littoral states have 10 years starting from their ratification of the convention to make claims to extend their outer limits of the continental shelf up to 350 nautical miles from the baselines from which the breadth of the territorial sea is measured. Art 245 emphasises that marine scientific research therein shall be conducted only with the express consent of and under the conditions set forth by the coastal state.

Under the treaty, 10 signatories, including China, have set up research stations.

Thirdly, as an observer state of the Arctic Council, China can be invited to the meetings of the Arctic Council, observe the work of the Arctic Council, propose projects through an Arctic State or a permanent participant and make statements, present written statements, submit relevant documents and provide views on the issues under discussion.

C. China's Obligation to Address Climate Change Issues

Climate change is declared to be of 'common concern to mankind'. The international community has been working together to minimise the risks that would be brought about by climate change through international laws and regulations. With an ultimate objective of stabilising greenhouse gas (GHG) concentrations at a level that would prevent dangerous anthropogenic interference with the climate system and based on the common but different responsibilities principle, the United Nations Framework Convention on Climate Change (UNFCCC) was adopted in 1992.[30] Both developed and developing countries under the convention accepted a number of general commitments in accordance with their common but different responsibilities, respective capacities and their social and economic conditions.

Under the UNFCCC, all convention parties are required to develop national inventories of anthropogenic emissions by sources and removals by sink of all GHGs and launch national strategies for climate change mitigation and adaptation to expected impact. They would also take climate change into account in their relevant social, economic and environmental policies; co-operate in scientific, technical and educational matters; and promote technology transfer, sustainable management, education, public awareness and the exchange of information related to climate change.[31]

As mentioned earlier, China is the largest CO2 emitter. Even without a compulsory reduction target, it is expected to take on a greater reduction responsibility to combat climate change. The melting Arctic is a prominent phenomenon caused by climate change. In addition, according to the UNCLOS, China has the obligation to protect and preserve the marine environment. In this regard, China has the responsibility to deal with environmental issues in the Arctic by cutting its emissions at home.

[30] United Nations Framework Convention on Climate Change, 12 June 1992, in force 21 March 1994, 31 *International Legal Materials* 849 (1992) (UNFCCC).

[31] ibid.

IV. CHINA'S APPLICATION OF THE INTERNATIONAL LAW IN THE ARCTIC

Considering the above-mentioned factors, China began to take an active part in Arctic region affairs after the Russian flag was planted on the seabed at the North Pole in 2007. In spite of the intentions, the Chinese government is being cautious with respect to Arctic issues and there is no authoritative statement of policy from the Chinese government on the Arctic. However, China's official silence should not be seen as indicating that it does not take a view on Arctic sovereignty and maritime rights.

A. The Chinese Government's Position on the Arctic

There is no one department within the Chinese government that deals exclusively with Arctic affairs. Rather, the government handles Arctic and Antarctic matters jointly as polar affairs. The office of the Chinese Arctic and Antarctic Administration (CAA) under the State Oceanic Administration (SOA) directly manages polar affairs.[32] The SOA reports administratively to the Ministry of Land and Resources. China's polar activities are funded by several ministries and agencies, which include the National Development and Reform Commission, Ministry of Finance, the Ministry of Science and Technology and the National Natural Science Foundation, administered by the State Council, China's highest governmental body. The Ministry of Environmental Protection implements international co-operation between China and the Arctic States in the fields of climate change and environmental protection. In addition, the Ministry of Foreign Affairs is the lead organisation on issues related to Chinese international Arctic co-operation.

There is no authoritative statement of policy from the Chinese government on the Arctic. Chinese officials from the departments have on several occasions expressed that China shall safeguard and protect its Arctic sovereignty and rights by adhering to international law, the two most relevant treaties of which are the UNCLOS and Svalbard Treaty. Some of their speeches are as follows:

> Sun from SOA said in 2008: 'China's primary attitude is actively participating'.[33]

[32] For more details, see the website of Chinese Arctic and Antarctic Administration: www.chinare.gov.cn/en/.

[33] Z Honghui, '国际海洋局领导视察极地中心和"雪龙"号' ['Director of the SOA inspected the Polar Research Institute of China and "Xue Long"'] 3 June 2008.

> Li from the State Council said in 2009: 'China focuses on scientific value and climate change in the Arctic and the principle is international co-operation'.[34]
> Hu from MFA said in 2009: 'China does not have an Arctic strategy'.[35]
> Hu from MFA said in 2009: 'UNCLOS is the primary legal mechanism for Arctic activities as well as the basis for international co-operation'.[36]
> Song from MFA said in 2012: 'Co-operation has become the mainstream in Arctic affairs which began with environmental protection along with co-operation on sustainable development'.[37]

It can be seen from these public statements and speeches that the Chinese government is being cautious in Arctic issues. The approach of the Chinese government is to avoid sensitive issues in the Arctic. For China, the UNCLOS is the primary legal mechanism for Arctic activities and the basis for international co-operation. China always insists that respect for state sovereignty should be a guiding principle of international relations. On the other hand, China would like to see the Arctic states recognise the interests of non-Arctic states. The treaty is regarded as another justification for China's Arctic presence. China should have a legitimate right to participate in Arctic governance as the melting Arctic has global impacts and offers both opportunities and challenges for non-Arctic states as well. In line with the governing principles in international affairs, China wishes to see disputes related to sovereignty resolved peacefully through dialogue. Instead, China prefers to talk about climate change, the environment, co-operation and scientific co-operation. China emphasises the global rather than regional implications of the melting ice.

There are two reasons for concern leading to the current low-profile attitude. First, there are unsettled sovereignty disputes among the eight Arctic states and uncertain factors in the delimitation of the outer continental shelf. Some Arctic littoral states submitted outer continental shelf claims to the UN agency. It is estimated that the high seas area will shrink by two-thirds if all the outer continental shelf claims by Arctic states were to be approved.[38] China is at a disadvantage because it is neither an Arctic littoral state—it has no Arctic coast, and so no sovereign rights to

[34] H Yanji, '李克强：极地考察关系我国的长久利益' ['Polar Expedition influences the Interests of China in Long Term'] (20 November 2009) news.xinhuanet.com/politics/2009-11/20/content_12508072.htm.

[35] X Ning, '地球未来的缩影—外交部部长助理谈"北极研究之旅"' ['A Microcosm of the World's Future—Assistant Minister of Foreign Affairs Talks about "High North Study Tour"'] (2009) 349(19) *Shijie Bolan* 58. See also Jakobson (n 10).

[36] ibid.

[37] '中国愿为北极地区和平稳定可持续发展做出贡献' ['China is Willing to Make Contribution to Peace, Stability and Sustainable Development'] http://news.sohu.com/20120416/n340709408.shtml, 16 April 2012.

[38] Jakobson and Peng, 'China's Arctic Aspirations' (n 9) 18.

underwater continental shelves—nor an Arctic council member state with the right to participate in the discussion of Arctic policies. As a consequence, China prefers to adopt a wait-and-see approach to Arctic development.

As a matter of fact, the Chinese government seeks to avoid sensitive issues in the Arctic. Under international law, China's rights in the Arctic are limited. On the one hand, China has no legal basis to contest existing sovereignty claims or to make any Arctic claims of its own. China therefore supports the rights of Arctic states over the resources within each nation's EEZ.

On the other hand, the government, academics, commercial entities and army in China are increasingly showing interest in the region, and suggesting policies and actions for the state. Some of them consistently hold the view that China should see the Arctic international waters as the treasure of mankind, suggesting that it could oppose some of the Arctic states' sovereignty claims and that China has a legitimate right to play a part in Arctic resource exploration.[39] As a result, China is seen as a threat due to its status as a rising major power.

Against this background, China started applying for permanent observer status in the Arctic Council in 2006. The application, however, was refused due to the objections of some members. Afterwards, China tried again to submit the application, but was again deterred. Facing this situation and following the Arctic Council's second deferral of decisions on permanent observership applications, Chinese Arctic scholars have become more subdued in public.[40] Chinese officials are certainly well aware of the suspicions that China's interest in the Arctic evokes and of the sensitive nature of Arctic politics, especially in the realm of resources and sovereignty.[41] Thus, China wants to change its image from 'a threat' to 'a co-operative actor' by avoiding sensitive issues. Meanwhile, the Arctic Council has adopted a manual for observers that defines their role in greater detail, making it easier for the Council to accept new observers. Consequently, China was finally accepted as a permanent observer after a wait of seven years in May 2013, and it also needs to acknowledge the existing Arctic Council member states' sovereignty and sovereign rights in Arctic waters.

B. Comparison between Sovereignty Stances on the South China Sea, East China Sea and the Arctic

China always insists that respect for state sovereignty should be a guiding principle of international relations, thus keeping a hardline stance on

[39] See eg Huang Zhixiong, '北极问题的国际法分析和思考' ['Arctic Issues from the Perspective of International Law'] (2009) 11(6) *International Forum* 12.

[40] Jakobson and Peng (n 9) 15.

[41] ibid.

sovereignty issues of the South China Sea and the East China Sea. This is because China has legitimate and reasonable rights to claim sovereignty over the South China Sea and the East China Sea from a historical, geopolitical or legal perspective. Nevertheless, China is only a near Arctic state or an Arctic stakeholder, thus making it difficult for China to question the mineral and territorial rights of the Arctic states.

C. China's other Arctic Actors

Other actors are showing increasing interest in Arctic issues, and thus may somehow influence China's Arctic activities. Academics discuss Arctic issues to help policymakers understand the changing Arctic from their specialised perspectives and to suggest policies and actions for the state. Generally speaking, their attitudes and opinions range from the hawkish to negotiable.

Although China and scholars have an increasingly clear-sighted view of the economic opportunities that the melting Arctic potentially offers industries, the relevant commercial sector has just started to notice the interests. Shipping and fishing industries are expected to be the first to benefit from a seasonally accessible Arctic. However, China's largest state-owned shipping companies have adopted a wait-and-see approach to the Arctic. Presumably, the region may be commercially unprofitable for shipping companies, at least in the short term, due to high insurance premiums, lack of infrastructure and harsh conditions.[42] It is unlikely that China's shipping industry will prioritise developing new shipping routes in the short term.

The untapped resources opened up by the melting Arctic will also stimulate Chinese energy companies to invest in the resources sector in the Arctic. To date, Chinese companies have been most active in Greenland and a number of energy companies, including private and state-owned resource companies, are starting to explore resources in the Arctic.

Arctic tourism is also a promising industry to attract Chinese travellers. Some Chinese businessmen are trying to expand tourism into the Arctic region.[43]

D. China's Arctic Activities

Although China has not yet formulated any concrete Arctic policy, the Chinese government and scholars are aware of the need and imperative to protect China's high interests in the ice-free Arctic. But it also has a realistic

[42] Jakobson and Peng (n 9) 7.
[43] ibid, 9.

awareness of its territorial disadvantages, limited maritime rights and scientific and technological capacity to exploit the Arctic resources. Under these circumstances, the purpose of China's activities in the Arctic region is 'peace, science, co-operation and environmental protection'.[44]

China highly values scientific exploration in the Arctic, the core content of which is based on climate change and the ecological environment. Moreover, the focus of the Arctic exploration has shifted to research. A new roadmap of polar exploration has been formulated for the period between 2011 and 2015, namely the 12th Five-Year Plan for China's Polar Research[45] and a chapter on polar exploration in the 12th Five-Year Plan for the Development of Marine Affairs.[46] A second icebreaker vessel is being built. More funds have been allocated to Arctic research. The central government has allocated a more generous budget to the research of polar issues during the 12th Five-Year Plan period. With the increased funds from the Ministry of Finance, five Antarctic expeditions and three Arctic expeditions will be carried out. In spite of that, compared to the Antarctic, the Arctic is of low priority.

At the same time, China pays attention to bilateral co-operation with littoral states in many fields, such as Arctic scientific research, shipping technology and expertise and oil exploitation how-know. China also wants to ensure that its voice is better heard in the international forum and has become a permanent observer state in the Arctic Council.

V. SEVERAL APPROACHES PROPOSED TO SAFEGUARD ARCTIC MARITIME RIGHTS

In spite of limited maritime rights and territorial disadvantages, the Chinese government has realised the potential benefits as well as challenges that a changing Arctic environment would bring about. Under these circumstances, there are several approaches suggested to safeguard and extend Arctic maritime rights.

First, sensitive issues, including sovereignty, resource exploration and shipping routes, are avoided. It is expected that the topic of climate change, which is a 'common concern of humanity' and of low political sensitivity, will assist China in playing an active role in Arctic issues. China is the largest emitter, and thus is expected to take on more responsibilities in addressing

[44] http://jjckb.xinhuanet.com/opinion/2011-12/27/content_351013.htm

[45] '中国极地考察"十二五"发展规划' [12th Five-Year Plan for China's Polar Research] August 2011.

[46] Section 2, ch 13 of the 12th Five-Year Plan for the Development of Marine Affairs, '国家海洋事业发展"十二五"规划' www.soa.gov.cn/zwgk/fwjgwywj/shxzfg/201304/t20130411_24765.html.

climate change issues. Paying attention to Arctic issues should start from climate change.

The first way to safeguard and extend the Arctic maritime rights should be to get involved in the Arctic issues. Due to the fact that China is merely a state near the Arctic, co-operation is a feasible way for China to tap into potential benefits from the Arctic. China can co-operate with the Arctic states in political, economic, technological and other aspects. In addition, co-operation with the non-Arctic states is an alternative option for China to get more involved in Arctic issues. The co-operation can also include the Arctic indigenous people with a view to understanding their demands and lifestyle.

With regard to Arctic issues, China may change from an outsider to a participant. There are overlapping applications due to the Arctic states' outer continental shelf claims. China is seeking to become more involved in the international forum on Arctic issues and the discussion of future Arctic activities through scientific co-operation, diplomacy and joint co-development projects with Arctic states.

VI. A COMPARATIVE STUDY OF CHINESE AND FINNISH LEGAL PERSPECTIVES ON ARCTIC GOVERNANCE

There are similarities and differences between the Chinese and Finnish legal perspectives on Arctic governance.

Finland and China are both states with strong interests in being part of Arctic governance, expecting certain benefits from opportunities created by the changing environment. Neither belongs to the group of Arctic littoral states, that is, those with a strong legal and political stake in the region.

First, the two countries have different maritime rights in the Arctic. Finland is not an Arctic coastal state, but it is an Arctic state with a membership in the Arctic Council. Thus, Finland is eligible to develop Arctic-specific legally binding agreements under the auspices of the Council. China is a country near the Arctic and has observer status of the Council. Therefore, China has a different level of power than Finland in discussing Arctic issues in the international forum.

Secondly, Finland has traditionally been a supporter of international law, perceiving international law as crucial and generally beneficial to smaller states. On the other hand, Finland is also an EU member state. The EU has taken more radical stances on Arctic governance; earlier, it even advocated an Arctic Treaty on the lines of the Antarctic Treaty to govern the region. In spite of the fact that China advocates its adherence to the international law to deal with international affairs, it has an international image of viewing many traditional areas of international law with suspicion. In addition, China, contrary to Finland, has not produced a comprehensive strategic document on its Arctic policy.

Thirdly, China's Arctic activities are still closely watched by other countries. Finland is a small European state, while China is a rising superpower whose role in the Arctic is continuously questioned. China has sustained an 8–10 per cent annual gross domestic product (GDP) growth rate since the 1980s.[47] Now, China is the largest manufacturing and export nation. The economy of China is still growing at a rate of 7.5 per cent on average.[48] The potential shipping routes and untapped natural resources in the Arctic are significant opportunities for China's international trade and energy security in the future. Besides, China's vast territories are vulnerable to natural disasters resulting from climate change. Under its national circumstances, it is reasonable to believe that China has a stronger economic motivation to participate in Arctic affairs as a 'stakeholder' and to suspect the role China wants to play in the Arctic region.

Fourthly, the two countries have different strategies and attitudes towards the Arctic. As a traditional Arctic state, Finland is a member state of the Arctic Council. In addition, as one of the Nordic countries, Finland is a member state of the European Union. The double memberships have shaped Finland's distinctive national Arctic strategy. Unlike the national strategies of the littoral 'Arctic Five', the priorities of Finnish Arctic strategy are neither sovereignty nor national security, but comprehensive security and stability based on regional co-operation, as well as economic interests.[49] Therefore, Finland supports the acceptance of new observer states from Asia and Europe into the Arctic Council. China is a near Arctic state and one of the new observer states of the Arctic Council. Thus, although there is no officially published strategy in China, it is clear that China has not made any claims on Arctic territories or challenged the sovereignty rights of Arctic states. In spite of that, in order to get involved in Arctic affairs, China often advocates that Arctic issues are not only regional, but also international.

Fifthly, in spite of realising the future importance of the melting Arctic, the two countries have different capacities in exploring the Arctic. As an Arctic state, Finland takes the lead in knowledge, research, technology and know-how regarding the Arctic, such as shipbuilding and drilling in harsh weather.[50] What Finland desires to do in coming years is to further enhance its capacity and develop trans-boundary co-operation in new forms. On the contrary, China has limited capacities in exploring the Arctic. Since the mid-1990s, the Chinese Arctic and Antarctic Administration (CAA) has

[47] Rates of GDP Growth from 1950–2013, http://intl.ce.cn/zhuanti/data/s/Chinadata/201403/14/t20140314_2485387.shtml.

[48] Report of the Work of the Government, available at http://lianghui.people.com.cn/2014npc/n/2014/0305/c376646-24532570.html.

[49] Finnish Arctic strategy.

[50] '芬兰宣布修订北极战略' ['Finland Declared to Adjust Arctic Strategy'] http://news.xinhuanet.com/world/2013-08/24/c_117076691.htm.

conducted only six Arctic research programmes,[51] the research of which has developed in recent years. In addition, the available funding allocated to the Arctic programmes is comparatively much lower than to the Antarctic. Consequently, international co-operation is the only effective and feasible solution for China to step into the Arctic region.

At present, China has yet not formulated an Arctic strategy. Respect for sovereignty rights and international co-operation are the principles of China's Arctic strategy. China respects the sovereignty rights of Arctic littoral states based on international law, while China also wants to be a 'stakeholder' of the Arctic. Thus, addressing climate change in the Arctic and international co-operation based on international law are expected to be the major activities in China's involvement in the Arctic region.

[51] For more details, see http://www.chinare.gov.cn/en/index.html?pid=science.

Part II

Comparison between Finland and China

6

China and Finland in the Globalised Arctic

Asymmetry with Common Interests?

LASSI HEININEN

IT IS POLITICALLY relevant and scientifically interesting, even exciting, to find the former marginalised periphery on the top of the world, and on the upper edge of the Mercator map, becoming the subject of growing interest both within the Arctic states and internationally. In brief, the Arctic has become global; what happens in the region matters on a global scale. Even though we know that most of the main reasons behind this are material-based and hegemony-oriented, and largely based on (new) realism and the resource models of (classical) geopolitics, this is fascinating for political sciences and political scientists—particularly so, as this development also involves immaterial things, such as human capital (eg traditional/local environmental knowledge) and political innovations. The current position of the Arctic is one of the paradoxes of international politics and international relations: the region and its peoples on the top of the Earth, colonised and marginalised for centuries, have suddenly become attractive to the rest of the world.[1]

I. POST-COLD WAR ARCTIC GEOPOLITICS—INTRODUCTION

For a long time the Arctic region has been known to be rich in natural resources, particularly energy. During the Cold War it was heavily militarised by the nuclear weapon systems of the two superpowers. Unlike the

[1] L Heininen, '"Arctic Paradoxes"—a State of Arctic (Resource) Geopolitics' (A presentation at University of Southern California, Los Angeles, California, 6 March 2014)—on file with the author.

traditional and somewhat naive interpretation of the Arctic region as an isolated northernmost periphery with pristine nature, the destination of brave expeditions and mapping efforts in the early twentieth century, in the 1980s the Arctic, particularly the northern seas, came to be known as a sink of long-range air and water pollutants (caused by industry, agriculture and cities mostly located in lower latitudes, and the military), such as radioactivity, heavy metals, persistent organic pollutants (POPs), greenhouse gases (GHGs) and black carbon. Later it became an area where the physical impacts of rapid climate change, such as the thawing of permafrost and the melting of sea ice and glaciers) are visible and cumulative, and thus threaten human security. Growing pollution and risks of nuclear accidents were the main reasons why northern indigenous peoples and civilian organisations became concerned about the state of the environment and, inspired by the Murmansk speech by Gorbachev, pushed governments to start environmental co-operation.

The Arctic states, in co-operation with indigenous peoples, civil societies and universities, managed to transform the confrontational spirit of the Cold War into international and interregional co-operation, mainly in the field of environmental protection based on the Arctic Environmental Protection Strategy (AEPS), in order to build intergovernmental and other international co-operative forums and networks, such as the Arctic Council (AC), the International Arctic Science Committee (IASC) and the Northern Forum (NF).

Through this broadening and deepening cross-border co-operation, the Arctic stakeholders involved in the process managed to achieve a state of high political stability and peace within the region and between the Arctic states. The result of this transformation is illustrated by two powerful trends: first, the increasing circumpolar co-operation by indigenous peoples, subnational governments and northern universities and research institutions; and second, region-building by nation-states, with the Arctic Council (AC) as the best-established circumpolar forum. As an emerging trend, a new kind of relationship is developing between the Arctic and the rest of the world.[2]

The Arctic of the 2010s is a region with an increasingly dense network of transnational actors, including indigenous peoples (organisations) energetically emphasising their cultural and political identities; sub-national governments in charge of regional development seeking collaboration both within and beyond national borders; NGOs with their concerns and ambitions to shape the discourse; as well as academic communities producing

[2] L Heininen, 'Circumpolar International Relations and Geopolitics' *AHDR 2004 (Arctic Human Development Report)* (Akureyri, Stefansson Arctic Institute, 2004) 207–25.

knowledge, and thus shaping our understanding of the region. Consequently, the Arctic region has high political stability and is without military conflicts, whether current or emerging. Following on new knowledge of long-range and regional pollution in the region, the Arctic states have called for robust international treaties concerning the environment, signed agreements on pollution prevention and worked towards better industrial management to minimise environmental risks. However, so far the implementation of such mitigation efforts has been weak. Furthermore, the states have not always been willing to adopt stricter environmental regulations against the offshore petroleum industry, despite their political rhetoric to the contrary.

In the early twenty-first century, the Arctic region, particularly the Arctic Ocean, has become recognised as an environmental linchpin globally: a sink of long-range pollutants[3] and a target area of rapid climate change.[4] The local environmental impacts of industrial activities have also received political attention. These developments pose new and more dangerous environmental and societal risks to the Arctic and its people(s),[5] but also have feedback effects on the social, technical, economic and political dynamics of global energy and natural resource systems. Moreover, the Arctic plays a key role in the global ecosystem and bio-geophysical processes that are heavily impacted by climate change and other global changes, and are closely integrated with current global economics and related energy security dynamics, as they relate to world politics. The past, present and future of the region are closely linked to global megatrends, such as migration, increasing resource demand as exemplified by rapidly, sometimes aggressively, expanding exploitation of minerals and (offshore) hydrocarbon resources, and growing use of northern sea routes.[6] Over the past several years there has been an increase in proposed activities regarding energy and mineral resource development in the Arctic region. At the same time, there is increasing global attention and scrutiny over such activities and their potential impact on global climate change, habitat degradation, community health and welfare, as well as apprehensions over offshore drilling that have arisen from, for example, the Gulf of Mexico oil spill in 2010.

It is in this context that Finland, one of the Arctic states, adopted its first Arctic strategy, and China became a new observer country of the Arctic Council.

[3] eg Arctic Monitoring and Assessment Program, *Arctic Pollution: Persistent Organic Pollutants, Heavy Metals, Radioactivity, Human Health, Changing Pathways* (Oslo, Arctic Monitoring and Assessment Program, 2002).

[4] eg Arctic Council, *Arctic Climate Impact Assessment (ACIA), Scientific Report* (Cambridge, Cambridge University Press, 2005) available at www.acia.uaf.edu.

[5] G Hoogensen Gjörv, DR Bazely, M Goloviznina and AJ Tanentzap, *Environmental and Human Security in the Arctic* (Tonbridge, Routledge, 2014).

[6] eg Nordic Council of Ministries, 'Megatrends' (2011) *TemaNord* 527.

The aim of this chapter is to discuss China and Finland in the Arctic context, both as Arctic stakeholders and in terms of their national interests and policies in, and dealing with, the Arctic region. The underlying assumption is that the globalised Arctic is geopolitically, (geo)economically and environmentally interesting, as well as strategically important, for these two countries. Indeed, Finland is located in the region and is one of the Arctic states with relevant Arctic expertise, although that interest has not always been so obvious.[7] Without a direct geographical connection to the Arctic region, China, along with a few other eastern Asian states, has become interested in the Arctic and involved in Arctic affairs. China's interest is motivated by the global fact that changes in the Arctic region 'have significant effects on China's ocean, climate, eco-environmental system and socio-economic development'.[8]

This is not a comparative study per se. For a proper comparison it is necessary to have equal indicators, or factors, such as documented policies and priorities, or interviews, which you can compare with each other. Indeed, the positions of China and Finland—and their major features in the world and world politics—are asymmetrical, which will be discussed first in this chapter. Secondly, this chapter discusses China and Finland as stakeholders in Arctic co-operation and affairs, in which they do not have the same kind of position but share the same interests. China has not adopted any national strategy or policy on Arctic affairs, unlike Finland, but has an obvious Arctic agenda and is interpreted to have an emerging Arctic policy.[9] Thirdly, there will be discussion, or a slight comparative study, on the national (official and potential) interests of the two states in the major fields of Arctic politics and affairs: in the case of China mostly based on literature, and in the case of Finland based on the adopted strategies and literature. Finally, the two states will be briefly discussed in the context of the Global Arctic.

II. CHINA AND FINLAND—ASYMMETRIC PARTIES

In the twenty-first century, the brand and image of a country play an important role in its international relations and world politics. China has recently invested much time and effort into building its national image and country brand as a 'big developing country' or 'responsible developing country'

[7] L Heininen, 'Finland as an Arctic and European State' in RW Murray and AD Nuttall (eds), *International Relations and the Arctic. Understanding Policy and Governance* (New York Amherst, 2014) 321–47.

[8] Ministry of Foreign Affairs, People's Republic of China, *Statement to Ministry of Foreign Affairs, The Kingdom of Norway* (Beijing, 22 November 2006).

[9] eg M Lanteigne, '*China's Emerging Arctic Strategies: Economics and Institutions*' (2014) 201 *Institute of International Affairs, The Centre for Arctic Policy Studies, Occasional Papers*.

in international negotiations on climate,[10] as well as a growing economy and welfare state with an economically and politically stable system. This was first manifested by the 2008 Beijing Olympic Games, and again seen in how China hosted and organised the APEC Summit in November 2014 in Beijing.[11] Its image as a developing country is, however, 'a-changing', and China has emerged as a major power. This was manifested, on the one hand, by the official announcement of China's exact goals—for the first time—to stop the increase of its GHGs (by 2030) at the APEC Summit in November 2014. China and the USA are the two biggest producers of GHGs/CO_2 emissions. China's new status as a major power was bolstered when the USA also made a similar announcement at the Summit. On the other hand, this was manifested by the conciliatory rhetoric that China's President Xi Jinping has recently adopted towards the increasing tensions across the Asia-Pacific region, particularly in the South China Sea.[12] All this means that China is seeking (geo)politically a more active role in international politics and has already become the counterpart to the USA as a major power, as the Soviet Union was in the Cold War period. Based mainly on a Confucian approach China is also trying to develop itself as a soft power and part of that is a Chinese international relations model that Chinese academics are working on.[13] Consequently, China should also be a responsible international actor and a member of the international 'community' (whatever that may mean).

Correspondingly, Finland is a small state whose specific political weight is light. Finland has, however, also been an initiator, even a forerunner, in international politics for decades: Finland has achieved several success stories in its foreign policy, from the hosting of the European Security and Cooperation Summit (in 1975) to the initiative of the Arctic Environmental Protection Strategy (in 1989) and that of the EU's Northern Dimension (in 1997).[14] Finland is a modern, democratic welfare state with a strong civil society and belief in education. In the 1990s, just before and after Finland joined the European Union (EU), the government frequently stated that Finland is a European country, next to Germany (in the North)—the statement was supported by the political and business elites.[15] Within the EU,

[10] S Kopra, 'With Great Power Comes Great Responsibility? China's Responsibility in International Climate Politics' (A seminar paper at the PhD course 'Global Engagement of East Asian Countries' in Turku, 11–12 December 2014—on file with author).

[11] Among others, nearly 900 factories in the surrounding Hebein province were temporarily closed due to the air pollution they produce.

[12] T Mitchell and D Pilling, 'Xi Tones Down Rhetoric in Conciliatory Nod to Neighbours' *Financial Times* (2 December 2014) 3.

[13] eg J Kallio, 'Watching a Dragon's Egg Hatch' (2012) 74 *The Finnish Institute of International Affairs—FIIA Working Paper*; Kopra, 'With Great Power Comes Great Responsibility?' (n 10).

[14] J Mäkinen, 'Puolustajasta pelinrakentajaksi' (2014) 2 *Ulkopolitiikka* 19–23.

[15] See L Heininen, 'Finland as an Arctic and European State' (n 7).

the closest political and economic alliance, Finland worked hard to ensure that the Northern Dimension would be one of the major external policies of the Union, as well as to turn the Union into a (global) Arctic stakeholder, and was mainly successful in these efforts.[16] Ironically, although Finland vigorously promoted the establishment of the Arctic Council, this intergovernmental forum was for long underestimated by the Finnish political and economic elites, who interpreted it to be of marginal relevance for Finland. Finland is, however, influential in this forum and has a right to be involved in making and voting on decisions. And there is no risk of losing any campaign (to become a member of an important decision-making body), unlike the failure of Finland's campaign to become a member of the UN Security Council at the beginning of the 2010s.

Furthermore, when discussing some of the geographical, geopolitical, cultural and identity features of China and Finland, it is obvious that in spite of the asymmetry between the two countries they have a few things and interests in common.

Geographically China is an eastern Asian state, and Finland is located in the northernmost part of Europe. Thus, the two states are located on the two edges of Eurasia. According to classical geopolitics China can be defined as a land power, which it is but with a modern navy. On the other hand, Finland is almost an 'island'—when looking a map this becomes surprisingly obvious—though it is not a real island state.

They are both coastal states: China is bordered by the Pacific Ocean, and Finland by the Baltic Sea. China's energy security is vulnerable, since it is still deeply dependent on energy transportation. Finland's trade, particularly export, is heavily dependent on sea transportation, and on icebreakers during most of the wintertime.

China is an old civilisation, with patience and an empire, which has economically and politically become a major power, challenging the USA. It is culturally heterogeneous as it has several nations with their own identities and languages. Finland is a small state that used to be an insular nation. Despite greater mobility and immigration, Finland remains a culturally homogeneous, protestant nation, where the rare ethnic privileges are based on history.

China is a politically and militarily non-aligned country with a communist political system and an economic system based on a market economy, or state capitalism. Finland is a democracy with an economic system based on a market economy or capitalism. Militarily Finland is, so far, non-aligned, but it is politically and economically aligned with the European Union as its member state.

[16] eg Prime Minister's Office, Finland, 2010, 'Finland's Strategy for the Arctic Region' (2010) 8 *Prime Minister's Office Publication.*

China with its huge population—the biggest in the world—has become the world's 'manufacturing house'. Largely based on its human capital, it is the second biggest, and still growing economy in the 2010s. Finland, with its small and well-educated population, is (almost) a former industrial country and a post-modern service-economy society whose economy has stagnated in the 2010s. China is both the biggest producer of global carbon emissions, GCEs (29 per cent of CO_2) and the largest producer of solar and wind power. Finland is reducing its production of GCEs (0.14 per cent of CO_2) and is a relatively big producer of biofuels.

As a result we have several pairs of largely mismatching characteristics. There are more differences than similarities between China and Finland in terms of their size, scale and geopolitical situation, as well as their status, power, capabilities, society and political system. Thus, there is asymmetry between the two countries. One is the second-largest economic and political power and civilisation, located in middle of Asia. The other is a small coastal state and insular northern nation at the periphery of Europe. In the twenty-first century, this is, of course, a greatly simplified, and partly old-fashioned stereotypical picture of the two countries. It is to a great extent derived from classical geopolitics and hegemonic studies based on (new) realism, a picture too-often presented in the mainstream media.

It would be worthwhile, if not to compare China and Finland with each other, to discuss them and their policies and interests in the Arctic and Arctic affairs. The two countries seek political stability and believe in economic growth. This is not surprising, as political stability is the main paradigm of the post-Cold War world and economic growth is a tenet of both capitalism and communism. Furthermore, although China is traditionally an Asian land power (unlike for example Japan) and Finland is not an island state (unlike for example Iceland), they are both coastal states and sea powers that are heavily dependent on sea transportation and shipping, when it comes to trade (both in export and imports). Behind is the trend that 'mobility' has become strategically, as well as economically, so important, indicating a transition from classical geopolitics towards critical geopolitics. Furthermore, in the age of globalisation and in the world of interdependence, the geographical, geopolitical and strategic position of a country does not determine its national, economic, or foreign policy interests. Some of these features can be (re)defined to be similar, thereby serving as foundations for common interests in the future.

Finally, and a bit ironically, both China and Finland have become—and officially (re)defined themselves as—Arctic stakeholders. China, which was accepted as an observer country of the Arctic Council in 2013, (re)defined itself as a 'near Arctic state'. Even in the case of Finland—the country 'here under the North Star' in the words of the famous Finnish author Väinö Linna, with its obvious 'northern' identity and 'Arctic ambience'—explicit self-identification as an 'Arctic nation' is very recent, with the first statement to that effect being made in 2010.[17]

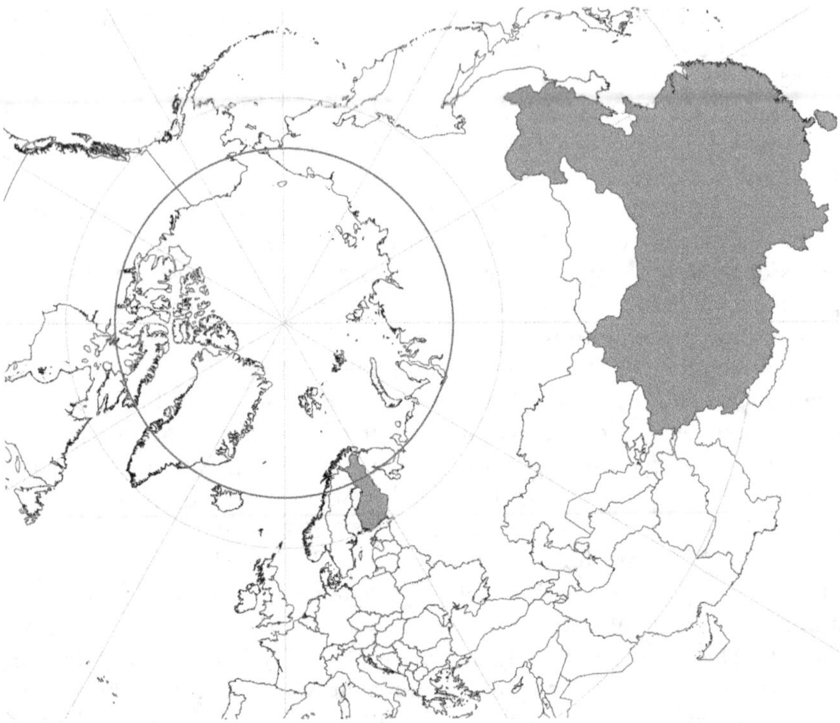

Figure 6.1: World map

III. CHINA AND FINLAND AS ARCTIC STAKEHOLDERS

All the Arctic states, including Finland, have adopted a strategy or policy on the Arctic region. They all emphasise economic development as the major national priority ahead of environmental protection, and many of them also prioritise sovereignty.[18] In spite of their internal competition (within the region), the Arctic states have seemingly sought to make their position stronger, and more influential in the region, against 'outsiders'—big Asian

[17] Heininen (n 7).

[18] For more details, see L Heininen, *Arctic Strategies and Policies—Inventory and Comparative Study*, updated April 2012 (Akureyri, The NRF and University of Lapland, 2011) available at www.nrf.is/arctic-strategies; also AJK Bailes and L Heininen, *Strategy Papers on the Arctic or High North: A Comparative Study and Analysis* (Reykjavik, Institute of International Affairs at University of Iceland, 2012).

powers and the EU—before allowing them to join the Arctic Council. At the Kiruna Ministerial Meeting in May 2013 the Arctic states accepted six new observers of the Council, five from Asia, including China.[19] Now even the first non-Arctic states, such as Germany and the UK, have accepted their national Arctic strategies/policies, and others, including China, have become involved in Arctic affairs as observers of the Council. This shifting emphasis mirrors the 'boom' in the regional and international interests of the Arctic states and observer countries of the Council, as well as their state-owned enterprises (SOEs), in trying to benefit from better access to energy resources and improve their energy security.[20]

A. Where Do China and Finland Stand Here?

China is a non-Arctic state and an Arctic Council observer country. Finland is an Arctic state and an Arctic Council member state. Both states are parties to the Svalbard Treaty, the only international treaty concerning a territory in the Arctic (see also QIN Tianbao in this volume). The two states are also parties of the United Nations Convention on the Law of the Sea (UNCLOS), the most meaningful, and frequently referred to, legally binding agreement in and concerning the Arctic and Arctic Ocean. They are also members of the International Arctic Science Council (IASC).

However, China is obviously not one of the coastal states of the Arctic Ocean, and neither is Finland. Thus, they do not belong to the 'inner' circle of the Arctic, the Arctic 'Five' (see also Duyck in this volume).

China has, like a few other eastern Asian states, become interested in the Arctic, though it has no direct geographical connection to the region. China is a newcomer in the Arctic with a clear interest in the impacts of rapid Arctic climate change (to the mainland of China) and investments in climate research in the Arctic. By active research in the Arctic and reaching observer status of the Arctic Council—among the first Asian countries—China can be seen as an Arctic 'stakeholder', not a local but a global one. Thus, obtaining observer status can be taken as an achievement for China, though status without decision-making power is not enough for China in the long run (also QIN Tianbao in this volume). However, China has to play by the rules, or try to change them. Therefore, China might soon try to strengthen its position in the Council by, for example, becoming active in the working groups of the Council, proposing a broader mandate for the observers, or seeking to have greater influence on some of the Arctic states.

[19] See Arctic Council, The Kiruna Declaration (Kiruna, Sweden, 15 May 2013).

[20] H Nicol and L Heininen, 'Human Security, the Arctic Council and Climate Change: Competition or Co-existence?' (2014) 50(1) *Polar Record* 80.

Several scientific articles and publications on China and the Arctic, as well as China's interests in, and emerging policies for, the region have been published in English.[21] There are also a few modest comparative studies, such as 'Canada and China in the Arctic' (by Huebert in 2012) and 'China-Iceland Arctic Cooperation' (by Nielsson 2014).[22]

Finland is an 'active Arctic nation', an Arctic Council member state, an EU member state and one of the Nordic countries. Here the legacy is to a great extent based on the Finnish initiative for international environmental co-operation, with a great emphasis on scientific co-operation on the environment and climate change. Finland, the initiator of the AEPS, would like to influence the development of the region. It has also shown interest towards a more global perspective on the Arctic, and accordingly supported the acceptance of new observer states from Asia, including China, and vigorously lobbied for observer status for the EU, which has not been realised yet.[23]

In brief, China is an observer country in the Arctic Council. It is a non-Arctic state that has redefined itself as a 'near Arctic state', or a 'neighbouring country' to an Arctic state, and as a 'mildly revisionist power' in the Arctic.[24] Finland is an Arctic state that has defined itself as an 'Arctic country' and an 'active Arctic nation'.

IV. NATIONAL INTERESTS/POLICIES OF CHINA AND FINLAND IN THE ARCTIC

As mentioned earlier, all Arctic states adopted a national strategy or state policy on the Arctic region by 2011, and several of them, including Finland (as well as Denmark, Norway, Russia and the USA), have also updated

[21] eg O Alexeeva and F Lasserre, 'China and the Arctic' (2012) *The Arctic Yearbook—Arctic Strategies and Policies*; AM Brady, 'China Playing a Long Game in Polar Governance' (2014) *World Politics Review*, Briefing on 14 January 2014; L Jakobson 'China Prepares for an Ice-Free Arctic' (2010) 2 *SIPRI Insights on Peace and Security*; L Jakobson and J Peng, 'China's Arctic Aspirations' (2012) 34 *SIPRI Policy Paper*; S Kopra, 'China's Arctic Interests' (2013) *The Arctic Yearbook*; Lanteigne, 'China's Emerging Arctic Strategies: Economics and Institutions' (n 9); H Liu, 'China and the Arctic: the Path of Scientific Research, Law and Policy' (presentation paper, May 2012) on file with the author; A Tonami, 'China and Japan in the Arctic: Economic Security and the Role of Foreign Policy for the Developmental State' (A presentation at the Security in the Arctic panel session at the Arctic Circle in October 2013 in Reykjavik, Iceland) on file with the author; L Xing and RG Bertelsen, 'The Drivers of Chinese Arctic Interests: Political Stability and Energy and Transportation Security' (2013) *The Arctic Yearbook 2013—The Arctic of Regions vs. The Globalized Arctic*.

[22] R Huebert, 'Canada and China in the Arctic: a Work in Progress' (2012) 16 *Canadian Polar Commission—Meridian*; ET Nielsson, 'China-Iceland Arctic Cooperation' (Presentation at 'Asian Countries and the Arctic Future' seminar on 23–26 April 2014, Shanghai)—on file with the author.

[23] For details, see Heininen (n 7).

[24] See eg M Lanteigne, 'China's Emerging Arctic Strategies' (n 9) 41.

their strategies.[25] Furthermore, the first non-Arctic states and Arctic Council observer countries, namely Germany and the UK, have adopted and published their national policies on Arctic affairs. China is not among them. These national strategies and policies are mostly intended to protect national interests—sovereignty and national security in the case of the five littoral states, as well as economic interests in the case of all Arctic states—and to act as strategic guidelines for taking more concrete action and allocating funding, although many of them lack this kind of concrete approach.

The strategies and policies include most of the major fields of activity and functional sectors in Arctic affairs, such as state sovereignty, environmental security, economic activities, transport, environmental protection, indigenous peoples and science and research. They are either listed as sectors, or are emphasised as highlights or designated as priority areas. With these national strategies the Arctic states clearly seek to increase the political stability of, and institutional co-operation within, the Arctic region due to the impacts of globalisation and growing global interest towards the Arctic and its rich natural resources. They have also mentioned the environment and climate change, and strongly support, in rhetoric, environmental protection.[26]

A. Where Do China and Finland Stand Here?

China intends to have its own Arctic policy, and is interpreted to have an emerging Arctic policy, as mentioned earlier. However, the country has taken a cautious stance towards advocating Arctic policy for fear of causing alarm—and therefore, it 'prepares for an ice-free Arctic' and has a 'polar research agenda' on both the Antarctic and the Arctic.[27] The Antarctic was its first target area, and is still given the biggest emphasis by the authorities and research institutions, such as the Polar Research Institute of China (PRIC). Due to this cautiousness on sensitive issues, China particularly avoids addressing issues of sovereignty and the utilisation of Arctic resources, and instead emphasises research on climate change and scientific co-operation. The problem here is the fact that China has not adopted any Arctic strategy, or at least has not published an official policy on Arctic affairs, and might not do so in the near future.

In spite of this, China's interests in the Arctic are real. The country is playing 'a long game' in the Arctic and the Antarctic.[28] China has the office

[25] L Heininen, *Arctic Strategies and Policies—Inventory and Comparative Study* (n 18).
[26] ibid.
[27] Jakobson 'China Prepares for an Ice-Free Arctic' (n 21).
[28] Brady, 'China Playing a Long Game in Polar Governance' (n 21).

of Chinese Arctic and Antarctic Administration under the State Oceanic Administration in charge of managing polar affairs.[29] Based on the assessment of recent policy papers, as well as the above-mentioned academic publications and presentations (particularly the paper on the 'developmental' state by Tonami)[30], which I have applied here, it can be interpreted that China prioritises certain fields of activities. China uses them among the main instruments of its practice of economic diplomacy, as well as that of its Arctic policies. Among them are: first, resource development for extra access to energy and minerals; second, Arctic shipping (including energy transport) for free trade; third, polar research (including international co-operation on science and technology) to have an outside, or global, voice in Arctic governance and future development of the region; and finally, Arctic governance (including research and geopolitics) with an emphasis on a multilateral or global approach. China also strongly supports international co-operation in this respect.

The Finnish Arctic strategy document (of 2010) states, for the first time, that Finland is one of the northernmost nations of the globe and an Arctic country.[31] The four substantial chapters of the first Finnish strategy, *Strategy for the Arctic Region*, adopted by the government in 2010, are 'Fragile Arctic Nature', 'Economic Activities and Know-How', 'Transport and Infrastructure' and 'Indigenous Peoples'. These chapters define Finland's political objectives in those important sectors. They are followed by a chapter on 'Arctic Policy Tools', which includes policy activities at global and regional levels, bilateral co-operation and funding. The strategy has a specific focus on external relations, as the chapter entitled 'The EU and the Arctic Region' clearly indicates by listing Finland's policy objectives concerning the European Union's activities in the Arctic. The government adopted an updated version of this strategy as a resolution in August 2013.[32] It is based on the 2012 vision of the 'Arctic' Finland and consists of the four pillars of policy outlined by the government in October 2012:[33] Finland as an 'Arctic country' and 'Arctic expert' that complies with the principles of sustainable development and promotes 'international co-operation in the Arctic'. In addition, the updated strategy includes objectives and detailed actions for attaining them. Finland does not have a single department in charge of Arctic or polar affairs, and the Prime Minister's Office co-ordinates the management of Arctic affairs and has published the Arctic strategies.

29 Jakobson and Peng, 'China's Arctic Aspirations' (n 21).

30 Tonami, 'China and Japan in the Arctic: Economic Security and the Role of Foreign Policy' (n 21).

31 Prime Minister's Office, *Finland's Strategy for the Arctic Region* (n 16).

32 Prime Minister's Office, *Finland's Strategy for the Arctic Region* (Prime Minister's Office Publications 16/2013).

33 ibid.

In its Arctic strategy Finland states that the Arctic region is a stable and peaceful area, and adds that significant changes are taking place in the region, including climate change and increased transportation. As global interest in the region grows, so does its global significance. Finland states that it respects the principles of sustainability, although the environment is not necessarily Finland's first priority. Finland greatly supports, on the one hand, international regional co-operation in the Arctic, particularly environmental co-operation, and in economic activities with clear business interests, and on the other hand, the Arctic Council as the main international/intergovernmental body and platform in and dealing with the Arctic region. Finland is also among the member states that would like to develop the Council and broaden its mandate.

Deeper analysis of my previous study[34] shows that Finland's Arctic strategy covers most of the features of a modern strategy document in adopting a holistic approach, and all major indicators of national strategies can be found in Finland's two strategies. It can also be seen as reflecting and responding to the recent significant and multifunctional environmental and geopolitical change(s) in the Arctic region and in its worldwide approach to the Arctic. It has neither clear priorities nor priority areas, though there is an apparent preference for economic activities including transport, infrastructure and know-how and, in contrast, general objectives for international co-operation on Arctic issues based on international treaties.

Furthermore, in order to find out if there are common interests between China and Finland and to determine the extent of their differences, there is a need to discuss the national interests of the two states in the Arctic in general and particularly with respect to substantial and relevant fields of Arctic affairs. Here I discuss the interests and policies of China and Finland in relevant fields of Arctic affairs, and based on that I try to recognise potential common interests between China and Finland. To this end, I apply the indicators that I have used in my previous research on national strategies and policies of the Arctic states (as well as that of the EU).[35]

V. SOVEREIGNTY AND SECURITY

As mentioned earlier the national Arctic strategies and policies are intended to protect national interests, and although economic interests are a major concern, state sovereignty is the highest national interest. Indeed, the five littoral states heavily emphasise maritime sovereignty, unlike the three others, which do not even mention it and instead emphasise international

[34] Heininen (n 7).
[35] Heininen (n 18).

co-operation. Post-Cold War Arctic geopolitics and security are characterised by a high level of political stability. This includes, on the one hand, region-building by the nation-states, and the fact that there are only a few disputes between the Arctic states, and on the other hand, trans-border co-operation by states and 'deterritorialisation' of borders and regionalisation by non-state actors. Since the end of the Cold War, one significant structural change in state structures has occurred thus far in the region: the self-governing status of Greenland as part of the Kingdom of Denmark. Together with globalisation this means a power transformation from nation-states to supra-national and sub-national entities, and delegation of authority.[36] Despite a few disputes over maritime borders, such as that between Canada and the USA in the Beaufort Sea, growing global interest towards the region and populist headlines about expected conflicts in the Arctic, the level of stability has been strengthening. That said, the Ukrainian crisis and war in 2014 put this stability to the test and pose a threat to it for the first time.

Stability was also strengthened by the ad hoc ministerial meeting in May 2008 in Ilulissat, Greenland between the five littoral states of the Arctic Ocean—Canada, Denmark, Norway, Russia and the USA. The three countries that were not invited to participate did not like that. This agreement[37] readily shows, even manifests, the common interests and mutual understanding of sovereignty shared by the five Arctic states.[38] It is also a practical way to control the Arctic Ocean and the resources of its shelves based on the UNCLOS without a 'need to develop a new comprehensive international legal regime to govern the Arctic Ocean'. Actually, none of the eight Arctic states, not even Finland, currently support the establishment of a new kind of regime, which makes the position of the five littoral states even stronger.

Although there is high stability in the post-Cold War Arctic, and no military conflicts, some parties disagree that this is the case. There are at least two major discourses on Arctic geopolitics: the first emphasises stability, the lack of rearmament in the Arctic and the limited modernisation of the Arctic states.[39] The second discourse, which is already partly outdated, challenges this by predicting emerging conflicts and arguing that the Arctic

[36] For more details, see M Ackren, 'Greenlandic Paradiplomatic Relations' in L Heininen (ed), *Security and Sovereignty in the North Atlantic* (Basingstoke, Palgrave Macmillan, 2014) 42–61; RG Bertelsen, 'Devolution and Withdrawal: Denmark and the North Atlantic, 1800-2100' in L Heininen (ed), *Security and Sovereignty in the North Atlantic* (Basingstoke, Palgrave Macmillan, 2014) 9–27.

[37] 'Ilulissat Declaration' (Arctic Ocean Conference, 28 May 2008) available at arctic-council.org/documents—Ilulissat Declaration.

[38] At the meeting the 5 littoral states of the Arctic Ocean stated 'their sovereignty, sovereign rights and jurisdiction in large areas of the Arctic Ocean' and that they 'have a stewardship role in protecting' the unique ecosystem of the Arctic Ocean (Ilulissat Declaration, 2008).

[39] eg L Heininen, 'Arctic Security—Global Dimensions and Challenges, and National Policy Responses' (2013) 5 *The Yearbook of Polar Law* 93–115.

states, particularly the five littoral states, are preparing for a conflict. A more interesting feature of Arctic security is, however, the coexistence of several concepts of security, from traditional to human security, largely as a result of environmental problems and risks, such as pollution and rapid climate change. These concepts are closely related to each other, making 'Arctic security' a special kind of phenomenon that simultaneously influences the region and its geopolitics.[40]

A. Where Do China and Finland Stand Here?

Among the Arctic states, and the Arctic Council observer states, there is a consensus, at least in official rhetoric, that there are no (military) conflicts in the Arctic region, not even emerging ones, but instead a high level of stability based on multilateral co-operation. China and Finland have agreed on this.

China has disputes with its neighbours, particularly in the South China Sea, but has recently adopted more conciliatory rhetoric towards the increasing tensions, as was discussed earlier. China has also been cautious not to touch the sensitive sovereignty issues in the Arctic region for fear of causing alarm among the Arctic states (this was particularly the case before the Kiruna 2013 ministerial meeting). It has neither made any claims on territories nor emphasised potential conflicts, but has instead promoted stability and international Arctic co-operation. On the other hand, China also holds that it has 'legitimate interests in the Arctic' because it is a party to the Svalbard Treaty and the UNCLOS, and has Arctic Council observer status (also QIN Tianbao in this volume).

It is not, however, easy to say if China really supports the discourse and point of view of comprehensive security—either emphasising environmental security and/or human security—in, and dealing with, the Arctic. This is particularly hard to determine in the light of the increasing military budgets and the ongoing modernisation of the Chinese army. An interesting notion, which speaks on behalf of a growing interest towards environmental or human security, is that one of the main reasons why China has become interested in the Arctic is to engage in research on climate change. The current Xi administration of China has emphasised the importance of the environment and environmental protection, and considers that environmental conflicts are potentially dangerous for the national stability of China.

Finland is a sovereign state within the Arctic region that is politically aligned, but militarily non-aligned. Finland's sovereignty in the Arctic, which includes the region of Lapland, is firm. Responsibility for the defence

[40] eg Hoogensen Gjörv et al, *Environmental and Human Security in the Arctic* (n 5).

of the region has been assigned to Finland's armed forces. Finland neither has any disputes with other Arctic states, nor has it recently made any claims in the Arctic region.[41] The current belief in Finland's sovereignty in the Arctic is actually so firm that neither sovereignty nor national security is mentioned as a national priority of its Arctic policy. Instead, Finland emphasises comprehensive security and stability based on international co-operation. Finland has clearly stated that it supports comprehensive security, recognises the security aspect of climate change and supports international co-operation (together with economic and business interests) as a means to increase security in the Arctic region.

All in all, there is a clear difference between the two states, as well as two different points of view, on how (state) sovereignty and national security are defined as priorities, although both are independent states with their own defence. However, they have no great differences on the importance of high stability in the Arctic region. That said, there are clear differences between China and Finland in how they define security and in their emphasis on the environment. The gap might, however, be narrowed if China were to place greater emphasis on the importance of environmental protection in its foreign and domestic politics, as several signs indicate. Due to long-range air pollution, the most influential deed to mitigate rapid climate change in the Arctic region that China can do is to dramatically decrease its own GHGs/ CO_2 emissions.

VI. ECONOMIC ACTIVITIES AND TRANSPORT

Economic activities and business are defined as the most important priority by the national strategies/policies of the Arctic states. The reason behind this is almost self-evident: natural resources, particularly non-renewable hydrocarbons, and their mass-scale utilisation, and consequently resource governance, play an important role in the globalised Arctic. This seems to be a worldwide trend, since resource-rich countries are aggressively promoting extractive industries (oil and gas, mining) to be able to benefit economically. Consequently, many parts of the world—eg Africa, Latin America and the Arctic—are now at the forefront of this exponential boom in global extraction. Resource geopolitics, including energy security, has a long history in shaping and impacting the entire North, both regionally and in a broader geographical context. It should go without saying that the Arctic is rich in natural resources, particularly minerals. Indeed,

[41] As part of the peace treaty negotiations after World War I, the newly independent state of Finland made a claim on Petsamo, a short coastal area of the Barents Sea which became the other 'arm' of Finland between the two World Wars.

resource geopolitics shapes and impacts the Arctic region of the twenty-first century through the growing international interest towards the region and its resources. In particular, there is a focus on resource extraction activities by the Arctic states, as well as by many non-Arctic Asian and European states, and their SOEs. This has caused a significant transformation in many sectors, making the Arctic region increasingly interesting strategically and economically, both within the region and to parties outside the region.

A reason behind the recent growth in interest towards the Arctic by the Arctic states and their SOEs, as well as by non-Arctic/Arctic Council observer states and their SOEs, is that they seek to benefit from the better access to energy resources and thus to guarantee energy security. Rapid climate change has also made Arctic shipping attractive and caused a frenzy to exploit new global sea routes on the top of the world. As a result, big industry and petroleum, shipping, icebreaking and insurance companies (both TNCs and NOCs) have become active and influential actors in the Arctic. Aggressively expanding and growing extractive industries, particularly the petroleum industry, are also bringing new kinds of environmental risks to the region, since they face significant risks and opportunities from climate change and increased deep-water drilling worldwide.

A. Where Do China and Finland Stand Here?

If the Chinese Dragon is globally hungry for resources, as it has been in Africa and the Indian Ocean area, one can predict that the country will follow the same policy in the Arctic region.[42] The Chinese government prefers to increase Chinese investments abroad, even aggressively, particularly in resource development projects, which can be interpreted to be in line with the government's efforts to consume its large surplus of capital and to increase the country's energy security. This is clearly indicated by, for example, the agreement between China National Petroleum Corporation and the Russian company Rosneft on the exploration of three offshore oil fields in the Russian Arctic, the free-trade treaty with Iceland, as well as Chinese initiatives and activities in mining, particularly concerning rare earth metals in Greenland.

China strongly supports and promotes Arctic shipping, as clearly indicated by the voyage of the first Chinese commercial ship, *MV Yong Sheng*, in September 2013 through the Northern Sea Route. The reason behind China's interest is the simple geographical fact that the use of Arctic sea

[42] eg J Kaiman, 'China Pours Cash into Melting Arctic in Bid to Win Influence. China's Growing Economy Needs Minerals and Oil—and its Gaze is Increasingly Focused Northwards' *The Guardian* (20 March 2013).

routes will dramatically shorten trade routes between China and Europe, as well as between China and North America. Being able to use (and control) trans-Arctic sea routes for transportation would strengthen China's energy security.

For the Finnish Swan—the swan is the national bird of Finland—economic activities in the Arctic are said to be driven by know-how, such as technology-based expertise on shipping, icebreaking, energy and mining.[43] Finland is the superpower of icebreaking, and one of the leading countries in planning and building icebreakers and other vessels for icy waters and cold, harsh climates. Finland also prioritises transport in the Arctic. Finland and its SOEs actively participate in Arctic shipping and would like to leverage know-how and business opportunities, as well as sell icebreaker services. If one had to interpret Finland's aims in the Arctic and identify the country's top priority, it would be economic activities, including technology-based know-how and services for offshore utilisation of hydrocarbons.

All in all, China and Finland to a great extent share the same growing interest towards economic activities in the Arctic. Finland prioritises economic activities, coupling them with know-how, while China emphasises resource development. Both states agree on the strategic and commercial importance of northern sea routes, and consequently prioritise Arctic shipping.

VII. ENVIRONMENT, CLIMATE CHANGE AND GOVERNANCE

In addition to long-range pollution, militarisation and rapid climate change, the mass-scale utilisation of resources is also heavily impacting the Arctic region. There are great interrelations between the physical impacts of climate change (due to its rapid speed), search for new sea routes (due to melting sea ice), growing mass-scale exploitation of hydrocarbons (due to the estimated abundance of hydrocarbons and better access to resources), more traffic in sea routes (due to more economic activities), emphasis on traditional resource geopolitics (due to growing expectations of national economic interests), more GHGs/CO_2 emissions (due to an increase in utilisation of hydrocarbons), and, consequently, better opportunities for the oil and gas industry in offshore drilling (due to less sea ice) etc. All of this results in the so-called 'Arctic paradox'.[44] Indeed, Arctic offshore drilling involves big environmental and societal risks due to several uncertain and dangerous factors.

[43] Prime Minister's Office, *Finland's Strategy for the Arctic Region* (n 16).

[44] eg T Palosaari, 'The Amazing Race. On Resources, Conflict, and Cooperation in the Arctic' (2011) 40(4) *Nordia Geographical Publications Yearbook* 13–29.

Accordingly, sustainable development is neither truly integrated into the national strategies and their implementations of Arctic strategies, nor will it be implemented in the northernmost parts of the Arctic states in the near future. It seems that the Arctic states have not been able, or are hesitating, to create and adopt stricter environmental regulations against the mass-scale utilisation of natural resources, particularly for the offshore petroleum industry. The reasons behind this political inability include the importance of (global) energy security, particularly in the current fiscal, economic, political and moral crisis, and related to that the growing economic interest in the hydrocarbons of the Arctic. Even an option to access these resources means power to an Arctic state and its SOEs, if the country can provide a rough estimate of the resources located in its territory, waters or the EEZ of the country, and that there is technology for drilling.

This new geopolitical situation driven by neoliberal globalisation, together with the continuity of traditional resource development, poses a danger to the unique Arctic ecosystem and also challenges the human security of Arctic peoples, nations and civil societies, and even the traditionally defined sovereignty of the Arctic states. All these dangers could materialise despite the high stability of the post-Cold War Arctic and its institutionalised international co-operation on environmental protection and sustainable development. There is even an assumption that this situation has been caused by resource geopolitics and economic development supported by the Arctic states and the Arctic Council observer states. The underlying reason is the failure to implement the two aims and pillars of the Arctic Council: environmental protection and sustainable development, as stated in the Ottawa Declaration (in 1996)[45] by the Arctic states to affirm their 'commitment to the well-being of the inhabitants ... to sustainable development in the Arctic ... to the protection of the Arctic environment'.

Under the auspices of the Council, however, two legally binding agreements concerning the Arctic region have been adopted, such as the Search and Rescue Agreement and the Arctic offshore oil and gas guidelines. In addition, there are national measures for critical infrastructure protection, as part of the changes in the security environment, and measures for industrial management, such as an ecosystem-based management plan by the Norwegian government to minimise environmental risks. However, there are no strict environmental regulations limiting or stopping offshore oil drilling in the Arctic Ocean or other icy Arctic waters.

[45] 'Ottawa Declaration, Declaration on the Establishment of the Arctic Council' (Ottawa, Canada, 19 September 1996).

A. Where Do China and Finland Stand Here?

China as a new Arctic Council observer country should play by the home rules of the Council, including the promotion of environmental protection and sustainable development in the Arctic. As mentioned earlier, on of the main reasons why China has become interested in the Arctic is climate change, particularly its (direct and potential) impacts on mainland China and agriculture there. Accordingly to this, China conducts research on climate change in the Arctic. In November 2014, China, the biggest producer of GHGs/CO_2 emissions, announced for the first time its exact goals for stopping the growth of its emissions (by 2030), but the country's current position is ambivalent: in 2012, when it was the world's largest producer of solar and wind power, it consumed almost four billion tons of coal[46] and polluted accordingly.

Due to its geographical location and sovereignty within the Arctic region, Finland has, on the one hand, definite rights to utilise Arctic resources and, on the other hand, responsibilities for environmental protection and upholding good governance in the Arctic. Finland, as the initiator of the Arctic Environmental Protection Strategy, has (re)defined itself as an 'Arctic expert' that 'complies with the principles of sustainable development', as mentioned earlier. Thus, Finland should be one of the forerunners in Arctic environmental protection. Finland's Arctic policy does not, however, clearly emphasise the environment/environmental protection as the country's first priority—or this aim is at least challenged by the country's emphasis on the importance of economic activities in the region.

If Finland, having sovereignty over the Arctic region, is an example of being directly in charge of Arctic governance, China can be taken as an example of how a non-Arctic state can, and maybe would like to, improve the Arctic governance mechanism and realise its goals.[47] It is often seen and interpreted by Chinese civil servants and scholars that China has 'legitimate interests' in the Arctic based on the principle of common concern for humanity and combined with the UNCLOS and the Svalbard Treaty,[48] both of which have been signed by China. Based on this, the Chinese approaches based on the (global) commons can be interpreted to mean a soft and indirect way to think about claiming rights for resource utilisation in the Arctic region. Finally, Finland as an Arctic Council member state and China as an

[46] eg B Walsh, 'Time for Change on the Climate' *TIME* (22 October 2014).

[47] J Yang, 'The Arctic Governance and the Interactions between Arctic and Non-Arctic Countries' (Asian Countries and the Arctic Future International Conference, Shanghai, 23–26 April 2014, Co-sponsor: Shanghai Institute for International Studies, Fridtjof Nansen Institute, supported by China-Nordic Arctic Research Centre) 1–9.

[48] See Qin in this volume, Ch 2.

Arctic Council observer country have accepted, and thus are in charge of implementing, the main aims and two pillars of the Council. Consequently, they have responsibilities for protecting the Arctic ecosystem and using the resources in a sustainable way. However, neither China nor Finland has made a clear statement on stricter environmental regulations for limiting the (offshore) utilisation of Arctic resources.

VIII. INDIGENOUS PEOPLES

In the Arctic there are not only states, state policies and SOEs, but also indigenous peoples and their organisations emphasising their own cultures, identities and livelihoods; sub-national governments in charge of regional development; non-governmental civil organisations with their concerns and interests; and universities and the scientific community conducting studies, updating data and creating new knowledge. If and when peoples and civil societies have become concerned about the environment, they have become subjects of (their) human security. The northern indigenous peoples also have their own understanding of sovereignty, particularly when it comes to how to use resources and land. From this it follows that there are claims, progress and results by these nations in the implementation of their rights to the land and waters, self-determination and self-governance, and the reconceptualisation of (state) sovereignty in terms other than inter-state relationships.

The Arctic Council is thus not only by and for the Arctic states, but also by and for northern indigenous peoples, such as the Saami in Finland. After becoming concerned about their environment and pushing governments to start co-operation on environmental protection and sustainable development, the next step is to implement a right to self-determination and self-governance to land and natural resources. It could be said that if the voices of indigenous peoples, as well as civil societies, would be heard, or if they would be louder, sustainable use of resources and regional development would include elements and aspects such as culture, democracy, equality, power and sovereignty.

A. Where Do China and Finland Stand Here?

China has shown interest towards, and in its rhetoric supports, the northern indigenous peoples (see Stepien in this volume). Finland supports the Saami and emphasises the status of the Saami as the only indigenous peoples with the European Union, and safeguards human security within the country including the Saami area. However, neither Finland nor China has ratified the ILO 169 Convention.

IX. SCIENCE, RESEARCH AND SCIENTIFIC CO-OPERATION

As discussed above, in the Arctic region there are not only states and material things, but also other influential actors and immaterial values, such as innovations in political and legal arrangements, and human capital. It is even possible to say and claim that what matters in the Arctic is not only material factors (based on classical geopolitics and realism), such as physical space, natural resources, and state power, but also immaterial factors (based on critical geopolitics and constructivism). This has a direct bearing on science and research, as well as education, done in universities and other research institutions within the region, such as the University of the Arctic. Furthermore, there is also the interplay between human security, people and resource development. All this, and the fact that there are more educated people and the 'de facto' epistemic community, makes the region more resilient and regional actors more mature. There is also more knowledge-based potential and willingness to implement sustainable development and prioritise sustainable use of resources and, if needed, to redefine sustainability.

A. Where Do China and Finland Stand Here?

China and Finland are members of the International Arctic Science Council (IASC) and have their own national Arctic research institutions. In the 2010s both China and Finland are active in Arctic research, as well as polar research in general. Both countries support, as well as invest in, scientific research in, and dealing with, the region. China and Finland started their active research on the Antarctic in the 1980s, and became consultative members of the Antarctic Treaty System.[49]

China has done systematic research in the Antarctic since then and has four research stations there. In Arctic affairs, China has been involved since the 1990s and started its systematic research in the Arctic in the International Polar Year and opened its station in Svalbard in 2004. By 2012, China had organised five scientific expeditions in the Arctic. The research is mainly focused on climate change in the Arctic region and its impacts within the region (eg to sea ice), as well as its direct and potential impacts to the mainland of China. China's polar research is run and co-ordinated by the PRIC.[50]

[49] Interestingly, both states became interested in the Antarctic at the time, when the utilisation of natural resources had not as yet been banned by the 1990 Protocol on Environmental Protection as part of the Antarctic Treaty System.

[50] Liu, 'China and the Arctic: the Path of Scientific Research, Law and Policy' (n 21).

Finland, as an 'Arctic expect', has a long tradition of Arctic research and makes a substantial contribution to Arctic science in many fields. Finland's scientific expertise is seen among others in technology (icebreaker and ship design and building, cold climate), in natural sciences (climatology, geology, forest research) and in social sciences and humanities (anthropology, philology, Saami studies, political sciences, security studies). The Finnish national research institutions mostly concentrate on the Arctic region, with a focus on Arctic studies combining research and education. Finland established a research station in Svalbard in the 1950s, but does not use it any more.

As a conclusion of this exercise, as long as China has not adopted an official national strategy or policy on the Arctic/Arctic affairs, it is not possible to have a proper comparative study of China and Finland. Thus, as described above, the situation between China and Finland remains asymmetrical, though this does not dominate relations in Arctic affairs. However, it would be good to have one more way, as well as a new context, to discuss the two states and their policies in the globalised or global Arctic.[51]

X. NEW CONTEXT: THE 'GLOBAL' ARCTIC

The starting point is the statement that globalisation is nothing new in the Arctic region due to the impacts of several flows of globalisation, such as whaling, fur trade, polar exploration, militarisation and long-range pollution.[52] That said, the current understanding of the Arctic in the context of globalisation is incomplete and contradictory among the Arctic states, as well as among the Arctic Council observer countries—where some have emphasised new opportunities, others see new threats and bigger risks.[53] Furthermore, there has as yet not been much discussion on what happens in the globalised Arctic has significant and multi-dimensional implications worldwide. This global view is also mirrored in the Arctic Council's vision paper at the ministerial meeting in May 2013 in Kiruna, Sweden.[54]

Due to this and the growing global interest towards the Arctic region and its (energy) resources, as well as the rapid climate change and the consequent Arctic paradox the geostrategic and geoeconomic importance of the Arctic region has increased, and is most probably still increasing, in world

[51] eg see the *GlobalArctic* project: www.globalarctic.org.

[52] For more details, see L Heininen and C Southcott (eds), *Globalization and the Circumpolar North* (Fairbanks, University of Alaska Press, 2010).

[53] eg see generally *The Arctic Yearbook 2013—The Arctic of Regions vs. the Globalized Arctic* (Thematic Network on Geopolitics and Security, and Northern Research Forum, 2013) available at www.arcticyearbook.com.

[54] See Arctic Council Secretariat, 'The Kiruna Vision for the Arctic' (15 May 2013) hdl.handle.net/11374/287.

politics and governance and the global economy. The scientifically more interesting context here is the globalised Arctic.

This is seen in at least two different and controversial ways: first, there have been, and partly still are, media-sexy headlines on the utilisation of Arctic resources and Arctic governance in general—to a great extent due to rapid climate change but also after the Russian expedition to the North Pole in August 2007—such as 'The Battle for the North Pole' by *Der Spiegel* (on 19 September 2008). In general, such headlines state that there is a 'scramble' in the Arctic, predicting a military or other conflict within the region. At the same time, the Arctic has been very stable and peaceful over the post-Cold War period, and there are serious political discussions and scientific studies on how to strengthen and deepen the high level of stability and co-operation as well as, even more urgently, how to maintain the achieved stability in the event of regional crises and conflicts, such as the Ukrainian crisis and war (in 2014), as one of the Valdai Discussion Club's reports, '*Russian Strategies in the Arctic: Avoiding a New Cold War*', puts it.[55] Even the biggest geopolitical change, the self-governing status of Greenland (in 2009) was very calm and peaceful, and done in full agreement by the Danish government in Copenhagen and the Greenlandic home government in Nuuk. This clearly shows, even manifests, on the one hand, that the post-Cold War Arctic is highly stable, and on the other hand, that post-World War Two Nordic devolution and self-determination are proceeding smoothly.

Secondly, while the Arctic Council has published a number of valuable assessments, including the Arctic Monitoring and Assessment Program (AMAP), Arctic Climate Impact Assessment (ACIA) and Arctic Marine Shipping Assessment (AMSA) reports, adopted the first legally binding agreements and the Kiruna vision paper for long-range planning in addition to normal declarations, and accepted new observer states, a comprehensive research programme examining the impacts of mass-scale economic activities, as well as linkages between industry, society and the environment has been lacking. Also, there is no clear focus on the linkages to global geopolitical shifts. The Arctic states are paying more attention to natural and social scientists working in extractive industrial development, transportation and other economic activities in the Arctic.[56] This new state of resource geopolitics demonstrates a shift in the Arctic Council's focus, as well as that in the policies of these states, from environmental protection towards 'economic

[55] As at January 2015 there was no direct connection between the Ukrainian crisis and the Arctic, but reflections via sanctions and counter-sanctions. In the background can be seen the cohesion of the Arctic multilateral international co-operation and high stability as its achievement, as 'human capital' for the future. See L Heininen, H Exner-Pirot and J Plouffe, 'Introduction: Human Capital in the North' (2014) *The Arctic Yearbook*.

[56] eg Arctic Council, 'Arctic Marine Shipping Assessment' (2009).

development'. Furthermore, this political inability stands in stark contrast to the two aims of the Arctic Council: environmental protection and sustainable development. Regardless of whether these new activities are interpreted as threats, challenges or opportunities, they are likely to influence sustainable use of resources and human security in the region, and create obstacles for reaching some politically agreed goals.

Even though a large share of the conventional hydrocarbons will probably not be utilised, and progress is slow due to hesitation among oil and insurance companies and other investors, the huge environmental risks involved have led to growing concerns over the maritime environment among the peoples and other non-state actors of the Arctic states, particularly the people living in the region, and many outside it. These actors have also ushered in a new kind of pressure for environmental protection. The Arctic littoral states also have growing concerns about their maritime sovereignty due to the physical impacts and related uncertainties of rapid climate change. As a consequence, and as response to this, more recently there has been a trend towards reconceptualisation of sovereignty, particularly in terms of resource sovereignty, by the northern indigenous peoples[57] with the argument that the Arctic agenda is no longer only about inter-state relationships and economic activities, but also about harnessing the knowledge-based potential to use resources sustainably. The reason behind this is that the Anthropocene, including the 'Arctic paradox', has already arrived in the Arctic.[58] This challenges the unique Arctic ecosystem, the human security of peoples, and even traditionally defined state sovereignty, as well as the implementation of sustainable development.

Does all this mean that the Arctic states, including Finland, and the Arctic Council observer states, including China, have not realised the full significance of this new situation and the serious consequences and increased risks of current resource development, and that the Arctic has become an important part of the global resources and transportation economy? Is it even possible to claim that these states, particularly China and Finland, are in charge of the 'Arctic paradox' and other impacts of the Anthropocene in the Arctic? And would they be willing to withdraw their support for the mass-scale exploitation of (offshore) Arctic resources and instead start to decrease their own GHG emissions and thus mitigate climate change?

[57] Inuit Circumpolar Council, 'Inuit Declaration, A Circumpolar Inuit Declaration on Sovereignty in the Arctic' (adopted on 28 April 2009).

[58] M Finger, 'The Arctic, Laboratory of the Anthropocene' in L Heininen (ed), *Future Security Of The Global Arctic. Defense, Sovereignty and Climate* (Basingstoke, Palgrave Macmillan, 2016).

A. Where Do China and Finland Stand Here?

The starting point here is that China and Finland, as relevant and credible Arctic stakeholders, have taken a firm stance and are in charge of the situation, as well as have consequent responsibilities with respect to the issue. This is supported, at least, by the global approach that is part—or at least an underlying element—of their Arctic agendas.

China has a global perspective on the Arctic and (therefore) strongly supports international co-operation in the region. The reason behind this is that the Arctic has been seen as a new global resource area, and even as the 'global pivot'. Accordingly, one of the Chinese approaches in Arctic affairs and governance is to rely on discourse on the (global) commons, or 'an object of global concern'.[59] The main argument is that the Arctic should be shared by humankind; the five littoral states of the Arctic Ocean should not be allowed to monopolise Arctic governance. There are also voices in China pointing out that Arctic management involves paradoxes, such as between resource exploitation and ecological protection, and between the sovereignty rights of the Arctic states and the common inheritance of humankind, and that therefore China's participation in Arctic management should include ethical values.[60] All these are signals that China would like to be included in discussions on Arctic (resource) governance, although officially China seeks to be cautious in advocating its Arctic policy for fear of causing too much alarm within the Arctic states and the entire Arctic region. On the other hand, as a large and fast-growing economy, as well as the biggest producer of global carbon emissions, China could do better, and provide greater support to Arctic environmental protection by starting mitigation. Furthermore, the point of the global Arctic is that by decreasing GHGs at home China makes the biggest contribution to environmental protection in the Arctic.

Correspondingly, the Finnish Arctic strategy has a worldwide, global perspective. Finland, as a small, stagnating economy that is already decreasing its GHGs, and a pragmatist problem-solver and expert in sustainable development, could also do much better. By 2017, when Finland will start its chairmanship of the Arctic Council, it could once again become the forerunner in the environmental protection of the Arctic.

[59] See Qin in this volume, Ch 2.

[60] J Yang and B Cheng, 'The Development Trends in Arctic Management Mechanism and China's Participation' (Paper presentation in 2013) on file with the author.

XI. CONCLUSIONS

The main conclusion of this chapter is dualistic. There is a clear 'asymmetry' between China and Finland in terms of their size, scale, geographical location and geopolitical position, as well as their status, power, capabilities, societies and political systems in general. At the same time, China and Finland have certain common interests, such as in terms of their agendas and policies in the Arctic and Arctic affairs. Furthermore, despite their asymmetry, it makes sense to have this kind of discussion on, and even a slight comparative study between, China and Finland in the globalised Arctic, mostly due to the exceptional features of the Arctic and the special status of the 'Global' Arctic.

The two states are defined as Arctic stakeholders: in the case of Finland this is very obvious, since the country is one of the eight Arctic states, though interestingly Finland's self-identification as an 'Arctic country' is rather recent. China is a new Arctic Council observer country, and as a 'neighbouring country' to an Arctic state, has very recently (re)defined itself as a 'near Arctic' state.

Based on the statements and policies concerning China's interests, the fields that China will potentially prioritise in 'the ice-free Arctic' are: (polar) research on climate change, including international co-operation on science and technology; Arctic shipping and (energy) transport, including free trade; governance, including resource development and economic activities; as well as international co-operation, both in fields such as research and technology and within the Arctic Council.

Based on Finland's national Arctic strategies, as well as their evaluations, its objectives in the Arctic are: the environment, including climate (change) and environmental protection; economic activities including know-how; transport and infrastructure, including shipping; and indigenous peoples, including the Saami. In addition, Finland has rhetorically redefined itself as an 'Arctic expect' that complies with the principles of sustainable development and promotes international co-operation in the region. When it comes to the Arctic environment Finland is clearly conscious of the importance of environmental protection in the Arctic, although it assigns a greater priority to economic activities.

As a final conclusion, the potentially common interests and fields of activities between China and Finland in the Arctic/Arctic affairs can be interpreted to be: science, research and scientific co-operation; transportation and shipping; resource governance; and international co-operation. Climate science and research on climate might be their top common interests, since both China and Finland explicitly emphasise the importance of rapid climate change (in the Arctic), both nationally and particularly scientifically.

What can be expected as further contributions in Arctic affairs from these two states—China as a new observer country in the Arctic Council, and

Finland as the Council's forthcoming chair (in 2017–19)—depends greatly on how responsible each of the states are as actors, and how they (re)define themselves in and dealing with the Arctic and globally. If they would be, or become, responsible Arctic stakeholders, as well as responsible members of the international community, they would stop supporting the mass-scale exploitation of (offshore) Arctic resources and instead start decreasing their own GHG emissions and thereby mitigate climate change, as well as to promote, not only research on climate (change), as they already do, but also multilateral governance in the global Arctic.

7

A Common Heritage—the Place of the Arctic in the Chinese and Finnish Discourses

TAPIO NYKÄNEN

I. INTRODUCTION

WHAT IS *THE Arctic region* and which states and other actors should be seen as being part of the *Arctic*? Should the definition be based on relevant scientific categories such as certain latitudes, treeline or average temperatures?[1] Who can decide which factors are significant and which not? The question is not simple and the answer not straightforward. Instead, the definition of the Arctic is deeply political and as such is affected by multiple competing and aligned uniting needs, interpretations, power relations and transitions. *What is the Arctic?* is a question that lies at the very heart of the ongoing political development and thus the future of the region.

In this chapter I analyse and compare Chinese and Finnish ways of defining the Arctic and their own places in this definition. I start from the supposition that China and Finland represent slightly different discourses that are associated with their different geographical/geopolitical locations as well as with their role in the Arctic and global politics.

First, China is a major global power and one of the world's power centres, exercising great influence in international relations. However, as many international observers have indicated, China's top priorities lie in its internal economic growth and 'national rejuvenation', not in its global political influence—even if the second goal is naturally connected to the first one.[2]

[1] See eg National Snow and Ice Data Center (NSIDC), 'What is the Arctic?', www.nsidc.org/cryosphere/arctic-meteorology/arctic.html.

[2] J Kallio, 'Chinese Dream, Other's Nightmare?' (The Finnish Institute of International Affairs, 2008) *FIIA Briefing paper* 153; Z Wang, 'Not Rising but Rejuvenating: The "Chinese Dream"' *The Diplomat* (5 February 2013) www.thediplomat.com/2013/02/chinese-dream-draft/.

Hence, the international politics of China are primarily intended aims in the first place to secure and support its domestic development. In the Arctic, China is a contracting party of the Svalbard Treaty and has an observer status in the Arctic Council. It is located in the northern hemisphere but does not extend into the Arctic Circle or even up to latitude 60°, which is defined as the southernmost borderline of the Arctic. China's northernmost point is at latitude 53°30′N, slightly north of Germany and Poland.

Finland in turn is a small country that traditionally emphasises co-operation and multilateral negotiations in international relations. It is one of the founding members of the Arctic Council and it also represents itself as a plenipotentiary Arctic state.[3] According to many definitions Finland or parts of it are located in the Arctic region. The whole country is north of latitude 60°, and the Arctic Circle—perhaps the most often used marker line of the Arctic at latitude 66°—cuts through the country at the city of Rovaniemi in Lapland. The area to the north of this line is the size of England. However, Finland does not have a shoreline in the Arctic Ocean and thus is not one of the six Arctic Ocean coastal states.

Despite their different characteristics and roles in international politics, Finland and China have adopted a similar tone in their Arctic politics in several respects. Both countries have emphasised that (1) it is important to respect international law and existing conventions like the UN Convention on the Law of the Sea (UNCLOS); (2) the environment in the Arctic region should be carefully protected; (3) the national sovereignty and legal rights of other states should be respected and (4) there is room and need for both multinational and bilateral co-operation in Arctic regions.

Both also see many economic and scientific possibilities in the Arctic region, even if they claim to be worried about climate change, the very phenomenon that makes these possibilities accessible. For Finland these premises are fundamental points of its Arctic strategy. China in turn endorsed these principles (from the legal perspective at least) when it applied and was accepted as an observer of the Arctic Council. In public talks China has demanded a bigger role in Arctic governance, but it has also clearly and repeatedly emphasised that it wants to do this in co-operation and by respecting the sovereignty of the Arctic states.[4]

It is crucial to see that national definitions of the Arctic are nationally heterogeneous, even contradictory. This applies especially to Finland, where arguments about this issue have led a minister to resign from her post, an

[3] Finland's Strategy for the Arctic Region 2013, government resolution on 23 August 2013, vnk.fi/documents/10616/334509/Arktinen+strategia+2013+en.pdf/6b6fb723-40ec-4c17-b286-5b5910fbecf4.

[4] See eg K Sun, 'China and the Arctic: China's Interests and Participation in the Region' (2013) *CIGI East Asia-Arctic Relations Papers*, www.cigionline.org/sites/default/files/no2a.pdf.

event that I will analyse in a more detailed manner later. The discussion inside China has not been monolithic or dogmatic either.[5] There has been support for a more hawkish approach as well as for more cautious ones. For example, Chinese academics in international law and political science—whose tasks include providing information and understanding for policymakers—have taken different approaches to Arctic issues.[6] This is not surprising from the perspective of internal political discussion in China in general. As Marc Lanteigne stresses:

> [T]here is much internal discussion within the Chinese Communist Party (CCP) over the degree to which the country should continue to follow the oft-cited Deng Xiaoping-era doctrine of 'tao guang yang hui' (韬光养晦), meaning to avoid openly demonstrating one's capability and instead keeping a low profile, as opposed to becoming a more traditional great power with a greater willingness to challenge global regimes and norms, as well as build opposing ones as the Soviet Union attempted to do in the twentieth century.[7]

In this chapter I seek to draw a more nuanced picture on the discourses that construct the Arctic in China and Finland. *What is the Arctic, who it is for and why should we be interested in it?* I am not interested only in representations but rather in the political struggle—both national and international—and political aims that lie beneath the parlance that gives the Arctic its shape in the political sphere. My theoretical contribution rises from *critical geopolitics* and especially so-called struggle analysis. Next, I will introduce this approach in a more detailed manner.

II. CRITICAL GEOPOLITICS

In short, critical geopolitics is a theory tradition where researchers have been interested in political discourses that shape and create geopolitical spaces. Actual geographical locations are considered to be important as well, but the primary interest is on the discursive structures that define the possibilities of understanding. The history of critical geopolitics is in critiques

[5] DC Wright, *The Dragon Eyes the Top of the World: Arctic Policy Debate and Discussion in China* (Newport, Rhode Island, China Maritime Studies Institute—Naval War College, 2011).

[6] L Jakobson and J Peng, 'China's Arctic Aspirations' (2012) 34 *SIPRI Policy Paper*.

[7] M Lanteigne, 'China's Emerging Arctic Strategies: Economics and Institutions' (Institute of International Affairs, University of Iceland, 2014) www.ams.hi.is/wp-content/uploads/2014/10/ChinasEmergingArcticStrategiesPDF.pdf. See also D Chen and J Wang, 'Lying Low No More? China's New Thinking on the Tao Guang Yang Hui Strategy' (2011) 9(2) *China: An International Journal* 195; M Mattlin and M Nojonen, 'Conditionality in Chinese Bilateral Lending' (2011) 4 *BOFIT Discussions Papers—Institute for Economies in Transition, Bank of Finland*; Kallio, 'Chinese Dream' (n 2).

of traditional geopolitics, an often openly ideological and political form of analysis. As Gearóid Ó Tuathail and John Agnew famously put it in 1992:

> Geopolitical theory from Ratzel to Mackinder, Haushofer to Bowman, Spykman to Kissinger was never an objective and disinterested activity but an organic part of the political philosophy and ambitions of these very public intellectuals. While the forms of geopolitical writing have varied among these and other authors, the practice of producing geopolitical theory has a common theme: the production of knowledge to aid the practice of statecraft and further the power of the state.[8]

Ó Tuathail and Agnew suggested that geopolitics should be 'critically re-conceptualised' as a discursive practice by which 'intellectuals of statecraft' spatialise international politics.[9] The (critical) study of geopolitics is then the study of the spatialisation of international politics by core powers and hegemonic states. This, in short, is the approach that I utilise in this chapter. I am not interested in 'hard truths, material realities and irrepressible natural facts'[10] but in the way Chinese and Finnish discourses spatialise the Arctic.

'Discourse' in this language is a structure of rules that form the possibilities for understanding and action.[11] Discourses are created in social processes and their content is associated with the will of power. This can mean simply individual, powerful actors or the collective action of the ruling elite of political, economic and ideological spheres. An actor seldom has the power to reshape discourses instantly and quickly: the transformations of the discourses take place in social processes. This, of course, to some extent depends on the political system and the social reality that it shapes. To put it bluntly, in democratic systems it takes more time to reform existing hegemonic discourses, no matter whether the origin of reformation is in the will of power or in political resistance. The democratic process itself is in a hegemonic discursive position and it is difficult to change things without using means that are considered democratic. This in turn takes time and creates several opportunities for the opposition to prevent, mitigate or undermine the reform efforts. Authoritarian and centralised systems are more effective in creating new political discourses that do not just take the form of slogans or euphemisms but may actually reshape the social reality of common people relatively quickly. In twentieth-century China, such discourses were created successfully several times. Maybe the best known is the Cultural

[8] GÓ Tuathail and J Agnew, 'Geopolitics and Discourse. Practical Geopolitical Reasoning in American Foreign Policy' (1992) 11(2) *Political Geography* 190.

[9] ibid.

[10] ibid.

[11] ibid. For classical (Foucauldian) definitions, see eg M Foucault, *Security, Territory, Population: Lectures at the Collège de France, 1977–78* (Basingstoke, Palgrave MacMillan, 2007); M Foucault, *Discipline and Punish: the Birth of the Prison* (New York, Random House, 1975).

Revolution, which of course was a euphemism for harsh political struggle but which without a doubt created new and powerful discursive practices amongst the rallying and protesting masses.[12] It could be emphasised here that also different variations of political systems themselves are discursive practices that need to be protected, supported and responded to. The more problematic the system is in the eyes of the people and/or other states, the more work is needed to keep it functional in the long run.

At the international level, discourses are created in the information game and public and hidden political debate between states and other significant actors. Powerful states with abundant economic and military resources are also powerful in diplomacy, intelligence and communications, so they play a central role in shaping the international discursive reality. Also intergovernmental organisations (like the UN), smaller states, big corporations and especially in the world of mass and social media NGOs, civil society organisations, individual activists, journalists, analysts and scholars have their part to play.

Furthermore, like Finnish scholar Sami Moisio,[13] I separate 'rhetoric' from discourse when studying political speech. While discourse is a hegemonic structure of understanding, rhetoric is intentional action that is intended to achieve certain goals that are often in opposition to the goals of the political enemy.[14] Rhetoric does not have limitless possibilities: it is directed and limited by discursive obstacles and frames. Still, skilful rhetoric can affect discourses, transform them and create them. Such a discursive change is always a significant conceptual change that is associated with transformations in power relations. For example: when China is urging for the right to participate in the governance of the Arctic, it wants to change the discursive structure in which only so-called Arctic states and indigenous organisations can be justified rightholders of the Arctic.[15] Likewise, before indigenous organisations like the Inuit Circumpolar Council (ICC) achieved the status of permanent participant in the Arctic Council, they needed to struggle for a fundamental discursive change in Arctic politics. Mary Simon and other indigenous pioneers had to convince state rulers that nation-states are not

[12] In China, political slogans and campaigns have often been used as symbols for an entirely new political direction and sometimes harsh transformations in societal practices. Well-known examples are the Great Leap Forward and Cultural Revolution and, with less dramatic consequences, slogans like 'Two Whatevers' and 'Three Represents'. See M Dillon, *China. A Modern History* (London, I.B. Tauris, 2012) 325, 355, 401.

[13] S Moisio, *Geopoliittinen kamppailu Suomen EU-jäsenyydestä* (Turku, Turun yliopisto, 2003) 69.

[14] ibid.

[15] AM Brady, 'China Playing a Long Game in Polar Governance' (2014) *World Politics Review*, www.worldpoliticsreview.com/articles/13492/china-playing-a-long-game-in-polar-governance.

the only rightful rightholders in the Arctic.[16] Successful politics require a transition in discursive structures that frame the world around us.

When I study political speech in China and Finland, I study both the rhetoric used and also the discursive structures that form the framework for rhetoric. I see politics as intentional action aiming to affect discursive structures through the use of innovative rhetoric. This means that I do not only study representations but rather the political struggle that can be found lurking under their surface.[17]

In general, the dimension of geopolitics is very relevant when studying the Arctic. The Arctic is, amongst other dimensions, by definition a particular geographical area, though its boundaries are in practice defined in political processes, 'spatialisation'. Both Finland and China are interested in the Arctic because of its location on geographical, geopolitical and geoeconomical maps, and also the definitions of the Arctic are connected to these locations.

III. CHINA

China has no explicit, overarching Arctic strategy similar to those published by members of the Arctic Council and the observer states Germany and United Kingdom. Instead China's Arctic 'strategy' can be interpreted based on many documents and statements as well as the actions the country has taken. The first ones include general strategies for foreign policy and statements by the high officials of the Communist Party. Furthermore, it is possible to sketch China's possible strategic interests and anticipate its future actions by reading Chinese academic or semi-academic journals. Like in many countries, also in China there are semi-academic journals that are close to government think-tanks and journals that are funded directly by the administration's departments.[18] In addition to engaging in academic discussion, the role of these journals is to create understanding for the policymakers.[19] It is worth emphasising that I understand these statements, including those made by scholars, as 'political' in the sense that they participate in challenging and reframing the existing discourse on the Arctic. In other words, scholars giving recommendations for foreign policy also participate in the international power struggle, and may even do so in a very open manner. Moreover, the People's Liberation Army's (PLA) affiliates,

[16] J English, *Ice and Water. Politics, Peoples and the Arctic Council.* (Toronto, Penguin, 2013).

[17] Moisio, *Geopoliittinen kamppailu* (n 13) 71.

[18] For more precise examples, see Jalo and Nykänen, Ch 4 in this volume.

[19] See DC Wright, 'China's Growing Interest in the Arctic' (2014) *Journal of Military and Strategic Studies, North America*, www.ciaonet.org/catalog/30238.

Chinese media reports and overseas diplomats have argued on what China's Arctic course of action should be.[20]

In general, the Arctic rhetoric in China has so far been rather cautious. According to Linda Jakobson the reason behind this is that China does not want to provoke the established Arctic states. '[A]ctive overtures would cause alarm in other countries due to China's size and status as a rising global power'. Furthermore, 'China's insistence on respect for sovereignty as a guiding principle of international relations deters it from questioning the territorial rights of Arctic states'. These choices can actually be seen as a backbone of China's Arctic strategy: it wants to advance carefully and convince other players that it respects their sovereignty in the Arctic.[21]

Secondly, according to many foreign observers, the Arctic is not a top priority in China's foreign politics, but this does not mean it is not important for China. As David Wright says, for China the Arctic is a 'geopolitical pivot' and economic crossroads in the world of climate change.[22] Wright also claims that China is much more concerned about economic possibilities and security issues in the Arctic than the negative impacts of climate change, even if China has taken note of these as well.

It is interesting that discussions on the Arctic inside China have had various and different phases. Such discussion was practically non-existent before 2007 but then began to gain traction and in 2009 and 2010 there were tens of articles in prominent Chinese academic journals talking about China in the Arctic. Many of these covered Arctic policy and strategy and also legal issues. Some of them were relatively hawkish and ambitious in political terms.[23] After this the discussion started to slow down significantly. David Wright assumes that the Chinese government instructed scholars to cool their rhetoric on the Arctic.[24] However that may be, the multiple tones in the articles show that there is an inner struggle and discussion on Arctic politics inside China. Official foreign policy is not decided or openly practised by scholars, but they have a significant role in shaping the political rhetoric that constructs both domestic and international discourses.

A. Definitions

So, what could be said about the definitions of the Arctic used in the somewhat active, if changing, Chinese discussion? Perhaps the most important

[20] TC Wright, 'China's New Arctic Stratagem: A Strategic Buyer's Approach to the Arctic' (2013) 15(1) *Journal of Military and Strategic Studies* 1.

[21] L Jakobson, 'China Prepares for an Ice-Free Arctic' (2010) 1 *SIPRI Insights on Peace and Security*.

[22] Wright, 'China's Growing Interest' (n 19) 53.

[23] ibid, 53.

[24] ibid, 54.

statement so far is the one made by Hu Zhengyue, China's assistant minister of foreign affairs in 2009. According to him, China intends to respect the international norms in the Arctic. The Arctic region beyond the 200-nautical mile exclusive economic zone (EEZ) of the A5 states belongs to all humankind, the minister said.[25] In addition, he asserted that:

> The Arctic occupies an unique position for all of us as humankind who live on the blue planet. The changing natural environment in the Arctic is enormously influential toward the existence and environment of all humankind. The Arctic is a sensitive region in global climate change. The entire planet in turn reacts to natural changes in the Arctic, especially the climate of the northern hemisphere.[26]

The minister makes it clear that the Arctic is deeply meaningful to all of humankind, especially those living in the northern hemisphere. In this rhetoric the Arctic is not in the first place a *remote* area with no interesting possibilities for humans. Instead it seems to be close to all of humankind, although it is not clear if it is in the *centre*: rather it has a unique and somewhat unidentified position. At the same time the Arctic is a very vulnerable region, representing the remaining colours of life on the blue planet. It is a bit like a small green roof garden in a gigantic Chinese city made from concrete, glass and steel. Pollution generated by modernisation and development are besieging the garden, which we need to protect with care.

The minister's short statement illuminates several issues. First, China, as represented by Hu Zhengyue, stresses that the Arctic outside the EEZs is very meaningful to all of humankind. This implies that the whole of humankind, including China and the Chinese, is legitimately and naturally interested in what happens to and in the Arctic.

Secondly, environmental protection and climate change are indeed important to China. There are hawks who emphasise economic growth and international influence over economic issues,[27] but this is not the whole picture. For China, climate change and environmental problems like pollution of the air and water are a clear and present reality that is taken extremely seriously. They are also becoming a matter of national security and stability, which are very important to the Chinese Communist Party. In 2014 China started 'a war on pollution',[28] which included plans for massive cuts in coal consumption[29] around the country. Also environmental legislation was reformed

[25] ibid, 53.

[26] As cited in Wright, 'The Dragon Eyes the Top of the World' (n 5).

[27] See also Wright (n 19).

[28] D Stanway, 'Beijing Cuts Coal Use by 7 Percent in First Half of Year' *Reuters/China Daily* (13 August 2013).

[29] For more information about China's energy consumption, see US Energy Information Administration, 'China', www.eia.gov/countries/cab.cfm?fips=ch.

in a far stricter direction.[30] Of course the speech about 'the blue planet' is indeed political rhetoric intended to change the existing power relations and discourses, but it is also associated with actual political problems in China.

The environmental aspect in the development of the Arctic is naturally only one—and possibly not even the most important—issue addressed in Chinese political talk. If one wants to examine where the actual emphasis of Beijing may really lie, the articles published in the Chinese semi-official *World Affairs* can be illuminating.[31] Most of them do not discuss environmental issues but instead have a very traditional focus on the military aspects of northern development. In this perspective big state actors take their place in the focus of interest. The Arctic is seen as the arena of military competition between the USA, Russia and Canada, and China seems to be worried about its possible militarisation. In addition, the Arctic is represented as a field for harsh economic competition between the A5 countries, that is, Norway, Denmark, USA, Russia and Canada.[32] Iceland, Sweden and Finland get only little attention in the articles: the world is seen through competition between those states that are in the most powerful position in military, economic and legal respects.[33] Even if the political reality is seen in very (neo)realistic terms in *World Affairs*, the authors seem to be emphasising good possibilities for peaceful co-operation in the Arctic.

For my theme it is important to note that one article in *World Affairs* defines the Arctic as a 'common property' of humankind[34] and another article calls it the 'world refrigerator', owned by all human beings.[35] Furthermore, the development of this common property also has common, that is, global effects. The most important of them is climate change. If development in polar areas accelerates climate change, all the states that are affected should be able to participate in politics that regulate this development. This argument is familiar from previous studies that discuss Chinese policy in Arctic regions.[36]

Now, it is important to see that 'climate change' here is a deeply political concept that is used to emphasise the Arctic region as a geopolitical area where many states have legitimate interests. It also makes a good argument:

[30] SL Wee, 'China to Impose Tougher Penalties on Polluters under New Law' *Reuters* (24 April 2014). See also E Ryan, 'The Elaborate Paper Tiger: Environmental Enforcement and the Rule of Law in China' (2014) *Duke Environmental Law and Policy Forum*, papers.ssrn.com/sol3/papers.cfm?abstract_id=2420677.

[31] See also Jalo and Nykänen, Ch 4 in this volume.

[32] See eg X Zhāng Xīnbō and Z Li, 'The Arctic Countries Accelerate the "'Tug of War"' (2013) 17 *World Affairs*; C Shǐ, 'The Five Arctic Countries Compete for the North Pole. Who Will Win?' (2010) 22 *World Affairs*.

[33] See also Jalo and Nykänen, Ch 4 in this volume.

[34] F Yu, 'Increasingly Fierce Disputes in Arctic Council' (2012) 6 *World Affairs*.

[35] Shǐ, 'The Five Arctic Countries' (n 32).

[36] See Jakobson and Peng,' China's Arctic Aspirations' (n 6).

it is difficult to deny that a big state like China could not have legitimate rights in crucial decisions that affect the lives of its people.

This is the point where scientific research gets political. If China can show that it has done prominent polar research, it has new political resources to participate in the discussion concerning climate change and the Arctic region's role in it. Through this, its position in Arctic governance in general will get stronger. So, emphasising the relation of climate change and the Arctic and on the other hand China's knowledge about the issue may create a door that China can use to enter into Arctic governance in a broader way. All in all, the rhetoric of common property and climate change in the Arctic are intended to reconstruct the discourse on Arctic governance. This is not to say that climate change and environmental questions will not be important for China as such: climate change will have a very deep impact on China and the research in Arctic regions is certainly based on actual worries about the future. But in politics, substantial questions are often associated with power struggles and transitions and long-term plans of governance: often one does not exist without the other.

It is a well-known and for this chapter very important fact that in another context China has defined itself as a 'near-Arctic' state.[37] China is far below the Arctic Circle line and even latitude 60°, so it would indeed be somewhat difficult to claim that it is an actual Arctic state. But it does also require an imaginative leap to claim that it is near the Arctic region. After all, between China and the established Arctic region there are the vast forests and ambitious political plans of Russia.

It is important to see that geopolitical borders are not drawn in the plateaus and mountains between Beijing and Moscow but in the minds of those who can influence political discourse and who on the other hand have the power to decide which countries are accepted to the Arctic Council. In this context the definition of 'near-Arctic' state takes on a different tone and, if we take a closer look, also political plausibility. After all, China is undeniably in the northern hemisphere and even relatively far north compared to for example India or even Korea. It is also clearly one of the stakeholders in the development of the Arctic regions: the future development of the transport business in the Northern Sea Route depends not only on climate change but also on trade between China, other Asian states and Europe. Last but not least China is a fast-growing economic powerhouse, which means that its face on the geopolitical and geoeconomic maps is evolving constantly: its location is not stable, but rather pulsing, radiating and fluid. In world politics, China is much more than a corner, if a big one, in Asia. However, even

[37] eg SIPRI, 'China Defines itself as a "Near-Arctic State", says SIPRI' (10 May 2012) www.sipri.org/media/pressreleases/2012/arcticchinapr.

with these premises in mind, the status of the near-Arctic status of China is not all that obvious. This can be seen when Chinese scholar Fu Yu asserts in *World Affairs* that China is not 'near' the Arctic area, but nevertheless has legitimate rights in the area through international conventions such as the Svalbard Treaty and UNCLOS.[38]

All in all, on the surface of China's rhetoric the Arctic is seen more or less in a traditional light. It is a certain geographical zone with certain natural features. Basically four main arguments are asserted: (1) the Arctic is a common property of humankind that needs to be accessible by all (excluding EEZs); (2) the Arctic should not be militarised further; (3) climate change is affecting the whole world and the Arctic may be in a crucial role in climate change, so the whole world has a right to participate in Arctic governance and (4) China already has many rights in the Arctic through international conventions such as the Svalbard Treaty and UNCLOS. China's discourse here is twofold: one needs to respect international conventions, peaceful development and the sovereignty of other states, but one must also share the global commons with everyone.

When China's rhetoric is inserted into the context of critical geopolitics, the image is more interesting and versatile. The Arctic is not explicitly located in the 'West' or 'East', sometimes not even in the 'North'—rather it is a 'global pivot', to use David Wright's very illuminating term. The whole world and especially the northern hemisphere are turning around the Arctic. Because China is part of the (northern) world and also an important political and economic power, it is both one of the actors and one of those that are heavily affected by this movement. China wants to form a team, grab the pivot and turn it in the right direction of development. On this map, the borders of the states and streams of co-operation are more fluid and mobile and the question of who is near and who is far is more negotiable.

IV. FINLAND

If China's stances and definitions are relatively difficult to define clearly, the opposite is true of Finland. As a founding participant of the Arctic environmental protection strategy—the predecessor of the Arctic Council—and proactive member of the Arctic Council,[39] Finland has an explicit and very detailed Arctic Strategy that was updated in 2013.[40] In this chapter, I will not analyse the strategy in a detailed manner. Instead, I will try to show how the Arctic and Finland's place in it are defined in the text.

[38] Yu, 'Increasingly Fierce Disputes' (n 34).

[39] For more information about Finland's active role in the process that led to the founding of the Arctic Council, see English, *Ice and Water* (n 16).

[40] Finland's Strategy for the Arctic Region (n 3).

In the beginning, the strategy states Finland's 'Arctic vision':

> Finland is an active Arctic actor with the ability to reconcile the limitations imposed and business opportunities provided by the Arctic environment in a sustainable manner while drawing upon international cooperation.[41]

Furthermore, the strategy represents the 'four pillars of policy':

> [...] an Arctic country, Arctic expertise, sustainable development and environmental considerations and international cooperation.[42]

This is indeed an illuminating summary of Finland's foreign policy not only in the Arctic but also more generally. Finland typically represents itself as a negotiator that wants to co-operate in politics and business at both the multi- and bilateral levels. At the same time it often emphasises environmental issues. Geopolitically Finland is here an 'Arctic actor/country' with 'Arctic expertise'. It is not in the West or East but rather in the North, where it has special 'expertise'. Later the strategy defines this expertise more clearly: Finland has knowledge in northern environmental protection/sustainable development and on the other hand various business sectors such as maritime industry and shipping, oil recovery, energy efficiency, mining, tourism, renewable resources (especially wood), information networks and digital communications. Furthermore, Finland has special knowledge of the fields of indigenous politics/research and, for example, cold climate expertise, which could be sold to the 'partners' of the Finnish Defence Forces.

In this strategy, the Arctic is a vulnerable and at the same time 'preserved' area, which should be protected even as it is being utilised. One cannot define the Arctic with a single definition but rather through different factors and criteria—all of which Finland itself fulfils:

> Finland is an Arctic country
>
> The Arctic identity of Finland has been shaped by climate, nature, geography, history and experience. Finland as a whole is a truly Arctic country: after all, one third of all the people living north of the 60th parallel are Finns. The Saami's status as the only indigenous people within the European Union is duly recognised and their participation in issues affecting their status as indigenous people is ensured. The northern parts of Finland must remain a stable and secure operating environment.[43]

In addition, the Arctic is also 'highly exceptional' in terms of its nature.

> It is extremely sensitive, regenerates slowly and its ecosystems and species have adapted to extreme weather conditions and short growing periods. This means that human action—when detrimental in its impact either globally or locally—may result in permanent changes in the Arctic region.[44]

[41] ibid, 7.
[42] ibid, 7.
[43] ibid, 17.
[44] ibid, 38.

Here Finland also calls upon the 'international community'. Policymaking in the Arctic may rely upon Arctic states, but the conditions in the Arctic are important to all of us.

> Globally speaking, the conservation of the Arctic environment is of intrinsic value. For this reason, Finland's Arctic policy focuses on understanding the effects of climate change and transboundary pollutants; the sustainable use of Arctic natural resources; the identification of the constraints imposed by the environment; and environmental protection in all areas of activity. It lies in the best interest of Finland and the entire international community to conserve the Arctic land and sea areas, and to promote ecologically sustainable economic and social development, a principle that Finland upholds.

Here, even the concept of the 'common property' or 'common interest' could be used. Finland points out that the preservation of the Arctic should be in the interests of all the states, not only Arctic ones. The message is clearly aimed at all parties that are interested in Arctic resources and also to those whose actions in other regions may have an effect on the Arctic.

Even if Finland is represented as an explicitly Arctic actor, the strategy also contains hints of the country's western and perhaps Scandinavian geopolitical association. First, Finland wants to strengthen the position of the Arctic Council, which is of course a multilateral organisation but actually has seven 'western; member states (Finland, Sweden, Norway, Iceland, Denmark, Canada, United States) and only one 'eastern' state, Russia. On the geographical map the situation looks rather balanced, since Russia alone has approximately as much Arctic Ocean shoreline as all other Arctic states together. However, in political decision-making 'western' countries seem to have a somewhat strong position here, if you take a look at the numbers of member states. On the other hand, Finland emphasises the meaning of the regions and regional organisations such as the Barents Euro-Arctic Council, which creates nuances in the big picture.[45]

A very important statement from the perspective of the geopolitical landscape of Finland is the emphasis that is given to the European Union at the end of the summary part of the strategy:

> In 2010, Finland launched an Arctic partnership with Russia, which represents a strong economic and practical approach responsive to the needs of enterprises operating on a commercial basis. Finland is also considering other bilateral Arctic partnerships as well as multilateral partnerships with Norway and Sweden.
>
> The European Union plays a key role in Finland's Arctic policy. Finland cooperates with Sweden and Denmark to clarify and reinforce the European Union's Arctic policy. The European Union's observer status in the Arctic Council serves this purpose.[46]

[45] ibid, 19.
[46] ibid, 15.

This resonates with the previous and other Finnish statements. Russia is an important (commercial) partner, but politically Finland is strongly engaged to the European Union.[47] Also, the recent political tension between Russia and the West due to the crisis in Ukraine and the Russian invasion in Crimea clearly illuminated the Finnish stance. Finland supported strongly the EU's mutual policy and financial sanctions on Russia even if they were harmful to Finland. However, at the same time Finnish political leaders wanted to maintain bilateral relations with Moscow[48] and were somewhat cautious concerning suggestions to join NATO.[49]

A. Dualisms

If there are certain tensions in the Finnish role between bi- and multilateral co-operation, an even more obvious dualism can be found in the relationship between environmental protection and exploitation of the natural resources. First it seems that Finland's Strategy for the Arctic Region 2013 gives a clear message: Finland sees Arctic nature as unique, vulnerable and indispensable. At the same time Finland wants to participate in the utilisation of the vast natural resources of the Arctic. The magic word here is, of course, 'sustainability'. Exploitation should not exceed natural limits and should not threaten the Arctic environment.

However, in practice it is difficult to define the acceptable level of exploitation. The Arctic environment is not only vulnerable but also challenging to operate in, which creates risks that are not easy to control. The climate is harsh and cold, and icy conditions create significant problems for shipping and oil drilling. In addition, the 'Arctic paradox'[50] is always present: the more climate change advances, the more we can utilise Arctic possibilities, such as mineral resources and fish. This, in turn, will enhance climate change. Because climate change in general will have more negative than positive effects, this is not a good thing.

Based on Finland's Arctic Strategy, it is rather difficult to draw obvious or only a single kind of conclusion on how we should operate in the Arctic. Instead, it is possible to emphasise either environmental protection or economic exploitation, and in Finland there are prominent supporters for both policies. This became a hot topic in autumn 2013, when the minister

[47] See also Moisio (n 13).

[48] See eg K Mackrael, 'Finland Urges Mending of Relations between Russia and the West' *The Globe and Mail* (12 October 2014).

[49] See eg Yle, 'Tuomioja: Natosta seuraisi ongelmia' (12 April 2014) www.yle.fi/uutiset/tuomioja_natosta_seuraisi_ongelmia/7188027.

[50] See eg T Palosaari, 'The Amazing Race. On Resources, Conflict, and Cooperation in the Arctic' (2011) *Nordia Geographical Publications Yearbook* 13.

responsible for ownership steering issues, Heidi Hautala (Green Party), had to resign her post after public debate on Arctic operations. Hautala had opposed the participation of Finnish icebreakers in Arctic offshore oil drilling operations. According to her, the risks of the operations are too great. A possible disaster in oil drilling would be very harmful to nature, and it could also become very expensive to Finnish taxpayers if the companies that had participated in the drilling operations would have to pay for the clean-up. Hautala also claimed that Finland in general should not support processes that clearly accelerate climate change.[51]

The reasons behind Hautala's resignation were complicated. She had already lost some of her political capital in previous outcries related to her political actions and personal history, and the debate on Arctic oil drilling also had various dimensions. According to some accusations, the problem was not her opinion on Arctic operations but rather the way in which she 'directed' the state-owned company Arctia Shipping in a case where the company wanted to press charges against Greenpeace. However, the debate on the issue itself, oil drilling in the Arctic, doubtlessly played a role in the process as well. Like in China, economic growth has been an unquestioned goal for the Finnish state's policy and it is likely that this will remain so. At the same time there are also those that question the costs of economic growth and thus also Arctic exploitation. Also in the Hautala case, she was not totally alone with her opinions: in addition to her colleagues from the Green Party, the Minister of Transport Merja Kyllönen from the Left Alliance party also questioned the relevance of Arctic oil drilling. Kyllönen especially doubted the economic possibilities of the Arctic: according to her, the offshore operations have not been that beneficial for Arctic shipping.[52]

B. Geoeconomic Hub

For my theme, one interesting recent discourse has concerned logistical development in the northern hemisphere. In this discourse the northern hemisphere is represented as a 'new super-continent' with easier, faster and cheaper transportation connections between Europe and Asia. In this scenario, Finland has the role of a *hub,* a geoeconomical link used by global streams of people, data, transport and money on their way between the geographical East and West, especially the European Union.[53] Even if hubs also

[51] See eg A Teivainen, 'Hautala's Resignation Sparks Debate on Arctic Drilling' *Helsinki Times* (17 October 2013).

[52] ibid.

[53] M Aaltola, 'Analyysi Ukrainan opetuksista Suomelle: Mennyt ei enää palaa' (2014) www.politiikasta.fi; M Aaltola and M Loescher, 'Arktinen myrsky. Globaalin logistiikan muutokset ja Suomen nousu maailmankartalle' (2013) www.aalto.fi.

attract unwanted phenomena such as international crime and uncontrolled immigration, they are seen as centres of global wealth and concentrations of regional power, which interests Finland. In the geoeconomic map of the northern hubs, Finland is in an important location for new transport systems, that is, the Northern Sea Route, TransAsian railroad and possible high-speed data connections between continents.[54]

A visualised example of this hub thinking can be found from the website of the Arctic Corridor project (www.arcticcorridor.fi). Arctic Corridor is a business project that seeks to tempt companies and states to invest in Arctic business and perhaps to convince financiers (like the state of Finland) that the railway to the Arctic Ocean from Finland is worth building. According to the site the Arctic Corridor is 'a new cross-border economic area as well as a transport and development corridor', which 'links the Baltic region with the deep-water ports around the Arctic Ocean, oil and gas fields and the Northern Sea Route to the west'. Financiers of the project were three municipalities in Northern Lapland, the City of Rovaniemi and the Regional Council of Lapland. The project also received funding from the European Union.

The website of the project is full of geoeconomic vocabulary and terms. It openly locates the Finnish Lapland in a new, central position on the world map:

> Arctic Corridor is centrally located among Arctic Europe's natural resources, on the borders with Russia and Norway. It has excellent transport links, high-quality western infrastructure and services, and politically stable and competitive business environment. Abundant metal and mineral resources, Lapland's favourable public profile along with other international travel destinations and skilled workforce creates large range of possibilities for growth.[55]

Perhaps the most interesting material on the Arctic Corridor's website is a video that markets the Corridor and as part of it a railway from Finland to the Arctic Ocean. The railway does not exist yet, but the policymakers in Lappish municipalities and cities and also a number of politicians in state politics want to see it built as quickly as possible. In the marketing video, the most visible objects on the dark world map are moving, colourful lines that represent transport routes and goods, and the people and information using them. These lines travel from Asia, North America and Northern Europe to the City of Rovaniemi in Finland. Their routes go through Arctic regions where huge natural resources such as gas and oil are just waiting for somebody to pick them up. Fires in the oil rigs burn, colossal buildings of steel rise, big machines lift items and healthy and modern looking workers control everything. A dramatic soundtrack gives the action a dynamic rhythm.

[54] ibid, 4–5.
[55] See the website of the Arctic Corridor: www.arcticcorridor.fi.

In the world of the Arctic Corridor there are no real obstacles, only opportunities linked to economic growth. Environmental problems are absent. The world map itself is characterised by *movement* and *streams*: these, not stable borders or geographical facts, are the reality in the world of the future. Of course the video is marketing material—made with a bit of melodramatic bombast—that aims to tempt investors to Finnish Lapland and the Barents region. In spite of this, it reflects precisely the thinking where Finland would be a state-sized corridor and hub that could serve as a global airport, harbour and railway station.

It is probably worth noting here that even if the economy plays a growing role in international relations, according to many observers the geopolitical 'realities' and borders between nation-states are yet not insignificant. The Arctic is, of course, also very important from the point of view of traditional geopolitics for Finland as well. During the Cold War the Arctic was the playing field of Russian and American nuclear submarines. Russia still has a powerful naval fleet in the Arctic Ocean, very close to the Finnish border, and recent geopolitical tensions—Russian intervention in Ukraine—imply that Russia has not rejected the traditional geopolitical game close to its borders. For Finland it is very important to foster stability in its neighbourhood through international law and existing conventions: the country has no resources (or the will) to participate in the power game with military means.[56] This is one of the reasons why the country has strong interests in investing in international, peaceful co-operation, also in the Arctic.

A significant detail is that the discussion on whether Finland should join NATO will probably continue and, due to the situation in Ukraine, even accelerate in the future. Joining the western military alliance could change the geopolitical map around Finland, and it is impossible to fully foresee how Russia would react and how co-operation in the Arctic region could be affected. In practice, Finland is already part of the western geoeconomical systems, but in the eyes of Russia it may still be an important geopolitical piece in its game against the West.[57] According to many commentators the geoeconomy cannot, after all, give us a holistic explanation of the world of international relations. Instead it is often a political concept that is used to (over)emphasise the meaning of the economic interdependence.[58] If we take this seriously, we should also not overemphasise the geoeconomic explanations of the world but rather read them as political constructions that are

[56] Finland's Strategy for the Arctic Region (n 3) 40–47.

[57] Aaltola, 'Analyysi Ukrainan opetuksista Suomelle' (n 53).

[58] S Sassen, *The Global City* (Princeton, Princeton University Press, 2001); S Sassen, *Territory, Authority, Rights: From Medieval to Global Assemblages* (Princeton, Princeton University Press, 2008); D Cowen and N Smith, 'After Geopolitics? From the Geopolitical Social to Geoeconomics' (2009) 41(1) *Antipode* 22.

intended to change the world. This applies at least to openly political texts and marketing materials such as the Arctic Corridor project.

V. CONCLUSION

The rhetorical discourses on the Arctic in China and Finland share many similarities. In both countries there are two hegemonic discourses: (1) the Arctic has huge economic possibilities with transportation and natural resources; and (2) the Arctic is a vulnerable place of indispensable environmental importance. Both discourses locate the Arctic much closer to the centre of the map than it used to be. It is no longer a hostile and remote region with polar bears, dangerous icebergs and odd Inuit folk. Instead it is the blue heart of the northern hemisphere that promises a lot to the new world order in terms of economic development and aesthetic experience. The relationship between the environment and natural exploitation/climate change remains unclear in these discourses.

There are also some differences. China emphasises the 'common' nature of the Arctic at least outside the EEZs, which means that resources in these areas are free for everybody to utilise. This message is dressed up in the clothes of environmental worries about 'common' nature. These worries about the environment are likely to be real, but also serve as a tool to achieve economic and, very importantly, political goals. After all, the Arctic is also a possible scene for new militarisation and tensions between East and West, which is not in China's interests.

China also clearly represents itself as a great power, although a cautious one: it is a significant global actor that has many legitimate interests around the world. The Arctic is just next to its backyard, so it is very interested in what is happening there.

Finland also recognises the 'common' nature of the Arctic. However, it strongly emphasises the role of the Arctic countries (in practical terms, the Arctic Council; in 2013 Finland suggested that the Arctic Council could be developed into an intergovernmental organisation) and their expertise in Arctic operations and policy. Finland also emphasises the roles of the European Union and Scandinavian co-operation.[59] Another and more unorthodox way of seeing the Finnish geopolitical and geoeconomic location comprises visions of the world of streams and mobility, where Finland could serve as a hub. It is not yet clear if this dream will actualise in the future.

[59] See also Foreign Ministry of Finland, 'Finland and Norway Intensify their Arctic Cooperation' (12 May 2014) www.formin.fi/public/default.aspx?contentid=305992&contentlan=1&culture=fi-FI.

Interestingly the rhetoric and thus discourses on the Arctic are not heterogeneous in either of the countries. Instead, there are different tones. In China, the greatest differences seem to be associated with China's political *style* and the means whereby China could achieve its goals in Arctic politics. There is support for both more hawkish and more cautious approaches. In Finland, the differences have perhaps to a greater extent concerned substantial issues. The most controversial one is the crucial question: how should we exploit the Arctic resources and/or should we leave them alone? Both countries claim to be worried about climate change and the environment, but nevertheless seem to agree on the use of Arctic resources. This means that they are also positioning companies from their own country into the developing Arctic race.

Part III

Comparison between the EU and China

8

China as an Observer in the Arctic Council

TIMO KOIVUROVA, WALIUL HASANAT, PIOTR GRACZYK AND TUULI KUUSAMA

I. INTRODUCTION

INTERGOVERNMENTAL CO-OPERATION IN the Arctic has been developing and expanding into a wide range of circumpolar issues for more than 20 years.[1] Today, due to climate change consequences, including new opportunities to exploit natural resources and increase shipping activities, and geopolitical/globalisation processes,[2] its premier institution—the Arctic Council, established in 1996—is at a turning point and undergoing important changes.[3]

Given these changes, and following Arctic states' discussions on the place of the Arctic Council in future Arctic governance, states and political entities from outside the region are expressing a growing interest in participating in decision-making processes and in the Arctic Council as the premier intergovernmental institution. The only way currently for the non-Arctic states and the European Union to get involved is to obtain observer status at the Council. This makes the Arctic Council the focal point of debate on who should govern an area undergoing profound transformation and in what manner. Therefore, admission of new observers on a more permanent basis[4]

[1] T Koivurova and DL VanderZwaag, 'The Arctic Council at 10 Years: Retrospect and Prospects' (2007) 40(1) *University of British Columbia Law Review* 121–94.

[2] L Heininen and C Southcott (eds), *Globalization and the Circumpolar North* (Fairbanks, Alaska, University of Alaska Press, 2010).

[3] W Hasanat, 'Reforming the Arctic Council against Increasing Climate Change Challenges in the North' 22(1) *Michigan State International Law Review* (2013) 195–240; T Koivurova, 'Limits and Possibilities of the Arctic Council in a Rapidly Changing Scene of Arctic Governance' (2009) 46(2) *Polar Record* 146–57.

[4] It is important to point out that there are no permanent observers in the Arctic Council, as many scholars erroneously call them, as their status can also be terminated, with the revision process.

has become one of the more pertinent issues in the debate on the shape and role the Arctic Council should play in regional governance structure.

Given that China's Arctic interests have increased greatly (see the Introduction to this volume), it is no surprise that China applied for observer status in the Arctic Council already in 2007. It is also no secret that within China there have been discussions over why China will have to satisfy itself with the role of an observer.[5] After all, as the sea ice retreats, the Arctic Ocean will gradually open itself to navigation, fishing and other commercial activities—activities in which China enjoys guaranteed rights under the law of the sea and the United Nations Convention on the Law of the Sea (UNCLOS).[6] If the Arctic states have all these rights in the Arctic, why then cannot China and other states that are not members proper of the Arctic Council gain a better status than an observer? Yet, before the Arctic Council or Arctic governance in general transforms into another organisation, it will be the Arctic Council with its rules and procedures that all states and other entities need to abide by. Since only the eight Arctic states are members of the Arctic Council, and other states can only apply for observer status, this is the status that China had been trying to obtain. Finally, in 2013 at the Kiruna ministerial meeting, China—among other applicant states[7]—was accorded this status.

This chapter examines what China has been able to do with its observer status, both with its ad hoc observer status and its current full observer status. China was given ad hoc observer status in 2007, and, as stated above, the country is now a full observer of the Council. The main research question is: how has China performed as an observer in the Arctic Council? This is studied in two dimensions. First of all, it is important to examine whether China is living up to the criteria required of those seeking to become observers to the Council. Given that the Council established criteria for observers in 2011 at the Nuuk ministerial meeting, it is useful to ask whether it has been able to live up to those general requirements, which it is expected to continue to satisfy. The second level of study is to examine what China has actually been doing as an observer in the Arctic Council. Has it participated in the meetings of the Council and its working groups, or not? If it has, in what way has it done so?

Interviews have been conducted among Arctic Council officials, Chinese officials and Chinese academic scholars to provide an answer to what China has been doing as an ad hoc observer and full observer, and whether there are plans in China for how to make use of its observer status. Most of these

[5] See QIN Tianbao's chapter in this volume.

[6] The US is not a party to the Convention on the Law of the Sea. eg the Ilulissat Declaration of 2008 refers to the 'law of the sea' rather than to the UNCLOS. Both bodies of law co-exist since also the US accepts that most of the UNCLOS codifies customary international law.

[7] The other states accorded the status were: India, Italy, Japan, Republic of Korea and Singapore.

interviews were confidential, given that our interviewees could only give this information to us under these terms. We will open up the interview method, and some other information on the interviews to the extent that it is possible without disclosing the identity of the interviewees. Some interviewees have given permission to use their name and the date of interview.[8]

In order to research these issues, we deem it necessary to understand, first, how observership has evolved in Arctic-wide co-operation (both Arctic Environmental Protection Strategy (AEPS) and the Arctic Council stages) throughout the over 20-year existence of this co-operation. This co-operation commenced between the eight Arctic states (the Russian Federation, the United States, Canada, Denmark, Iceland, Finland, Norway and Sweden) in 1991. It is useful to show what have been the major changes in this co-operation,[9] so that it is possible to locate the changes in the observer status in the context of the general changes in Arctic-wide co-operation. By examining the evolution of observer status, we can understand better how observer status can be achieved today, and why it has come to include the particular privileges that it has.[10] Only after knowing these basics is it possible to move to studying the core question: how has China performed as an observer in the Council?

A. Introduction to Arctic-wide Co-operation

The Arctic Environmental Protection Strategy (AEPS) was adopted by the eight Arctic states[11] in 1991 in Rovaniemi, Finland to combat six priority environmental problems[12] identified in the strategy. All this was done, but there was no unequivocally defined boundary for Arctic co-operation. The countries that were invited to take part in this co-operation were states that had areas of territorial sovereignty above the Arctic Circle.[13] However, the

[8] Timo Koivurova conducted 2 semi-structured interviews, Waliul Hasanat 5 semi-structured interviews, Piotr Graczyk 1 discussion-type interview and Tuuli Tanninen 3 semi-structured interviews.

[9] See T Axworthy, T Koivurova and W Hasanat (eds), *The Arctic Council: Its Place in the Future of Arctic Governance* (Toronto, Munk-Gordon Arctic Security Program, 2012); W Hasanat, 'Towards Model Arctic-Wide Environmental Cooperation Combating Climate Change' (2009) 20 *Yearbook of International Environmental Law* 125–27.

[10] Since the Arctic Council is a soft law forum, we intentionally avoid the use of the terms 'rights' and 'obligations' that associate with proper legal relations, and use instead 'privileges' and 'duties'.

[11] The Soviet Union (not yet Russia) was the signatory to the AEPS that was signed on 14 June 1991.

[12] These were: Persistent Organic Contaminants, Oil Pollution, Heavy Metals, Noise, Radioactivity and Acidification. See Declaration on the Protection of the Arctic Environment (Rovaniemi, Finland, 14 June 1991) ch 4, available at http://library.arcticportal.org/1542/.

[13] Iceland also has areas of territorial sovereignty above the Arctic Circle, as its territorial sea extends above the Circle. For an analysis of the various definitions, see T Koivurova,

Arctic Circle has not been used as a boundary in the everyday work in the Council, since all the Arctic states and the working groups have defined 'the Arctic' differently for their own purposes. The Arctic Council was established in 1996 on the Canadian initiative, and during the period from 1996 to 1998, the AEPS was merged into the Arctic Council.[14]

The four initial working groups of the AEPS co-operation—Conservation of Arctic Flora and Fauna (CAFF), the Protection of the Arctic Marine Environment (PAME), Emergency Prevention, Preparedness and Response (EPPR) and the Arctic Monitoring and Assessment Programme (AMAP)—were integrated as part of the Arctic Council. Yet, another new working group was established when the Arctic Council was adopted, the Sustainable Development Working Group (SDWG). The mandate of the Council was defined in a broad manner to include all common issues facing the Arctic. However, military issues were excluded from the agenda. Hence, at first sight, there seemed to be a clear departure from the AEPS, which had its focus on environmental protection. However, the AEPS also worked on sustainable development issues via its Task Force on Sustainable Development and Utilisation (TFSDU),[15] which had on its agenda more high-level and controversial sustainable development issues that the SDWG eventually came to deal with.[16] Overall, therefore, there was no real change in the mandate of the AEPS and the Council, given that both in practice dealt with environmental protection and sustainable development issues.

Institutional forms have also not changed much during the transition. The AEPS had Senior Arctic Affairs Officials (SAAOs) to co-ordinate the work within the Council, SAAOs being normally high-level civil servants from the national line agencies. SAAOs also prepared the ministerial meetings of the AEPS, which took place in Nuuk (1993), Inuvik (1996) and Alta, Norway (1997, the final one). Almost the same structure has been retained in the Arctic Council compared to the AEPS, although its organisation has been made clearer with rules of procedure (Rules of Procedure 1998). Yet, it is still the Senior Arctic Officials (SAOs), with only a slightly changed name, that co-ordinate the work in the Council. The SAOs prepare the ministerial

Environmental Impact Assessment in the Arctic: A Study of International Legal Norms (Farnham, Ashgate Publishing, 2002) 25–28.

[14] T Koivurova and W Hasanat, 'Climate Policy of the Arctic Council' in T Koivurova, C Keskitalo and N Bankes (eds), *Climate Governance in the Arctic* (Hanover, Springer-Verlag, 2009) 52–58.

[15] To be more specific, the TFSDU was agreed to be promoted to the status of a working group just before the Arctic Council was established, at the Inuvik ministerial meeting of the Arctic Council in March 1996: para 5: 'In view of this, we agree to establish a Working Group on Sustainable Development and Utilization (SDU)'; see library.arcticportal.org/1272/1/The_Inuvik_Declaration.pdf.

[16] C Keskitalo, *Constructing the Arctic* Acta Universitatis Lapponiensis 47 (Rovaniemi, Finland, Lapland University Press, 2002) 113–58.

meetings in the same way as the SAAOs did in the AEPS, and ministerial meetings take place after the end of a country's chair period.[17] The secretariat services for the Arctic Council have been provided by the chair state, but now this has been changed as will be described below.

The only clear change that took place when moving from the AEPS to the Arctic Council during the transition period 1996–1998 was an improvement in the status of membership accorded to the region's indigenous peoples, more specifically, their international organisations that represent either one people living in many Arctic states or many indigenous peoples living in one state.[18] They were transferred from the status of observers to becoming permanent participants.[19]

The level of commitment from the member states was low in Arctic co-operation from the beginning up until 2007. This is manifested in the lack of a stable funding mechanism, the function of the Council as a type of soft law intergovernmental forum that was unable to make legally binding decisions and the fairly uncontroversial questions that were taken up in the Council. Funding has, from the beginning, been ad hoc in the sense that no permanent contributions are required from the eight Arctic states or other participants. The funding system has improved since the so-called Project Support Instrument (PSI) became operative, and the Arctic Council actors—not observers—have made contributions to it.[20] This PSI is intended for project preparation activities that aim at Arctic pollution prevention and mitigation. There has been no serious discussion to date over changing the funding system from the present ad hoc system to a stable permanent funding mechanism, that is, stable funding contributions from the Arctic states to the Arctic Council.[21]

Another factor signalling the low level of commitment in the early years of Arctic co-operation is the way the AEPS and the Arctic Council were established. The 1991 Rovaniemi Declaration, by which the AEPS co-operation was commenced, was signed by the representatives of the eight Arctic

[17] These have taken place in Iqaluit (Canada 1996–98), Barrow (USA 1998–2000), Inari (Finland 2000–02), Reykjavik (Iceland 2002–04), Salekhard (Russia 2004–06), Tromsø (2006–09), Nuuk (2009–11) and Kiruna (2011–13). After a full rotation, the chairmanship returned to Canada in 2013 and will be assumed by the US in 2015.

[18] Declaration on the Establishment of the Arctic Council (Ottawa, Canada, 19 September 1996) para 2 (Ottawa Declaration).

[19] By the end of the AEPS, a practice started where the indigenous peoples' status started to be called 'AEPS permanent participants', but this still needed to be negotiated during the establishment of the Arctic Council; P Graczyk and T Koivurova, 'A New Era in the Arctic Council's External Relations' (2014) 50(3) *Polar Record* 225, 227.

[20] Currently, only the Sámi Council and Arctic states, excluding Canada and Denmark, have made contributions to this instrument run by the Nordic Environment Finance Corporation (NEFCO) (interview by Waliul Hasanat, 20 October 2014). See generally at www.nefco.org/financing/arctic_council_project_support_instrument.

[21] Evidently, the Arctic states do support the secretariat of the Arctic Council with stable financial contributions.

states. In a similar vein, the Arctic Council was established via the signed Ottawa Declaration. Both forms of co-operation were thus created not by an international treaty, but through a signed declaration, thus effectively keeping the co-operation as a type of soft law arrangement. According to Evan Bloom, the US Department of State representative in the meetings of the Arctic Council and the US negotiator on the establishment of the Arctic Council, these types of co-operative forms were an objective for the US, given the enhanced flexibility they provide.[22]

Yet, it is fair to say that in recent years, the Arctic Council has strengthened its mode of operation. The political profile of the Council has become stronger. New biennial deputy ministers' meetings were established in addition to regular ministerial meetings taking place every other year. Moreover, two legal agreements have been negotiated under the auspices of the Arctic Council. The Agreement on Cooperation on Aeronautical and Maritime Search and Rescue in the Arctic (SAR) was signed during the May 2011 ministerial meeting. The agreement is meant to strengthen search and rescue co-ordination and co-operation efforts in the Arctic by allocating responsibilities to each Arctic state in its own jurisdiction and by establishing procedures for states to co-operate in cases of emergency. An agreement on marine oil pollution preparedness and response for the Arctic was signed during the May 2013 ministerial meeting. Moreover, a permanent Secretariat for the Council was established in Tromsø, Norway.

Overall, it can be concluded that even though there was indeed a rapid shift from the AEPS to Arctic Council co-operation, the nature of the co-operation remained very much the same. The Arctic Council was more detailed in its organisational structure, and some moderate changes took place, but the basics of the co-operation did not change in this transition. Real changes are starting to take place recently, meaning, for some, that the Arctic Council is transforming as an institution from a decision-shaping to decision-making body.

II. THE EVOLUTION OF THE OBSERVER STATUS IN ARCTIC-WIDE CO-OPERATION

The observer category first appeared during the preparatory meetings for the 1991 AEPS proposed by Finland. At that time, the group embraced three types of actors: non-Arctic states, indigenous peoples' organisations and intergovernmental and non-governmental organisations. Accordingly, the reasons for engagement varied among them. Nonetheless, the Arctic states

[22] ET Bloom, 'Establishment of the Arctic Council' (1999) 93(3) *American Journal of International Law* 712, 721.

deemed that those invited as observers were crucial for the prospective cooperation due to their knowledge, experience and resources that would help in protecting the Arctic environment. This remains the case today. Yet, nowadays, an increasing number of states all over the world want to become observers in the Council. Reasons include the increasing awareness that all states enjoy various types of rights in the maritime Arctic, or that most pollution originates from states and regions outside of the Arctic. This section briefly traces the evolution of the observer category under both the AEPS and the Arctic Council and discusses its present status.

A. Observers within the AEPS

Nine entities[23] observed the first ministerial meeting, the conference on the Protection of the Arctic Environment, in Rovaniemi in June 1991, wherein the AEPS was adopted. The most striking difference between the Rovaniemi Process (alternatively called the AEPS) and the Arctic Council was that, at least formally, indigenous peoples' organisations fell into the observer category in the AEPS.[24] Their status was still better than that of other observers since the aboriginal inhabitants were recognised as essential in implementing the AEPS.[25] Other observers were not given so much attention in the official documents, except for a vaguely formulated criterion that 'the decision to invite the observers should be based on a pragmatic and functional evaluation of their involvement in and contribution to Arctic environmental questions'.[26]

There was not much guidance, hence, for deciding who can be invited as observers. As mentioned, indigenous peoples' enjoyed a privileged position in the sense that the Arctic states committed to invite them in the future. With respect to the non-Arctic states and organisations (both intergovernmental and non-governmental), decisions were taken based on their commitment to protect the Arctic environment. In practice, this applied to a limited number of countries that had conducted research in the Arctic for years and were de facto present in the region. Environmental organisations'

[23] These included 3 states (the Federal Republic of Germany, Poland, the United Kingdom), 3 indigenous peoples' organisations (Inuit Circumpolar Conference—ICC, the Nordic Sámi Council, the USSR Association of Small Peoples of the North) and 3 organisations (International Arctic Science Committee—IASC, United Nations Economic Commission for Europe—UN ECE and the United Nations Environment Programme—UNEP); OR Young, *Creating Regimes: Arctic Accords and International Governance* (Ithaca and London, Cornell University Press, 1998) 90.

[24] P Graczyk, 'Observers in the Arctic Council—Evolution and Prospects' (2011) 3 *Yearbook of Polar Law* 590.

[25] The AEPS (n 12) 6.

[26] ibid, 42.

interest in the situation in the Arctic had been rising since Alaskan oil exploration got under way, and mounted even more rapidly after the spill from the *Exxon Valdez* supertanker off the coast of Alaska in 1989. However, works under AEPS were observed by only two intergovernmental organisations (UN Economic Commission for Europe (UN ECE) and the United Nations Environmental Programme (UNEP)) and one scientific organisation (International Arctic Science Committee (IASC)).

Throughout the AEPS process accredited and ad hoc observers could participate in ministerial conferences, SAAOs meetings as well as works of the working groups.[27] Individual working Groups could also accredit additional observers, which were, however, restricted only to the particular working group and could not be extended to other AEPS meetings.[28] The AEPS documents did not specify an actual role and way of engagement for observers. Nevertheless, their potential and capabilities were not fully exploited and their possibility to participate was severely limited, since the Arctic countries did not look favourably on any political involvement of external actors.[29] Decisions based on functional and pragmatic evaluation may suggest that the contribution of the non-Arctic actors must have been considered from the perspective of the Arctic states' but no precise procedures for evaluation of candidates for observership were specified.[30] In light of their constrained participation on political levels in SAAOs and ministerial meetings observer states focused their efforts on working groups' projects.[31]

Observers' commitment to research and protection of the Arctic environment evinced throughout the AEPS collaboration enhanced their presence within both the region and its major co-operative forum. It is fair to say that it favourably influenced the shape of the observer status in the AEPS' successor—observers were seamlessly transferred into the new process as full observers.[32]

[27] HR Nilson, *Arctic Environmental Protection Strategy (AEPS): Process and Organization, 1991–97*, No 103) (Oslo, Norwegian Polar Institute, 1997) 54.

[28] ibid, 56. Peculiarly, definitions of working group members differed among the working groups. Eg in the Arctic Monitoring and Assessment Programme (AMAP) only representatives of the 8 Arctic states were considered as members, while the Conservation of Arctic Flora and Fauna (CAFF) also included other national delegates, permanent participants (IPOs), AEPS accredited observers, working group accredited observers and ad hoc observers in this category.

[29] The AEPS (n 12) 6.

[30] Graczyk, 'Observers in the Arctic Council' (n 24) 591.

[31] Non-Arctic states could accentuate their engagement by allocating substantial scientific and financial support for the research and activity of AMAP (Germany and the Netherlands, who hosted an AMAP meeting in 1997) and CAFF (Great Britain). It was particularly significant compared to the modest contribution from the biggest Arctic states as financial support from Germany and the Netherlands was more generous than from the US and Russia combined; Young, *Creating Regimes* (n 23) 136. See also D Scrivener, *Environmental Cooperation in the Arctic: From Strategy to Council* Security Policy Library, 1/1996 (Oslo, The Norwegian Atlantic Committee, 1996).

[32] Graczyk and Koivurova, 'A New Era' (n 19).

B. Observers at the Arctic Council

The establishment of the Arctic Council was intended to widen and intensify Arctic co-operation and to provide it with a better institutional framework.[33] During negotiations on a new institutional arrangement in the Arctic it became apparent that the form of participation—place in the structure, right to speak and vote—is a highly politicised issue that revealed the increasing importance of the region in the Arctic states' policies.[34] With regard to observers, it was decided that a system of self-selecting accredited and ad hoc observers developed during the AEPS implementation should be maintained also in the Arctic Council.[35]

Operation of the Arctic Council is guided by the Rules of Procedure that apply to all its subsidiary bodies, being relatively well developed for a forum which is not a formal intergovernmental organisation based on a legally binding treaty.[36] There are three categories of participants in the Council: 'Arctic states', which are the member states of the Arctic Council (eight Arctic nations), 'permanent participants', which are six indigenous peoples' organisations,[37] and 'observers'.[38] Unlike the AEPS, the Ottawa Declaration clearly defines categories of actors that may apply for observer status. Accordingly, it is open to non-Arctic states, intergovernmental and inter-parliamentary organisations, global and regional, and non-governmental organisations on the basis of their application and the evaluations made by the Arctic states. Before decisions regarding observers were taken at the Nuuk ministerial meeting, there were no clear and comprehensive criteria that the observers had to fulfil in order to become observers. The only requirement was that they should contribute to the Council work as determined by the member states.[39]

Since the early 2000s the Arctic has been brought into the global limelight by a number of different factors, creating a geopolitical debate on the

[33] Ottawa Declaration (n 18).

[34] Scrivener '*Environmental Cooperation in the Arctic*' (n 31); Graczyk (n 24).

[35] Scrivener (n 31) 26.

[36] Bloom, 'Establishment of the Arctic Council' (n 22) 712–22.

[37] 3 indigenous organisations are recognised as permanent participants in Art 2 of the Declaration: The Inuit Circumpolar Conference (ICC), the Sámi Council and the Association of Indigenous Minorities in the Far North, Siberia, the Far East of the Russian Federation (renamed later as Russian Association of Indigenous Peoples of the North—RAIPON). The other 3IPOs were included later: in 1998, the Aleut International Association (AIA), and in 2000, the Arctic Athabaskan Council (AAC) and Gwich'in Council International.

[38] Ottawa Declaration (n 18) art 2.3; Arctic Council Rules of Procedure as adopted by the Arctic Council at the First Arctic Council ministerial meeting (Iqaluit, Canada, 17–18 September 1998) revised by the Arctic Council at the Eighth Arctic Council ministerial meeting (Kiruna, Sweden, 15 May 2013) r 1.

[39] Arctic Council Rules of Procedure as adopted by the Arctic Council at the First Arctic Council ministerial meeting (Iqaluit, Canada, 17–18 September 1998).

Arctic.[40] Several powerful external actors also expressed their interest in economic opportunities in the Arctic and, as a consequence, in regional governance structures.[41] These developments exposed the Council for the new regional situation and gave a clear signal for the need for change in this respect.[42] As Arctic Council observer status is the only way to gain access to its proceedings and to get formal recognition as a stakeholder in Arctic governance processes, outside actors centred their efforts on obtaining this position by following the official procedure. At the same time, those already involved as observers in Arctic co-operation raised the question of improving their position within the Council.[43] Accordingly, the number and role of observers, and the justifications for their presence, emerged as one of the main problems in the debate on the Council's reform.[44]

The work on new rules concerning observers was carried out in a highly politicised context, affected by several factors. The considerable reluctance expressed by the Arctic states during the formulation of the observer criteria[45] stemmed primarily from a concern over their own interests and an anxiety that they could put their regional position in jeopardy and challenge the current consensus on governance principles in the Arctic based on the law of the sea (and Law of the Sea Convention) and the Arctic Council as the two anchors.[46] Another reason and instrument of blocking unwanted applications is the practical argument that the number of entities will grow too large, which could be more of a hindrance than a help.[47] Furthermore, the wording of the criteria was arguably influenced by some external actors' policy statements such as different views on the legal status of parts of the northern passages and delimitation processes on the Arctic Ocean expressed by China and the EU (however, being in line with American stance).[48]

[40] OR Young, 'Whither the Arctic? Conflict or Cooperation in the Circumpolar North' (2009) 45(1) *Polar Record* 73–82; T Koivurova and P Graczyk, 'How Outside Actors Hold Sway within the Arctic Council: Benefits of Cooperation and the Problems When Improving Them' in R Ramesh, M Sudhakar and S Chattopadhyay (eds), *Scientific and Geopolitical Interests in Arctic and Antarctic* (New Delhi, LIGHT Research Foundation, 2013) 33–54.

[41] Koivurova, 'Limits and Possibilities of the Arctic Council' (n 3).

[42] P Graczyk, 'The Arctic Council Inclusive of Non-Arctic Perspectives: Seeking a New Balance' in T Axworthy, T Koivurova and W Hasanat (eds), *The Arctic Council: Its Place in the Future of Arctic Governance* (Toronto, Munk-Gordon Arctic Security Program, 2012) 261, 278.

[43] Graczyk (n 24).

[44] Senior Arctic Official (SAO) Report to the Ministers (Tromsø, Norway, April 2009); Senior Arctic Official (SAO) Report to the Ministers (Nuuk, Greenland, May 2011).

[45] Graczyk and Koivurova (n 19).

[46] AH Hoel, 'Do We Need a New Legal Regime for the Arctic Ocean?' (2009) 24 *International Journal of Marine and Coastal Law* 443–56.

[47] Graczyk, 'The Arctic Council Inclusive of Non-Arctic Perspectives' (n 42).

[48] L Jakobson, 'China Prepares for an Ice-free Arctic' (2010) 2 *SIPRI Insights on Peace and Security*.

Finally, the accredited observers voiced concerns about the role of the status as being rather symbolic compared to their abilities, aspirations and interests, and not corresponding precisely to their vision of involvement in Arctic affairs.[49]

Arctic countries, aware of these concerns, decided to carry out (under the Danish chairmanship) the first comprehensive review of observer engagement to evaluate their performance, and, if applicable, to make any amendments to the list of observers, including the reaccreditation of Arctic Council observers or withdrawal of observer status.[50] The survey was also meant to determine the stances of the member states and permanent participants on observers' role in the Arctic Council. The new Arctic Council member states' policy towards observers at the forum was based on the results of this study and the outcome had to be aligned with all the Arctic states' interests.

The rules concerning observers adopted at the seventh ministerial meeting in Nuuk, Greenland in May 2011 introduced several important innovations to principles and rules concerning the admission and role of observers at the Arctic Council. There are three key documents defining the status of different actors in the Arctic Council: the Declaration on the Establishment of the Arctic Council,[51] (Revised) Arctic Council Rules of Procedure and the AC Observer Manual for Subsidiary Bodies.[52] The Revision of the Rules of Procedure (in parts related to observers) and the latter document emanated from the debate on involvement of external actors in AC activities that had been carried out since powerful actors—China, the EU, Italy, Japan and South Korea—had applied for the status, and already accepted observers raised questions about increasing their role within the Council.[53] Because of the new rules for admission it was possible to use them at the ministerial meeting in 2013 to evaluate pending applications and admit the candidates at the same time as the Revised Rules of Procedure were adopted. Also at the Nuuk ministerial meeting, the Arctic states established a Task Force on Institutional Issues (TFII) chaired by Sweden, which was responsible for revising the Arctic Council.

Based on the criteria for observer admission and the description of the role of observers at the Council, the TFII proposed amendments to the Arctic Council Rules of Procedure (RoP) and compiled the Arctic Council Observer Manual for Subsidiary Bodies as guidance for the chairs of working groups and task forces on how to involve observers in work at this level. The changes introduced to the RoP along with the Manual have clarified

[49] Graczyk and Koivurova (n 19).

[50] SAO Report, April 2009 (n 44) 36.

[51] Ottawa Declaration (n 18).

[52] Arctic Council Observer Manual for Subsidiary Bodies adopted by the Senior Arctic Officials and endorsed by the Arctic Council at the Eighth Arctic council ministerial meeting, Kiruna, Sweden, 15 May 2013.

[53] Graczyk and Koivurova (n 19).

the position of observers at the Council. First, ad hoc observer status was abolished. It was originally intended for entities wishing to attend an individual meeting, and was only later associated with the applicants for full observer status.[54] Secondly, the role of observers—hitherto rather vaguely stated—was clarified to mean: observing the work of the Arctic Council; contributing at the working group level; making statements at meetings at the discretion of the chair (primarily at the working level); submitting relevant documents; and providing views on issues under discussion. Furthermore, observers are entitled to propose projects through an Arctic state or a permanent participant, but their financial input cannot be greater than that of the member states.[55] Importantly, the amended Annex 2 of the RoP has no list of admitted observers (as it had before), underpinning the assumption that observer status lasts as long as there is consensus among the Arctic States. Now it contains criteria for admitting observers, arguably putting the Council in a new position in the Arctic governance system.[56]

Observer status, even as a 'full' observer, lasts as long as there is a consensus on this issue among the Arctic States, and the entity that holds it has not engaged in activities that are in conflict with the Ottawa Declaration.[57] This means that a state (or organisation) may be deprived of that status when one Arctic country withdraws its acceptance of a certain entity as observer at the Council.[58] Officially, participation of observers is provided at all levels of the Council.

An important thing to note in this context is that there is also a prohibited area for observers not anchored in official documents, which is still crucial for the functioning and effectiveness of the Council. The practice of having closed meetings of Heads of Delegations comprising Arctic governments' representatives and leaders of permanent participants during ministerial and SAO meetings allows frank discussions, which have proven useful in making sure that no additional controversial points will be taken up during formal sessions. Such a form proved to be a particularly efficient way of resolving contentious issues and seamless conduct of conferences, even if these clearly diminish the power of observers.[59] In a similar manner, the increasing use of task forces prevents participation of observers and permanent participants, as it was the case when the SAR agreement was negotiated under a task force. According to SAOs, task forces may be necessary for specific initiatives that require unique expertise and, in those instances, the composition

[54] Rules of Procedure (n 38) r 37.
[55] ibid, 38.
[56] Graczyk and Koivurova (n 19).
[57] ibid, 37.
[58] Graczyk (n 24) 603.
[59] T Fenge, *Canada and the Arctic Council: Our Turn to Conduct the Arctic Orchestra* (2012) *Policy Options/Options Politiques* 54–58.

and mode of operation of the task force would be determined on a case-by-case basis.[60]

i. Observer's Role

While the Rules of Procedure provide exclusively a single line on observers' role concerning making statements and submitting relevant documents to the meetings that the Council determines can contribute to their work,[61] the definition presented in Nuuk clarifies several issues related to their engagement in Arctic Council activities. Besides the above-described rules that pertain to statements, the Arctic States set limits to the involvement of external actors.

First, they stipulate that decision-making at all levels within the Council is the exclusive right and responsibility of the eight Arctic States with the involvement of the permanent participants.[62] Furthermore, it is emphasised that the primary role of observers is to observe the work of the Arctic Council and to make relevant contributions, primarily at the level of working groups.[63] Finally, the new definition illuminates the issue of proposing projects, which observers may do through an Arctic state or permanent participant. However, a caveat was included that observers' financial contributions to any given project may not exceed the financing from Arctic States, unless otherwise decided by the SAOs.[64]

Although the rules underline that observers should focus on involvement at the working level, there is a lack of entries determining procedure and criteria for incorporation of non-Arctic scientists into working groups' projects. The Observer Manual complementing the Rules of Procedure does not seem to suffice to solve the problem of rather modest observer participation in the Council. The purpose of this instruction is to bolster the performance of subsidiary bodies by facilitating meeting logistics and exchange of information between different actors.[65]

The Observer Manual does not establish any uniform framework that promotes observers' applications for participation in working groups' projects. On the other hand, it may help to work out a common practice that would make it possible. By the same token, the rules pertaining to sponsoring new initiatives seem rather elusive, as they impose on observers an additional need to persuade the Arctic States to provide appropriate funding, which proved to be problematic within the Council.

[60] SAO Report (May 2011) (n 44) 49–50.
[61] Ottawa Declaration (n 18).
[62] ibid, 50.
[63] Rules of Procedure (n 38) r 38.
[64] ibid.
[65] Observer Manual (n 52) 1.

ii. Criteria for Admission

As stated earlier, the Arctic Council has formulated a set of criteria that could be seen as prerequisites for an interested entity to apply to become an observer of the Arctic Council. The main criteria for admitting an observer are whether the applicant:

(a) accepts and supports the objectives of the Arctic Council defined in the Ottawa Declaration;
(b) recognises Arctic States' sovereignty, sovereign rights and jurisdiction in the Arctic;
(c) recognises that an extensive legal framework applies to the Arctic Ocean including, notably, the Law of the Sea, and that this framework provides a solid foundation for responsible management of this ocean;
(d) respects the values, interests, culture and traditions of Arctic indigenous peoples and other Arctic inhabitants;
(e) has demonstrated a political willingness as well as financial ability to contribute to the work of the permanent participants and other Arctic indigenous peoples;
(f) has demonstrated its Arctic interests and expertise relevant to the work of the Arctic Council; and
(g) has demonstrated a concrete interest and ability to support the work of the Arctic Council, including through partnerships with member states and permanent participants bringing Arctic concerns to global decision-making bodies.[66]

Arguably the most remarkable part of the new set of rules are criteria for admitting observers that may have wider ramifications for the Arctic Council's role in Arctic governance—and also for China's role as an observer.[67] Until the ministerial meeting in Nuuk, there were no official entries in any document determining on what basis decisions are made with respect to applications for observer status. This raised frequent concerns among both observers and permanent participants as the existing general criteria were indefinable and to a large extent created an interpretational space that could be influenced by changing tides of politics.[68] Also, as the above-mentioned survey carried out by the Danish chairmanship revealed, there was a significant discrepancy between the Arctic states and permanent participants; the new criteria had to reconcile many diverging interests. Therefore, the

[66] Rules of Procedure (n 38) Annex 2, s 6.

[67] There were also criticisms of these criteria as too strict, if one compares these criteria to other intergovernmental forums and organisations; see eg P Guo, 'An Analysis of New Criteria for Permanent Observer Status on the Arctic Council and the Road of Non-Arctic States to Arctic' (2012) 4(2) *International Journal of Maritime Affairs and Fisheries* 21–38.

[68] Graczyk (n 24) 604.

criteria can be divided into three categories: (1) confirming the existing ones; (2) underpinning the position of permanent participants; and (3) introducing a political benchmark, and thus assigning new roles to the Council.

As before, therefore, applicants are assessed based on the extent to which they accept and support the principles of the Ottawa Declaration and have demonstrated their Arctic interests and expertise relevant to the work of the Arctic Council as well as a concrete interest and ability to support its work.[69] This criterion is further strengthened by reference to their input into bringing Arctic concerns to global decision-making bodies in partnerships with both the member states and permanent participants.[70] In general, it is a detailed description of the standards recorded in the Ottawa Declaration and the Rules of Procedure. Something of a novelty is an emphasis on applicant standards recorded in the Ottawa Declaration and the Rules of Procedure.

A new feature that has emerged in recent years—also in relation to the increased political self-awareness of permanent participants and their concerns that new powerful actors could possibly dilute their current role—is the introduction of norms pertaining precisely to their position. Therefore, a successful applicant to observer status must respect the values, interests, culture and traditions of Arctic indigenous peoples and other Arctic inhabitants.[71] It comes as no surprise that these requirements primarily are the result of the restrictions on the marketing of seal products imposed by the European Union, which despite inclusion of exceptions for seal products derived from indigenous peoples' traditional hunting have caused a collapse of the seal products market.[72] The second criterion that falls under that category is the requirement to demonstrate a political willingness as well as financial ability to contribute to the work of the permanent participants and other Arctic indigenous peoples.[73]

The third grouping of criteria represents the differing views on jurisdictional and legal issues in the Arctic expressed by some of the current applicants to observer status. Given that the Arctic states attach much attention to their sovereignty and leading role in regional affairs, it becomes more and more apparent that they decided to harmonise their actions and protect common interests against external actors, despite differences between themselves in this regard. First of all, an applicant to the status is supposed to recognise Arctic States' sovereignty, sovereign rights and jurisdiction in the Arctic.[74]

[69] Rules of Procedure (n 38) Annex 2, s 6a.

[70] ibid, 6g.

[71] ibid, 6d.

[72] L Carter, 'Canadian Seal Hunt "Collapsing"' *BBC News* (Toronto, 18 June 2009) available at news.bbc.co.uk/2/hi/8106539.stm; A Peter, 'The European Parliament Shuts down Seal-Product Imports—Again' *Above & Beyond* (May/June 2010).

[73] Rules of Procedure (n 38) Annex 2, s 6e.

[74] ibid, 6b.

This implies that these issues will need to be taken and decided upon by the Council—an advancement that has not been present before. Since the Arctic States do not fully agree on certain issues among themselves it still remains unclear how they will assess the recognition of their sovereignty. Furthermore, it has not been determined yet whether sovereignty questions related to non-Arctic actors will be debated at the Council's meetings.

The second criterion that falls into that category obligates applicants to recognise that an extensive legal framework applies to the Arctic Ocean, including, notably, the Law of the Sea, and that this framework provides a solid foundation for responsible management of this ocean.[75] This standard implies that the Arctic countries have formally and de facto included the principles of the Ilulissat Declaration of the five Arctic Ocean coastal states from May 2008, thereby bridging the gap that had opened between the Arctic Five and Arctic Eight.[76] According to the member states these measures will strengthen the Arctic Council and solve the observer question while maintaining the key role of the Arctic states and permanent participants.[77]

Without doubt the revised new set of rules pertaining to observers has added to understanding of the reasons taken into consideration when assessing applications for observer status and has helped to clarify ambiguities in interpretation and application of the Rules of Procedure and the Ottawa Declaration regulating observers' participation in the Council's work. Candidates and already admitted actors are being evaluated according to the degree to which they are not a challenge to Arctic regional interests.[78] In these terms, the new observer guidelines have elucidated the picture of political requirements that must be met by the applicants. Since the criteria have a highly political profile, they also involve some important implications for the role of the Arctic Council in regional sovereignty and legal discourses, in which the forum has not engaged before.

The current observer status gives an opportunity to follow the vast majority of the Council's work and enables participation in the projects and activities of the subsidiary bodies. It is important, however, to realise that the Arctic States left themselves much discretion in determining the activity of observers within the Arctic Council. Their fairly broad access to the

[75] ibid, 6c.

[76] Graczyk and Koivurova (n 19). When the Arctic Ocean coastal states organised their first meeting in Ilulissat, Greenland in 2008, and the second one in Canada in 2010, there was considerable discussion whether the Arctic 5 would become the predominant forum for Arctic governance.

[77] SAO Report (May 2011) (n 44) 3.

[78] Peculiarly, definitions of working group members differed among the working groups. eg in the Arctic Monitoring and Assessment Programme (AMAP) only representatives of the 8 Arctic states were considered as members, while the Conservation of Arctic Flora and Fauna (CAFF) also included other national delegates, permanent participants (IPOs), AEPS accredited observers, working group accredited observers and ad hoc observers in this category (ibid).

Council's activities may be verified and to some extent restricted, depending on the importance of the projects or enterprises, and policies carried out by the Arctic countries towards specific issues. It may be perceived as a justified anxiety about national interests and intention to maintain control over the situation in the forum and the region. A numerous and robust observer corps could dilute or hinder it considerably, making it difficult to govern circumpolar collaboration.

An observer issue has been present since the inception of the Arctic Council and been frequently pointed out throughout its history as one of the pending issues.[79] Though better developed and coherent compared to the AEPS, final specific decisions concerning observer involvement have been left at the discretion of the member states.[80] Different views of the Arctic states and permanent participants have for a long time hindered efforts to define clearly the role of observers in the Council. The paramount emphasis is placed on their ability to contribute at the working level, which may reveal their real intentions and actual interests related to the Arctic Council. Bearing in mind observers' statements, it is difficult to assess whether they will be satisfied by the enhanced and more efficiently executed rights guaranteed to them in the Rules of Procedure. Financial support and major economic interests in the Arctic (handled in bilateral relations with the Arctic states) may become the main argument of actors such as China, especially in relation to modest financing provided by the member states. It is critical, therefore, to develop an appropriate and constructive mechanism for introducing non-Arctic actors into the working groups' activities and to commence unequivocal co-operation between them and the Council—issues that we will turn to next.

III. CHINA AS AN OBSERVER IN THE ARCTIC COUNCIL

China was granted an ad hoc observer position in 2007 and a 'full' observer position in 2013. It seems that before 2013, there were also concerns among Chinese officials over the Nuuk criteria, as an interview by Jacobson and Peng demonstrates:

> While Chinese officials have not publicly commented on these, officials have privately expressed displeasure with some of the criteria: the stipulations that an applicant must have demonstrated the 'political willingness and financial ability to contribute to the work of the Permanent Participants' and 'recognize Arctic states' sovereignty, sovereign rights and jurisdiction in the Arctic'.[81]

[79] Bloom (n 22); P Haavisto, *Review of the Arctic Council Structures* (Helsinki, The Finnish Institute of International Affairs, 2001); Koivurova (n 3).

[80] Graczyk (n 24) 605.

[81] See L Jacobson and J Peng, *China's Arctic Aspirations* (2012) SIPRI Policy Paper No 34, 14.

Academic commentators were also suggesting that with the current peculiar criteria, it would be better for China to influence Arctic governance via other routes.[82] It is rather odd that China, even against many who doubted whether its observer application would be accepted, and the other Asian nations were accepted as observers but the EU's application was deferred. The EU's presence in the Arctic is very strong, given that its Arctic presence in terms of environmental protection, research, social cohesion policy and other such issues is significant in the European side of the Arctic, which is reflected in the fact that the Commission is one member of the Barents Euro-Arctic Council and has its own Northern Dimension policy, with Canada and the United States as observers, and its internal evolving pan-Arctic policy.[83] Moreover, three EU member states are also members proper (Finland, Sweden and Denmark) in the Arctic Council, while most state observers in the Council are member states of the EU. The reason for this was the so-called seal ban, which prohibits placing into the EU's market most seal products, which aggravated Canada and its commercial sealers and Inuit.[84]

A. China and the Criteria for Observer Status

As was explained in the introduction, the Nuuk criteria are important when we are studying how observer non-Arctic states are behaving. There is an expectation from those that have been accepted as observers that they continue to fulfil the Nuuk criteria, which will be examined from time to time by the Arctic Council (in fact, according to the revised Rules of Procedure of the Arctic Council, the activities of each observer state are to be reviewed every four years).[85] Hence, it is useful to examine how China is currently conducting itself from the perspective of these criteria.

In the following, we will examine—on the basis of anonymous interviews—how China has contributed to the Arctic Council's work in regard to the above listed observer criteria. The focus will be on criteria dealing with how far the observer has demonstrated a concrete interest and ability to support the work of the Arctic Council and brought Arctic concerns to global decision-making bodies.

[82] Guo 'An Analysis of New Criteria for Permanent Observer Status' (n 67).

[83] The EU's presence is well summarised in its Joint Communication to the European Parliament and the Council, Developing a European Union Policy towards the Arctic Region: Progress Since 2008 and Next Steps (Brussels, 26 June 2012, JOIN (2012) 19 final), eeas.europa.eu/arctic_region/docs/join_2012_19.pdf. See also the extensive 'Strategic Assessment of Development of the Arctic: Assessment Conducted for the European Union', at www.arcticinfo.eu/en/.

[84] See the Regulation and implementing legislation, at ec.europa.eu/environment/biodiversity/animal_welfare/seals/seal_hunting.htm.

[85] See Rules of Procedure (n 38) Annex, s 5.

The government of China has expressed that it accepts and supports the objectives of the Council as defined in the Ottawa Declaration.[86] In fact, it is difficult to assess what 'accepting and supporting the objectives of the Arctic Council'—environmental protection and sustainable development in the Arctic—means, given that it is so generally worded. It would seem to be enough that China has clearly expressed strong political commitment in this regard. According to the SAOs and the secretariats of the working groups, China is an effective global partner of the Arctic Council.[87]

China recognises the sovereignty of Arctic States and their sovereign rights and jurisdiction in the Arctic subject to the principles and norms articulated in international law. This general recognition is likely the only thing that the Arctic Council member states want to obtain from the observer candidates, given that they themselves have differing legal views over certain issues as regards the status of land sovereignty (Hans Island) and the legal status of certain maritime areas.[88] In academic literature, some scholars have asserted that China might behave in the Arctic in a similar way as it does in the South-China Sea, making controversial maritime claims, but these views seem to tell us more of a fear of rising China in general than any reality of international politics.[89]

i. Respects the Values, Interests, Culture and Traditions of Arctic Indigenous Peoples and other Arctic Inhabitants

In fact, China affirms its respect to the values, interests, cultures and traditions of Arctic indigenous peoples and other inhabitants in principle. China maintains close contact with Arctic indigenous peoples as an observer state of the Arctic Council, and has committed to enhancing its relationship with Arctic indigenous peoples' organisations and taking part in projects concerning their interests and exploring possibilities for co-operation to make contributions to their well-being.[90] Adam Stepien analyses in his chapter China's stance in this respect. Currently, as he argues, China is trying to gain knowledge of the Arctic indigenous peoples.

[86] One recent express official stance on this was by G Jia, 'China in the Arctic' (2014) 3 *The Circle* magazine 14–15. Guide Jia is the Director-General of the Department of Treaty and Law, Ministry of Foreign Affairs of China.

[87] Interviewee Q (4 March 2014).

[88] Most of the Northwest Passage is perceived by Canada as its historic internal waters, while the US maintains that it is a strait that can be used for international navigation.

[89] RD Kaplan, *Asia's Cauldron: The South China Sea and the End of a Stable Pacific* (New York, Random House LLC, 2014); B Hayton, *The South China Sea: The Struggle for Power in Asia* (New Haven, Yale University Press, 2014).

[90] Updated Information Regarding the Application for Observer Status in the Arctic Council by China (as of March 2013) para 10.

ii. Has Demonstrated their Arctic Interests and Expertise Relevant to the Work of the Arctic Council

China is keen to demonstrate its Arctic interests primarily via scientific research.[91] China recognises that the Arctic Council plays an important role in scientific research concerning emerging issues in the Arctic, such as environmental protection in the region, enhancing economic co-operation and social development in the region, along with global issues like climate change and maritime transportation. And China considers the Arctic Council to be a common platform for the Arctic and non-Arctic states to jointly address relevant international issues.[92] China has developed bilateral relationships with all Arctic states due to its Arctic interests in general and scientific interests in particular.[93]

iii. Has Demonstrated a Concrete Interest and Ability to Support the Work of the Arctic Council, Including through Partnerships with Member States and Permanent Participants Bringing Arctic Concerns to Global Decision-making Bodies

The answer to this section has been partly discussed in the previous section. Moreover, China seems to appreciate also the forceful measures taken by the Arctic states to protect the Arctic environment, and their positive roles in global environmental co-operation.[94]

[91] eg China established a scientific research station in the Arctic in 2004—the Yellow River Station—and has been conducting several marine scientific expeditions in the Arctic since 1999, some of which include scientists from Canada, Finland, Iceland, Russia and the US, along with Chinese scientists. China implemented its *Polar Action Plan* under the International Polar Year (IPY) Programme 2007–10, and also participated in a number of international Arctic scientific expeditions and international Arctic science programmes mainly connected to Arctic climate change and its role in global climate change, the dynamic processes of the Arctic Ocean and their impact on global ocean circulation, the Arctic environment process and ecosystem evolution. Updated Information (as of March 2013) (n 90) para 1.

[92] 'China and the High North', speech by Chinese Ambassador Zhao Jun at the Arctic Frontiers Conference (21 January 2013).

[93] eg China held a bilateral meeting with Canada on Arctic affairs in 2008; with Norway in 2009 and 2010 and jointly organised a workshop on Arctic scientific co-operation in 2010; with the United States in 2010, 2011 and 2012; and with Finland in 2011. In 2012, legal advisers from the Chinese and Russian ministries of foreign affairs exchanged views on Arctic affairs; then, the Chinese Premier and the Prime Minister of Iceland had a meeting about bilateral co-operation regarding Arctic issues in 2012 where a Framework Agreement on Arctic Cooperation between the Chinese and Icelandic governments, and a Memorandum of Understanding on Cooperation in the field of Marine and Polar Science and Technology were signed. China also organised 2 joint workshops on marine and polar co-operation in 2011 and 2012; senior officials in charge of Chinese polar affairs visited Denmark in 2012 and talked about polar co-operation; and China exchanged views with Sweden on Arctic affairs and the Arctic Council at diplomat level in 2012; Updated Information (2013) (n 90) para 5.

[94] 'China and the High North' (n 92).

China is evidently an independent player in international politics, has vast resources and also the capacity to make efforts to create and share Arctic knowledge. It joined the International Arctic Science Committee in 1996, and was co-initiator (with Korea and Japan) of establishing the Asian Forum on Polar Science (AFoPS) in 2004. In 2005 it hosted the Arctic Science Summit Week. Chinese experts participated in the 'Melting Ice: Regional Dramas, Global Wake-up Call' conference and the Task Force on Melting Ice in 2009. China has developed scientific collaboration between Chinese research institutions[95] and conducted active exchanges and co-operation on Arctic scientific research with relevant scientific institutions of different Arctic states (eg Denmark, Iceland, Russia and the United States).[96] The Chinese Arctic and Antarctic Administration is a member of the Ny-Ålesund Science Managers Committee (NySMAC) and China established the China-Nordic Arctic Research Centre in Shanghai within a year of gaining observer position.

China has not yet, to our knowledge, brought Arctic concerns—together with member states and permanent participants—to global decision-making bodies. The expectation is clearly there. In the most recent statement by Canada as the chair of the Arctic Council to the UNFCCC Conference of the Parties (XIX), on behalf of the Arctic Council States and the six Arctic Council indigenous permanent participant organisations, it was stated that:

> Earlier this year, the Arctic Council welcomed several new observer States. We are confident in their abilities, tools, knowledge, and desire to make major strides in the fight against climate change. We look forward to working with them, to make even greater progress on addressing climate change and its impacts.[97]

B. How China Has Performed as an Observer in the Actual Work in the Arctic Council

It is of great importance to examine what China has been doing as an observer in the Arctic Council, given that it has already been an ad hoc observer since 2007, and has now received full observer status. It is relevant to seek an answer to what China has been doing as an ad hoc observer and

[95] They are The Polar Research Institute of China, China Geological Survey, Chinese Academy of Sciences and Chinese Academy of Geological Sciences.

[96] Updated Information (2013) (n 90) para 2.

[97] See www.arctic-council.org/index.php/en/resources/news-and-press/news-archive/818-statement-to-the-unfccc-cop-xix (accessed April 2015). See also www.arctic-council.org/index.php/en/our-work2/8-news-and-events/143-statement-copxix.

full observer, and whether there are plans in China on how to make use of its observer status in the future.

First of all, China has regularly attended meetings at different levels of the Arctic Council. China has been participating in all SAO meetings since 2007, participated in ministerial meetings in 2009 and 2011 as an ad hoc observer and in 2013 as an observer; and also in the deputy ministerial meeting (as an ad hoc observer) in 2012.

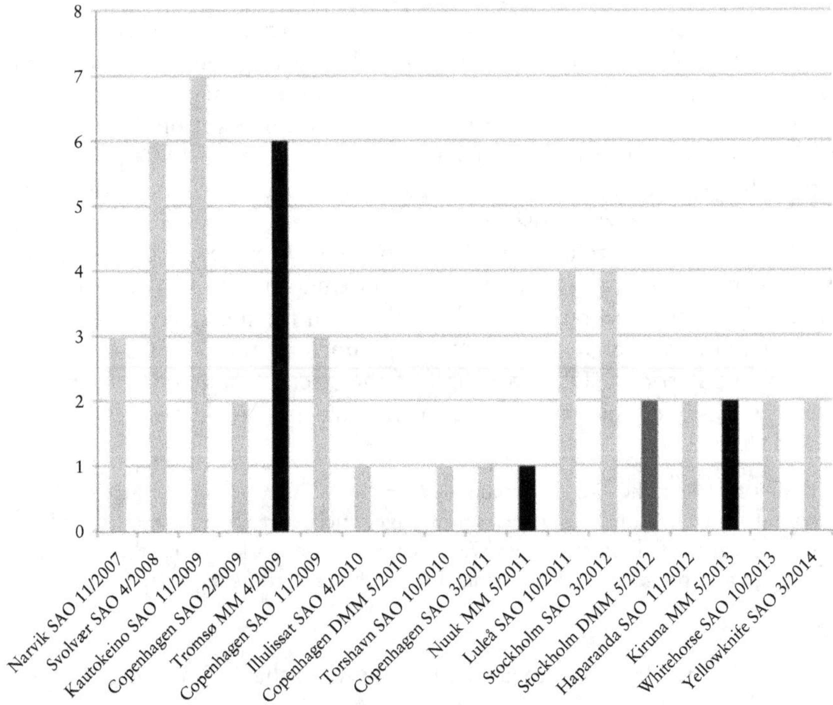

SAO = SAO Meeting, MM = Ministerial Meeting, DMM = Deputy Ministers' Meeting.
From May 2012, a cap was imposed by the Arctic Council on observers' delegations, thus stabilising the seize of Chinese delegations.

Figure 8.1: Number of Chinese representatives at the AC meetings

As one can see from Figure 8.1, the activity of China in the Arctic Council Meetings has varied over time. China sent its biggest delegations in the years following its ad hoc observer status in 2007, partly driven by the intention to better understand the Council. To this end, Chinese delegations consisted of representatives of various fields and institutions, resulting in about 30 different delegates that represented China during SAO, ministerial or deputy ministers' meetings. The delegates include diplomats (from the Ministry of Foreign Affairs, Ministry of Transport, Ministry of Land and Resources); researchers or representatives from different institutions (Chinese Arctic and Antarctic Administration, China Academy of Meteorological Sciences or the National Energy Administration).[98] In one case only Chinese diplomats in their local post attended a meeting with their attaché.[99]

The Arctic states gradually became concerned about the considerable observer delegations, particularly from the Asian states (for instance, the Korean delegation to the SAO meeting in Kautokeino, Norway in November 2008 was larger than that of some of the Arctic states), and started to impose limits for observer delegations: two delegates for full observers and one for ad hoc observers. The official explanation referred to practical and logistical reasons—accommodation facilities in the remote locations of the meetings were not sufficient for such numbers of people and Arctic states and permanent participants had to be prioritised. Therefore, the level of Chinese participation has stabilised to one or two delegates per meeting and the size of delegation depends on the location and imposed limits.

What is of more concern is that at least for the SAO meetings there seemed to be a high level of diversity among representatives (two-thirds of the representatives have attended the meetings only once). The problematic aspect in this is that there does not seem to be continuity in how certain persons gain expertise in the work of the Arctic Council.[100] Going forward, it is preferred that there will be some sort of continuity in the Chinese delegations, at least in the form of institutions sending representatives.[101] It seems that China has now appointed a number of Chinese experts who will be working on a permanent basis to different working groups of the Arctic Council appropriate to their expertise.[102]

In the scheme of the Arctic Council, the main work of the observers is expected to be undertaken in working groups, where most work of the Council is conducted in any case. Thus, it is useful to evaluate to what extent China seems active at the working group level of the Arctic Council. The representatives of the working groups pointed out that they follow the same invitation process as all the observers. For the time being, China has shown its interest mainly at the SAO level where the delegates have networked with the representatives of the working groups.[103] According to the working groups, there are no obstacles to China's full engagement as an observer from their side.[104] Thus far, the Chinese activity at the working group level has been very limited. The interviewed representatives of the working groups welcome all experts who can support their work. One task force representative informed us that they had invited China to their

98 Participant lists of the meetings.
99 Participant lists, SAO meeting in Copenhagen, Denmark, February 2009.
100 Interviewee P (27 February 2014).
101 Interviewee A (13 October 2014).
102 Interviewee X (7 March 2014).
103 Interviewee B (13 October 2014) and Interviewee C (14 October 2014).
104 Interviewee C (14 October 2014).

meetings but no Chinese delegate has been present thus far;[105] however, two Chinese engineers attended the Task Force on Arctic Marine Oil Pollution Prevention in Oslo in January 2014.[106]

One example of ACAP meeting will shed light on the process. China participated for the first time in an ACAP meeting in September 2014. China had showed its interest even before getting observer status during the Swedish chairmanship, and it was advised to wait for the official decision. The Embassy of China made the first contact, after which the Foreign Ministry of China took the leading role. China did not react right after the Kiruna ministerial meeting, but in late summer 2014.[107]

According to the interviewees, China can best contribute to Arctic affairs by joining the working group meetings and projects.[108] The representatives of the working groups mentioned that it is of utmost importance that China joins the meetings in situ.[109] Thus far China has sent one delegate to an ACAP meeting.[110] In addition to that, two Chinese delegates participated in the Black Carbon Steering Group.[111] China has not yet participated in any EPPR meetings. Some Chinese representatives were in contact with the EPPR at a SAO meeting, where China demonstrated its interest in the work of the EPPR.[112] The SDWG Working Group does not currently have any projects or research field with a direct Chinese relevance.[113] China hosted the former chair of AMAP and its Executive Secretary when they visited Beijing and Shanghai (Ocean Administration and Polar Institute) last year. AMAP has not received any scientific data from China although China has presented its activities related to Arctic monitoring and assessment to the AMAP Working Group.[114] Expert members of China attended the AMAP Working Group in 2010 for the first time, in which Chinese experts introduced the activities of China relating to Arctic monitoring and assessment.[115] China has so far participated in one workshop of the PAME Working Group.[116]

China has not yet attended any CAFF Working Group meeting (to date) although it has nominated several experts to the CAFF.[117] In fact, China has participated substantively in the Arctic Migratory Birds Initiative (AMBI)

105 Personal communication (9 October 2014).
106 Participants list of the meeting.
107 Interviewee A (13 October 2014).
108 Interviewee B (13 October 2014) and Interviewee C (14 October 2014).
109 Interviewee A (13 October 2014).
110 Interviewee A (13 October 2014).
111 Interviewee B (13 October 2014).
112 Interviewee C (14 October 2014).
113 Personal communication (8 October 2014).
114 Interviewee R (5 March 2014).
115 ibid.
116 Interviewee Q (4 March 2014).
117 Interviewee Y (20 March 2014).

that was initiated by CAFF in 2013 with a goal of improving the status and securing the long-term sustainability of the declining Arctic breeding migratory bird populations. The initiative improving the status and securing the Arctic countries themselves and with countries outside the Arctic that host Arctic birds during the non-breeding season, such as China.[118]

The working groups representatives stated that China will bring added value to the Arctic Council in many ways. Scientific potential is a main factor. The areas of co-operation stated by interviewees include mostly natural sciences and technical engineering.[119] China's know-how concerning chemical compounds and their injurious effects is widely recognised.[120] The country's contribution in eliminating emissions will be another potential field of co-operation. A third area will be the development of technological solutions, because in some core geographical areas even small developments are effective.[121] It is of utmost importance that China shows its sincere interest in solving major environmental problems. An interviewee hoped that China's increasing engagement would even activate some Arctic players to act in a more responsible way and be more active in the Arctic co-operation.[122]

At the moment there is no sign according to the interviews that China would support financially the work of any working group. Neither has China thus far made any direct commitments to the working groups.[123] At this point it was mentioned that China is supposed to need more time to build up the structure needed for efficient engagement in the Arctic Council and its working groups.[124] It was mentioned that there is already bilateral co-operation between the Arctic states, especially Finland, and China. This co-operation will hopefully evolve into practical Arctic co-operation.[125]

China evidently decides for itself the composition of the delegation.[126] A single problem mentioned in the interviews was that the Chinese delegates did not perfectly match the needs and interests of the respective working group. However, it was mentioned that the first delegates have a big role in reporting about procedures and working at the meetings. It was emphasised that China did send substantive experts compared to some other observer states, which sent diplomats to the working group meetings. It is of great

118 Arctic Migratory Birds Initiative (AMBI) www.caff.is/arctic-migratory-birds-initiative-ambi; see also Senior Arctic Official (SAO) Meeting of the Arctic Council, Yellowknife, Canada, 26–27 March 2014, Final Report, 10 (section 5.4.2, Arctic Migratory Birds Initiative (AMBI)).

119 Interviewee B (13 October 2014) and Interviewee C (14 October 2014).

120 Interviewee A (13 October 2014).

121 Interviewee B (13 October 2014).

122 Interviewee A (13 October 2014).

123 Interviewee A (13 October 2014) and Interviewee C (14 October 2014).

124 Interviewee B (13 October 2014).

125 Interviewee A (13 October 2014).

126 Interviewee A (13 October 2014).

concern to the working group representatives that all the delegates have substantive knowledge. What is even more important, the delegates need a mandate from their home country to contribute to the work of the respective working group. The role of working groups' projects and expert groups should not be underestimated, because as one of the interviewees said: 'Science and politics meet at the Working Group level'. Another factor complicating practical scientific co-operation is the lack of common standards.[127]

As mentioned above, China is actively involved in one project—the migratory bird species project—and tries to provide the requested information. A similar situation is also observed in the Arctic Contaminants Action Program ACAP—China has nominated experts for the climate change project of ACAP.

Nevertheless, the working groups of the Council are likely to be beneficial for China when it receives more information and valuable data in the future and it is also important for the Council to get China involved in the activities of the Council as a global partner.

IV. CONCLUSIONS

Observer status in the Arctic Council, as it has evolved and as was demonstrated above, does give some limited room for observers to influence the work of the Arctic Council, in particular in the working groups. Much depends on how active an observer is, especially in the working groups. China, even though it had been an ad hoc observer for some time, has only with its full observer status started to become more serious about its involvement in the Arctic Council. This is reflected in our interviews. In the past, China has actively taken part in various meetings in the Council, but has not provided much in the way of substantive contributions. There is only one project that we could identify where China has been more actively involved. On the other hand, compared to other Asian observers, it would seem that China is developing its Arctic interests more intensely than, for instance, Japan.[128]

Why then has China not been more active in the Arctic Council, since even ad hoc observer status would have made that possible? One Chinese academic interviewee was of the opinion that China has been too cautious. In his opinion, China already possesses possibilities to make substantial contributions but, according to this person, the governmental agencies are very cautious since they are afraid of being seen as imposing them on the Arctic states.[129] This idea came through in effect in many interviews that

[127] Interviewee B (13 October 2014).

[128] A Tonami, 'The Arctic Policy of China and Japan: Multi-layered Economic and Strategic Motivations' (2014) 4(1) *The Polar Journal*, 105–26.

[129] Interview by Timo Koivurova (October 2014).

this overall 'China threat' feared by other nations and peoples influences the way the Chinese operate. Yet, it seems that China has been able to establish itself better as a stakeholder in the Arctic by being proactive in conveying a constructive approach to Arctic affairs. According to Kai Sun, this is thanks to the positive and active image building and positive discourse dissemination by Chinese media and Chinese scholars/officials in international forums in responding to negative images of China as a threat. The international community is thus slowly accepting China as a 'legitimate stakeholder' in Arctic affairs.[130]

According to most interviewees, both academic and governmental, China is still in the early stages of learning about Arctic realities, not only in terms of what is happening in the region, but also how to co-ordinate Arctic affairs internally between various government agencies in a consistent manner. China is also aiming to learn better how the Arctic Council functions and who should hence represent China in various working groups and task forces. The co-ordination of Arctic Council co-operation is in the hands of the Chinese Ministry of Foreign Affairs, also via the State Oceanic Administration, but they are still struggling with how to send the best qualified persons to different meetings. One concrete example was the recent meeting of the Scientific Cooperation Task Force—SCTF task force, where a natural scientist represented China even though the discussions were more related to international negotiations and diplomatic relations, which were not his area of interest and expertise (he could not have contributed regardless, as observer states were not invited to do so, as is the case in the task forces).[131] The fact that China is still learning is visible in its fairly modest activities in the working groups, the main project being the Arctic Migratory Birds Initiative under CAFF.

Currently, as our interview with the State Oceanic Administration of China demonstrates, China is very much on the learning curve of the Arctic realities. More and more social and natural science research is being conducted in the Arctic, and China expects that by first becoming more aware of the realities of the region, it is in a better position to engage also in the work of the Arctic Council. The appointment of Chinese delegates to various bodies of the Arctic Council will have the same effect, since this will steer the country's policy towards having most qualified experts to represent China in different bodies of the Arctic Council.[132] The various government

[130] K Sun, 'Practice of Engagement, Discourse Interaction and Identity Recognition: Understanding China's Participation in Arctic Affairs' (2014) 7 *World Economics and Politics* 42-62 (in Chinese). We thank Kai Sun for his summary of the main ideas in his article.

[131] Discussion by Piotr Graczyk with a Chinese representative in the task force meeting.

[132] Guide Jia argues that 8 representatives have now been nominated Jia, 'China in the Arctic' (n 86) 14–15.

agencies having responsibilities in activities that also take place in the Arctic have not yet co-ordinated their positions in the Arctic. This co-ordination between the government agencies may be the next future step in China's evolving Arctic policy, which will likely enhance its possibilities to play a stronger role as an observer in the Arctic Council.[133]

China has been a full observer only for a very limited time, from the year 2013, and hence it can be expected that it will gradually take a stronger role as its capacity in Arctic affairs increases. Importantly, by being an observer in the Council, China is exposed to the science and environmental protection-driven realities of the Council, which are likely to boost awareness in China of the seriousness of climate change in general, as Guide Jia, Director-General of the Department of Treaty and Law (Ministry of Foreign Affairs of China) argues.[134] This increase in awareness of climate change and the reality of other environmental problems will hopefully play a small part in the evolution of China's own environmental policies.

[133] Interview by Timo Koivurova on 15 October 2014, from 8 to 10 am at the premises of the State Oceanic Administration in Beijing. Timo Koivurova interviewed, and the officials responded under the lead of Haiwen Zhang, Director General (Department of International Cooperation) in the State Ocean Administration. The general method was a semi-structured interview, proceeding from Timo Koivurova's questions to where the respondent wanted to take the discussion. See also Kai Sun's argument that issuing a policy paper on China's main positions on Arctic issues should be thought about, in K Sun 'Practice of Engagement' (n 130) 42–62.

[134] See Jia (n 86) 14–15.

9

Conservation of Marine Living Resources and Fisheries Management in the Arctic

Perspectives from Non-Arctic Actors

SÉBASTIEN DUYCK

I. INTRODUCTION

IN 2013, THE Conservation of Arctic Flora and Fauna (CAFF) Working Group of the Arctic Council released its first comprehensive scientific assessment of the present status and expected future trends for Arctic flora and fauna.[1] The key message of the report combined a negative assessment of ongoing trends with a more positive call for action.

> Arctic biodiversity is being degraded, but decisive action taken now can help sustain vast, relatively undisturbed ecosystems of tundra, mountains, fresh water and seas and the valuable services they provide.[2]

The report highlighted that improved access to the Arctic and rising global demand for natural resources lead to an increase in economic activities in the region—including shipping and fossil fuels extraction—which increases risks for local biodiversity. The regulation of both of these activities has been the subject of most of the recent academic and policy debates dedicated to the future governance of the Arctic. The first two legally binding agreements adopted under the auspices of the Arctic Council have also addressed respectively shipping and oil spill preparedness.[3]

[1] Conservation of Arctic Flora and Fauna (CAFF), *Arctic Biodiversity Assessment: Report for Policy Makers* (Akureyri, 2013).

[2] ibid, Key Finding 1, 8.

[3] Agreement on Co-operation on Aeronautical and Maritime Search and Rescue in the Arctic, 12 May 2011, in force 19 January 2013; Agreement on Co-operation on Marine Oil Pollution Preparedness and Response in the Arctic, 15 May 2013, not yet in force.

The Arctic Biodiversity Assessment however also insisted on the need to avoid addressing these stressors in isolation, highlighting not only the interconnected nature of the stressors threatening regional biodiversity but also on the importance of international co-operation to address them.[4] The report thus emphasised the relevance of the conservation of marine living resources in the Arctic, including in areas beyond national jurisdiction. Governmental and non-governmental actors have also recently put forward proposals for the establishment of a protected area in the High Arctic, such as the call by the European Parliament to protect the international sea area around the North Pole and the proposal for the creation of an 'Arctic Sanctuary' suggested by Greenpeace.[5]

The conservation of marine ecosystems in the High Arctic constitutes a specific challenge for Arctic co-operation as the interests and rights of non-Arctic states must be taken into consideration. This chapter will describe relevant ongoing efforts—both global and regional—to define a legal framework for the protection of marine living resources in the High Arctic. Considering that this area is located in areas beyond national jurisdiction (ABNJ), this chapter will also emphasise to what extent the position of non-Arctic actors might be relevant to these processes.[6]

The first section of the chapter provides a review of the current legal framework and ongoing political processes related to the conservation of marine fauna and flora in the high seas. Both protection of biodiversity and conservation of fish stocks in areas beyond national jurisdiction are discussed. The second section describes relevant initiatives by the Arctic states—through the Arctic Council as well as outside of its framework—and defines the current state of play with regards to this issue. Finally, the third section highlights the policies and positions adopted by two key non-Arctic players that might potentially have an important say in the design of Arctic marine conservation in Arctic ABNJ: China and the European Union. These two actors have indeed the capacity to contribute to Arctic developments through their economic activities (as producers, consumers and investors in the exploitation of natural resources) and

[4] *Arctic Biodiversity Assessment* (n 1) Key Finding 9.

[5] European Parliament Resolution on the EU strategy for the Arctic, 10 March 2014, 2013/2595(RSP) para 38. See also N Hamilton, 'Global Commons, Environmental Protection and Future-Proofing' (2014) www.greenpeace.org/international/Global/international/publications/oceans/2014/Arctic%20Sanctuary.pdf. This proposal is also promoted by Finland. See Finland's Strategy for the Arctic Region 2013.

[6] Considering the ongoing process through which 4 of the Arctic states are submitting claims to an extended continental shelf, this chapter only addresses the issue of marine conservation in the water column of the high seas. According to art 77 of UNCLOS, issues related to the conservation of living organisms belonging to sedentary species located on the continental shelves fall within the jurisdiction of the coastal states.

have also consistently expressed their interest in becoming involved in Arctic governance, both participating in the Arctic Council as observers.[7]

The designation of Marine Protected Areas (MPAs) and the establishment of regional instruments for fisheries management do not constitute the only policy options contributing to the conservation of marine living resources. From the perspective of non-coastal states, these two approaches are however especially relevant given the opportunity for these actors to take part in any related governance framework. Additionally, ongoing intergovernmental processes related to both of these policy options render their study particularly timely. This chapter will therefore consider opportunities to protect Arctic marine ecosystems primarily through the option to designate Arctic MPAs in ABNJ and the possibility for interested states to establish a regional fisheries management instrument.

II. CONSERVATION OF MARINE LIVING RESOURCES IN THE HIGH SEAS

The conservation of the marine environment in the high seas is regulated by the 1982 UN Convention on the Law of the Sea (UNCLOS).[8] However, the provisions of the convention left many uncertainties with regards to the applicable legal framework. Consequently, additional negotiations were required in order to address these uncertainties with regard to environmental conservation. The first subsection will provide a short outline of relevant international norms and of the ongoing efforts to further define the legal regime applicable to the conservation of marine living resources in ABNJ. The international community has partly provided a response to the gaps related to the more specific issue of the management of fish stocks in areas beyond national jurisdiction. The second subsection will introduce the current legal regime for the management of fish stocks in the high seas and the questions that remain unanswered.

A. Protecting Biodiversity in Areas beyond National Jurisdiction

Part XII of UNCLOS reiterates the legal obligation for all states to protect and preserve the marine environment,[9] and to prevent, reduce and control

[7] According to a decision reached at the Kiruna ministerial meeting, the application of the EU to observership to the Council remains pending until the confirmation by Canada that the EU has adequately addressed concerns related to its ban on placing seal products on the EU market. See Kiruna Declaration (Arctic Council, 15 May 2013) 6. In the meantime, the EU remains an observer 'in principle'. 7 member states of the EU also have been granted observer status to the Council: France, Germany, Italy, the Netherlands, Poland, Spain and the United Kingdom.

[8] United Nations Convention on the Law of the Sea, 10 December 1982, in force 16 November 1994, 21 *International Legal Materials* 1261 (1982).

[9] ibid, art 192.

pollution of the marine environment from any source under their control or jurisdiction.[10] These obligations are however conditioned by the respect of the rights of other states defined in the other sections of the convention.[11] Consequently, any environmental regulation applicable in the high seas must take into account the relevant legal regime defined by the convention. Part VII of the convention provides that 'the high seas are open to all States' and offers a non-comprehensive list of activities covered by the freedom of the high seas, including freedom of navigation and overflight, freedom to lay submarine cables and pipelines, freedom to construct artificial islands and other installations, freedom of fishing and freedom of scientific research.[12]

Furthermore, the convention emphasises the relevance of international co-operation to the conservation of marine living resources. In relation to fisheries, it highlights the need for states whose nationals exploit identical living resources, or different living resources in the same area, to enter into negotiations with regards to the management of these stocks.[13] In relation to marine conservation, this duty to co-operate is underlined in the context of opportunities for regional co-operation and taking into consideration 'characteristic regional features'.[14] Despite the emphasis on the duty to co-operate, the provisions of UNCLOS fall short of specifying a legal framework for the development of instruments or mechanisms to exploit and conserve natural resources in the high seas.

Given the absence of reference to protected areas in UNCLOS, there is currently no universal definition of Marine Protected Areas. However, the definitions adopted by the Convention on Biological Diversity (CBD) and the International Union for the Conservation of Nature (IUCN) are commonly used to fill this vacuum. The provisions of the CBD define a protected area as 'a geographically defined area, which is designated or regulated and managed to achieve specific conservation objectives'.[15] The IUCN adopted shortly afterwards a specific definition for MPAs:

> any area of intertidal or subtidal terrain, together with its overlying water and associated flora, fauna, historical and cultural features, which has been reserved by law or other effective means to protect part or all of the enclosed environment.[16]

Considering that most of the expected protected areas should be established within national jurisdiction, individual states are responsible for their identification and establishment. Consequently, the international community

[10] ibid, art 194.2.
[11] ibid, art 194.4.
[12] ibid, art 87.
[13] ibid, art 118.
[14] ibid, art 197.
[15] Convention on Biological Diversity, 5 June 1992, 31 *International Legal Materials* 822, art 2.
[16] IUCN, 'Guidelines for Protected Area Management Categories', Resolution 19/46 (1994).

has not further regulated the establishment of protected areas but has instead relied on the adoption of global political targets related to the areas that should be placed under protection. The World Summit on Sustainable Development committed countries to promote the establishment of MPAs, including the development of 'representative networks' by 2012.[17] The parties to the CBD adopted in 2010 a set of specific targets—the Aichi targets—which include a quantitative objective for the establishment of MPAs:

> By 2020, at least 17 per cent of terrestrial and inland water, and 10 per cent of coastal and marine areas, especially areas of particular importance for biodiversity and ecosystem services, are conserved through effectively and equitably managed, ecologically representative and well connected systems of protected areas and other effective area-based conservation measures, and integrated into the wider landscapes and seascapes.[18]

These targets are ambitious given the current state of play. In 2010, the IUCN reported that only 1.17 per cent of the total surface of the oceans was covered by a MPA.[19]

Additionally, the large majority of these MPAs are located within national jurisdiction, with only a very limited number of MPAs having been established up to now in ABNJ. The parties to the Convention for the Protection of the Mediterranean Sea established in 2001 the first MPA partly comprising of high seas areas.[20] The effectiveness of this MPA has however been impaired by a lack of effective management.[21] More recently, the OSPAR Convention established the only existing network of MPAs in ABNJ.[22] However, as OSPAR lacks a mandate to address specific uses of the ocean, such as shipping and fisheries, the organisation needs to co-operate with

[17] Plan of Implementation of the World Summit on Sustainable Development, Johannesburg, 4 September 2002, UN Doc A/CONF 199/L.6/Rev.3, para 32c.

[18] Framework for monitoring implementation of the achievement of the 2010 target and integration of targets into the thematic programmes of work. 2006, COP8 Decision VIII/15, Annex II.

[19] C Toropova, I Meliane, D Laffoley, E Matthews and M Spalding, *Global Ocean Protection: Present Status and Future Possibilities* (Gland, IUCN, 2010) ch 3.

[20] UNEP/MAP. Report of the twelfth ordinary meeting of the Contracting Parties to the Convention for the Protection of the Mediterranean Sea against Pollution and its Protocols, Monaco, 14–17 November, 2001,UNEP(DEC)/MED IG.13/8, 30 December 2001, Annex IV.

[21] J Rochette, S Unger, D Herr, D Johnson, T Nakamura, T Packeiser, A Proelss, M Visbeck, A Wright and D Cebrian 2014, 'The Regional Approach to the Conservation and Sustainable Use of Marine Biodiversity in Areas beyond National Jurisdiction' (2014) 49 *Marine Policy* 109, 112.

[22] OSPAR Decision 2010/1-6 on the Establishment of the Milne Seamount Complex, the Charlie Gibbs South, the Altair Seamount High Seas, the Antialtair Seamount High Seas, the Josephine Seamount High Seas and the Azores High Seas Marine Protected Area. See also generally E Molenaar and AO Elferink, 'Marine Protected Areas in Areas beyond National Jurisdiction: The Pioneering Efforts under the OSPAR Convention' (2009) 5(1) *Utrecht Law Review* 17–19. See also D Freestone, D Johnson, J Ardron, K Killer, I Morrison and S Unger, 'Can Existing Institutions Protect Biodiversity in Areas beyond National Jurisdiction? Experiences from Two On-going Processes (2014) 49 *Marine Policy* 167.

other intergovernmental organisations with the relevant competences, such as the International Maritime Organization (IMO) and North-East Atlantic Fisheries Commission (NEAFC).[23] The limited number of MPAs established in ABNJ can be explained by the lack of an international framework regulating protected areas in the high seas, which prevents regional organisations from effectively adopting measures applying to third states.

In addition to these few precedents, several intergovernmental organisations have adopted sectoral measures to protect the marine environment within a defined geographic area of the high seas. The MARPOL Convention provides, for instance, the adoption of Special Areas[24] and the IMO adopted guidelines for the identification of Particularly Sensitive Sea Areas (PSSAs)[25] in which maritime activities are particularly regulated. The International Whaling Commission (IWC) also established 'whale sanctuaries' in which whaling is strictly prohibited.[26] Nevertheless, these measures are not fully comparable to MPAs as their scope is limited to the regulation of only some of the human activities potentially interfering with the marine environment.

Given the fragmented nature of ocean governance, the UN General Assembly (UNGA) is the only global forum with an undisputed mandate to discuss issues of biodiversity beyond national jurisdiction.[27] The UNGA has established two parallel processes under which the issue of MPAs has been discussed. In 1999, the UNGA launched the United Nations Open-ended Informal Consultative Process on Oceans and the Law of the Sea (UNICPOLOS) in order to review annually developments related to ocean affairs and to identify areas that might benefit from further international co-operation.[28] The issue of MPAs was mentioned repeatedly during UNICPOLOS sessions, but UNICPOLOS has fallen short in proposing consensual solutions to address this particular issue.

In 2004, the UNGA established a second relevant process with a mandate explicitly focused on this particular issue: the Ad Hoc Open-ended Informal Working Group to study issues relating to the conservation and sustainable use of marine biological diversity beyond areas of national jurisdiction (BBNJ WG). The proceedings of the BBNJ WG encountered initial

[23] See Convention for the Protection of the Marine Environment of the North-East Atlantic, Paris, 22 September 1992, in force 25 March 1998, Annex V, art 4.

[24] ibid, Annex 1, 2, 4 and 5.

[25] See IMO Resolution A.982(24) 2005: Revised guidelines for the identification and designation of Particularly Sensitive Sea Areas.

[26] IWC, 31st Report (1979) s 9 of the Chairman's Report; IWC, 46th Report (1994) s 12.3 of the Chairman's Report.

[27] See eg the recognition of this mandate by the Conference of the Parties to the Convention on Biological Diversity, Decision X/29 on Marine and Coastal Biodiversity, s 21.

[28] UN General Assembly Resolution 54/33, 'Results of the review by the Commission on Sustainable Development of the sectoral theme of "Oceans and seas": international coordination and cooperation', adopted on 24 November 1999, UN Doc A/RES/54/33, para 2.

difficulties due to the strong divergence of positions between northern and southern countries.[29] In 2011, the BBNJ WG was however able to make a substantial step forward with the adoption of a package deal covering at least some of the proposals put forward by each country, thus opening the door to a compromise between the positions of different negotiating players. This package includes several issues that should be dealt with as a whole: Marine Genetic Resources—including questions on the sharing of benefits, measures such as area-based management tools—including MPAs and Environmental Impact Assessments (EIAs), capacity building and the transfer of marine technology.[30] The package did however not specify the nature of the instruments and principles that should be implemented in relation to each of these issues.

With the BBNJ WG making only slow and limited progress towards the adoption of a framework to protect biodiversity in ABNJ, several countries attempted to secure a political mandate for the opening of negotiations towards the adoption of an implementing agreement through the Rio+20 summit on sustainable development. The Rio 1992 Conference on Environment and Development had offered a precedent for the use of such a conference to launch negotiations towards an implementing agreement under UNCLOS. Through the adoption of Agenda 21, governments had agreed to convene an intergovernmental conference to consider the issue of straddling fish stocks and highly migratory fish stocks.[31] Several countries opposed however the adoption of a concrete decision on the issue of biodiversity in ABNJ at the 2012 conference. The outcome of the Rio+20 conference thus could only stipulate that countries will take a decision on the opportunity for an international instrument before August 2015,[32] thus indicating a clear deadline for the conclusion of the work of the BBNJ WG. The BBNJ WG concluded its work with the adoption of a recommendation to develop an international legally binding instrument under UNCLOS. Building on these conclusions, the UNGA established a preparatory committee to consider substantive issues related to this future instrument and to make a proposal regarding core elements of the future agreement. This committee met twice in 2016 and is expected to conclude its work in 2017.

The current legal framework and political processes related to the conservation of biodiversity in the high seas highlight the important role of

[29] For an account of BBNJ history, see E Druel, J Rochette, R Billé and C Chiarolla, 'A Long and Winding Road: International Discussions on the Governance of Marine Biodiversity in Areas beyond National Jurisdiction' (2013) 07/13 IDDRI study.

[30] Letter dated 30 June 2011 from Co-Chairs of the Ad Hoc Open-ended Informal Working Group to the President of the General Assembly, para I. 1 (a) and (b).

[31] 'Agenda 21', United Nations Conference on Environment & Development, UN Doc A/Conf.151/26 (1992) ch 17, para 49e.

[32] 'The Future We Want', outcome of the Rio+20 Conference on Sustainable Development, UN General Assembly Resolution 66/288, UN Doc A/RES/66/288 (2012) para 162.

third states in any co-operation aimed at conserving living resources in the High Arctic. First, in the absence of a legal framework, any instrument or mechanism to protect biodiversity in the high seas—such as the establishment of an MPA—would need to be particularly cognisant to the rights and interests of third states and to the justification of the selection of the area placed under protection.[33] In this context, regional arrangements lack the mandate to comprehensively regulate activities taking place in the high seas. Any measures adopted by a regional organisation would also fail to apply to third states. Secondly, non-Arctic states, such as China and the EU, have an important role to play in contributing to the BBNJ process and shaping the emergence of a future legal framework on this issue.

B. Regulating Fish Stocks in the High Seas

The weakness of the legal regime defined in 1982 by UNCLOS with regards to fish stocks located in the high seas caused tensions between fishing nations, in particular in relation to straddling fish stocks moving in between exclusive economic zones (EEZs) and high seas. Consequently, governments had agreed through the adoption of Agenda 21 to convey a conference to address specifically the issue of highly migratory and straddling fish stocks.[34] The conference resulted in the adoption in 1995 of an UNCLOS implementing agreement on Conservation and Management of Straddling Fish Stocks and Highly Migratory Fish Stocks.[35] The agreement mainly commits its parties to adopt measures to ensure the long-term sustainability of straddling and highly migratory fish stocks based on best scientific knowledge and on the precautionary principle.[36]

The agreement also insists on the duty for states to co-operate, specifically identifying Regional Fisheries Management Organisations (RFMOs) or arrangements as the preferred mechanism for co-operation.[37] The agreement stipulates that membership to such RFMOs or arrangements must be open to all states having a real interest in the fisheries concerned.

[33] IU Jakobsen, 'Marine Protected Areas as a Tool to ensure Environmental Protection of the Marine Arctic: Legal Aspects' in E Tedsen, S Cavalieri and A Kraemer (eds), *Arctic Marine Governance: Opportunities for Transatlantic Cooperation* (Heidelberg, Springer, 2014) 220; Y Tanaka, *The International Law of the Sea* (Cambridge, Cambridge University Press, 2012) 331.

[34] Agenda 21 (1992) ch 17.49(e).

[35] 1995 UN Agreement for the Implementation of the Provisions of the United Nations Convention on the Law of the Sea of 10 December 1992 relating to the Conservation and Management of Straddling Fish Stocks and Migratory Fish Stocks, in force 11 December 2001, 34 *International Legal Materials* 1542.

[36] ibid, arts 5 and 6.

[37] ibid, art 8.3.

The agreement establishes two innovations compared to the provisions of UNCLOS in relation to enforcement. First, it allows members of RFMOs to board and inspect vessels flying the flag of another country—including those flying the flags of countries not parties to the RFMO—[38] and it sets new rights for port states to inspect fishing vessels and adopt relevant measures.[39] These specific rights provide a strong incentive for coastal states and other states interested in a given stock to co-operate and establish RFMOs.

The provisions of the Fish Stocks Agreement nevertheless left several questions unaddressed. First, the scope of the agreement only applies to straddling and highly migratory stocks, thus excluding other fish stocks occurring in the high seas such as discrete high seas fish stocks. Secondly, the agreement does not provide a legal framework for the adoption by RFMOs of comprehensive conservation measures regulating other uses of the seas such as the establishment of MPAs.

Following the entry into force of the Fish Stocks Agreement, an informal process was initiated by the UNGA in order to consider the regional and global implementation of the agreement.[40] The process is meant to provide recommendations to the UNGA as well as to prepare the Review Conference mandated in the agreement.[41] The issue of MPAs in ABNJ was mentioned in the first sessions of the consultations but was removed from the agenda once the BBNJ WG was conveyed so as to avoid overlap between the two processes.[42]

III. CURRENT STATUS OF MARINE CONSERVATION IN THE ARCTIC

The overview of the legal framework applicable to the conservation of marine living resources in ABNJ highlights both the importance of regional co-operation and the need to consider the rights and positions of all states claiming a specific interest in the issue. The present section reviews relevant regional processes for international co-operation in the Arctic. Governance of Arctic marine living resources is addressed through two parallel processes. While the Arctic Council—the most prominent forum for regional co-operation—has considered the conservation of Arctic flora and fauna, issues related to fisheries in the High Arctic have been discussed recently

[38] ibid, art 21.

[39] ibid, art 23.

[40] UN General Assembly Resolution 56/13, 'Agreement for the Implementation of the Provisions of the United Nations Convention on the Law of the Sea of 10 December 1982 Relating to the Conservation and Management of Straddling Fish Stocks and Highly Migratory Fish Stocks', adopted on 28 November 2001, UN Doc A/RES/56/13, para 6.

[41] 1995 UN Fish Stocks Agreement, art 36.

[42] Informal Consultations of States Parties to the UN Fish Stocks Agreement; see for more information: www.un.org/depts/los/convention_agreements/fish_stocks_agreement_states_parties.htm.

by the five Arctic coastal states through a more informal platform. Consequently, marine conservation and fisheries management will be addressed in two subsections.

A. Regional Co-operation on the Marine Conservation in the Arctic

The Arctic states emphasised the importance of co-operating on the establishment of protected areas in the Arctic before the establishment of the Arctic Council. The Arctic Environmental Protection Strategy (AEPS) already described as one of its priorities the development of a network of protected areas.[43] The second AEPS ministerial meeting in 1993 considered the implementation of this principle. Ministers requested CAFF to prepare a plan for developing a network of Arctic protected areas, including the identification of a common process through which each Arctic state could promote the establishment of such areas.[44] This mandate became the priority for CAFF during the following years,[45] with CAFF focusing on the development of a series of reports to support the development of the Circumpolar Protected Areas Network (CPAN).[46] Building on this work, CAFF adopted in 1996 the CPAN Strategy and Action Plan, which identified as the main objective support for countries in addressing the gaps in the establishment of Arctic protected areas in their territory and filling remaining gaps within the area covered by the AEPS.[47] Through its second priority, CPAN could have played a particularly important role in addressing the fragmentation of conservation in the Arctic and guaranteeing the protection of large transboundary natural areas.[48] The Strategy and Action Plan identified 17 actions to be undertaken at the national level and seven actions at the circumpolar level.[49] Responding to a request by the ministers, CAFF prepared in 1997 a comprehensive progress report to assess the implementation of the CPAN Strategy in each of the Arctic states.[50]

1997, however, constituted a turning point in the work of CAFF as the working group developed a more comprehensive programme of work,

[43] Arctic Environmental Protection Strategy—The Declaration on the Protection of the Arctic Environment (Rovaniemi Declaration) (Rovaniemi, Finland, 14 January 1991) para 2.2(viii).

[44] Report of the AEPS second ministerial meeting (Nuuk, 16 September 1993) 13.

[45] T Koivurova, 'Governance of Protected Areas in the Arctic' (2009) 5(1) *Utrecht Law Review* 44, 49.

[46] CAFF Habitat Conservation Reports 1–5 (1994 and 1996). These Habitat Conservation Reports can be downloaded at www.caff.is/expert-groups-series/21-circumpolar-protected-areas-network-cpan.

[47] CAFF Habitat Conservation Report no 6 (1996).

[48] K Bastmeijer, "Protecting Polar Wilderness: Just a Western Philosophical Idea or a Useful Concept for Regulating Human Activities in the Polar Regions?' in G Alfredsson and T Koivurova (eds), (2009) 1 *Yearbook of Polar Law.*

[49] CAFF Habitat Conservation Report no 6 (1996) 20 and 21.

[50] CAFF Habitat Conservation Report no 7 (1997).

including a Co-operative Strategy for the Conservation of Biological Diversity in the Arctic Region.[51] Consequently, the CPAN project lost its prominence among the activities of CAFF.[52] In 2003, participants to the CAFF managerial board meeting noted that, despite its importance, CPAN had become mostly inactive.[53] Participants also noted that the establishment of protected areas was a domestic matter, in relation to which CAFF had only a very limited role to play, except in relation to marine areas. The simultaneous resignation of all three chairs of CPAN in 2004 brought the project to a halt, CPAN becoming almost dormant up to 2010.[54] In 2010, CPAN was finally discontinued as it was recognised that its mandate overlapped with other CAFF projects.[55]

The CAFF working group and its CPAN project were indeed not the only initiatives adopted by the Arctic Council with relevance to the establishment of MPAs in the Arctic. The opportunity to establish MPAs was also referred to in the activities of the Protection of the Arctic Marine Environment WG (PAME). Up to 2004, PAME did not address directly the establishment of MPAs. The issue was however mentioned in its Arctic Marine Strategic Plan (AMSP)—one of the most significant outcomes of the work of PAME.[56] The AMSP contained a list of strategic actions, which referred among other actions to the establishment of MPAs, including representative networks of protected areas.[57] This strategic action was suggested as a contribution to the Plan of Implementation adopted at the 2002 World Summit on Sustainable Development. The experience gathered through CPAN provided the impetus for the inclusion of this reference in the AMSP.[58] The key recommendations contained in the AMSP related however to integrated ocean and coastal management and to the implementation of an ecosystem-based ocean management approach. The actions suggested in the biennial work plans of the working group since 2004 have consequently focused on these two principles. The successive work plans have all lacked specific references to the opportunities for PAME to contribute to or promote the establishment of MPAs.[59]

More recently, the Arctic Biodiversity Assessment emphasised the importance of establishing MPAs to protect Arctic biodiversity. The recommendations

[51] Report of the CAFF WG to the Arctic Council SAO (1997) on file with the author.
[52] Koivurova 'Governance of Protected Areas in the Arctic' (n 45) 51.
[53] CAFF Managerial board meeting 2003, 16.
[54] Koivurova (n 45) 52.
[55] Information is available on the webpage of the CAFF WG: www.caff.is/expert-groups-series/21-circumpolar-protected-areas-network-cpan.
[56] Arctic Council, 'Arctic Marine Strategic Plan' (24 November 2004).
[57] ibid, para 7.3.2.
[58] Koivurova (n 45) 55.
[59] The work plans of PAME are available at www.pame.is/index.php/shortcode/pame-work-plan.

contained in the assessment included the following suggestion to protect large areas of ecologically important marine habitat:

> build upon existing and on-going domestic and international processes to complete the identification of ecologically and biologically important marine areas and implement appropriate measures for their conservation.[60]

The importance of establishing MPAs, including representative networks, in the Arctic was thus repeatedly emphasised in the projects of the Arctic Council during the past two decades. This emphasis failed however to result in any concrete actions being taken by the working groups of the Council. Consequently, no MPA has yet been established in ABNJ of the Arctic.

B. Towards a Regional Instrument to Govern Fisheries

Considering its very broad mandate to offer a platform for co-operation on 'common Arctic issues, in particular issues of sustainable development and environmental protection in the Arctic', the Arctic Council could consider issues related to Arctic fisheries.[61] To date, the Council has however avoided directly discussing matters related to Arctic fisheries.[62] In 2007, the US Senate highlighted the relevance of the issue with the adoption of a joint resolution calling for a moratorium on Arctic fisheries until an adequate instrument is adopted.[63] The US representative brought this resolution to the attention of the meeting of Arctic Senior Arctic Officials (SAOs) in November 2007. The SAOs however simply concluded that 'there was strong support for building on and considering this issue within the context of existing mechanisms'.[64]

Shortly after this decision not to tackle Arctic fisheries through the Arctic Council, the relevance of regional fishing co-operation was brought back in the context of another regional forum. While the Arctic states had always used the Arctic Council as the main venue for regional co-operation on Arctic matters, the five Arctic coastal states initiated a parallel co-operation process focused on maritime issues in 2008 through the convening of the first Arctic Ocean Conference. The Ilulissat Declaration resulting from this event affirmed the opinion of the Arctic coastal states that no new comprehensive

[60] Arctic Biodiversity Assessment (2013).

[61] Ottawa Declaration on the establishment of the Arctic Council (1996) art 1.

[62] E Molenaar, 'Arctic Fisheries and International Law' (2012) 6(1) *Carbon & Climate Law Review* 63, 70.

[63] US Senate Joint Resolution 17, Directing the United States to initiate international discussions and take necessary steps with other Nations to negotiate an agreement for managing migratory and transboundary fish stocks in the Arctic Ocean 110th Congress, 5 October 2007.

[64] Final Report of the Narvik SAO Meeting 2007; available at oaarchive.arctic-council.org/handle/11374/380 SAO report (Narvik, November 2007) 12.

legal instrument was required to govern the marine Arctic.[65] The Declaration also highlighted the commitment of the five coastal states to take appropriate steps to protect the Arctic marine environment.

> The Arctic Ocean is a unique ecosystem, which the five coastal states have a stewardship role in protecting.
>
> We will take steps in accordance with international law both nationally and in cooperation among the five states and other interested parties to ensure the protection and preservation of the fragile marine environment of the Arctic Ocean.[66]

The conference met strong opposition from the other participants in the Arctic Council (the three Arctic states lacking direct access to the Arctic Ocean as well as permanent participants), which denounced their exclusion from this new process.[67] While this criticism was met with sympathy by some of the coastal states,[68] the co-operation process among the five coastal states has nevertheless continued, albeit with a lower profile, more limited publicity and a more focused scope.

The next ministerial meeting of the Arctic coastal states took place in Canada in spring 2010. The ministers considered then more specifically the issue of future commercial fisheries in the Arctic. While they noted that 'large-scale commercial fishing in most of the Arctic Ocean is not imminent', the ministers also affirmed their 'unique interest and role to play in current and future efforts for the conservation and management of fish stocks in this region'.[69] This ministerial meeting was rapidly followed by another meeting at the level of senior officials, which concluded that there is a need to follow developments related to Arctic fisheries closely in order to prevent possible negative effects on fish stocks in the area.[70] The senior officials also initiated a process of scientific meetings on Arctic fish stocks to inform their discussions related to the governance of Arctic fisheries. Following a first scientific meeting, the senior officials emphasised that, while the scientific meeting

[65] The Ilulissat Declaration (2008) available at oceanlaw.org/downloads/arctic/Ilulissat_Declaration.pdf.

[66] ibid.

[67] See eg the concerns raised by the Icelandic government prior to the Arctic Ocean Conference, Final Report of the Narvik SAO Meeting 2007. See also the response to the Ilulissat Declaration by the Inuit Circumpolar Council: Statement issued by Inuit Leaders at the Inuit Leaders' Summit on Arctic Sovereignty, Kuujjuak, Canada (6–7 November 2008): 'Arctic Sovereignty Begins with Inuit'; available at www.sikunews.com/art.html?artid=5711&catid=2.

[68] See press reports of comments made by Secretary of State Hilary Clinton blaming Canada for not having invited 'those who have legitimate interests in the region' to the second Arctic coastal states ministerial meeting.

[69] See statement adopted at the ministerial meeting of the 5 Arctic coastal states, Churchill, 29 March 2010.

[70] See chair summary of the meeting of senior officials of the 5 Arctic coastal states, Oslo, 22 June 2010.

had confirmed the unlikelihood of High Arctic commercial fisheries in the short term,

> there was also general recognition of the desirability of addressing the possibility that commercial fishing could, at some point in the future, take place in the high seas area of the central Arctic Ocean.[71]

Consequently, the senior officials decided that, while no RFMO would be established in the short term, interim measures would be adopted in order to protect Arctic fish stocks. The interim measures were further elaborated in spring 2014. According to the interim measures, the coastal states commit to allowing vessels to fish in the high seas portions of the Arctic Ocean only within the framework of existing RFMOs.[72] Additionally, the interim measures include the commitment of the coastal states to co-operate in initiating research and in monitoring activities in the area. The senior officials called upon third states to apply similar interim measures.

The meeting also reaffirmed that other states may have an interest in this topic and announced that the Arctic 5 will broaden these discussions, involving additional states before the end of 2014. The purpose of the consultations would be to further develop a set of interim measures, including commitments by additional states. The Arctic 5 also indicated that these consultations might result in the initiation of a process towards the adoption of a regional legal instrument.[73] The senior officials emphasised that these consultations could result in a binding international agreement.[74] In summer 2015, the five coastal states adopted a formal ban on high Arctic fisheries. Following this decision, additional meetings were held in 2016 to consider how to secure the commitment of other fishing nations—including China and the EU—in these arrangements. Consultations with non-coastal states will continue to be crucial in order to guarantee the effectiveness of any measures or instrument that the coastal states might wish to adopt in order to regulate fisheries in the High Arctic beyond their respective EEZs.

IV. PERSPECTIVES OF NON-COASTAL STATES ON THE PROTECTION OF MARINE LIVING RESOURCES

While the international legal framework for the management of living resources in ABNJ emphasises the role of non-coastal states, regional co-operation in the Arctic has so far been driven only by Arctic states, in

[71] Chairman's Statement at Meeting on Future Arctic Fisheries, Washington, 29 April 2013, available at www.state.gov/e/oes/rls/pr/2013/209176.htm.

[72] Meeting on Arctic Fisheries, Nuuk, Greenland, 24–26 February 2014, Chairman's Statement.

[73] ibid.

[74] ibid.

particular the five coastal states. The study of the positions of key non-Arctic actors is therefore useful to assess the potential consequences of their deeper involvement in the governance of Arctic matters. Among non-Arctic actors, the positions of China and of the EU will be of particular relevance to the conservation of biodiversity in the High Arctic. China and the EU are indeed major global players in relation to the use of marine living resources.[75] Both have also emphasised their interest in becoming involved in Arctic governance, for instance through their application to the status of observer at the Arctic Council and their involvement in the activities of the Council.

A. China: Promoting the Perspective of Developing Countries and the Concept of Rational Use

The role of China as a distant water fishing nation has increased considerably since 1985 and the depletion of its domestic halieutic resources.[76] Marine living resources are perceived by the Chinese government as the largest stock of proteins, hence of particular long-term importance to feeding the country. The Chinese fishing industry has for instance been a pioneer in Antarctic krill fishing, an experience that might provide the country with a particular interest and stake in Arctic fish stocks. Future Arctic fish stocks were recently described by the former Chinese ambassador to Norway as the 'world's largest storehouse of biological protein'.[77] The position of the country on the management of fish stocks in the high seas and on conservation of biodiversity in ABNJ can thus be expected to influence the regime applicable to any future fisheries in the High Arctic.

The Chinese government has not made publicly available its official strategies or positions in relation to either Arctic fisheries or the negotiations currently ongoing in the BBNJ WG. Consequently, the future position of China on efforts to conserve marine living resources in the High Arctic must be deduced from its interventions in the working group as well as its positions in other related marine conservation and fisheries processes.

i. Biodiversity in Areas beyond National Jurisdiction

When negotiating under the BBNJ WG, China takes part in the G77/China coalition, which represents the perspectives of 133 developing countries.

[75] China is the world's largest fish producer and exporter and the EU is the most important importer of fishery products, representing 40% of total world imports (about half of these imports relate to intra-European trade). Food and Agriculture Organization, *The State of World Fisheries and Aquaculture* (2012) 16.

[76] T Mallory, 'China's Distant Water Fishing Industry: Evolving Policies and Implications' (2013) 38 *Marine Policy* 99, 101.

[77] ibid.

The country therefore does not need to make systematic interventions in order to promote its own positions but can often rely on the interventions made on behalf of the G77/China. Additionally, the position of China has evolved along the stages of the discussions in the working group. Consequently, and in the absence of an official policy position available publicly, isolated statements provide only limited insights with regards to the future priorities of the country.

The position of China on the opportunity for a new instrument to address issues related to BBNJ has evolved over the meetings of the working group. During the first sessions of the working group, China emphasised the need to fully implement UNCLOS and to deepen co-operation rather than to negotiate a new instrument.[78] At the seventh meeting of the working group, China however argued that 'the recognised gaps in the current legal framework and its fragmented nature demonstrate the need for a new instrument'.[79] In June 2014, it reiterated its support while requesting that consensus on the scope, parameters and feasibility of the agreement should be found before initiating the negotiations.[80]

Several other themes have been repeatedly emphasised in the interventions of the Chinese delegation. Throughout the process, China positioned itself as a champion of the interests of developing countries. The country repeatedly argued for the importance of considering capacity building and technology transfers for developing countries.[81] China also specifically emphasised the need to ensure the participation of developing countries in the governance of MPAs in ABNJ[82] and the importance of taking into consideration the legitimate concerns of developing countries about the use of BBNJ.[83]

Additionally, China repeatedly stressed the importance of promoting sustainable development in the high seas and avoiding any overemphasis on protection over sustainable use of marine biodiversity in ABNJ.[84] In relation

[78] Summary of the Second Meeting of the Working Group on Marine Biodiversity beyond Areas of National Jurisdiction: 28 April–2 May 2008 25(49) *Earth Negotiations Bulletin*; Third Meeting of the Working Group on Marine Biodiversity beyond Areas of National Jurisdiction: 1–5 February 2010 *Earth Negotiations Bulletin*, available at www.iisd.ca/oceans/marinebiodiv3/.

[79] Summary of the Seventh Meeting of the Working Group on Marine Biodiversity beyond Areas of National Jurisdiction: 1–4 April 2014 *Earth Negotiations Bulletin,* available at www.iisd.ca/oceans/marinebiodiv7/.

[80] Summary of the Eighth Meeting of the Working Group on Marine Biodiversity beyond Areas of National Jurisdiction: 16–19 June 2014 *Earth Negotiations Bulletin*, available at www.iisd.ca/oceans/marinebiodiv8/.

[81] Summaries of the Second, Third and Seventh Meetings of the BBNJ-WG (respectively 2008, 2010 and 2014).

[82] Summary of the Third Meeting of the BBNJ-WG (2010).

[83] Summary of the Fourth Meeting of the Working Group on Marine Biodiversity beyond Areas of National Jurisdiction: 31 May–3 June 2011 25(66) *Earth Negotiations Bulletin.*

[84] Summaries of the Third, Fourth, Fifth and Sixth Meetings of the BBNJ-WG (respectively 2010, 2011, 2012, and 2013).

to the establishment of MPAs in ABNJ, the country insisted on the need for any MPA network to be 'limited to a rational proportion of the Convention area so as not to compromise national use'.[85]

These main themes are also reflected in the Chinese interventions or positions adopted in other international processes. The emphasis of China on the specific needs of developing countries is also the most consistent theme of the interventions of the country in the UNICPOLOS. China insisted on the need for technology transfer to and capacity building of developing countries in six of the sessions of the UNICPOLOS.[86]

ii. Management of Fisheries in Areas beyond National Jurisdiction

The emphasis of China on rational use of marine living resources was also reflected in the positions promoted by the country in several Regional Fisheries Management Organisations (RFMOs). This position received much publicity when advocated in the context of the Commission for the Conservation of Antarctic Marine Living Resources (CCAMLR). The CCAMLR, established in 1980, has been successful at conserving some of the resources under its scope through the adoption of measures in specific geographic areas.[87] The CCAMLR worked during the past decade to establish a network of MPAs when carrying out the Johannesburg Plan of Implementation. In 2012, the establishment of MPAs in the Ross Sea and the East Antarctic was suggested to the Commission. These proposals would have effectively established a network of MPAs in the Southern Ocean. The suggestions were rejected amidst concerns raised by several countries. China in particular questioned the legal competence of the CCAMLR to establish MPAs in areas beyond national jurisdiction.[88] During a special meeting of the Commission conveyed to consider the issue of MPAs, China emphasised the definition of the concept of 'conservation' under the CCAMLR as including 'rational use'.[89] China thus underlined the need for any MPA to take into account the legitimate right of all parties to conduct fisheries in the convention area as well as the importance of securing sufficient scientific data prior to the adoption of any MPA.[90]

[85] Summary of the Sixth Meeting of the BBNJ-WG (2013).

[86] Chinese interventions during the Fifth (2004), Eighth (2007), Eleventh (2010), Twelfth (2011), Fourteenth (2013) and Fifteenth (2014) sessions of UNICPOLOS. See reports of the Earth Negotiating Bulletin of the sessions of the UNICPOLOS, available at www.iisd.ca/oceans/.

[87] C Brooks, 'Competing Values on the Antarctic High Seas: CCAMLR and the Challenge of Marine-protected Areas' (2013) 3(2) *The Polar Journal* 277, 280.

[88] ibid, 289.

[89] Convention on the Conservation of Antarctic Marine Living Resources, 1980, 19 *International Legal Materials* 841, art II.2.

[90] CCAMLR, Report of the Second Special Meeting of the Commission, CCAMLR-SM-II, 10.

China is not a party to the Fish Stocks Agreement, which has important relevance to Arctic fish stocks.[91] The country signed the agreement but refused to ratify it due to disagreement over enforcement authorisation and use of force during inspections of fishing vessels by authorities other than the flag state.[92] The country nevertheless joined most RFMOs established to regulate highly migratory fish stocks.[93] China is also participating actively in the informal consultation process and has taken part in the Fish Stock Agreement review conference in 2010 as a non-party bureau member. The country has however denounced the current interpretation of the agreement as 'first come, first served', which favours countries joining regional fisheries instruments in their earlier stages. It called for a more equitable share of global fisheries.[94] This concern could motivate the country to join any Arctic co-operation mechanism in its early stages.

In its assessment of Chinese distant water fishing, Mallory concluded that, despite capacity challenges, China has generally demonstrated its willingness to participate and to co-operate with RFMOs.[95] This participation has however been described as generally passive, the country proposing few initiatives within these regimes.[96] Mallory also emphasised that distant water fishing practices of developed countries play an important role in shaping China's own practices.[97] While Chinese fisheries do contribute significantly to global Illegal, Unreported, and Unregulated (IUU) fishing, these activities are concentrated in regions with poor levels of governance.[98] Consequently, it is rather unlikely that the Chinese fleet undermines any regional management mechanism in the Arctic through IUU activities.

This analysis thus suggests that China is likely to become involved in—as well as comply with—any regional mechanism established to manage High Arctic fisheries. The review of the interventions by China at the BBNJ WG thus highlights that the country has promoted two key themes throughout this process. First, China has advocated for the consideration of special interests for developing countries. Secondly, the country has repeatedly emphasised rational use rather than conservation. The positions adopted by China in other processes confirm this assessment.

[91] Information obtained from www.un.org/Depts/los.

[92] Declaration of China upon signature of the Fish Stocks Agreement www.un.org/depts/los/convention_agreements/fish_stocks_agreement_declarations.htm#CHINA.

[93] R Blomeyer, I Goulding, D Pauly, A Sanz and K Stobberup, 'The Role of China in World Fisheries' Study commissioned by the European Parliament, Directorate General for Internal Affairs (2012) 70.

[94] Summary of the Eighth Round of Informal Consultations of States Parties to the UN Fish Stocks Agreement: 16–19 March 2009 7(64) *Earth Negotiating Bulletin*.

[95] Mallory, 'China's Distant Water Fishing Industry' (n 76).

[96] Blomeyer, Goulding, Pauly, Sanz and Stobberup, *The Role of China in International Fisheries* (n 93) 70.

[97] ibid, 107.

[98] Mallory (n 76) 7.

B. The EU: A Strong Supporter of a Framework to Conserve Marine Ecosystems in Areas beyond National Jurisdiction

The EU is undeniably another key international actor with a particular interest in Arctic governance. While three member states of the EU are members of the Arctic Council, the EU is also in a position similar to that of China as it is also a non-coastal actor in the Arctic.[99] The relevance of the EU as an actor in the Arctic—as opposed to the role of its individual member states—must be understood in the context of the division of competences between the Union and the member states.[100] The Treaty on the Functioning of the EU stipulates for which policy areas the EU has exclusive competence (the EU makes decisions on behalf of all its member states), shared competence (decisions are made jointly by the EU and its individual member states) or complementary competences (the EU might only support policies of its member states but refrain from decision-making in these areas). According to this treaty, the EU has exclusive competence with regards to the conservation of marine biological resources under the common fisheries policy[101] and shared competence in relation to other fisheries matters and the protection of the environment.[102] Consequently, the EU itself (rather than its individual member states) has a particular role to play in contributing to the governance of marine ecosystems.

Compared to that of China, the position of the EU with regards to the conservation of marine living resources in the Arctic can be inferred not only from the positions promoted by the EU in international forums but also from its official policy papers and frameworks. Policy documents produced by the EU in relation to both Arctic governance and marine policy provide information relevant to the current research.

i. Biodiversity in Areas beyond National Jurisdiction

Since the establishment of the BBNJ WG, the EU has championed proposals for the adoption of a new implementing agreement under UNCLOS. At the first meeting of the working group, the EU advocated for the adoption of an agreement fully implementing the precautionary principle and providing a legal framework for the establishment of MPAs in ABNJ.[103]

[99] Sweden and Finland do not have direct access to the Arctic Ocean and Greenland (through which Denmark possesses its access to the Arctic Ocean) is not part of the EU.

[100] T Koivurova, K Kokko, S Duyck, N Sellheim and A Stepien, 'The Present and Future Competence of the European Union in the Arctic' (2012) 48(4) *Polar Record* 361.

[101] Consolidated version of the Treaty on the Functioning of the European Union OJ C 83 (30 March 2010) art 3.1(d).

[102] ibid, art 4.1(d) and (e).

[103] Summary of the First Meeting of the Working Group on Marine Biodiversity beyond Areas of National Jurisdiction: 13–17 February 2006 25(25) *Earth Negotiations Bulletin*.

The EU also suggested that priority be given to this proposal in order to facilitate the adoption of such an agreement in the short term. Faced with the difficulty of securing broad support for this proposal, the EU modified its position at the second meeting of the working group, suggesting that the adoption of an agreement should be considered as a mid-term priority.[104] It also acknowledged the importance of implementing other measures while the agreement is negotiated and made pragmatic proposals in discussions about additional issues such as access and benefit sharing of marine genetic resources—a theme particularly important to many developing countries.

Building on this pragmatic approach, the EU formed at the fourth session of the working group a coalition with the G77/China and Mexico to propose the adoption of a package approach to the negotiations in order to ensure that several issues would be addressed in parallel.[105] This package approach gave assurances to many countries that the issues most important for them would remain on the agenda and facilitated the reaching of a consensus. Since then, at each session the EU has continued to urge all countries to support the opening of negotiations towards an implementing agreement under UNCLOS to address, inter alia, conservation of marine ecosystems in ABNJ, including through the establishment of a network of multi-purpose MPAs in ABNJ.[106]

The proposal of an implementing agreement on BBNJ and work towards the establishment of MPAs in the high seas are also two of the key elements identified in the EU Integrated Marine Policy to promote European leadership in International Maritime Affairs.[107]

In its Arctic policy documents, the EU institutions have repeatedly emphasised the importance of promoting the establishment of a network of MPAs in the Arctic.[108] The 2008 Arctic Communication of the European Commission also highlighted the role that the EU could play to promote the negotiations taking place at the BBNJ WG.[109] The most recent resolution adopted by the European Parliament on the Arctic provides the most concrete proposal with regards to the conservation of Arctic marine ecosystems, calling EU and EEA countries (Norway and Iceland) to support the achievement of

[104] Summary of the Second Meeting of the BBNJ-WG (2008).

[105] Summary of the Fourth Meeting of the BBNJ-WG (2011).

[106] See eg the EU intervention to the BBNJ-WG on 16 June 2014, available at euccnews.files.wordpress.com/2014/07/eu-bbnj-june-meeting-openingstatementbydranastasiastrati1.pdf.

[107] European Commission, 'An Integrated Maritime Policy for the European Union' COM(2007) 575 final, 14, 10 October 2007.

[108] European Commission, 'The European Union and the Arctic Region' COM(2008) 763 final, 20 November 2008; Council of the European Union, 'Conclusions on Arctic Issues', 2985th Foreign Affairs Council meeting (2009); European Parliament, 'Resolution on a Sustainable EU Policy for the High North' (2011) 2009/2214(INI).

[109] European Commission, 'The EU and the Arctic Region' (n 108).

the Aichi target in the Arctic and emphasising the need to protect the high seas located around the North Pole.[110]

ii. Management of Fisheries in the High Arctic

In their Arctic policy documents, EU institutions have repeatedly highlighted their commitment to the full implementation of the precautionary principle with regards to High Arctic fisheries, urging the adoption of a legal framework before any fisheries are established in the area.[111]

Between 2008 and 2012, the EU expressed its preference for the extension of the mandate of existing RFMOs, such as the NEAFC and the Northwest Atlantic Fisheries Organisation (NAFO), over the establishment of a new regional arrangement.[112] In its 2014 resolution dedicated to the Arctic, the European Parliament expressed its support for the approach adopted by the five coastal states.[113] The EU institutions have also highlighted the role and responsibility of the EU not only as fishing nations but also as the largest consumer of Arctic fish products.[114]

In line with its emphasis on the implementation of the precautionary approach to new fisheries, the EU also attempted to raise the issue of Arctic fisheries in the context of the UNGA discussions in 2009 on oceans and on sustainable fisheries.[115] This proposal to single out Arctic fisheries was, however, not reflected in the UNGA resolutions.

V. CONCLUSION

While the Arctic coastal states have emphasised their stewardship with regards to the protection of the Arctic marine environment, there is currently no legal mechanism established specifically to protect marine living

[110] European Parliament Resolution (n 5). This proposal had also been previously endorsed by Finland in its 2013 Arctic Strategy. See Finland's Strategy for the Arctic Region 2013, Government Resolution of 23 August 2013, 59.

[111] European Commission, 'The EU and the Arctic Region' (n 108); Council of the EU, 'Conclusions on Arctic Issues' (n 108); European Parliament Resolution (n 108); European Commission, 'Joint Communication: Developing a European Union Policy towards the Arctic Region: Progress since 2008 and Next Steps' JOIN(2012) 19 final; European Parliament, 'Resolution on the Arctic' (n 5).

[112] European Commission, 'The EU and the Arctic Region' (n 108); Council of the European Union, 'Conclusions on Arctic Issues' (n 108); European Commission, 'Joint Communication' (n 111).

[113] European Parliament, 'Resolution on the Arctic' (n 5).

[114] European Commission, 'The EU and the Arctic Region' (n 108); European Commission, 'Joint Communication' (n 111).

[115] Molenaar, 'Arctic Fisheries and International Law' (n 62).

resources in the High Arctic. The thawing of the summer sea ice might offer promises of new economic opportunities further North than at any time in the past, thus making international co-operation on marine conservation in the High North increasingly relevant. While commercial fishing is unlikely to take place on a large scale in the High Arctic in the short term, the coming years offer opportunities for coastal states—and other potentially interested actors—to establish an effective mechanism to manage any future fisheries in the region.

Legal options to protect biodiversity in the high seas areas of the Arctic Ocean are likely to be influenced by the ongoing process initiated by the UNGA. At the time of the writing of this chapter, the content of the recommendations prepared by the BBNJ WG remains uncertain, especially with regards to the opportunity to initiate negotiations towards an implementing agreement under UNCLOS. Even if the preparatory committee was to conclude its work successfully in 2017, this process would require many years to be concluded, with additional time required afterwards prior to the entry into force of any legal outcome.

Negotiations for a regional solution could offer a satisfactory approach in the meantime. Any such regional agreement could then be 'upgraded' once a potential implementing agreement on BBNJ has entered into force in order to be brought in compliance with the provisions of the new implementing agreement.[116] Until a global agreement is adopted, strengthening co-operation through existing organisations could already improve the international framework for conservation of BBNJ.[117]

In both cases, the provisions of UNCLOS suggest that the rights and perspectives of any state with an interest in Arctic marine living resources will need to be taken into consideration in the development of regional mechanisms or instruments. While the Arctic Council—the most prominent forum for circumpolar co-operation—has institutionalised (limited) opportunities for non-Arctic states to voice their perspectives, no such opportunity is currently provided in the context of the co-operation among the five Arctic coastal states on matters related to the Arctic Ocean.

The review of the positions promoted by China and the EU in relation to marine conservation and fisheries management in ABNJ highlighted that non-coastal states are likely to have significantly different perspectives on how the Arctic marine ecosystems should be governed. China has, for instance, repeatedly highlighted the need for a pragmatic approach to the conservation of biodiversity in the high seas—emphasising rational use of

[116] See Rochette et al, "The Regional Approach to the Conservation of Marine Biodiversity' (n 21) 116.

[117] J Ardron, R Rayfuse, K Gjerde and R Warner, 'The Sustainable Use and Conservation of Biodiversity in ABNJ: What Can Be Achieved Using Existing International Agreements?' (2014) 49 *Marine Policy* 98.

resources over conservation. The country also stressed the importance of taking the specific interests of developing countries into consideration—a theme that has been absent from Arctic co-operation up to now. On the other hand, the EU has championed more principles-based approaches, suggesting stronger legal frameworks and a key role for the implementation of the precautionary principles.

If they intend to regulate effectively the conservation of Arctic marine living resources, the Arctic states will thus need to recognise the rights of non-coastal states and to enable the participation of any interested state in related regional processes. Given the diverging views existing among non-Arctic states on these issues, the five coastal states would need to accommodate a diversity of interests and positions supported by key non-Arctic players and play a facilitating role in the development of regional marine governance.

10

Incentives, Practices and Opportunities for Arctic External Actors' Engagement with Indigenous Peoples

China and the European Union

ADAM STEPIEN

I. INTRODUCTION

THE CHAPTER COMPARES the European Union—an actor that is fairly experienced in engaging with Arctic indigenous peoples—to China, a recent newcomer to Arctic affairs. The chapter also discusses reasons why such engagement is needed and advantageous for both Arctic peoples and external actors.[1] That is particularly important to highlight for China, as comparatively a newcomer to Arctic affairs. The discussion is based on the EU's and China's stances regarding Arctic indigenous peoples, as well as general statements and actions referring to indigenous rights and issues globally. That includes positions on indigenous rights within the UN system, as well as guidelines/policies relevant for development co-operation or overseas activities of European and Chinese state and private actors. This is particularly interesting for this research project due to the lack of comprehensive Chinese Arctic policy statements.

In order to provide background for the discussion, first an overview of the role of the indigenous peoples in Arctic governance is presented. Then, the reasons why external actors should engage with Arctic indigenous peoples are identified: the requirements arising from the observer status in the Arctic Council as well as the relevance of non-Arctic actors for Arctic

[1] The term 'external actors' is used here despite the elements of a more direct presence of the EU and China in the region.

peoples primarily due to their environmental footprint and economic leverage. Building on this background, China's and EU's engagement with Arctic indigenous peoples and their organisations is discussed. That is followed by the analysis of stances towards indigenous rights and problems in general, including relevant standards guiding behaviour of private actors. The chapter concludes with general recommendations, with a particular emphasis on issues relevant for China's future presence in the region.

II. INDIGENOUS PEOPLES: ACTORS NOT TO BE NEGLECTED IN ARCTIC GOVERNANCE

Indigenous peoples constitute about 10 per cent of the population of the Arctic within the boundaries defined by the Arctic Human Development Report[2] and contribute significantly to Arctic cultural diversity. Different groups vary greatly in terms of their livelihoods, economic situation, legal situation and participation in decision-making.

From the inception of the global indigenous movement in the 1970s, the world's indigenous peoples have achieved much at the international and national level.[3] This is clearly visible in the incorporation of indigenous dimensions into international documents, such as the 1992 Convention on Biological Diversity[4] (CBD, art 8j on traditional knowledge and practices), and especially in the adoption of two international instruments dealing specifically with indigenous rights: the 1989 ILO Convention 169 on the Rights of Indigenous and Tribal Peoples in Independent Countries[5] (replacing the earlier ILO Convention 107, which displayed an assimilationist approach) and the 2007 UN Declaration on the Rights of Indigenous Peoples.[6]

The Arctic regions have been from the beginning at the forefront of the normative, legal and governance shift towards acknowledgement of indigenous rights and establishment of participatory decision-making mechanisms. That can be attributed to the existence of capable indigenous elites, and comparative vitality of Arctic cultures coupled with the development of major resource extraction projects affecting indigenous lands in the region. At the same time, Nordic and North American states gradually endorsed minority and indigenous rights and started to address indigenous demands.

[2] Arctic Human Development Report (AHDR) (Akureyri, Stefansson Arctic Institute, 2004).

[3] R Niezen, *The Origins of Indigenism* (Oakland, University of California Press, 2003).

[4] Convention on Biological Diversity, 1760 UNTS 79/31 *International Legal Materials* 818 (1992).

[5] International Labour Organisation (ILO) Convention no 169 concerning Indigenous and Tribal Peoples in Independent Countries, Geneva, 27 June 1989, in force 5 September 1991, 1650 UNTS 383.

[6] UN Declaration on the Rights of Indigenous Peoples. General Assembly Resolution, 61st Regular Session, New York, 13 September 2007.

Concurrently, the region saw the rise of indigenous movements.[7] The Arctic indigenous organisations, most notably the Inuit Tapiriit Kanatami (ITK—association of Inuit in Canada), Inuit Circumpolar Council (ICC, earlier Conference established in 1977), the Sámi Council (functioning since 1956) and the Russian Association of the Small Peoples of the North, Siberia and Far East (RAIPON, from the end of the 1980s), have gradually become influential actors both in domestic politics and internationally. The first meeting of indigenous peoples from around the circumpolar North took place in Copenhagen in 1973 and preceded the first global indigenous summit in Port Alberni, Canada in 1975.[8]

As a result, starting from the 1970s the way in which the North is governed has been changing. In 1971, the development of oil and plans to construct a pipeline for the transport of oil from Prudhoe Bay fields resulted in the Alaska Native Claims Settlement Act (ANCSA), giving Alaskan native communities ownership over large areas previously controlled by the federal government, thereby engaging them into the market economy. In Canada, land claims settlements, especially in the Inuit regions (a prominent example being the Inuvialuit Final Agreement in the Western Arctic), introduced co-management structures throughout Arctic Canada. In the case of the Nunavut Land Claims Agreement (covering the Eastern Arctic), the settlement also led to the establishment of a new territory, Nunavut, with an Inuit majority and a number of autonomous policy areas under Inuit-controlled territorial government.[9] Greenland gained home rule from Denmark in 1979 and self-government in 2009, and thus the government in Nuuk currently has a broad spectrum of powers and competences. In Finland, Norway and Sweden, Sámi parliaments were established as elected representative institutions. Sámi Parliaments are primarily consultative bodies, including in matters relevant for land use planning or extractive industries, but over time have also gained decision-making powers in areas such as education, culture and language. In addition, the 2005 Finnmark Act established an (ongoing) process of defining the rights to land in Norway's northernmost county, with the Sámi Parliament and Sámi reindeer herders playing a vital role in the process.[10] In Russia, the position of the indigenous peoples is comparatively the weakest, especially in the context of oil and gas developments. The main indigenous organisation—RAIPON—had recently experienced a major setback in its relations with the authorities, as its activities had

[7] See eg AHDR (n 2).

[8] Niezen, *The Origins of Indigenism* (n 3).

[9] BS Zellen, *Breaking the Ice: From Land Claims to Tribal Sovereignty in the Arctic* (Plymouth, Lexington Books, 2008).

[10] A Stepien et al, 'Arctic Indigenous Peoples and the Challenge of Climate Change' in E Tedsen, S Cavalieri and RA Kraemer (eds), *Arctic Marine Governance: Opportunities for Transatlantic Cooperation* (Heidelberg, Springer, 2014).

been temporarily suspended. However, also in Russia indigenous actors are present and active at the local and regional governance levels.[11]

These developments have been reflected in the venues of Arctic co-operation. During the Rovaniemi Process—the early years of the Arctic Environmental Protection Strategy[12]—indigenous organisations (ICC, RAIPON and the Sámi Council) were present as observers or members of state delegations. Following the 1996 Ottawa Declaration,[13] their status had transformed to that of permanent participants in the Arctic Council. Indigenous organisations gained equal participation in the discussion, although not in decision-making, which means that they have to be consulted before consensus decisions are made by the eight Arctic states and they have a role in agenda-setting.[14] The formal positioning of permanent participants in the Council is thus much stronger than for instance that of observer states, which constitutes one of the unique features of the organisation.[15] The role of indigenous organisations is even more prominent due to the consensual format of decision-making within the Council. If all permanent participants are strongly opposed to certain decisions (eg the content of policy recommendations based on scientific assessments), it is likely that at least one Arctic state supports the indigenous standpoint. Moreover, in order for projects to be accepted by the Council, the support of as many actors as possible is vital and the point of view of permanent participants may constitute a key leverage.[16] This is of particular importance for the observers, who can propose projects either through an Arctic state or a permanent participant, but also need to acquire broad support in the Council in order to see it eventually accepted. Consequently, the relationship with indigenous peoples is relevant for the effectiveness of the EU's and China's participation in the Arctic Council's work.

[11] See eg F Stammler, 'Oil without Conflict? The Anthropology of Industrialisation in Northern Russia' in A Behrends, S P Reyna, and G Schlee (eds), *Crude Domination: An Anthropology of Oil* (Oxford, Berghahn Books 2011) 243–69.

[12] Arctic Environment Protection Strategy (AEPS) 30 *International Legal Materials* 1624 (1991).

[13] Declaration on the Establishment of the Arctic Council (Ottawa Declaration) and Joint Communique of the Governments of the Arctic Countries on the Establishment of the Arctic Council, 19 September 1996, 35 *International Legal Materials* 1385–90 (1996).

[14] T Koivurova and L Heinämäki, 'The Participation of Indigenous Peoples in International Norm-making in the Arctic' (2006) 42 *Polar Record* 101; S Duyck, 'Polar Environmental Governance and Non-state Actors' in R Pincus and SH Ali (eds), *Diplomacy on Ice: Energy and the Environment in the Arctic and Antarctic* (London, Yale University Press, 2015, in press).

[15] An important role here can be attributed to the activities of the Indigenous Peoples' Secretariat, established in 1994 and currently being partly merged with the new Council's permanent secretariat in Tromsø. The secretariat supports logistically the work of permanent participants and facilitates communication between the Council and its working groups and permanent participants.

[16] Koivurova and Heinämäki, 'The Participation of Indigenous Peoples in International Norm-making in the Arctic' (n 14); M Tennberg, *The Arctic Council. A Study in Governmentality* Acta Universitatis Lapponiensis 19 (Rovaniemi, University of Lapland, 1998) 126–29.

Overall, as major non-Arctic or near-Arctic actors have become interested in the regional affairs, the indigenous peoples have gained a non-negligible level of influence on decision-making and governance throughout the Arctic. They are able to influence the ways in which particular development projects are conducted, decision-making at national level and assessment and decision-making processes in the Arctic Council, and are present in many international venues where regulatory frameworks of relevance for the Arctic are shaped. This has been the case for the Stockholm Convention on Persistent Organic Pollutants,[17] where Arctic indigenous organisations—particularly the ICC—played a crucial role in the negotiations and in the earlier assessment work within the Arctic Council.[18] The ICC is still active in the screening process for new substances listed as candidate persistent organic pollutants (POPs).[19]

III. CHINA'S AND EU'S IMPACT ON ARCTIC INDIGENOUS PEOPLES' LIVELIHOODS AND INTERESTS

China and the EU can influence the Arctic region and its indigenous communities through: (1) their environmental footprint, primarily connected with climate change and long-range pollution; (2) the economic leverage through which they play a role in shaping development trends in the region; (3) economic activities of companies subject to their jurisdiction, as well as (4) their influence on international legal frameworks of relevance for the Arctic. Furthermore, Arctic research programmes conducted by external actors are of interest for indigenous peoples.

The Arctic is a globalised space and especially changes in demand for resources originating from the Arctic have major influence on the region's economies. Although Arctic indigenous communities are diverse in their livelihoods and have undergone rapid processes of modernisation over the last century, they are in general still intimately connected and dependent on nature. This is primarily due to the relatively high consumption of food originating from harvesting, hunting, gathering or herding as well as the central position of traditional practices in indigenous cultures.[20]

The most widely discussed challenge for Arctic indigenous peoples is the changing climate, which affects the cryosphere and impacts both the

[17] Stockholm Convention on Persistent Organic Pollutants (adopted 22 May 2001, entered into force 17 May 2004) 2256 UNTS 119 (Stockholm Convention).

[18] DL Downie and T Fenge (eds), *Northern Lights against POPs: Combatting Toxic Threats in the Arctic* (Montreal, McGill-Queen's University Press, 2003).

[19] See 'Persistent Organic Pollutants' at ICC website, www.inuitcircumpolar.com/persistent-organic-pollutants-pops.html.

[20] Stepien et al, 'Arctic Indigenous Peoples and the Challenge of Climate Change' (n 10); ACIA 2005, *Arctic Climate Impact Assessment* (Arctic Council, Cambridge University Press, 2005); AHDR (n 2).

terrestrial and maritime environment.[21] Hunting, fishing and reindeer herding are dependent on the weather as well as ice and snow conditions. In some cases, traditional knowledge relevant for hunting or fishing becomes insufficient to conduct these activities successfully and safely in the light of the changing climate. Community infrastructure—including houses, water and power sources constructed on permafrost—become vulnerable. Coastal communities are exposed to storm surges and coastal erosion.[22]

In terms of influence on climate change, the footprints of China and the EU depend primarily on their CO_2 emissions. China is the largest emitter with 29 per cent of global emissions in 2012 (9900 million tonnes of CO_2, 7.1 tonnes of CO_2 per person). The EU is responsible for roughly 11 per cent of global emissions (3700 million tonnes, 7.4 tonnes per person). However, the EU and China bear different historical responsibility for the current levels of CO_2 in the atmosphere,[23] and much of China's emissions are connected with the production consumed, inter alia, in Europe. In addition, the emissions of black carbon from both inside the region and more southerly latitudes (especially north of the 40th parallel north) affect the Arctic through changing the albedo of the snow and ice surfaces, contributing to increased melting and greater absorption of solar energy.[24] Both China and the EU are major black carbon emitters. Europe is the largest contributor to surface black carbon in the Arctic (due to high latitude and proximity to the region) while East Asia is the largest contributor to black carbon in the upper troposphere owing to air transport directions.[25]

Similarly to black carbon, POPs and other long-range pollutants like mercury can be transported by wind or ocean currents into the Arctic, a region which, due to wind and current patterns, may be considered a pollution sink.[26] POPs are deposited in the tissue of animals and humans and have noticeable effects on the health of Arctic indigenous communities, especially those highly dependent on traditional sources of food.[27] The Inuit

[21] M Strahlendorff et al, 'Climate Change in the Arctic' in A Stepien, T Koivurova and P Kankaanpää (eds), *Strategic Assessment of Development of the Arctic: Assessment Conducted for the European Union* (Arctic Centre, University of Lapland, 2014).

[22] Stepien (n 10).

[23] T Wei et al, 'Developed and Developing World Responsibilities for Historical Climate Change and CO_2 Mitigation' (2012) 109 *Proceedings of the National Academy of Sciences* 32, 12911.

[24] Arctic Monitoring and Assessment Programme (AMAP) (PK Quinn et al), *The Impact of Black Carbon on Arctic Climate* (2011).

[25] United States Environmental Protection Agency, *Report to Congress on Black Carbon* (2012) ch 3: 'Emissions of Black Carbon', www.epa.gov/blackcarbon/2012report/Chapter4.pdf.

[26] AMAP *Arctic Pollution 2009: Persistent Organic Pollutants, Radioactivity, Human Health* (2009) 1.

[27] AMAP reports: *AMAP Assessment Report: Arctic Pollution Issues* (1998); *Arctic Pollution 2002: Persistent Organic Pollutants, Heavy Metals, Radioactivity, Human Health, Changing Pathways* (2002); Downie and Fenge (eds), *Northern Lights Against POPs* (n 18).

have therefore emphasised that long-range contamination makes the very bases of their culture literally poisonous.[28]

While the global emissions of some POPs have decreased significantly, partly due to the adoption of the aforementioned Stockholm POPs Convention,[29] other pollutants are still of major concern for Arctic communities.[30] To give only a couple of examples, Europe contributed to 35 per cent of HCB (hexachlorobenzene) depositions over the Arctic while South-Eastern Asia is responsible for 12 per cent, and the EU is a source region for 42 per cent of SO_2 deposits while 11 per cent comes from East Asia. PCB-153 emissions from Europe constitute above 50 per cent of the total emissions affecting the Arctic.[31] Moreover, 'about half the mercury deposition to the Arctic is due to the atmospheric transport from anthropogenic emission sources, of which the greatest contribution is made by Asian (33%) and European sources (22%)'.[32] The recently adopted Minamata Mercury Convention[33] gives hope for the gradual decrease in the presence of mercury in the environment, but only in a long-term perspective.

Apart from long-range pollution and climate change, Arctic external actors impact the Arctic environment also locally, via the actions of their extractive, shipping and tourist companies or the economic influence they have on a wide spectrum of Arctic developments. Here, the policies shaping demand on resources or products originating from the region are of key relevance. For example, the EU's final demand for products from SO_2-intensive Arctic industries has been estimated at 38 per cent of the global demand, final demand for products from mercury-intensive Arctic industries at 36 per cent, and the EU's final demand for products from the Arctic oil and gas industry at 24 per cent.[34] The demand for oil, gas and minerals is particularly critical for indigenous livelihoods, as it drives hydrocarbon and mineral developments, which are of major concern for indigenous communities and the Arctic environment. This demand is generated primarily by markets outside of the region, such as the EU and China.

[28] Downie and Fenge (n 18).

[29] Stockholm Convention (n 17).

[30] See eg AMAP, *AMAP Assessment 2009: Human Health in the Arctic* (2009).

[31] Ecologic Institute et al (S Cavalieri et al) *EU Arctic Footprint and Policy Assessment* (European Commission, 2010) arctic-footprint.eu.

[32] O Travnikov, 'Contribution of the Intercontinental Atmospheric Transport to Mercury Pollution in the Northern Hemisphere' (2005) 39 *Atmospheric Environment* 7541.

[33] Minamata Convention on Mercury (adopted 10 October 2013 at Kumamoto). On the status of the Convention, see the UNEP website of the Minamata Convention on Mercury at www.mercuryconvention.org.

[34] Ecologic Institute et al, *EU Arctic Footprint and Policy Assessment* (n 31); for methodology and data, see the full report; see also A Neumann and B Rudloff, *Impact of EU Policies on the High North. The Cases of Climate Policy and Fisheries*, Standard Briefing (European Parliament, Directorate-General for External Policies of the Union, 2010); T Koivurova et al, 'The Present and Future Competence of the European Union in the Arctic' (2012) 48 *Polar Record* 361.

The EU has made an attempt to assess its environmental footprint (and associated economic leverage) by commissioning the EU Arctic Footprint and Policy Assessment study,[35] allowing for better understanding of the actual role and place of the EU in Arctic change, and consequently, its influence on the Arctic peoples. For instance, EU tourists constitute between 25 per cent and 30 per cent of all tourists visiting the Arctic, the EU's share in fish imports from Arctic countries is at 39 per cent,[36] and vessels flying EU member states' flags or owned by EU-based companies can be estimated to constitute between 30 and 50 per cent of Arctic shipping.[37]

Chinese actors may affect Arctic habitats and peoples more directly through the investments of Chinese companies in places like Greenland, northern Canada or Siberia. Projects such as pipelines, mines, shipping or transport infrastructure have numerous impacts on lands and territories used by indigenous communities and have proven to significantly affect their livelihoods and wellbeing over the last century. A good example is the planned iron ore mine near Nuuk, Greenland. The project is—as of July 2016—run by a Chinese company the General Nice Group, after the previous operator's bankruptcy. The investment would entail a range of environmental impacts as well as flying in a couple of thousand workers during the construction phase (in a country with a population of 56,000), likely from China. However, the project would also contribute to expanding the economic autonomy of Greenland in relation to Denmark and provide work for more than 450 Greenlanders in a country troubled by unemployment and an education gap.[38] In any case, the social implications—positive and negative—of the investment are likely to be significant, both in terms of relations between fly-in workers and locals as well as long-term economic and social viability. It is unclear how the prospective Chinese investors and contractors would take these complex issues into account.

Eventually, both China and the EU have influence on international regulatory developments affecting the Arctic and relevant for its indigenous communities. These include the aforementioned POPs Convention, Convention on International Trade in Endangered Species (where recently trade in polar bear products, of importance for Inuit communities, was discussed),[39] the Convention on Biological Diversity or the International Whaling Commission.

[35] Ecologic Institute et al (n 31).

[36] No data for Arctic and sub-Arctic fisheries as such.

[37] Ecologic Institute et al (n 31).

[38] P Jun, 'China's Arctic Mining Adventure Left Out in the Cold' *CaixinOnline* (26 October 2013) english.caixin.com/2013-11-26/100609861.html; London Mining, Company factsheet (2013) www.londonmining.com/media/48900/2013_02_28_-_london_mining_isua_factsheet.pdf (last accessed in November 2014, no longer available online, on file with the author).

[39] See the address of John E Scanlon in Moscow in December 2013 at the CITES website at cites.org/eng/news/sg/2013/20131204_polar-bear.php.

IV. ARCTIC COUNCIL: REQUIREMENTS REGARDING OBSERVERS' ENGAGEMENT WITH INDIGENOUS PEOPLES

In recent years, the Arctic states and indigenous organisations have stressed that engagement with permanent participants is an important element of effective participation in the Council's work. For example, the President of Iceland Ólafur Ragnar Grímsson underlined that 'the respect given to the region's indigenous peoples and their involvement internationally' constitutes one of the 'Arctic house rules' for the newcomers to Arctic regional co-operation.[40]

Even though the Arctic Council is not an organisation making binding decisions,[41] it has established itself as a primary intergovernmental forum for discussing Arctic affairs. In recent years, participation in the Council's work has come to be seen as a symbolic acknowledgement of the actors' interest in and relevance for Arctic matters. Presence in the Council allows external actors to take part in the shaping of common understanding of the Arctic state of affairs and also encourages these actors to share this common understanding. Involvement in the projects conducted within the Council's working groups is particularly important in this context.

Both China and the European Union applied for observer status in the Arctic Council before the 2009 Tromsø ministerial meeting and acted, until 2013, as ad hoc observers.[42] At the Kiruna ministerial meeting, China was accepted as an observer. The EU's situation is more complex, as the Arctic Council 'received the application of the EU for observer status affirmatively',[43] with a final decision on the observer status awaiting 'final decision on implementation', but with the EU being invited to observe Council proceedings on an equal basis to other observers, becoming a so-called 'observer-in-principle' and acting in practice like any other observer. In autumn 2014, after reaching a partial agreement with Canada on the seal ban issue, the EU would be well on its way to acquiring formal observer status (that is, the Kiruna decision to be 'finally implemented'), but for the Ukrainian crisis and tensions with Russia.

[40] ÓR Grímsson (President of Iceland), 'Preface: The Arctic House Rules' (2013) *Arctic Yearbook*, www.arcticyearbook.com.

[41] Although it has served as a catalyst for 2 binding agreements on search and rescue and oil spills.

[42] ie given access to Council meetings on a meeting-by-meeting basis. See Ch 8 by Koivurova et al in this volume.

[43] 'The Arctic Council receives the application of the EU for observer status affirmatively, but defers a final decision on implementation until the Council ministers are agreed by consensus that the concerns of Council members, addressed by the President of the European Commission in his letter of 8 May are resolved, with the understanding that the EU may observe Council proceedings until such time as the Council acts on the letter's proposal'; Arctic Council, Kiruna Declaration (Eighth ministerial meeting of the Arctic Council, 15 May 2013).

Importantly, observer status in the Council is not permanent and is reviewed by Arctic states every four years, subjecting observers to regular scrutiny regarding their alignment with the requirements Arctic states put on observers.[44] These requirements were listed in the so-called 'Nuuk observer rules' (role and criteria for observers adopted during the 2011 ministerial meeting), of which several refer directly to indigenous peoples and permanent participants:

— Respect the values, interests, culture and traditions of Arctic indigenous peoples and other Arctic inhabitants.
— Have demonstrated a political willingness as well as financial ability to contribute to the work of the permanent participants and other Arctic indigenous peoples.
— Have demonstrated a concrete interest and ability to support the work of the Arctic Council, including through partnerships with member states and permanent participants bringing Arctic concerns to global decision-making bodies.[45]

In addition, the Senior Arctic Officials in their report to ministers for the Nuuk meeting emphasised that '[t]he involvement of observers should enhance and complement the unique and critical role of Permanent Participants in the Arctic Council'.[46]

The reasons for the inclusion of such strong language safeguarding the position of permanent participants were the concerns of Arctic indigenous organisations regarding their status in the Council in the light of the presence of powerful observer states, as well as expected changes in the way how the Council functions and its rising international significance.[47] To understand these concerns one has to take into account that circumpolar Arctic co-operation had been shaped in the conditions of relatively limited global attention to the Arctic. Focusing primarily on environmental protection and later also sustainable development and being at the time rather peripheral intergovernmental forums, the Arctic Environmental Protection Strategy and the Arctic Council were open to non-state actors. The extraordinary status indigenous organisations gained in the Council is a result of that initial set-up of Arctic co-operation. The evolution of the Arctic Council towards a more institutionalised, more prominent forum, with much higher international profile than in the 1990s may therefore be a concern

[44] P Graczyk and T Koivurova, 'A New Era in the Arctic Council's External Relations? Broader Consequences of the Nuuk Observer Rules for Arctic Governance' (2014) 50 *Polar Record* 225.

[45] Senior Arctic Officials (SAOs), *Report to Ministers* (Nuuk, Greenland, May 2011) 50–51.

[46] ibid, 50.

[47] Personal Communication with the staff of Indigenous Peoples Secretariat, April and October 2013. Most likely the particular issue of the EU seal ban played a key role in the wording of the Nuuk observer rules referring to indigenous and local communities.

for indigenous organisations.[48] In addition, the presence of powerful actors such as China, the EU, India or Japan may be thought to undermine the special position indigenous organisations enjoyed in the Council. The executive director of Gwich'in Council International, Bridget Larocque, provided a good summary of indigenous hopes and concerns in her commentary in the *Arctic Yearbook* 2012:

> The Permanent Participants are very cautious about some applications, as it is not enough to say that Observers will be sensitive to the needs and rights of the indigenous peoples; they also need to show their track record. New Observers have to accept the Arctic Council's governance structure, as this is the only international forum that guarantees that the voice of the Arctic People gets heard.[49]

Three years after the Nuuk meeting it is still unclear what the 'respect for the values, interest, culture and traditions' or the 'contribution' and 'support' for permanent participants mean exactly. The indigenous leaders themselves are not sure what they can expect and demand from the observers.[50]

However, the case of the European Union is illustrative in understanding what the observers' *respect* and *support* for indigenous peoples may constitute. The opposition of Canada[51] and the Inuit to the EU observership had been connected with the ban on placing seal products on the EU market owing to concerns over the welfare of animals (humane treatment) during the hunt.[52] Although traditional harvesting conducted by indigenous groups has been exempted from the regulation, the Inuit argue that the law led to the collapse of the global market for seal products (as Europe was the key market), and that the certification schemes introduced are not feasible. The Inuit are also opposed to the view of seal hunting as being as such an inhumane activity.[53] If these arguments are accepted, the case could be made that the EU has failed to 'respect the values [...] and traditions of Arctic

[48] Moreover, while the position of permanent participants is very strong in the working groups, there is a risk for weakening their overall standing due to increasing use of task forces in the work of the Council. Task forces use their own terms of reference, which leads eg to limiting the involvement of observers. So far, the permanent participants have been engaged in task forces' proceedings, but their inclusion in more sensitive issues in the future is not certain. See Duyck, 'Polar Environmental Governance and Non-state Actors' (n 14).

[49] B Larocque (2012), 'A Voice from the Arctic' *Arctic Yearbook* (2012) arcticyearbook.com.

[50] Personal communication with ICC and Sámi Council activists (October 2014). That was also visible during the meeting among Arctic Council observers in Warsaw in April 2013 where a representative of permanent participants was present.

[51] Canada has agreed on the 'final implementation' of the decision of awarding the EU observer status in the Arctic Council in autumn 2014.

[52] Regulation (EC) No 1007/2009 of 16 September 2009 on trade in seal products, OJ L 286, 31.10.2009, p 36–39.

[53] D Cambou, 'The Impact of the Ban on Seal Products on the Rights of Indigenous Peoples: A European Issue' (2013) 5 *Yearbook of Polar Law* 389; K Hossain, 'The EU Ban on the Import of Seal Products and the WTO Regulations: Neglected Human Rights of the Arctic Indigenous Peoples?' (2013) 49 *Polar Record* 154.

indigenous peoples and other Arctic inhabitants' (including the traditions of non-indigenous, so-called 'commercial sealers'), resulting in Canada's earlier opposition to granting the EU official observer status. The next section discusses how the EU has attempted to address the backlash from the seal ban and the anger of Arctic indigenous communities.

V. CHINA'S AND EU'S ARCTIC-SPECIFIC STATEMENTS AND ACTIONS

Due to the influence of powers like China and the EU on Arctic developments and owing to the position of permanent participants within the Arctic Council, it is in the interest of both state observers and indigenous organisations to establish channels of communication and eventually collaborate. By submitting their applications for observer status in the Arctic Council, China and the EU implicitly agreed to respect indigenous values and interests and to support permanent participants. As discussed in the previous section, it is unclear if and how such respect and support is to materialise. The EU has taken the first steps to respond to this challenge, while China, even though it made contact with permanent participants following its application, has so far shown comparatively limited interest in engaging with the permanent participants.

Chinese activities may be also juxtaposed with the statements referring to indigenous peoples and actions of other Asian state applicants prior to the Kiruna ministerial meeting, for example Japan and Singapore.[54] A Singaporean representative not only stated that the development of 'human capital' in the Arctic regions is the country's 'Arctic interest',[55] but indigenous communities have been directly engaged by arranging visits of Singapore's officials to Arctic towns such as Iqaluit or Nuuk, as well as by inviting Arctic indigenous leaders to Singapore to showcase the country's achievements.

Such statements and activities, while in themselves not reality-shaping (and some activities—such as showcasing Singaporean success—have limited usefulness for Arctic indigenous actors), are important for trust-building. That is particularly relevant for China as it has not yet elaborated its Arctic policy and there are few instances of Chinese direct engagement in the region.[56] Consequently, Arctic actors may lack knowledge and

[54] See eg China's and Japan's statement at the Stockholm observers' meeting with the AC chair in November 2012, www.arctic-council.org: statement by HE Ambassador Lan Lijun at the meeting between the Swedish chairmanship of the Arctic Council and observers, 6 November 2012, Swedish Ministry of Foreign Affairs. Italy is another example of an observer making strong statements regarding indigenous peoples.

[55] S Tan (Senior Parliamentary Secretary), 'Singapore in the Arctic', speech at the Arctic Circle General Assembly (12 October 2013) www.mfa.gov.sg/content/mfa/media_centre/press_room/pr/2013/201310/press_20131014_01.printable.html?status=1.

[56] Apart from research activities focused chiefly on earth sciences and climate change. See Ch 3 by Ren in this volume.

understanding of Chinese interests, the role China wants to play in the region and the standards it would follow in asserting that role. This is especially the case as the resource dimension is prominent (particularly in the West)[57] in the discussion on Chinese Arctic interests. Resource extraction is among the most problematic issues for indigenous communities, so the aforementioned concerns may be exacerbated.

China has thus far made little reference to indigenous peoples in its official international statements and declarations referring to the Arctic or Arctic Council, apart from confirming their important role within Arctic regional co-operation.[58] However, following the adoption of the 'Nuuk observer rules' Chinese officials (primarily from the embassies in Nordic countries—particularly in Helsinki) have contacted the Sámi Council (one of the participants), the Sámi parliaments and the Indigenous Peoples Secretariat regarding indigenous perspectives and the expectations of permanent participants regarding observers.[59] Chinese officials also approached indigenous leaders during Arctic Council meetings, especially in the Sustainable Development Working Group.[60] On the other hand, there was apparently no contact established with the Inuit Circumpolar Council, perhaps the most influential Arctic indigenous organisation,[61] which shows uneven commitment, likely dependent on the particular interest of specific embassies or officials. Moreover, there was no follow-up on these interactions after the 2013 Kiruna ministerial meeting.

Currently, there is ongoing work among Chinese policymakers and scholars to better understand Arctic indigenous perspectives, with the China Institute for Marine Affairs (part of State Ocean Administration) conducting a project on Arctic indigenous peoples following a request from Chinese officials.[62] Chinese policymakers and scholars argue that before any actions are taken or proposals made, there is a need first to learn more regarding Arctic indigenous affairs.[63] That resonates well with the declaration by Feng Gao,

[57] See eg a commentary by F Perreault, 'Can China Become a Major Arctic Actor' (2012) RSIS Commentary No 073/2012; L Xing and RG Bertelsen 'The Drivers of Chinese Arctic Interests: Political Stability and Energy and Transportation Security' (2013) *Arctic Yearbook* www.arcticyearbook.com; Ch Seidler, 'The Resource Race: China Dips Toes in Arctic Waters' *Spiegel Online* (25 January 2013) www.spiegel.de; 'Polar Bearings: China Pursues Its Interest in the Frozen North' *The Economist* (12 July 2014).

[58] Statement by HE Ambassador Lan Lijun at the Meeting between the Swedish Chairmanship of the Arctic Council and Observers (n 54).

[59] Personal communication with IPS staff (April 2013) and Sámi Council staff (October 2014).

[60] ibid.

[61] Personal communication with one of the ICC leaders (October 2014).

[62] Personal communication, interview by Timo Koivurova with officials from the China's State Oceanic Administration (Haiwen Zhang, Director General of the Department of International Cooperation) and scholars from the China Institute for Marine Affairs (Dr Fu Yu) (Beijing, 15 October 2014).

[63] ibid, based also on discussions during the project seminars in Rovaniemi (March 2014) and Wuhan (September 2014).

the head of the Chinese delegation to the Kiruna ministerial meeting, who said that 'understanding the Arctic' is one of the priorities in Chinese governments' current activities within the Arctic Council.[64] Limited reference in Chinese statements to Arctic indigenous (and other) inhabitants can be also attributed to the focus in Chinese declarations on Arctic climate change and its significance for China, rather than on China's resource interests and the impacts of China on the region.[65]

In comparison to China, the EU's direct engagement with Arctic indigenous peoples goes back much further and is more substantial. There are several factors explaining the EU's more proactive approach. First, the presence of the Sámi population within the EU territory (the only Arctic indigenous people in the EU) means that the Sámi are internal stakeholders in the context of EU policymaking. Second, as the difficult situation of indigenous peoples around the globe is seen as historically a result of European colonisation and its legacies, Europeans are often reminded of their moral responsibility for indigenous groups around the globe.[66] Third, the EU has always emphasised its principal commitment to human rights and group rights.[67] Fourth the EU has been faced by a major obstacle in entering the Arctic forums due to the ban on seal products introduced in 2009/2010.[68] Very strong opposition to the EU's presence from the side of the Inuit, supported by other Arctic peoples and Canada, forced the EU to seek dialogue with Arctic indigenous leaders and to highlight indigenous issues in its policy documents. In terms of improving the quality of EU Arctic policy, this can be seen as a 'blessing in disguise'.

Since 2007, when Arctic issues entered the EU agenda and simultaneously the debate on the ban on seal products entered into a decisive phase, European Commission officials have attended various indigenous meetings (eg Barents Indigenous Peoples' Congress)[69] and visited northern communities (eg in Nunavut).[70] Primarily, the European Commission organised meetings in the format of Arctic Dialogue (in 2010, 2013, 2014, and 2016 in Brussels and, in addition, a side-event during a conference in Tromsø in

[64] A Tonami (2014), 'The Arctic Policy of China and Japan: Multilayered Economic and Strategic Motivations' (2014) 4 *The Polar Journal* 105.

[65] See other chapters in this volume.

[66] See eg M Lister, *The European Union and the South: Relations with Developing Countries* (New York, Routledge, 1997).

[67] eg the Charter on Fundamental Rights of the European Union (OJ C 364/1, 2000/C, 18 December 2000). Art 21 of the Charter prohibits discrimination on the grounds of race, ethnic or social origin, genetic features, religion or belief, language and membership of a national minority, which are all applicable to indigenous persons.

[68] Regulation (EC) No 1007/2009 (n 52).

[69] The Norwegian Barents Secretariat, Indigenous Peoples in the Barents Euro-Arctic Region, www.beac.st/en/Working-Groups/Working-Group-of-Indigenous-Peoples.

[70] Personal communication with the European Commission DG Mare officer (Brussels, May 2011).

January 2011). A gesture showing the commitment of the EU to dialogue with the Arctic indigenous peoples was the presence of Maria Damanaki—a commissioner responsible for maritime affairs and fisheries, one of the key units of the European Commission involved in shaping the EU Arctic policy—at the 2013 meeting. The downside of the meetings was that the participation of the indigenous representatives was rather incidental and lacking continuity. As a result, the 2010 meeting lacked proper follow-up and the discussions in 2013 were largely disconnected from the results of earlier meetings. The meetings were focused more on the format of dialogue than specific EU policies and consisted to a great extent of the presentation of various EU projects relevant for Arctic indigenous peoples. During the 2011 meeting, a number of possible ways to make the contacts between the EU and Arctic indigenous peoples more effective were proposed, including the possibility of creating an indigenous office in Brussels. However, there was no tangible follow-up on this discussion.

These discrepancies are currently being addressed. That reflects a larger learning process taking place in the EU institutions starting from the inception of the Union's Arctic policy in 2008.[71] The 2013 meeting was fairly well followed-up. With the October 2014 meeting, the Arctic Dialogue format is becoming regular and more focused. As there is greater continuity in indigenous participation, it becomes possible to have a more in-depth discussion on the issues critical for the Sámi, for example mining developments in Fennoscandia where the EU is among the key regulators.[72]

The EU representatives also try to involve Nordic Sámi parliaments on a more systematic basis.[73] A separate meeting between the European Commission officers, several Members of the European Parliament and the Sámi leaders took place in October 2014. One of the issues discussed was a more permanent representation of the Sámi in Brussels. This has been a long-standing postulate of Arctic indigenous peoples and the Commission has put forward a number of ideas. These entailed for instance including Sámi representation in already functioning offices of Nordic northern regions.[74] The Sámi Council responded with a comprehensive and advanced proposal to establish a representative office as a project under one of the EU's

[71] See T Koivurova and A Stepien, 'The EU and the Arctic: An Ongoing Learning Process' in Stepien, Koivurova and Kankaanpää (eds), *Strategic Assessment of Development of the Arctic* (n 71).

[72] Personal communication with the European Commission staff (September 2014) and indigenous leaders (Sámi Council) (Brussels, 14 October 2014).

[73] European Commission, 'Summary of "Arctic Dialogue" Workshop—9 March 2010—Brussels' MARE.C1/EH/ZB/2010; Personal communication with the European Commission DG Mare officer (Brussels, May 2013); Observations from Arctic Dialogue meeting in October 2013 (Brussels; Personal communication with a Sámi and Inuit leaders attending the October 2013 meeting, October–December 2013).

[74] This is a problematic issue as the relationship between indigenous peoples and regional authorities is not always unproblematic.

territorial co-operation programmes.[75] At the moment of submission of this volume the future of this proposal remains uncertain. Inputs of other Arctic indigenous organisations will likely remain limited to Arctic dialogue meetings and incidental participation in specific consultation processes.

The rights and interests of Arctic indigenous peoples are also emphasised in the EU Arctic policy documents. From the beginning of the official EU Arctic policy formulation—marked by the European Commission's Communication on the Arctic region[76]—the indigenous peoples' issues have been emphasised and the 'protecti[on] and preserv[ation of] the Arctic in unison with its population' defined as one of the main policy objectives. The issues of marine mammals, primarily due to debates about the welfare of seals and the management of whaling, have been taken up particularly broadly. Proposed actions included: engaging Arctic peoples in regular dialogue, supporting Sámi organisations and providing opportunities for development and protection of traditional lifestyle. These aims were supported by the Council in its 2009 Conclusions on Arctic issues, which positioned indigenous rights more clearly as the foundation of EU interactions with indigenous peoples.[77] The European Parliament in its 2011 Resolution, in turn, had a stronger emphasis on the coexistence of indigenous and non-indigenous populations in the region and the need for protection of the bases of indigenous livelihoods, primarily by safeguarding the Arctic environment.[78]

In the later series of EU documents—2012 Joint Communication from the European Commission and the High Representative[79] and 2014 European Parliament Resolution and Council Conclusions[80]—a 'constructive engagement and dialogue' with indigenous peoples is to be intensified and the EU is to identify 'appropriate ways of ensuring that the representatives of Arctic indigenous peoples are informed and consulted on the EU policies that affect them, and are given appropriate platforms to present their particular

[75] Personal communication with a Sámi Council staff member (October 2014).

[76] European Commission, 'The European Union and the Arctic Region' Communication COM(2008)763 final (2008).

[77] Council of the European Union. Council Conclusions on Arctic Issues (2985th Foreign Affairs Council meeting, Brussels, 8 December 2009).

[78] European Parliament, Resolution of 20 January 2011 on a sustainable EU policy for the high North, A7-0377/2010. See also the earlier resolution of the Parliament, European Parliament Resolution of 9 October 2008 on Arctic governance, 2010/C 9 E/07.

[79] European Commission (with High Representative), 'Developing a European Union Policy towards the Arctic Region: Progress Since 2008 and Next Steps'. Joint Communication of the European Commission and the High Representative of the European Union for Foreign Affairs and Security Policy to the European Parliament and the Council (Brussels, 26 June 2012, JOIN(2012) 19 final).

[80] European Parliament, 'Joint Motion for a Resolution on the EU Strategy for the Arctic' (2013/2595(RSP)) (2014) www.europarl.europa.eu/sides/getDoc.do?pubRef=-//EP//TEXT+MOTION+P7-RC-2014-0229+0+DOC+XML+V0//EN; Council of the European Union, 'Council Conclusions on Developing a European Union Policy towards the Arctic Region' (Foreign Affairs Council meeting, Brussels, 12 May 2014).

concerns to EU institutions and audiences'. The organisation of the 2013 and 2014 Arctic Dialogue meetings and the plans for further engagement can be seen as results of this objective. However, a clear shortcoming in the EU policy documents is that apart from the issue of Arctic marine mammals,[81] there are no specific policy areas or matters identified as themes for the future intensified dialogue.

Apart from the general policies towards the Arctic region, the EU has also a more direct role in influencing indigenous affairs, both in its own territory (northern Finland and Sweden) and in the states and territories where various EU programmes are implemented, including Greenland, Norway and Russia.[82] EU-funded programmes (including, until 2013, a separate Sápmi sub-programme) acknowledge the dynamic nature of indigenous cultures and many projects aim to develop creative industries and culture-based entrepreneurship as well as facilitate cultural co-operation, events and network-building. That is highly commendable considering the often naïve and simplistic approach to indigenous cultures.[83] A special EU-Greenland agreement provides resources for supporting education, vocational training and the enhancement of human resources, in line with the expectations of the Greenlandic government.[84]

It has been a longstanding postulate of indigenous peoples that any research taking place on their territories or concerning themselves and the environment they inhabit should have a participatory character and at least partly address their needs and problems.[85] Neither the EU nor China has so far established mechanisms to integrate and address the views and needs of Arctic communities in their research strategies and activities in the region. However, 'taking account of the needs of indigenous communities' in EU contributions to Arctic issues[86] could be interpreted as meaning the readiness to make such an effort in the long-term perspective. In turn, the Chinese draft (not yet adopted) Arctic Research Management Regulation includes

[81] eg the EU position regarding the aboriginal quota within the International Whaling Commission is of relevance to Greenlandic whaling.

[82] Many EU regulations are applicable to Norway and Iceland due to the existence of the European Economic Area Agreement (EEA Agreement 1994) and a number of EU-funded programmes extend both to these countries as well as to northwest Russia and Greenland.

[83] InterregIVA/North, 'Goals and Strategies', www.interregnord.com/en/about-the-programme/goals-and-strategies.aspx; Interreg IVA North 2014-2020 Document (in Finnish) www.interregnord.com/wp-content/uploads/Interreg-Pohjoinen-FIN-web.pdf.

[84] European Commission, 'Mid-term Review of the EU/Greenland Partnership 2007–2013' (8 May 2012) (on file with the author).

[85] T Søvndahl Pedersen (Head of Greenland Representation in Copenhagen), 'The Relevance of EU Policies on Indigenous Peoples in EC Cooperation with Greenland and the Arctic' (n/d), eu.nanoq.gl/Emner/EuGl/~/media/8E788A8FB50E486CA9CE602AB162B666.ashx.

[86] European Commission, 'Developing a European Union Policy towards the Arctic Region: Progress since 2008 and Next Steps' (n 79) 5.

respect for rights and customs of Arctic indigenous groups.[87] Moreover, comparing to China, the EU puts greater attention on Arctic social sciences, which is of key importance for studies relevant for indigenous peoples.[88]

VI. GENERAL APPROACHES TOWARDS INDIGENOUS RIGHTS AND ISSUES

As there is very little information on China's approach to indigenous peoples in the Arctic and the EU's actions are to a great extent preliminary, it is instructive to discuss the stances of China and the EU towards indigenous peoples and their rights in the global context. Especially in the case of China this could shed light on the format the future engagement could take.

A. Development of International Indigenous Norms

The People's Republic of China officially does not recognise the existence of an indigenous population within its territory,[89] as it considers the international legal emergence of the indigeneity and the distinguishing of the legal category of indigenous peoples as arising solely from European conquest and colonisation. As this perspective is taken, there cannot be any special indigenous rights in any other contexts than colonial or post-colonial.[90] Although China officially identifies 55 ethnic minority groups, none of these minorities is considered to have indigenous status. Interestingly, that includes the Evenki, who number over 30,000 and primarily inhabit the north of the Inner Mongolia province. The Evenki are recognised in the Russian Federation as a small-numbered indigenous people of the North. Groups from both sides of the border share cultural and livelihood features such as reindeer husbandry (around 230 Chinese Evenki are engaged in herding).[91]

[87] Legislative draft of 'Arctic Expedition Management Regulation' in preparation by the State Oceanic Administration since 2006. See Chs 2 and 3 by Qin et al and Ren respectively in this volume.

[88] That is visible, eg, from the content of the Arctic programme within the EU's Horizon 2020 research programme, partly due to the EU's direct presence in Fennoscandia. See European Commission, 'Horizon 2020—The Framework Programme for Research and Innovation' Communication COM(2011) 808 final) (Brussels, 30 November 2011) eur-lex.europa.eu/legal-content/EN/TXT/PDF/?uri=CELEX:52011DC0808&from=EN.

[89] That is different in Taiwan and adjacent islands, where Austronesian tribes are acknowledged as indigenous by the government of the Republic of China and enjoy certain rights arising from that status.

[90] T Lixiao, statement at the Third Committee of the 56th UNGA, on the Issue of Indigenous People (item 116) (29 October 2001) www.china-un.ch/eng/rqrd/xgwt/t85100.htm.

[91] The Evenki herders in China are members of the Association of World Reindeer Herders, which connects 20 indigenous reindeer herding peoples and 100,000 reindeer herders and has observer status in the Arctic Council (see the website of the International Centre for Reindeer

In the eight Arctic states, all Arctic groups considered currently indigenous have been subject to European colonisation and conquest and they are, moreover, recognised as indigenous by their respective states. That means that formally China recognises the indigenous status and rights of Arctic peoples.

Looking at the global context, China has often proven supportive of international developments within the indigenous rights framework. It has promoted the establishment of the UN Permanent Forum for Indigenous Issues (UNPFII),[92] voted in favour of adopting the 2007 UN Declaration on the Rights of Indigenous Peoples (UNDRIP), and expressed support for the World Conference on Indigenous Peoples. For instance,[93] a Chinese representative during the meeting of the Third Committee of the UN General Assembly stated that:

> *countries concerned and the international community are duty bound* to promote and protect the basic human rights and freedom of indigenous peoples, to secure the natural environment and resources they rely on for survival, and to cherish and safeguard their traditional cultures.
>
> the United Nations Declaration on the Rights of Indigenous Peoples [...] is a milestone on the road to justice, equality and development for indigenous peoples.[...]
>
> Although there are neither indigenous people nor indigenous issues in China, *we steadfastly support the promotion and protection of basic human rights and freedom of the world's indigenous peoples.* [...] In the future, the Chinese government will continue to work with others and play a proactive and constructive part in safeguarding the rights and interests of indigenous peoples, promoting their full participation in economic and social development, and pushing for the comprehensive implementation of the Declaration.[94] (emphasis added)

During the UN Permanent Forum for Indigenous Issues, the Chinese representative emphasised:

> efforts to promote and protect the rights of indigenous peoples and strengthen their comprehensive development still face serious challenges, *including the failure of some developed countries to earnestly implement the Declaration on the Rights of Indigenous Peoples.*[95] (emphasis added)

Husbandry at reindeerherding.org). The 2013 World Reindeer Herders Congress was organised in Genhe/Alogoya in northwest China.

[92] Z Xing, statement at the Third Committee of the 57th session of the General Assembly on Issues of Indigenous People (21 October 2002) www.china-un.ch/eng/rqrd/xgwt/t85186.htm.

[93] Similar statements have been uttered by Chinese representatives in various contexts. eg in the UN Permanent Forum for Indigenous Issues, see the Statement by Counsellor Shaojun Yao of the Chinese Delegation at the Interactive Dialogue on the Asian Region at the 13th Session of the Permanent Forum on Indigenous Issues, www.china-un.org/eng/chinaandun/socialhr/rqwt/t1164597.htm.

[94] H Qing, statement at the Third Committee of the 67th Session of the General Assembly on Agenda Item 66: Rights of Indigenous Peoples, www.china-un.org/eng/hyyfy/t982303.htm.

[95] Yao, statement (n 93).

The last statement could be interpreted as referring, although not openly, also to some of the Arctic states. Markedly, in its statements China pays special attention to the 'development of indigenous women, children, elderly persons and persons with disabilities'.[96]

On the other hand, a more direct engagement with indigenous organisations (that is, eg, entering into dialogue with indigenous representatives) appears to be limited. A prominent exception was hosting a pre-sessional meeting of the UN Permanent Forum on Indigenous Issues in Beijing in March 2007.[97]

The EU's engagement with indigenous actors goes back to the 1990s when the EU was designing its approach to indigenous peoples within the development policy.[98] EU development aid efforts include support for indigenous organisations and their participation in policymaking processes, support for indigenous rights advocacy including land rights in several countries, as well as typical development projects.[99] The EU has also developed standards for its activities in areas of key relevance to indigenous peoples around the globe, such as within the forest sector.[100] Interestingly, in the 1990s the Sámi had been involved in the formulation of the EU indigenous policy within development co-operation and the EU financed several projects supporting co-operation between the Sámi Council (Sámi umbrella NGO) and indigenous organisations in the Global South.[101] Currently, the attention to indigenous rights is highlighted in the European Consensus on Development, although without details on practical implementation.[102]

[96] Qing, statement (n 94); L Heng, statement at the Third Committee of the 68th Session of the General Assembly on Agenda Item 66: Rights of Indigenous Peoples (21 October 2013) www.china-un.org/eng/hyyfy/t1091938.htm.

[97] Informal pre-sessional meeting for Sixth Session of Forum, Beijing, China, 19–21 March 2007, undesadspd.org/IndigenousPeoples/MeetingsandWorkshops.aspx.

[98] See eg Council Resolution of 30 November 1998 on Indigenous Peoples within the Framework of the Development Co-operation of the Union and the Member States.

[99] See eg European Commission, 'Annual Report on the European Union's Development and External Assistance Policies and Their Implementation in 2012' (Directorate General Development and Cooperation—EuropeAid, 2013). However, a clear shortcoming is the lack of distinguishing projects that have an indigenous dimension in the report, as is the case eg in Norway.

[100] Ministry for Foreign Affairs of Finland, 'Development Policy Guidelines for Forest Sector' formin.finland.fi/public/default.aspx?contentid=288213&nodeid=15457&contentlan=2&culture=en-US.

[101] See eg European Commission. 'Project Report—Indigenous Peoples: International Human Rights Standards and the Policy Process, Ref No. B7-7020/MTR/VN/155/98' (2002); the website of the Sámi Council at www.saamicouncil.net; Personal communications with Sámi Council leaders (past and present) in Tromsø, Norway, Rovaniemi, Finland and Arusha, Tanzania (June 2011–March 2012).

[102] Joint statement by the Council and the representatives of the governments of the Member States meeting within the Council, the European Parliament and the Commission on European Union Development Policy: 'The European Consensus', OJ C46/2, 2006/C 46/01, 24 February 2006.

Similarly to China, the EU's overall strong commitment to human and indigenous rights is reflected in its strong support for international developments, such as the UNDRIP, UNPFII and currently the UN World Conference on Indigenous Peoples. The EU is also fairly active in such forums as the Expert Mechanism on the Rights of Indigenous Peoples under the Human Rights Council.[103] Participation of indigenous peoples in these and other international processes has been occasionally supported.[104] As a result, and despite the existence of a number of problematic issues, even some indigenous representatives called the EU a 'front-runner when it comes to establishing policies on the rights of indigenous peoples'.[105] Currently, the European Commission is considering how to implement the UNDRIP within the EU's development co-operation, human rights activities as well as within its Arctic policies, with a view to moving from declarations and general principles to practical action. So far, the EU's new Strategic Framework and Action Plan on Human Rights and Democracy reiterated the EU's 'commitment to the protection of the rights of indigenous peoples, particularly to combat discrimination'.[106] That is potentially important not only within the sphere of development co-operation but also in the EU's projects in Arctic Russia. However, it is clear that the implementation of the general indigenous rights principles is challenging for the EU.[107] It is, for example, undefined how, if at all, the principle of free, prior and informed consent is acknowledged and taken into account in specific projects or actions. The EU has been, for instance, criticised for allegedly undermining the status of UNDRIP as a human rights document within climate negotiations.[108]

B. Activities of Corporate Actors: Standards and Guidelines

The Chinese or European economic presence in the Arctic means that the actions of Chinese or European-controlled companies affect indigenous communities. Currently, companies are expected not only to abide by the

[103] Author participated in the EMRIP meeting in Geneva in July 2012.

[104] See eg the list of projects financed under the European Initiative for Democracy and Human Rights, http://ec.europa.eu/europeaid/sectors/human-rights-and-governance_en (last accessed November 2014); Annual Work Programme For Grants of the European Instrument for Democracy and Human rights (EIDHR) (2013).

[105] Søvndahl Pedersen, 'The Relevance of EU Policies on Indigenous Peoples in EC Cooperation with Greenland and the Arctic' (n 85).

[106] See Notes from the Third Committee (Social, Humanitarian and Cultural) of the Sixty-seventh General Assembly (GA/SHC/4045, New York, 22 October 2012) www.un.org/News/Press/docs/2012/gashc4045.doc.htm.

[107] Discussion during the Arctic Dialogue meeting, Brussels, 18 October 2013 (notes with the author).

[108] esp regarding reducing emissions from deforestation and forest degradation (REDD), RC Rÿser, 'Climate Talks Resume, Bolivia, China and Indigenous Peoples' (CWIS, 5 April 2011) cwis.org/FWE/2011/04/05/climate-talks-resume-bolivia-china-and-indigenous-peoples/.

laws and regulations of the state in which they operate, but to go beyond them by adopting codes of corporate social responsibility and guidelines for their employees. These cover not only environmental performance but also the interaction with local communities. Does the discussed official support for indigenous rights worldwide have therefore a practical reflection in the standard-setting regarding enterprises operating abroad? In the case of China, government-imposed standards and guidelines are particularly important as many companies are fully or partly owned and controlled by the state.

The issue is highly topical, as Chinese companies are increasingly active internationally. Inevitably, Chinese companies' or banks' activities are likely to also result in some adverse impacts on indigenous communities. The most illustrative—as usually connected with significant social and economic impacts—are examples of major hydropower and irrigation projects in Ethiopia, Gabon, Sudan, Cambodia or Myanmar, where some projects had to be suspended after resistance from local communities and NGOs.[109] A good example is the construction of dams in Ethiopia, financed by Chinese lenders and supported by China's export credit agency. The project is expected to have major social and environmental impacts, including on agriculture, grazing lands and fisheries, affecting 500,000 indigenous people and likely leading to ethnic conflicts over water and disappearing grazing lands.[110] In 2011, the UN World Heritage Committee asked the Industrial and Commercial Bank of China (ICBC) to put on hold the financial support for the project.[111] Also the presence of Chinese extractive companies in other African countries[112] is associated with controversies. For instance, in 2013, the Zambian government revoked a number of mining permits for Chinese companies after the latter had been criticised for poor worker safety and environmental performance. African governments are thought to allow for lowering standards in order to attract investors and Chinese companies

[109] International Rivers, 'The New Great Walls: A Guide to China's Overseas Dam Industry' (November 2012). It is important to highlight that most actors engaged in dam building experience major challenges, esp in areas affected by water scarcity. That is true also, eg, for Nordic companies and development agencies; see AD Usger (ed), *Dams as Aid: A Political Anatomy of Nordic Development Thinking* (London and New York, Routledge, 1997).

[110] For discussion, see P Bosshard, 'Chinese Loans Could Fuel Regional Conflict in East Africa' (blog entry, 14 January 2013) www.chinadialogue.net/article/show/single/en/5601-Chinese-loans-could-fuel-regional-conflict-in-East-Africa.

[111] World Heritage Committee, Decision 35COM 7B.3, whc.unesco.org/en/soc/313/?mode=doc, due to effects on heritage sites, primarily Lake Turkana. Moreover, the African Development Bank has indicated in its study that the project will result in major adverse environmental impacts.

[112] See eg H Wenbin and A Wilkes, 'Analysis of Approvals for Chinese Companies to Invest in Africa's Mining, Agriculture and Forestry Sectors' (2011) Centre for International Forestry Research Working Paper 81.

are blamed for making use of such poor regulatory frameworks.[113] In general, problematic issues in developing countries include the practice of Chinese companies of bringing own workers or reports of poor treatment of local workers, lack of social integration or proper mechanisms for consultations. These problems are coupled with limited domestic accountability for companies' actions abroad compared to the West, where companies are still more likely to be subject to various forms of public scrutiny.[114] These issues may be problematic also for Arctic communities.

A broad requirement to respect local laws appears to be the key binding principle regarding local context applicable within Chinese overseas foreign investment laws. Chinese governmental guidelines for foreign investments, including 'Nine Principles of the State Council on Encouraging and Regulating China's Outbound Investment' and the 2008 'Administrative Regulations on Contracting Foreign Projects' require enterprises to, inter alia, consider their social responsibility in their activities abroad.[115] In 2013, the Ministries of Commerce and Environmental Protection issued 'Guidelines on Environmental Protection in Foreign Investment and Co-operation'.[116] They focus on environmental problems and do not deal with indigenous issues directly. However, these documents take up potentially relevant matters: developing environmental strategies, management plans, proper conduct of the environmental impact assessments, or disclosure of environmental information to the interested public, including within the supply chain. In September 2014, the Ministry of Commerce produced also a revised document 'Measures for Foreign Investment Management', which calls for strengthened guidelines and regulations for oversees activities of Chinese companies.[117] Similar guidelines, although with more emphasis on social issues, have been developed by the China Banking Regulatory Commission. The so-called Green Credit Guidelines[118] highlight, among others, issues such as resettlement and land—issues of major concern for indigenous peoples. Some commentators highlight that because 'for Chinese

[113] M Noland, 'Comment on "Changing China, Changing Africa: Future Contours of an Emerging Relationship"' (2014) 9 *Asian Economic Policy Review* 198.

[114] See comment by T Levitt, 'China's Elitist Approach to Overseas Investments' (25 February 2013) www.chinadialogue.net/article/show/single/en/5736-China-s-elitist-approach-to-overseas-investments.

[115] International Rivers, 'The New Great Walls' (n 109).

[116] Guidelines on Environmental Protection in Foreign Investment and Cooperation, PRC Ministry of Commerce, english.mofcom.gov.cn/article/policyrelease/bbb/201303/20130300043226.shtml.

[117] Ministry of Commerce (PRC), 'Ministry of Commerce Introduces Newly Revised Measures for Foreign Investment Management', english.mofcom.gov.cn/article/newsrelease/significantnews/201409/20140900729955.shtml.

[118] China Banking Regulatory Commission, 'Green Credit Guidelines' (unofficial translation for internal use) pfbc-cbfp.org/docs/news/avril-mai-13/RDP12-Mars-2013/DCC-China%20Banking%20Regulation%20-%20Green%20Credit%20Guidelines.pdf.

companies, environmental risks have become business risks', the governmental guidelines are relevant and helpful.[119]

Some Chinese companies themselves also attempt to elaborate internal standards and guidelines. For example, the China International Contractors Association has issued a 'Guide on Social Responsibility for Chinese International Contractors',[120] including fairly high standards for community involvement and local development, although indigenous rights and issues are not mentioned. More progressive standards can be seen in the case of companies that have already encountered problems connected with their interaction with indigenous and local communities. This is the case with Sinohydro, which is engaged in a number of difficult hydropower projects in Africa.[121] The company has committed to: conducting proper environmental and social impact assessments; carrying out sufficient consultations with relevant stakeholders, including local communities; developing long-term relationships with communities and maintaining open communication, as well as establishing culturally appropriate grievance mechanisms. Moreover, the management is to ensure that the company's actions are consistent with the UNDRIP and that free, prior and informed consent is obtained from affected indigenous peoples as well as that access to cultural heritage sites is secured. While these latter standards go beyond industry average, their implementation would have to be scrutinised against actual conduct in the case of each project.

The EU is in a different position than China regarding its influence on industry's behaviour outside of Europe. The EU does not control any companies and standard-setting is largely the responsibility of EU member states, not all of which have drafted their own policy documents. Nevertheless, the European Commission has attempted to co-ordinate and encourage companies to develop and implement corporate social responsibility standards, for example via the European Alliance on Corporate Social Responsibility (CSR),[122] and has elaborated the EU CSR strategy.[123] Recently, increased attention has been given to human rights, including labour and employment practices or non-discrimination. The aim is to involve local civil society, human rights organisations and defenders in order to allow the companies to understand the challenges of operating in states that fail to protect their citizens' human rights. As in the case of China, EU actions are parallel

[119] P Bosshard, 'New Rules will Help Hold Chinese Overseas Investors to Account' (blog entry, 22 April 2013) www.chinadialogue.net/blog/5931-New-rules-will-help-hold-Chinese-overseas-investors-to-account-/en.

[120] 'Guide on Social Responsibility for Chinese International Contractors', China CSR Map website, www.chinacsrmap.org/.

[121] International Rivers (n 109).

[122] European Commission, 'Better Self- and Co- Regulation', ec.europa.eu/digital-agenda/en/communities/better-self-and-co-regulation.

[123] European Commission, 'A Renewed EU Strategy 2011–14 for Corporate Social Responsibility' Communication (COM(2011)681final (Brussels, 25 October 2011).

to those undertaken by European business actors, for example within the European Hub on Business and Human Rights.[124]

At the 2010 Arctic Dialogue meeting, it was indicated that corporate social responsibility could be one of the themes for EU-indigenous dialogue.[125] However, there has so far been no CSR discussion within the Arctic Dialogue format, nor has the issue of the performance of European companies been taken up in EU Arctic policy documents.

VII. CONCLUSION AND RECOMMENDATIONS

The discussion in this chapter allows for the formulation of some recommendations. These refer especially to China as a newcomer to Arctic affairs, and as an actor that does not have direct engagement with Arctic communities arising from a geographical presence in the region, as is the case for the EU due to its interaction with the Sámi. If China becomes a more active observer in the Arctic Council, its interaction or even co-operation with permanent participants at the level of working groups may be inevitable, unless the fears of indigenous leaders that the presence of powerful observers would undermine special indigenous status in the Council materialise.

Without an ongoing dialogue, even at a very superficial level, it is not possible to understand the problems and perspectives specific for indigenous communities. An Indian researcher, Sanjay Chaturvedi, commented in 2012 that:

> as the rising Asian powers prepare and push their cases for observer status in the Arctic Council, it is vitally important that they give due space and attention to the human dimension of Arctic governance. In most reasoning advanced so far, what is missing by and large is the engagement with indigenous peoples of the circumpolar North; their knowledge systems, world-views and aspirations. It is useful to be reminded that Arctic (both on land and at sea) is not a strategic void and it is the lived in geographies of the circumpolar North that are in the front line of adverse climate change consequences. What might appear as opportunities offered by climate change may in some cases pose serious threats to the livelihoods of Arctic communities; especially the indigenous peoples. It is vital in other words that the Asian efforts at confidence-building and alliance-making go beyond the state actors in the Arctic Council.[126]

[124] 'CSR Europe, Business and Human Rights', CSR Europe website, http://www.csreurope.org/business-and-human-rights/european-hub-business-human-rights.

[125] European Commission, *Summary of 'Arctic Dialogue' Workshop* (Brussels, 9 March 2010, MARE.C1/EH/ZB/2010).

[126] S Chaturvedi, 'Geopolitical Transformation: "Rising" Asia and the Future of the Arctic Council' in T Axworthy, T Koivurova and W Hasanat (eds), *The Arctic Council: Its Place in the Future of the Arctic Governance* (Munk-Gordon Arctic Security Program, 2012) gordonfoundation.ca, 251.

China and the EU, if they want to play a constructive role in the region as well as secure their political and economic interests, have to take into account the role of the indigenous peoples in the Arctic and their status at various levels of governance, from local and national to circumpolar. As a state supporting indigenous rights in a post-colonial context, China can be expected to engage in dialogue with indigenous organisations and support their activities. The Arctic Council appears to be a perfect venue for such a dialogue. There appears to be a shift from perceiving the presence of powerful external actors in the Arctic Council as a threat towards seeing it as an opportunity. This is especially true for actors with limited capacities, such as permanent participants, which can use the Arctic Council as a space where these major powers can be approached. Bridget Larocque from the Gwich'in Council International—quoted earlier in this chapter—stated that:

> The indigenous peoples appreciate the support offered by Observers of the Arctic Council and recognise that cooperation and collaboration not only advances their work but their indigenous agenda as well. However, as new applications have been submitted, the Permanent Participants' unwavering message is that prospective Observers clearly demonstrate how their presence will enhance the role and increase the participation of the Permanent Participants in the Arctic Council.

Furthermore, it would be highly valuable for the development of Chinese Arctic policy to assess the Chinese environmental footprint and economic imprint in the Arctic, similarly to what the EU has done by commissioning the EU Arctic Footprint and Policy Assessment study. The impacts related to indigenous and local communities should be part of such an assessment. Even though such studies are necessarily burdened with major approximations and may be speculative in character, they provide the policymakers with a general overview of the country's connection to the Arctic and show both to their own constituency (eg companies) and to Arctic actors their willingness to act responsibly in the region.

So far, Chinese companies planning on operating in the Arctic have not received a clear signal on how to deal with indigenous issues. This may cause problems both for Arctic communities and Chinese investors or contractors, despite the existence of general standards for overseas activities. Various levels of Arctic governance are interconnected, as exemplified by the case of the EU seal ban. Therefore, any problems occurring at the level of particular developments may affect the attitudes and behaviour of indigenous actors at the national or circumpolar level. While the influence of indigenous actors on Arctic governance is far from decisive, it is certainly not negligible. Thus, China may consider developing specific standards for companies which operate in the Arctic and which conduct activities potentially affecting livelihoods and interests of Arctic indigenous communities.

Due to the difficult relations with the Inuit in the aftermath of the seal products ban, resulting in resistance to acknowledgement of its Arctic actorness,[127] the EU has made major efforts in engaging with indigenous peoples. Consequently, the forms of engagement developed by the EU, such as Arctic dialogues or including indigenous issues and perspectives in assessment activities and policy considerations, are good examples of how external actors can, despite challenges, involve Arctic indigenous peoples.

The issues of limited resources and capacities of indigenous organisations need to be taken into account. Indigenous organisations often experience so-called participation overload, where various forms of engagement impose a financial and human resources burden that they increasingly cannot carry.[128] Therefore, the Arctic Council could be an appropriate venue for dialogue and a space where the indigenous peoples could turn to the European Commission or the Chinese government with any problematic issues. This may also include EU regulatory developments or challenges of working with Chinese companies operating in indigenous lands, not only the questions under discussion within the Council.

The European Union, as an actor much more experienced in engaging with Arctic stakeholders, should build on its experience and enhance already existing frameworks. This refers in particular to the Arctic dialogue format, by continuing the path taken in the 2013 and 2014 meetings and making the dialogue more regular, including continuous long-term participation of indigenous leaders. The discussions should be more focused and specific, including down-to-earth matters. Following China's example, the EU could be more open about European economic and strategic interests in the Arctic (for example, by discussing the EU's strategic interest in developing EU domestic resource extraction),[129] and incorporate the discussion on these interests within dialogues with Arctic indigenous peoples. Eventually, the idea of establishing a more visible and permanent Arctic indigenous presence in Brussels should be further explored, either for the Sámi or much more broadly for indigenous peoples in general, also including groups affected by EU development co-operation policy. Such representation has to be independent from state and regional authorities and would need to address the constraints of indigenous organisations' human and financial capacities.

[127] The question of EU actorness within international relations and in the Arctic in particular is broadly discussed in the literature and in the political debates. See eg A Niemann and Ch Bretherton (2013), 'EU External Policy at the Crossroads: The Challenge of Actorness and Effectiveness' (2013) 27 *International Relations* 261.

[128] See eg, H Huntington et al, 'Less Ice, More Talk: The Benefits and Burdens for Arctic Communities of Consultations Concerning Development Activities' (2012) 1 *Carbon and Climate Law Review* 33.

[129] Based on the discussion during the stakeholder workshop dedicated to social and cultural changes within the Strategic Assessment of Development of the Arctic (n 21) study, www.arcticinfo.eu.

11

China and the Development of International Law on Arctic Shipping

Challenges and Opportunities

NENGYE LIU AND KAMRUL HOSSAIN

I. INTRODUCTION

IN RECENT YEARS, the number of ships operating in Arctic waters, in particular through the Northern Sea Route, has been gradually on the rise.[1] This is mainly due to the fact that melting sea ice results in relatively easier access to Arctic waters and a comparatively longer period when shipping is feasible. It also diversifies the shipping routes for world trade. However, there are also a number of other factors behind this increase. Climate change-induced human activities open up diverse economic opportunities. The Arctic has already been acknowledged as a resource-rich region by a number of scientific research assessments.[2] Increase in fisheries, hydrocarbon practices and tourism development result in great attention towards the Arctic. Today the Arctic has emerged as a region of both economic and military importance as well as of environmental concerns.[3] The region is attracting greater attention from powerful international actors. Needless to

[1] A Staalesen, 'Arctic Change on Barents Agenda' *Barents Observer* (Kirkeness, 3 June 2013) available at www.barentsobserver.com/en/arctic/2013/06/arctic-change-barents-agenda-03-06. In 2009, 2 ships, the *Beluga Fraternity* and *Beluga Foresight*, made the trans-continental journey. In 2010, altogether 4 ships passed through the route. The following years have experienced even further increases: 34 ships in 2011, 46 ships in 2012 and around 80–100 ships in 2013.

[2] See generally *Arctic Climate Impact Assessment* (ACIA) (Cambridge, Cambridge University Press, 2005). See also USGS, 'Circum-Arctic Resource Appraisal: Estimates of Undiscovered Oil and Gas North of the Arctic Circle' (2008) pubs.usgs.gov/fs/2008/3049/.

[3] O Jensen, 'IMO Guidelines for Ships Operating in Arctic Ice-covered Waters: From Voluntary to Mandatory Tools for Navigation Safety and Environmental Protection' (2007) Fridtjof Nansen Institute Report 2/2007.

say, the world's major actors, such as the US, Russia and Canada, surround the Arctic Ocean. Both the US and Russia are permanent members of the United Nations Security Council. These two, with six other states, form the Arctic Council—an intergovernmental body of the eight Arctic states.

Among other actors—those from outside the region, but interested in it—China has been engaged in the Arctic's regional development more actively in recent years. In 2013, China was admitted as an observer in the Arctic Council along with South Korea, Japan, Singapore, India and Italy. China has already proved itself to be one of the world's major shipping nations. As of 1 January 2013, China is the largest ship-owning country in the world in terms of vessel numbers, with 5313 ocean-going merchant ships.[4] The Arctic shipping routes, especially the Northeast Passage (NEP)[5] are becoming important navigation routes for China that enable Chinese cargo ships to save nearly 5200 kilometres and nine days compared with the traditional voyage to Europe through the Strait of Malacca and the Suez Canal.[6] Moreover, at a meeting held in Yokohama on 25 August 2014, China joined the Republic of Korea and Japan, and adopted a joint declaration to promote co-operation on logistics systems and eco-friendly logistics services amongst these three nations—co-operation on launching services on the Northern Sea Route (NSR)[7] has been agreed.[8] Because of China's rapid economic growth, increased trade relations with the Arctic states,[9] as well as its willingness to have a greater voice in Arctic politics, China apparently has a huge stake in the region. Moreover, China as a party to the United Nations Convention on the Law of the Sea[10] (UNCLOS) has legitimate rights as

[4] United Nations Conference on Trade and Development, *Review of Maritime Transport 2013* (Geneva, United Nations Conference on Trade and Development, 2013) 42.

[5] The Northeast Passage is defined as the set of sea routes from northwest Europe around North Cape (Norway) and along the north coast of Eurasia and Siberia through the Bering Strait to the Pacific. See Arctic Council Arctic Marine Shipping Assessment 2009 Report, 34.

[6] 'China to Release Guidebook on Arctic Shipping' *Barents Observer* (20 June 2014) www.barentsobserver.com/en/arctic/2014/06/china-release-guidebook-arctic-shipping-20-06.

[7] The NSR is defined in Russian Federation law as a set of marine routes from Kara Gate (south of Novaya Zemlya) in the west to the Bering Strait in the east. Several of the routes are along the coast, making use of the main straits through the islands of the Russian Arctic; other potential routes run north of the island groups; see Arctic Council Arctic Marine Shipping Assessment 2009 Report, 23.

[8] 'Tripartite Logistics Ministers Meeting Adopts "Yokohama Declaration"' *Japan International Freight Forwarders Association Inc* (28 August 2014) www.jiffa.or.jp/en/news/entry-3067.html

[9] China has concluded an agreement (20 May 2014) on massive imports of natural gas from Russia as its economy is booming; see I Koch-Weser and C Murray, 'The China-Russia Gas Deal: Background and Implications for the Broader Relationship', *US-China Economic Security Commission* (9 June 2014) www.uscc.gov/sites/default/files/Research/China%20Russia%20gas%20deal_Staffbackgrounder.pdf.

[10] United Nations Convention on the Law of the Sea, 10 December 1982, in force 16 November 1994, 21 *International Legal Materials* 1261 (1982) (UNCLOS).

well as obligations over the Arctic Ocean including navigation. China has recently released the Guidance on Arctic Navigation in the Northeast Route (2014 Guidebook). The 2014 Guidebook includes the NEP's nautical chart, sailing methods, icebreaking providers and Arctic geography and climate, as well as laws and regulations of countries along the NEP in order to facilitate Chinese shipping through Arctic waters.[11]

However, vessel operation in Arctic waters is not the same as it is elsewhere in open marine waters. Despite the rapid melt of sea ice in both poles, the waters are not entirely clear for navigation even in the summer months. Floating ice may have potential to cause maritime safety problems, requiring special ship design technology to operate in Arctic waters. Moreover, unlike other traditional sea routes, Arctic sea routes do not have sufficient infrastructure, port facilities, near-shore safety mechanisms and search and rescue operation facilities. Unpredictable weather conditions may also make Arctic shipping difficult. The *Exxon Valdez* accident that occurred in 1989 gave some indications about special improvements for ship operation in frozen or semi-frozen waters, even though the accident itself did not occur exactly in Arctic waters. Nevertheless, it provides us with knowledge of the potential environmental catastrophe if such an accident occurs in Arctic waters. In addition to accidents, operational vessel source pollution may also cause devastating effects on the Arctic's marine biodiversity. A search and rescue operation, or pollution clean-up operation in case of an oil tanker accident, will no doubt be severely difficult in Arctic waters with ice present. The UNCLOS has addressed 'ice-covered areas' with Article 234. The importance of shipping through frozen water has also been placed within the International Maritime Organization (IMO) agenda since the 1990s, requiring specific policies and regulations both to limit the environmental impact on Arctic marine waters and to improve the safety of navigation. In 2002, the IMO adopted voluntary guidelines—Guidelines for ships operating in Arctic ice-covered waters—in order to respond to challenges in Arctic conditions. The application of the guidelines was later extended, with some modifications, to the other pole—the Antarctic—in the year 2009. The guidelines, known as the International Code (of Safety) for Ships Operating in Polar Waters (Polar Code), are now in the process of becoming mandatory.

Against the above-mentioned background, this chapter aims to look into the development of a maritime legal regime applicable to the Arctic and China's role in such development. While China, as mentioned, has taken an assertive stance towards potential Arctic shipping, particularly through the NEP, the chapter argues that China should play a proactive part in the

[11] 'Guidance on Arctic Navigation in the Northeast Route' *Maritime Safety Administration of the People's Republic of China* (18 September 2014) www.msa.gov.cn/Notice/PicNotice/5654288e-6b7e-4c8e-83b1-c8f7f924af69 (in Chinese).

adoption of the mandatory Polar Code within the IMO. The first part of this chapter looks into recent developments concerning Arctic shipping including the development of the Polar Code. The second part first discusses China's interest in Arctic shipping. Then it analyses challenges and opportunities for China's role in the development of international law on Arctic shipping, with a focus on (1) China and Article 234 of the UNCLOS; (2) China and development of the Polar Code within the IMO; and (3) China as a newcomer within the Arctic Council.

II. EXISTING LEGAL REGIME OF ARCTIC SHIPPING AND RECENT DEVELOPMENTS

The Arctic is dominated by the Arctic Ocean, which is surrounded by five coastal states. International law applies to the Arctic Ocean in the same way as it does elsewhere in any other marine areas around the world.[12] Given that the Arctic Ocean is becoming increasingly accessible, calling for compliance with existing international law and a need for new developments are of huge significance. Generally, the UNCLOS, which entered into force in 1994, creates the legal basis for regulating the world's oceans and seas, including shipping and navigation. However, given that UNCLOS only offers a general framework, shipping and navigation as well as obligations concerning protection of the marine environment are dependent upon specific subsequent legal measures to be developed under a separate body of law. The IMO has developed guidelines and conventions on shipping that are generally applicable to all marine areas including the Arctic Ocean. Since the 1990s, the IMO had started addressing specific issues concerning shipping in polar waters. This section briefly discusses the existing legal regime and recent developments relevant to Arctic shipping.

A. General Legal Framework

i. UNCLOS

The UNCLOS, which is designated as the constitution of the world's oceans and seas, provides the general legal basis for Arctic shipping. The UNCLOS applies to almost all the marine areas in the Arctic Ocean despite the fact that amongst the Arctic states, the US has not yet become a party. The US

[12] M Byers, *International Law and the Arctic* (Cambridge, Cambridge University Press, 2013) 4–5. See also D Rothwell, 'International Law and Arctic Shipping' (2013) 1 *Michigan State International Law Review* 22, 70.

however adheres to customary principles of the law of the sea, and since the UNCLOS largely is the reflection and codification of those customary norms, most of the provisions of the convention are also applicable to the US. The Arctic littoral states clearly articulated in their well-disseminated Ilulissat Declaration in 2008 that the law of the sea provides a basic legal framework for governing the Arctic. Although no reference to the UNCLOS was mentioned in the Ilulissat Declaration because the US is not a contracting party to it, it has now been generally observed, and adhered to, that the UNCLOS creates a legal framework for all activities associated with the marine domain, including shipping,[13] and therefore Arctic shipping is necessarily covered by the general framework of the UNCLOS. The convention designates specific maritime areas as belonging to coastal states' jurisdiction with specific obligations concerning, for example, protection of the marine environment. The UNCLOS guarantees rights of navigation to all other states in a manner consistent with its provisions. These include rights of innocent passage through the territorial sea, rights of transit passage through straits used for international navigation and freedom of navigation in the high sea. Consequently, the Arctic littoral states are under obligation to allow navigational rights to other states within their territorial sea and exclusive economic zones (EEZs). However, Arctic coastal states may reserve the rights to promulgate specific and stricter measures in order to protect the marine environment within their EEZs empowered under Article 234 of the UNCLOS. Article 234 allows coastal states to take stricter legal measures in ice-covered water. Therefore, although the freedom of navigation is generally applicable in all navigable Arctic waters, it can be restricted to some extent by coastal states by virtue of Article 234 as it applies to ice-covered waters.

ii. International Maritime Organization (IMO) Conventions

Specific supplementary regulations are set to give effect of the general provisions of the UNCLOS concerning shipping. The IMO has adopted a number of conventions that are also applicable to the Arctic; its ongoing legal development concerning the adoption of a set of polar-specific legal rules—the Polar Code—is an important milestone for Arctic shipping. Here in this section, IMO conventions are briefly discussed insofar as they are relevant to Arctic waters. These conventions and the ongoing legal development pertaining to polar-specific shipping are complementary to the general framework provided by the UNCLOS.

[13] Rothwell 'International Law and Arctic Shipping' (n 12) 74.

iii. MARPOL

The International Convention on the Prevention of Pollution from Vessels (MARPOL),[14] as amended by its 1978 Protocol addresses the core legal framework concerning vessel-sourced marine pollution globally. The convention put a limit on ships discharging oil and noxious substances at sea. It also regulates sewage, garbage and air pollution from ships. However, MARPOL has not addressed the disposal of wastes into the sea by dumping. Nevertheless, the specific measures under the convention set standards acknowledging the rights of coastal states to enact laws and regulations within their EEZs to prevent and control marine pollution from ships. In its Annexes I, II and V, the convention embodies special mandatory requirements for certain areas (special areas) concerning the prevention of operational discharges of harmful substances. This special area is identified as an area where special mandatory methods for the prevention of marine pollution by oil and/or by other ship-source harmful substances are required due to recognised technical reasons because of the area's oceanographic and ecological conditions and of the particular character of its traffic. Despite the fact that the Arctic Ocean has its own unique ecological characteristics that are sensitive to any sorts of pollution, it has not so far been recognised as a 'special area' under the MARPOL Convention, while the Antarctic has nonetheless been designated as a special area under Annexes I and V of the MARPOL.[15]

iv. SOLAS

The International Convention on the Safety of Life at Sea (SOLAS)[16] was adopted in 1974. While MARPOL addresses vessel-source marine pollution, SOLAS on the other hand regulates shipping operations at sea in order to ensure the safety of mariners. It sets up a number of operational standards for all shipping to ensure safety of life at sea. The convention ensures that flag states comply with these standards in regard to ship constructions, equipment and operation. SOLAS regulations establish navigational systems such as for ship routing, reporting and traffic service. These measures are particularly important for ships operating in Arctic waters because of the

[14] International Conference on Marine Pollution: International Convention for the Prevention of Pollution from Ships (1973) 6 *International Legal Materials* 12, 1319–444.

[15] Resolution MEPC 42(30), Adoption of Amendments to the Annex of the Protocol of 1978 Relating to the International Convention for the Prevention of Pollution from Ships, 1973, Designation of Antarctic Area as a Special Area under Annexes I and V of MARPOL 73/78, 16 November 1990.

[16] Inter-Governmental Maritime Consultative Organisation: International Convention for the Safety of Life at Sea 1974, (1975) 4 *International Legal Materials* 14, 959–78.

prevailing characteristics of the Arctic conditions; as indicated elsewhere in this chapter, navigation through the Arctic involves a number of risks due to, for example, unpredictable weather conditions, remoteness, coldness, lack of proper communication systems and lack of search and rescue services. Chapter V of the convention deals with safety of navigation, adopting some particular regulations[17] applicable to the Arctic, for example, obligations requiring ship masters to communicate ice information by all means at their disposal to ships in the vicinity, and also to the competent authorities.[18] Connected to the SOLAS Convention, a related instrument—the Convention on Standards of Training, Certification and Watchkeeping of Seafarers (STCW Convention)[19]—is also important to note here. The convention aims to maintain the safety of shipping, which is relevant in Arctic waters. The IMO's Sub-Committee on Standards of Training and Watchkeeping is now in the process of revising the convention in order to develop mandatory minimum requirements for the training and qualification of navigators serving on board ships operating in areas where ice or ice floes are likely to be present, so-called ice navigators, in Chapter V (Special training requirements for persons on certain types of ships) of the STCW Convention and in the STCW Code.

v. Other Relevant Regulatory Arrangements

There are a number of other international conventions applicable to Arctic waters as far as shipping is concerned. These include the International Convention on the Control of Harmful Anti-Fouling Systems on Ships (Anti-Fouling Convention),[20] the International Convention for the Control and Management of Ships' Ballast Water and Sediments (Ballast Water Management Convention),[21] the 1972 Convention on the International Regulations for Preventing Collisions at Sea,[22] the 1972 Convention on the Prevention of Marine Pollution by Dumping of Wastes and Other Matter (London Convention),[23] and the 1990 Convention on Oil Pollution, Preparedness,

[17] The most important one is reg 6 setting obligations on ice patrolling and observation of ice condition.

[18] eg reg 31 (Dangerous messages), reg 32 (Information required in dangerous messages).

[19] International Convention on Standards of Training, Certification and Watchkeeping for Seafarers, 1978 (with annex), UNTS No 23001, Vol 1361, 1984.

[20] International Conference on the Control of Harmful Anti-Fouling Systems for Ships, AFS/CONF/26, 18 October 2001, Agenda item 8.

[21] International Convention on Ballast Water Management for Ships, BWM/CONF/36, 16 February 2004, Agenda item 8.

[22] Convention on the International Regulations for Preventing Collisions at Sea, 1972, UNTS No 15824, Vol 1050, 1977.

[23] Inter-Governmental Conference on the Convention on the Dumping of Wastes at Sea: Final Documents (1972) 6 *International Legal Materials* 11, 1291–314.

Response and Co-operation (OPRC Convention).[24] The OPRC Convention has particular relevance for ships operating in the Arctic waters, forming the base convention for the Arctic Council Oil Spill Agreement. In addition, there are several non-legally binding guidelines applicable to Arctic shipping, such as the 2008 International Code on Intact Stability, the 2012 Guide for Cold Water Survival, the 2006 Enhanced Contingency Planning Guidance for Passenger Ships Operating in Areas Remote from SAR Facilities and the 2007 Guidelines on Voyage Planning for Passenger Ships Operating in Remote Areas.

B. Development of the Polar Code

The event that awakened focused attention on polar shipping was the *Exxon Valdez* oil tanker disaster off the coast of Alaska. The accident brought to the attention of nations the special requirements for ships operating in frozen water. Germany was the first country to propose that the IMO should add specific rules under Chapter II of the SOLAS Convention requiring ships operating in polar waters to have suitable ice-strengthening for polar conditions in accordance with the rules of a recognised classification society. This proposal was then supported by a large number of IMO member states. Consequently the matter was referred to the relevant IMO sub-committee—the sub-committee on ship design and equipment (DE). The sub-committee appointed Canada to lead an outside working group (OWG) of technical experts to develop special rules for ships operating in polar water. The OWG included a number of stakeholders in the process, ie representatives of shipping companies, classification societies, academics, engineers and national and regional maritime authorities. Since 1993, the OWG has met annually and developed a set of draft rules concerning navigation, construction and equipment. The draft was entitled 'International code of safety for ships in polar water' and submitted to DE's 41st session held in London in 1998. A year later in 1999 the Maritime Safety Committee (MSC) reviewed the draft, and decided that the code should only be confined to the Arctic, and that it needs to be further developed as voluntary guidelines with conformity to international law since the Antarctic Treaty Consultative Meeting (ATCM) expressed its concerns that the draft code was Arctic-centric and failed to address prevailing differences between the two poles in terms of environmental, operational, legal and political issues. The special conditions of the Antarctic were not reflected in the draft code—one reason for

[24] International Maritime Organization: International Convention on Oil Pollution Preparedness, Response and Co-operation 1990, and Final Act of the Conference (1991) 3 *International Legal Materials* 30, 733–61.

which was that the OWG drafted the code on the basis of the northern hemisphere.[25] In 2002 both the Marine Environment Protection Committee (MEPC) and the MSC approved the draft as 'Guidelines for ships operating in Arctic ice-covered waters' as voluntary guidelines. However, in 2004 the Antarctic Treaty Consultative Parties adopted the IMO's Arctic guidelines, which were then re-engineered by the Council of Managers of National Antarctic Programmes to incorporate Antarctic-specific factors to make them equally applicable to Antarctic shipping.[26] Thereafter in 2009, the IMO Assembly adopted Resolution 1024/26. It is not yet a binding document.

The development of a legally mandatory Polar Code is, however, on its way to encompassing existing elements of MARPOL, SOLAS and STCW in a rather strengthened form adapted to polar (Arctic) conditions with specific mandatory provisions that reflect additional challenges facing polar shipping.[27] In this respect, the Code is aimed at addressing inadequacies in the existing legal regime, including comprehensive aspects of search and rescue, safety of life, protection of property, prevention of marine pollution and the maintenance of ecosystem integrity upon which the bulk of polar scientific research relies. The IMO moves to recognise these aspects in the Polar Code so that comprehensive regulation for ships operating in polar waters can be developed.[28]

C. The Development within the Arctic Council Regarding Shipping

The Arctic Council is an intergovernmental co-operation body of eight Arctic states established by the Ottawa Declaration in 1996. This body is to date the most prominent forum to discuss the Arctic agenda. Even though its outcomes are not legally binding in nature, they offer influential guidance on Arctic matters. The Council has six working groups, each with a specific mandate. The two that are of importance to shipping are the Protection of the Arctic Marine Environment (PAME) and Conservation of Arctic Flora and Fauna (CAFF) Working Groups. In 2009 the PAME Working Group released a major report on Arctic marine shipping—the Arctic Marine Shipping Assessment (AMSA)—which analyses current and future trends in Arctic transport. The report is a message by the Arctic states to the world with a framework to address many complex challenges involved

[25] The draft code is also inconsistent with the existing international law of the sea in that it requires prior notification for ships entering into EEZs of coastal states, which contradicts a set legal right to navigation of other states in EEZs.

[26] Antarctic Treaty Secretariat, Antarctic Treaty Consultative Meeting Decision 4 (2004).

[27] J Jabour, 'Progress towards the Mandatory Code for Polar Shipping' (2014) 1 *Australian Journal of Maritime and Ocean Affairs* 6, 64.

[28] ibid, 65.

in protecting Arctic people and the environment in an era of expanding use of the Arctic Ocean. However, as mentioned, the recommendations developed are not legally binding, but certainly they contribute to the adoption of subsequent legal measures accounting for Arctic-specific conditions. It can therefore be observed that the two significant regional conventions concluded under the auspices of the Arctic Council—the 2011 Agreement on Co-operation on Aeronautical and Maritime Search and Rescue in the Arctic (SAR Agreement) and the 2013 Arctic Marine Oil Pollution, Preparedness, and Response Agreement—are the milestones in the development of a further legal mechanism concerning Arctic-specific challenges including, and connected to, shipping and navigation.

D. National Legislation

Due to increased shipping through the NSR, the Russian government has opened an office called NSRA (Northern Sea Route Administration) that has been assigned the authority to administer the NSR. In January 2013, the Ministry of Transport of the Russian Federation developed and approved the Rules of Navigation on Water Areas of the Northern Sea Route. The rules include procedures for the navigation of ships in the water areas of the NSR; icebreaker assistance for ships in the water areas of the NSR; pilot ice assistance for ships in the water areas of the NSR; assistance for ships in the seaways of the water areas of the NSR; navigational-hydrographic and hydrometeorologic support for the navigation of ships in the water areas of the NSR; radio communication during the navigation of ships in the water areas of the NSR; requirements set for ships with respect to the safety of navigation and protection of the marine environment from the pollution from ships; and other provisions in relation to the organisation of the navigation of ships in the water areas of the NSR.[29]

III. CHINA AND ARCTIC SHIPPING

A. China's Shipping Interest in the Arctic

China has emerged as a major shipping nation. With the growth of its economic power, China's maritime power is growing very fast. Consequently,

[29] ABS, 'Navigating the Northern Sea Route Status and Guidance', www.eagle.org/eagleExternalPortal WEB/ShowProperty/BEA%20Repository/References/Capability%20Brochures/NSR_Advisory.

China is becoming increasingly assertive in its maritime endeavours.[30] The shipping industry has made an important contribution to the rapid development of the Chinese economy. 90 per cent of China's export and import are carried out by maritime transport.[31] As mentioned above, in terms of vessel numbers, China is now the largest ship-owning country in the world. Moreover, as of 1 January 2013, Chinese ownership of vessels was ranked third in the world. Chinese shipowners control 11.78 per cent of the total world tonnage.[32] China has also emerged as the world's largest shipbuilder, and expanded its dry bulk shipbuilding capacity by a factor of six between 2008 and 2010.[33] Furthermore, China is now one of the world's biggest suppliers of seafarers.[34]

Therefore, it is not a surprise that China has a strong interest in using Arctic shipping routes.[35] MV *Xue Long*, the world's largest non-nuclear-powered icebreaker, became the first Chinese vessel to traverse the Northeast Passage in summer 2012, conducting research on sea ice, navigation and meteorology in the Arctic. Jianzhong Wang, Captain of the *Xue Long*, believes that the use of NEP is of significant importance for the development of the Chinese economy.[36] The Northeast Passage could be a new route between China and Europe, which may greatly save shipping costs.[37] Following the *Xue Long*, the COSCO[38]-owned vessel *Yong Sheng*, weighing 19,000 tonnes, has become the first Chinese commercial vessel to tackle the tough NEP, having set sail from the Chinese port of Taicang to Rotterdam in

[30] KY Zou, 'China's Ocean Policymaking: Practice and Lessons' (2012) 2 *Coastal Management* 40, 158.

[31] Ministry of Transport & Legislative Affairs Office of State Council, PR China, *The Legislative Interpretation of 2009 Regulation on the Prevention and Control of Marine Pollution from Vessels* (Beijing, China Communications Press, 2010) 1 (in Chinese).

[32] United Nations Conference on Trade and Development Review of Maritime Transport 2013 (n 4) 43.

[33] UNCTAD Review of Maritime Transport 2011; see also Ministry of Transport & Legislative Affairs Office of State Council, PR China, *The Legislative Interpretation of 2009 Regulation on the Prevention and Control of Marine Pollution from Vessels* (Beijing, China Communications Press, 2010) 146–47 (in Chinese).

[34] Seafarer supply covers two different employment groups: officers and ratings. China ranks first in the world with 90,295 ratings and a share of 12.1%. For supplying officers, China comes second in the world with 51,511 officers (UNCTAD Review of Maritime Transport, 2011); see also Ministry of Transport & Legislative Affairs Office of State Council, *The Legislative Interpretation of 2009 Regulation on the Prevention and Control of Marine Pollution from Vessels* (n 33) 158–59.

[35] Presentation of Mr Yunpeng Li, President, China Ocean Shipping (Group) Co (COSCO Group), 1st Arctic Circle, Reykjavik, Iceland, 13 October 2013.

[36] 'Interview with Captain of Xue Long, the Northeast Passage is Partly Navigable' *The Central People's Government of the People's Republic of China* (17 September 2012) www.gov.cn/jrzg/2012-09/17/content_2226556.htm, (in Chinese).

[37] ibid.

[38] China Ocean Shipping (Group) Company. It is the largest dry bulk carrier in China and one of the largest dry bulk shipping operators worldwide.

summer 2013.[39] This voyage took 27 days, which saved nine days and 2800 nautical miles compared to the traditional route via the Strait of Malacca and Suez Canal.

According to Malte Humpert,

> future shipping in the Polar region will mostly consist of seasonal destinational transport, delivering supplies into the Arctic for its increasing economic activity and transporting the region's natural resources to markets in East Asia. Arctic shipping routes will be unable to compete with the world's existing major trade routes. Thus, while climate change will, over the coming decades, transform the frozen north into a seasonally navigable ocean, Arctic shipping routes will not become a new silk road for China.[40]

Although this is echoed by some Chinese scholars, such as Chuanxin Wang and Baozhi Chen,[41] the Ministry of Transport (MOT), the competent authority of the Chinese government that is in charge of maritime transport, does not share this view. In September 2014, the China Maritime Safety Administration (MSA) of the MOT published China's first Guidebook for Arctic Shipping (Northeast Passage) (the Guidebook). Based on information from voyages conducted by the *Xue Long* and *Yong Sheng*, the Guidebook aims to provide detailed navigational information for commercial vessels sailing in the Northeast Passage. The Guidebook consists of four parts. These contain (1) relevant national/Russian legislation and applicable international conventions; (2) weather and meteorology conditions; (3) suggested safe routes for vessels; and (4) ice-strengthening measures.[42] During the *Xue Long's* voyage along the Northeast Passage, Captain Jianzhong Wang complained that although the Russian authority does provide weather, sea ice and piloting services for vessels sailing in the Northeast Passage, these are not convenient for Chinese vessels due to language barriers.[43]

In addition to potential cost-saving for shipping companies, the Ministry of Transport believes that the use of the Northeast Passage will improve China's energy security.[44] China was a net oil exporter until the early 1990s

[39] A Staalesen, 'First Container Ship on Northern Sea Route' *Barents Observer* (21 August 2013) www.barentsobserver.com/en/arctic/2013/08/first-container-ship-northern-sea-route-21-08.

[40] M Humpert, 'The Future of Arctic Shipping: A New Silk Road for China?' (Arctic Institute, November 2013) 15.

[41] Prof Chuanxin Wang from Tongji University, Shanghai: 'It is still quite limited for navigation in Arctic Sea Routes'. Dr Baozhi Chen from Shanghai Institute for International Studies: 'There is a lack of infrastructure, port facilities as well as search and rescue capacity along Arctic sea routes. Moreover, sea ice conditions in the summer are not certain. The use of Arctic sea routes also requires ice-strengthening vessels and specially trained seafarers'; 'China is Coming to the Arctic Sea Route' *China Water Transport* (newspaper published by Ministry of Transport) (28 July 2014) (in Chinese).

[42] '"Guidance on Arctic Navigation in the Northeast Route" Published' (n 11).

[43] 'Interview with Captain of Xue Long, the Northeast Passage is Partly Navigable' (n 36).

[44] 'China is Coming to the Arctic Sea Route' (n 41).

and became the world's second-largest net importer of crude oil and petroleum products in 2009.[45] However, China has been facing the 'Malacca Dilemma' over the years.[46] At present, approximately 60 per cent of China's crude oil imports originate in the Middle East, and this figure is expected to rise to 75 per cent by 2015. Oil from the Persian Gulf and Africa is shipped to China via the Malacca or Lombok/Makkasar straits. Over the past few years, Chinese leaders have come to view the straits, especially the Malacca Strait, as a strategic vulnerability.[47] The opening of new sea routes in the Arctic might reduce China's dependence on the Malacca Strait. Moreover, the Arctic contains vast oil and natural gas reserves. The US Geological Survey estimates the Arctic could contain 1670 trillion cubic feet (tcf) of natural gas and 90 billion barrels of oil, or 30 per cent of the world's undiscovered gas and 13 per cent of oil.[48] Climate change is gradually making access to the Arctic marine area easier, and as such, offshore hydrocarbon exploitation is anticipated to be a major future economic activity in the Arctic.[49] Therefore, the Arctic has the potential to become another Middle East as an important energy supplier for China. In the Strategic Review 2013, published by the Centre for National Defence Policy, Academy of Military Science, it is for the first time stated by the Military of China that the Arctic is very meaningful for the sustainable development of China because of new shipping routes and rich oil and gas reserves.[50]

B. China and Interpretation of Article 234 of the UNCLOS

At the beginning of the UNCLOS III, China was Mao's China and the notorious Cultural Revolution (1966–76) was ongoing. Diplomacy at the time was aimed at attacking the hegemony of the two superpowers—the Soviet Union and the USA. This policy guided the Chinese delegation at UNCLOS III. It was only after 1978 that the situation in China gradually improved and diplomacy was carried out in a more pragmatic manner.[51] Although

45 China, US Energy Information Administration (4 February 2014).

46 S Chen, 'China's Self-Extrication from the "Malacca Dilemma" and Implications' (2010) 1 *International Journal of China Studies* 1, 1–24.

47 I Storey, 'China's "Malacca Dilemma"' (2006) 6 *China Brief* 8.

48 'Opportunities and Challenges for Arctic Oil and Gas Development' *Wilson Center*, www.wilsoncenter.org/sites/default/files/Artic%20Report_F2.pdf.

49 K Hossain, T Koivurova and G Zojer, 'Understanding Risks Associated with Offshore Hydrocarbon Development' in E Tedsen, S Cavalieri and RA Kraemer (eds), *Arctic Marine Governance, Opportunities for Transatlantic Cooperation* (Heidelberg, Springer, 2014) 159, 160. See also YM Yusuf, 'The Environmental Problems Associated with Offshore Oil and Gas Activities' (2014) 1 *Oil, Gas & Energy Law* 12, 1–16.

50 'China is coming to the Arctic Sea Route' (n 41).

51 K Zou, 'Implementing Marine Environmental Protection Law in China: Progress, Problems and Prospects' (1999) 3 *Marine Policy* 23, 210.

Tommy Koh (President of the Third UN Conference on the Law of the Sea) suggested to China's then-Vice Minister of Foreign Affairs Huang Hua that China should pay more attention to its own interests during negotiations,[52] obviously the Chinese government did not anticipate the later growth of a booming Chinese shipping industry and that China might become a major shipping power in the years that followed. Needless to mention, China had nothing to do with the negotiation of Article 234 (Ice-Covered Area) of the UNCLOS,[53] which bolsters coastal state powers to regulate foreign shipping in order to prevent, reduce and control marine pollution in the Arctic.[54] The negotiation of Article 234 was concluded primarily by three northern states, Canada, the United States and Soviet Union.[55]

Nevertheless, the Arctic is changing. The United States National Oceanic and Atmospheric Administration (NOAA) suggests that summers in the Arctic will be nearly sea ice-free before the middle of this century.[56] Regardless of the current debate on how to define the ice-covered area in the Arctic,[57]it will be more and more difficult for Arctic coastal states to justify references to 'ice-covered area' in an ice-free Arctic. As a shipping power, China should bear in mind that the shipping industry is international in nature. Unilateral coastal state measures could be an extra burden for commercial shipping in any part of the world. Therefore, due to climate change, this is an opportunity for China to have a voice on the interpretation of Article 234 of the UNCLOS, with preference for international rather than national rules and standards applicable to future trans-Arctic shipping in

[52] Personal (Dr Nengye Liu) conversation with Ambassador Tommy Koh, at Ministry of Foreign Affairs, Singapore, 2008.

[53] It reads:

> Coastal States have the right to adopt and enforce non-discriminatory laws and regulations for the prevention, reduction and control of marine pollution from vessels in ice-covered areas within the limits of the exclusive economic zone, where particularly severe climatic conditions and the presence of ice covering such areas for most of the year create obstructions or exceptional hazards to navigation, and pollution of the marine environment could cause major harm to or irreversible disturbance of the ecological balance. Such laws and regulations shall have due regard to navigation and the protection and preservation of the marine environment based on the best available scientific evidence.

[54] Arctic Council Arctic Marine Shipping Assessment 2009 Report, 53.

[55] S Nandan and S Rosenne, *United Nations Convention on the Law of the Sea 1982 A Commentary*, (Dordrecht, Martinus Nijhoff, 1991) 393.

[56] 'Arctic Nearly Free of Summer Sea Ice during First Half of 21st century' *NOAA Arctic Theme* page (13 May 2013) www.arctic.noaa.gov.

[57] Such as (1) whether art 234 relates only to the EEZ (water beyond the territorial sea) or implies the application of art 234 landward of the outer limits of a coastal state's EEZ; (2) what is the meaning of the word 'where' (where particularly severe climatic conditions and the presence of ice covering such areas for most of the year create obstructions or exceptional hazards to navigation)? Is it spatial or temporal? See K Bartenstein, 'The "Arctic Exception" in the Law of the Sea Convention: A Contribution to Safer Navigation in the Northwest Passage?' Ocean (2011) 1 *Development and International Law* 42, 28–30.

the EEZ of Arctic coastal states, especially Canada and Russia. The challenge is obviously how to persuade Canada and Russia to give up their current position.

C. China and Development of the Polar Code

In May 2014, the Maritime Safety Committee (MSC) of the IMO approved, for consideration with a view to adoption at its November 2014 session (MSC 94), the draft new SOLAS Chapter XIV 'Safety measures for ships operating in polar waters', which would make mandatory the Introduction and part I-A of the Polar Code. The MSC also approved, in principle, the draft Polar Code, with a view to adoption in conjunction with the adoption of the associated draft new SOLAS Chapter XIV.[58] The Marine Environment Protection Committee (MEPC) is expected to further consider the environmental chapter at its next session in October 2014 (MEPC 67). Therefore, a mandatory Polar Code will emerge in the foreseeable future.

As mentioned above, China has a strong interest in shipping in the Arctic. Nevertheless, China seems to have nothing to do regarding the development of the Polar Code within the IMO.[59] In the following part, possible reasons for China's current position on the Polar Code are analysed. Then it is argued that China should be more proactive in the future development of the Polar Code.

Indeed, China is a shipping power in terms of vessel numbers and deadweight tonnages. However, so far China is not a powerful member within the decision-making process within the IMO. Chinese delegates attend most IMO meetings, but are normally quiet and not that active. China submitted a total of 88 proposals to different committees and sub-Committees of the IMO from 2000 to 2009. It ranks only ninth among 10 category (a) countries of the Council of the IMO in terms of the number of proposals submitted. In the same period, Japan submitted 640 proposals, Norway submitted 450, the UK submitted 627 and the US submitted 567.[60] China generally has a conservative reaction to the development of international law instead of taking initiatives. There has however been a noticeable increase in China's willingness to be more active in the decision-making process of the IMO.

[58] IMO, 'Shipping in Polar Waters: Development of an International Code of Safety for Ships Operating in Polar Waters (Polar Code)' www.imo.org/MediaCentre/HotTopics/polar/Pages/default.aspx.

[59] Interview with the EU's delegation to the IMO.

[60] D Sun (then Chinese representative to the IMO, Maritime Section of Chinese Embassy in the UK), 'Statistics and Analysis about Proposals submitted by IMO Category A Council Members' (2010) *China Maritime Safety* 8, 69 (in Chinese).

Nevertheless, China lacks a long-term strategic plan for increasing the effectiveness of its involvement in the decision-making process within the IMO.

Moreover, China's attitude to Arctic interests has to date been cautious and pragmatic. Chinese participation in the Arctic is limited within the scope of scientific research.[61] A Chinese diplomat has proposed that China's role in the governance of the Arctic is that of a 'near Arctic' country.[62] However, it will take time for both China and Arctic states to recognise this role. Furthermore, China lacks sufficient resources and capacity to share the burden of global governance.[63] This might be another reason why China is not active in the development of the Polar Code.

Nevertheless, China should have been proactive towards the adoption of a mandatory Polar Code. The draft Polar Code covers the full range of design, construction, equipment, operational, training, search and rescue and environmental protection matters relevant to ships operating in the inhospitable waters surrounding the two poles.[64] It will also harmonise the ice-strengthening standards for polar class vessels. In the authors' opinion, the Polar Code has the potential to define what exactly is meant by 'ice-covered areas' in Article 234 of the UNCLOS. The draft Polar Code includes mandatory measures covering safety (part I-A) and pollution prevention (part II-A) and recommendatory provisions for both (parts I-B and II-B).[65] So far, controversial issues, eg ban on heavy grade fuel oils in the Arctic, are mentioned only in the recommendatory part. In the future, the Polar Code might be developed to cover more issues in its mandatory part, such as anti-fouling and ballast water management for ships sailing in the Arctic. It is once again in China's interest as a flag state to deal with internationally agreed rules and standards rather than unilateral national legislation when sailing in the EEZ of Arctic coastal states, in particular Russia.

D. China as a Newcomer in the Arctic Council

China first submitted its application to be an observer of the Arctic Council in 2006. At the Kiruna ministerial meeting of the Arctic Council in May 2013, China was accepted as an observer, together with Japan, South Korea, India,

[61] H Liu, Y Dong and Y Chen, 'China and the Arctic: the Path of Scientific Research, Law and Policy', (2012) *Ocean Yearbook* 26, 374.

[62] Presentation of Mr Zhao Jun, Chinese Ambassador to Norway at 2013 Arctic Frontiers, Tromsø, Norway.

[63] B Chen, 'Arctic Governance, a Chinese Scholar's Perspective' (2012) 10 *Pacific Journal* 20, 69–70 (in Chinese).

[64] IMO, 'Polar Code' (n 58).

[65] ibid.

Singapore and Italy. According to Xinhua, China's official press agency, observer status in the Arctic Council is a milestone for China on its way to becoming a 'sea power'.[66] Once observer status has been granted, observers are invited to the meetings and other activities of the Arctic Council unless Senior Arctic Officials (SAOs) decide otherwise. In meetings of the Arctic Council's subsidiary bodies to which observers have been invited to participate, observers may, at the discretion of the chair, make statements after Arctic states and permanent participants, present written statements, submit relevant documents and provide views on the issues under discussion. Observers may also submit written statements at ministerial meetings.[67] Observers may also propose projects through an Arctic state or a permanent participant.[68] The current observer status gives an opportunity to follow the vast majority of the Council's work and enables participation in projects and activities undertaken by its subsidiary bodies. Nonetheless, Arctic states have left themselves notable discretion in determining the activity of observers.[69] It has to be pointed out that observers have no voting rights within the Arctic Council. It is however of symbolic significance for China to be officially involved in the most important regional forum for discussion of Arctic issues.

In any case, China could make use of this opportunity to influence decision-making processes within the Arctic Council to protect China's shipping interests in the Arctic. The authors believe that China shares similar shipping interests with Japan and South Korea on issues related to Arctic shipping. They should collaborate and invest resources together to shape the changing governance of Arctic shipping, at both regional (Arctic Council) and international level (IMO). As mentioned above, at a meeting held in Yokohama, Japan on 25 August 2014, China joined South Korea and Japan and adopted a joint declaration to promote co-operation on logistics systems, developing eco-friendly logistics services and achieving a good balance between safety and efficiency in logistics. One of the action plans is to launch services on the Northern Sea Route. Chaired by the Minister of Land, Infrastructure, Transport and Tourism Akihiro Ota of Japan, the meeting was joined by Chief Engineer Zhou Haitao of China's Ministry of Transport and Minister of Oceans and Fisheries Lee Ju-young of South Korea. They unveiled an action plan after exchanging views on international logistics

[66] 'China became an Observer of the Arctic Council, a Milestone to be a Sea Power' *Xinhua* (16 May 2013) news.xinhuanet.com/world/2013-05/16/c_124717385.htm (in Chinese).

[67] Arctic Council Rules of Procedure 1998, pt V: 'Other Matters'.

[68] ibid.

[69] P Graczyk and T Koivurova, 'A New Era in the Arctic Council's External Relations? Broader Consequences of the Nuuk Observer Rules for Arctic Governance' (2014) 3 *Polar Record* 50, 225–36.

policies. The action plan is made up of 12 proposals, which include a new route between Hakata, Japan and Busan, South Korea in the two nations' joint chassis service, in which those from one country are allowed to directly enter the other; a pilot project to visualise cargo movement in the Northeast Asia Logistics Information Service Network (NEAL-NET), which will be commenced in August; and a project to launch services on the Northern Sea route. The three ministers also agreed that the next meeting would be held in China.[70] This meeting is a good sign and starting point for three Asian economies/shipping powers to develop their joint Arctic shipping policy.

E. China and the EU: Common Interest towards Arctic Shipping Rules

The European Union (EU), though it has no coastal line in the Arctic, is inextricably linked to the Arctic region by a unique combination of history, geography, economics and scientific achievements.[71] Three Arctic countries are EU member states (Denmark, Sweden and Finland) and the EU maintains close relations with Iceland and Norway through the European Economic Area (EEA). The EU declared as a condition of joining the UNCLOS that maritime transport, safety of shipping and the prevention of marine pollution contained inter alia in UNCLOS Parts II, III, V, VII and XII are considered to be areas of shared competences between the EU and member states, but also subject to continuous development.[72] Like China, the EU plays a major role in today's shipping world, as 41 per cent of the world's total fleet (in dwt) is beneficially controlled by EEA companies. The EEA registered fleet is 224 million gross tonnage, representing 22 per cent of the world tonnage, the pure EU share being 19.3 per cent.[73] As almost 90 per cent of EU external trade is carried out via sea, the EU has significant experience in shipping, shipbuilding, satellite navigation, search and rescue as well as port infrastructure development.[74] Regarding the EU's Arctic shipping policy, the Commission proposes that the EU should (1) fully implement existing obligations concerning navigational rules, maritime safety,

[70] 'Tripartite Logistics Ministers Meeting Adopts "Yokohama Declaration"' (n 8).

[71] European Commission (2008) 'The European Union and the Arctic Region' COM(2008) 763 final, 20 November 2008, 2.

[72] Declaration Concerning the Competence of the European Community with Regard to Matters Governed by the United Nations Convention on the Law of the Sea of 10 December 1982 and the Agreement of 28 July 1994 relating to the implementation of Part XI of the Convention, Council Decision of 23 March 1998, OJ L179, 23 June 1998, 1.

[73] European Community Shipowners' Association Annual Report 2011–2012, 9, www.ecsa.eu.

[74] European Commission, 'Joint Communication: Developing a European Union Policy towards the Arctic Region: Progress since 2008 and Next Steps' JOIN(2012) 19 final, 4.

routes system and environmental standards in the Arctic, in particular those under the IMO; (2) stress the need to avoid discriminatory practices (fees, obligatory services) by any of the Arctic coastal states towards third countries' merchant fleets; (3) improve maritime surveillance capacities in the far North; (4) maintain the competitive lead of European shipyards in developing technology required for Arctic conditions; and (5) explore support for designating some Arctic navigation routes as Particular Sensitive Sea Areas (PSSAs).[75] Therefore, there is a common interest for both the EU and China to secure freedom of navigation for shipping in the Arctic. China could therefore possibly work together with the EU on issues such as interpretation of Article 234 of the UNCLOS and development of the Polar Code within the IMO.

IV. CONCLUSIONS

China has a strong shipping interest in the Arctic. As a global shipping power, China is interested in using new Arctic sea routes, especially the Northeast Passage, to save costs and improve energy security. China is however facing both opportunities and challenges concerning the development of international law in the Arctic. Due to climate change, it might be more difficult for Arctic coastal states to justify references to 'ice-covered areas' based on Article 234 of the UNCLOS in an ice-free Arctic. This is an opportunity for China, which played a limited role during the negotiation of the UNCLOS, to interpret Article 234 in favour of international rules and standards for shipping rather than more stringent unilateral legislation. Moreover, China should have been more proactive for the adoption of the mandatory Polar Code within the IMO, which will provide uniform rules and standards for future Arctic shipping. Furthermore, China could make use of its observer status in the Arctic Council, together with the EU and other Asian economies such as Japan and South Korea, to influence decision-making on shipping-related issues. Nevertheless, China so far has not even adopted its official Arctic policy. China's participation in the Arctic is limited to scientific research. Although a shipping power in terms of vessel numbers and deadweight tonnage, China is not very active in the decision-making process of the IMO. It seems that China still lacks the resources and capacity to share the burden of global governance, including the development of international law in the Arctic.

[75] European Commission, 'The EU and the Arctic Region' (2008) (n 71).

12

Concluding Chapter

Several Pathways to Arctic Engagement

SÉBASTIEN DUYCK, TAPIO NYKÄNEN,
TIMO KOIVUROVA AND QIN TIANBAO

I. INTRODUCTION

FOR MANY CENTURIES, the main actors of international relations either ignored the Arctic or considered the region to be peripheral, as symbolised by its position on the margins of the Mercator map. This situation began to evolve with the Cold War as the two superpowers of the time literally faced off against each other in the region. For a few decades, the Arctic thus became a region of uttermost strategic importance from a military standpoint and the theatre of robust militarisation. But even then, this face-off mainly concerned the two most powerful nations—the United States and the Soviet Union, both having an important coastline in the Arctic Ocean—and to a lesser extent the northern allies of the United States. For more distant nations, the Arctic only gained relevance with the growing understanding of the regional impacts of climate changes. In the past two decades, the increase in awareness of the consequences of human interference with the climate system has emphasised the potential importance of the region for the rest of the world.[1]

First, climate science highlighted that changes in the Arctic would have global implications. In the past, Arctic nations and peoples had already raised the alarm in relation to the impacts of distant economic activities on the most remote Arctic locations. For instance, Arctic indigenous peoples very effectively increased awareness of the contamination of the Arctic food web by Persistent Organic Pollutants (POPs) originating from thousands of

[1] See eg C Southcott, 'History of Globalization in the Circumpolar World' in L Heininen and C Southcott (eds), *Globalization and the circumpolar north* (Fairbanks, University of Alaska Press, 2010).

kilometres away.[2] In the context of climate change, however, this vulnerability of the region to external environmental stressors became a bidirectional phenomenon. As in the case of POPs, the circumpolar world remains under pressures resulting mainly from human activities taking place in distant areas. Similarly, the Arctic ice sheets and the polar marine ecosystems are impacted by greenhouse gases emitted anywhere in the world. The novel element associated with these environmental changes is that the implications are no longer contained to the region. The melting of the Greenlandic ice sheet, for instance, not only impacts communities and ecosystems located on the narrow coastal strip around the island, but also contributes to the global sea level rise with severe consequences for communities in low-lying coastlands or on islands anywhere else on the planet.

Secondly, the gradual increase of temperatures in the region has led to the expectation that new resources will become accessible. While sea ice has ensured that the region remains out of reach of large-scale industrial developments, the prospects of a gradual reduction in the extent of sea ice—and the likelihood of ice-free summers further into the future—suddenly revolutionised investors' and analysts' perceptions of the Arctic. At a time when very few regions of the world still remain outside the reach of man's extractive and industrial thirst, the possibility that such a large and resource-rich region would be rapidly opened to economic activities raised the interest of actors located far beyond the limits of the Arctic Circle. The fossil-fuels extraction and shipping industries in particular began to anticipate the potential revolution that these changes might usher in. The US Geological Survey estimated in 2008 that up to 20 per cent of the world's undiscovered oil and gas reserves could be located in the region.[3] Maritime transport experts also emphasised the unprecedented shortcut that an ice-free Arctic would provide for the transportation of goods between Asia and either the North American east coast or Europe, potentially reducing the shipping distance by up to 25 per cent compared to current alternatives. While experts caution against taking these figures at face value, emphasising the unique challenges that persist in the region, these numbers continue to shape the public perception of the Arctic as an area promising new potential.

As a logical response to these global implications of changes in the Arctic, regional neighbours and distant actors have become significantly more interested in the development of economic opportunities and regional governance in the region. Investments by foreign companies in the Arctic are rising steeply, as are the number and the diversity of applicants to observer status to the Arctic Council.

[2] T Fenge and DL Downie, *Northern Lights Against POPs: Combatting Toxic Threats in the Arctic* (Montreal, McGill-Queen's Press, 2003).

[3] DL Gautier et al, 'Circum-Arctic Resource Appraisal: Estimates of Undiscovered Oil and Gas North of the Arctic Circle' (2008) 3049 *US Geological Survey Fact Sheet*.

Throughout this edited volume, we have sought to further the understanding of the roles and interests of three policy actors in the Arctic: China, Finland and the EU. Each chapter provides additional insights that contribute to this general exercise. Some of these contributions seek to assess the extent to which non-Arctic states enjoy rights in the region and what role China has been and could be playing in the main forum involved in Arctic governance, the Arctic Council (Chapters 2, 3, 5 and 8). Other contributions analyse the construction of a domestic identity and the shaping of public narrative on the Arctic (Chapters 4, 6 and 7). The final chapters of the volume address the role of non-Arctic states, and of China and the EU more specifically, in relation to sectoral policies of high relevance to the circumpolar world: maritime security, marine environmental protection and relations with indigenous peoples (Chapters 9, 10 and 11).

In the present conclusions, we draw on these diverse contributions to provide a succinct analysis of the paths leading non-Arctic states to step up their involvement in Arctic governance. We begin by providing a short review of the state of play in the region related to the rights and obligations of states lacking coastal access to the Arctic Ocean. We then present the different strategies implemented by China, Finland and the EU to increase their presence in the Arctic. These three actors provide a very diverse set of experiences, each of them representing a unique position in relation to future Arctic developments. The comparison between the interests and strategies of these actors is fruitful, both in terms of allowing them to learn from each other's experiences and good practices as well as providing core Arctic players with an understanding of the perspectives and priorities that frame the engagement of these two crucial external actors as well as of Finland in Arctic developments. The response by Arctic actors to these interests is then described. Finally, we highlight four areas for additional research that could contribute to a better understanding of the role and status of non-Arctic states and the EU in the circumpolar world.

II. THE RIGHTS AND OBLIGATIONS OF NON-ARCTIC STATES

While the Arctic, and in particular the Arctic Ocean, remained for many years out of reach for most economic activities, the legal status of the region is however very far from that of a terra nullius. All land areas in the region fall within the territorial sovereignty of one of the eight Arctic states, with the miniscule exception of Hans Island. Additionally, the marine areas covered by the jurisdiction of the five Arctic coastal states contain the vast majority of the natural resources located in or under the Arctic Ocean—including Arctic offshore oil and gas reserves as well as any potential future fish stocks.[4]

[4] See eg OR Young, 'Governing the Arctic Ocean' (2016) 71 *Marine Policy* (online version).

There are therefore virtually no resources that non-Arctic states can expect to exploit in the short term outside of the jurisdiction of the coastal states. The positions of non-coastal states with regard to the Arctic Ocean and related economic opportunities—such as fisheries and the use of new shipping routes—is however less restricted. The customary law of the sea, as codified in UNCLOS, defines the rights and obligations of states with regard to activities taking place in the oceans.[5] The 1982 Convention builds to a large extent on the recognised principle of the freedoms of the seas. Not only are states free to engage in most economic activities in relation to areas beyond national jurisdiction—the high seas and the 'Area' (the area of the sea floor located beyond national jurisdiction)—but third states also enjoy limited rights to conduct peaceful activities within waters falling under the jurisdiction of the coastal states. Third states also benefit from specific rights related to shipping or scientific research for peaceful purposes that are explicitly protected under the UNCLOS. These rights come together with a limited set of obligations. UNCLOS provides a duty for all states to take national measures and to co-operate regarding the preservation of marine living resources in the high seas. The convention also provides a general duty for all states to protect and preserve the marine environment.

Additionally, the Svalbard archipelago is regulated under a unique legal framework building on the 1920 Spitzbergen Treaty. The treaty was adopted with the purpose of preserving peace over the archipelago, the legal status of which was then the subject of a dispute between Norway and other states. The provisions of the treaty grant Norway sovereignty over the islands while at the same time preserving the rights of other contracting parties with regard to commercial activities on the islands. Consequently, the more than 40 parties to the treaty have additional legally protected economic rights over the archipelago.[6]

While these rights provide an undeniable basis for third states to potentially benefit from opportunities in the Arctic, the characteristics specific to the region however warrant a strong role for the coastal states. For instance, while third nations can access the Arctic coastlines, subject to the rules of Canada and Russia, commercial traffic through the Northern Sea Route will nevertheless require strong logistical support from the Russian authorities in exchange for financial fees. The conduct of scientific activities in exclusive economic zones and on the continental shelf is also subject to approval by the coastal states (or by Norway, in relation to research conducted in the territory covered by the Spitzbergen Treaty) who thus retain a great deal of latitude in facilitating or impeding such activities.

[5] United Nations Convention on the Law of the Sea, 10 December 1982, in force 16 November 1994, 21 *International Legal Materials* 1261 (1982) (UNCLOS).

[6] See Ren in this volume, Ch 3.

III. PATHWAYS AND STRATEGIES TO PARTICIPATE IN ARCTIC GOVERNANCE

The approaches adopted by states interested in playing a greater role in the Arctic while lacking direct access to the Arctic Ocean differ in many respects. Those might build on various strategies involving rhetorical, economic, scientific and geopolitical elements.

Finland, as an Arctic state—albeit not an Arctic Ocean coastal state—occupies a very different position from China and the EU in relation to Arctic governance, thus providing a useful point of reference.

As a member of the Arctic Council, Finland has been actively involved at the core of circumpolar co-operation since the inception of the relevant processes. Finland, in effect, commenced the entire circumpolar co-operation process by convening the Arctic states to negotiate what became the 1991 Arctic Environmental Protection Strategy (the so-called 'Rovaniemi Process'), which was later merged into the 1996 Arctic Council. Additionally, Finland is also a member of other regional co-operation forums covering parts of the Arctic, such as the Barents Euro-Arctic Council and the Nordic Council.

Since 2008, co-operation by the five Arctic Ocean coastal states has to some extent undermined this position, as issues related to the Arctic Ocean—and in particular to fisheries—have been dealt with through this more exclusive forum. With the thawing of the summer sea ice, the Arctic Ocean is gradually occupying a more important place among issues related to Arctic regional co-operation,[7] a trend that could potentially weaken the role of Finland as an Arctic actor.

Perhaps as a consequence of these developments, Finland appears to have rediscovered in recent years the importance of the Arctic for its national identity, increasingly referring to itself as an Arctic nation and making references to its Arctic experience when intervening in global governance forums. Finland is for instance one of the only two Arctic states to have released two comprehensive Arctic strategies defining in great detail the policy priorities for the country in the Arctic.[8] The country has also defined its entire territory as being in the Arctic, and has suggested in its 2013 Arctic strategy the formalisation of the Arctic Council.[9]

China is in a very different situation as the country is located much more south of the Arctic Circle and thus did not participate in the regional

[7] P Kankaanpaa and OR Young, 'The Effectiveness of the Arctic Council' (2012) 31 *Polar Research* (online version).

[8] The US has as well, but its strategies are less comprehensive.

[9] Prime Minister's Office, *Finland's Strategy for the Arctic Region* (Prime Minister's Office Publications 16/2013).

processes initiated at the end of the Cold War. The country has nevertheless demonstrated a growing interest in the region.[10] In 2007, the country submitted a formal application for observer status at the Arctic Council, an application that was accepted six years later during the Kiruna ministerial meeting in 2013. When arguing for the legitimacy of its Arctic interests, the country has been prompt to put forward its experience in Arctic and polar research. In addition to this political involvement, the main presence of China in the Arctic relates to current and future economic developments, through possible investments in Arctic regions and an increased interest in Arctic shipping.

China has been seeking to make use of the current legal regime to enhance the benefits that the country might gain rather than to overtly question the existing governance framework. This approach is actually a good example of Deng's doctrine of 'keeping a low profile and hiding one's brightness' in Chinese foreign relations.

Additionally, China's involvement in the Arctic has been built more on bilateral relations with the relevant key actors, such as Canada, Norway, Iceland or Denmark, rather than through active participation in multilateral processes.[11] This trend is comparable to the approach used by China when dealing with other regional marine issues, for instance with regard to its interactions with other coastal states in the South China Sea where the country prefers bilateral relations rather than regional co-operation forums.

However, references by some Chinese civil servants and scholars to the concept of the 'global commons' when characterising the Arctic have raised concerns, as most of the region is actually already divided among the coastal states. These references have led to fears that China could seek to more openly question the existing framework of Arctic governance.[12]

Due to its specific nature, the presence and influence of the EU in the region is particularly complex. First, while the EU is generally referred to as a non-Arctic actor, two of its members (Finland and Sweden) possess Arctic territories and are themselves considered Arctic nations. The situation is more peculiar in relation to Greenland and Denmark. While Denmark, itself a member state of the EU, takes part in Arctic institutions such as the Arctic Council to represent Greenland, the island exited the European Union in 1985.[13] Many decisions adopted by the EU also have direct implications for two additional Arctic

[10] See F Lasserre, 'China and the Arctic: Threat or Cooperation Potential for Canada?' (2010) 11 *China Papers*. Centre for International Relations—The University of British Columbia and Canadian International Council.

[11] See eg D Degeorges, *The Role Of Greenland in The Arctic* (Paris, IRSEM, 2012); L Jakobson 'China Prepares for an Ice-Free Arctic' (2010) 2 *SIPRI Insights on Peace and Security*.

[12] See eg references in L Jakobson and J Peng, 'China's Arctic Aspirations' (2012) 34 *SIPRI Policy Paper*.

[13] See S Berglund, 'Prison or Voluntary Cooperation? The Possibility of Withdrawal from the European Union' (2006) 29(2) *Scandinavian Political Studies* 147, 157.

countries—Iceland and Norway—through the membership of these states in the European Economic Area. Moreover, the majority of the non-Arctic state observers of the Arctic Council are member states of the EU.

The role that the EU already plays and could be playing in relation to Arctic governance must be understood on the basis of the division of competence between the EU itself and its member states. According to the treaties establishing the European Union, the EU has exclusive competence in relation to several policy areas (among which the conservation of marine biological resources) and shares competence with its member states in other areas (such as fisheries, environmental and energy policies). In other matters, the EU has complementary competence to the one its member states have in defining their policies.[14]

The contribution of the EU to Arctic governance also builds on a longer history than most other observers. For many years, the EU has contributed to Arctic governance through its participation in regional forums such as the Barents Euro-Arctic Council.[15] Even more importantly, the EU has a strong presence in a number of areas crucially relevant for the Arctic: its economic presence, funding of Arctic research, active engagement in Arctic governance, significant environmental footprint and engagement with the region's indigenous peoples.

A unique feature of the EU's engagement in the Arctic consists of the consideration of its role as a consumer of Arctic goods and its impact on the regime. The EU has conducted an assessment of its social and environmental impact in the region, through its contribution to long-range pollution and its role as a consumer of Arctic goods.[16] The institutions of the EU highlight this exercise to demonstrate that the EU intends to be a responsible actor in relation to the Arctic, aiming at reducing the adverse impacts of its domestic activities on the region.

At the same time, the EU also decided to consider the ethical implications of some of its imports from the region, in particular in relation to the import of fur products and concerns regarding animal welfare. In 2009, the EU imposed a ban on these products, with the exemption of seal products from traditional Inuit hunts. The original modalities included in this regulation to prevent adverse impacts on indigenous communities did not suffice to adequately protect the Inuit from the social and economic consequences of this ban.[17]

[14] T Koivurova, K Kokko, S Duyck, N Sellheim and A Stepien, 'The Present and Future Competence of the European Union in the Arctic' (2012) 48(4) *Polar Record* 361.

[15] A Myrjord, 'Governance Beyond the Union: EU Boundaries in the Barents Euro-Arctic Region' (2003) 8(2) *European Foreign Affairs Review* 239.

[16] See Ecologic Institute and others (S Cavalieri et al), *EU Arctic Footprint and Policy Assessment, Final Report* (European Commission, 2010) arctic-footprint.eu.

[17] See N Sellheim, 'The Neglected Tradition?—The Genesis of the EU Seal Products Trade Ban and Commercial Sealing' (2013) 5(1) *The Yearbook of Polar Law Online* 417; N Sellheim,

This resistance has however forced EU institutions to consider a more subtle policy for the Arctic as well as prompted the Union to demonstrate the legitimacy of its Arctic interest. As a result, the EU attempted to present itself as an exemplary Arctic external actor. That is for instance visible in the balanced language used in the EU documents after 2009 in which EU institutions have somewhat downplayed their institutional proposals for the Arctic. The EU has also renewed its efforts to engage and co-operate with various Arctic actors, including Arctic indigenous peoples. It also increased the amount of resources allocated to a broad range of Arctic-relevant projects.

This review highlights the diversity of the approaches followed by the three policy entities to strengthen their position in the Arctic. As a consequence, governments interested in playing a more important role in the Arctic have the opportunity to learn from each other's experiences, both to identify good practices that could be replicated as well as to anticipate those activities that have resulted in additional tensions with Arctic actors. The diversity of approaches used by non-Arctic states might also pose additional challenges for Arctic states and other relevant actors when considering what role such distant nations could and will have in Arctic governance.

IV. RESPONSES BY LOCAL ACTORS TO THE INTERESTS OF DISTANT NATIONS

In relation to broader governance issues, the Arctic states, and in particular the five coastal states, have also proven reluctant to invite other states to participate too actively in regional co-operation. The main forum for regional governance—the Arctic Council—remains a body strongly focused on the role of the eight Arctic states and of the organisations representing Arctic indigenous peoples. Non-Arctic states have been relegated to the status of observers—a status granted based on the goodwill of the Arctic Eight. The Arctic states reacted to this surge of external interest by redefining the role of observers, listing the conditions under which non-Arctic states would be considered for observer status while refusing to reconsider the scope of opportunities offered to observers to engage in the Council.[18]

The Arctic interests of some of the most important non-Arctic actors have also faced particular suspicion and resistance from Arctic actors. China's

'The Goals of the EU Seal Products Trade Regulation: From Effectiveness to Consequence' (2015) 51(3) *Polar Record* 274.

[18] P Graczyk and T Koivurova, 'A New Era in the Arctic Council's External Relations? Broader Consequences of the Nuuk Observer Rules for Arctic Governance' (2012) 50(3) *Polar Record* 225, 230.

initiatives to gain a stronger foothold in the region have been opposed by host countries, for instance in relation to the potential purchase of property in Iceland and in Greenland.[19]

In relation to the increasing presence of the EU, the dispute over the import of seal fur has greatly undermined the relations between the Union and some of its Arctic partners. Canada, Norway and indigenous peoples' organisations took a very negative view of the consumer activism associated with this measure, denouncing in particular its impacts on local indigenous populations. This issue incurred direct implications for the status of the EU in Arctic governance.[20] In addition to the seal fur dispute, institutional proposals made by the EU Parliament with regard to Arctic governance have also been negatively perceived as intrusive on the matters related to the sovereignty or the environmental 'stewardship' of the Arctic states.[21]

Consequently, some of the Arctic actors have given the EU a cool welcome to the region. These concerns culminated with the rejection of the EU application as an observer to the Arctic Council. During the 2013 Kiruna ministerial meeting, the Arctic States suspended the approval of the application to the resolution of the seal dispute, a suspension particularly notable as the applications submitted by other actors with much less at stake and experience in the region were approved.[22]

On issues related only to the Arctic Ocean, the five coastal states have created an additional informal forum for political discussions in relation to which no role for any other actor is yet foreseen—not even for the three Arctic states lacking direct access to the Arctic Ocean. The relevance of this co-operation platform is currently much more limited in scope, ambition and degree of institutionalisation than the Arctic Council. The five coastal states have however initiated discussions through this channel on important developments that might affect the rights and interests of other nations in relation to the preventive regulation of fisheries. These specific developments tend to indicate that the three Arctic states lacking direct access to the Arctic Ocean (Finland, Iceland and Sweden) cannot take for granted the willingness of the five coastal states to address all Arctic-related issues through co-operation involving all eight Arctic states and the six organisations currently recognised to represent Arctic indigenous peoples. In other regions of the world, regional seas instruments also very seldom provide a role, either

[19] See DC Wright, 'China's Growing Interest in the Arctic' (2013) 15(2) *Journal of Military and Strategic Studies* 54.

[20] N Wegge, 'The EU and the Arctic: European Foreign Policy in the Making' (2012) 3(12) *Arctic Review on Law and Politics* 6, 20.

[21] See Graczyk and Koivurova, 'A New Era in the Arctic Council's External Relations?' (n 18) 226.

[22] PE Steinberg and K Dodds, 'The Arctic Council after Kiruna' (2013) 51(1) *Polar Record* 108.

as parties or as observers, for non-coastal states, providing therefore only limited precedents that would support more inclusive regional governance on marine issues.[23]

Besides the status of non-Arctic states in the Arctic Council, the response of the coastal states to the interest expressed by other countries in future economic activities in the region is also critical in shaping the ability of these other nations to make full use of the rights that they enjoy in the region under international law.

In turn, this reaction by the Arctic states—and in particular by the five Arctic coastal states—is based to a large extent on their perception of the strategies and activities implemented by external actors in the region and thus shaped significantly by the behaviour of these actors.

V. MOVING RESEARCH FORWARD: SUGGESTIONS FOR FURTHER RESEARCH

The research conducted in the preparation of the present volume suggested four areas in which additional research would be particularly warranted in order to further the understanding of the role and opportunities of non-Arctic actors in the region.

First, as the Arctic gradually becomes even more integrated in international economic structures, developments in the region become more dependent on international markets and thus on the role of external actors as consumers (and investors). This is particularly so as the region's most vital economic activities consist of primary industries particularly dependent on global commodity prices.

In this context, important external economic actors, such as China and the EU, have the potential to influence developments in the Arctic through their consumption of Arctic resources. The demand generated by these markets, also influenced by their domestic regulations and policies, plays a key role in shaping global prices and, consequently, the prospects (and profitability) for the extraction of these resources in the future.[24]

The role of the EU as a consumer of Arctic products has been studied at length in relation to its decision to ban imports of seal furs to its domestic

[23] 3 regional frameworks do provide examples of other inclusive approaches to regional marine instruments: the Convention for the Protection of the Mediterranean Sea Against Pollution (Barcelona Convention), the Convention on the Conservation of Antarctic Marine Living Resources (CCAMLR) and the Convention for the Protection of the Marine Environment of the North-East Atlantic ('OSPAR Convention'). See S Duyck, 'Legal Issues Related to Options for a Regional Seas-type Arrangement for the Arctic Ocean' Briefing Paper prepared for the Natural Resource Defence Council, available at papers.ssrn.com/sol3/papers.cfm?abstract_id=2517104.

[24] See the statistics provided in the introduction to this volume.

market as well as its impacts on Arctic indigenous communities. This EU policy is however rather unique as external actors have so far very rarely adopted decisions specifically targeting Arctic products. Little research has been dedicated to studying the role of external actors such as the EU and China in relation to Arctic developments through their broader domestic policies.[25]

Secondly, the role of domestic actors in shaping the national positions of non-Arctic states with regard to the region is generally little understood. However, the influence and priorities of the actors, both institutional and non-governmental, contribute greatly to shaping the engagement of non-Arctic states in the region. Furthermore, forthcoming changes in internal power relations and for example juridical statuses of indigenous peoples may affect the cohesion and direction of national policies. For instance, the Nordic Sami Convention could strengthen the internal status of the Sami in Nordic countries and create an even more unified cross-border Sami identity, which in turn could affect Sami policies and possibly national policies in many arenas.[26] Furthering the understanding of these domestic forces could help explain the differences between the interests and positions of various non-Arctic states.

This analysis could also help assess to what extent statements and claims by non-governmental actors, including NGOs, private actors and academics, are likely to contribute to influencing the positions of non-Arctic states. The governance structure of China and the EU present particular specificities that offer few points of comparison with other actors engaged in Arctic affairs, for instance with respect to the relations between the state, educational institutions and state-owned enterprises in China or with regard to the existence of three institutions at EU level.

In both cases internal institutional arrangements influencing decision-making relevant to the Arctic are not well understood by external partners, which might contribute negatively to the establishment of trust between Arctic actors on the one hand and external actors such as China and the EU on the other hand.

Thirdly, the importance of the co-operation among external players with regard to Arctic developments has received little academic attention up to now, with most focus being dedicated to the issue of co-operation among the Arctic states, or in some cases between Arctic states and some external actors.

Among the historical observers to the Arctic Council, Poland has played a specific role in convening meetings of the observers to consider opportunities

[25] The EU Footprint Study constitutes a notable exception to this assessment. See n 16.

[26] See T Koivurova, 'The Draft Nordic Saami Convention: Nations Working Together' (2008) 10 *International Community Law Review* 10 (2008) 279–93.

for further involvement and contribution to Arctic affairs. These meetings have enabled non-Arctic states to discuss their own priorities and perspectives with regard to Arctic affairs while at the same time avoiding appearing to be in conflict with the role of the eight Arctic states or of the Arctic Council. Additionally, other external actors have in some instances joined forces on specific scientific co-operation projects.

In the past, China was involved in Arctic co-operation with other non-Arctic actors only as far as scientific research was involved. More recently, the country signed a memorandum of understanding for co-operation on the safety of Arctic shipping with Japan and South Korea. It remains to be seen whether this co-operation will deliver practical results for the benefit of all participating countries. Such Asian co-operation on Arctic affairs could potentially provide added value to the Arctic states in strengthening their presence in the Arctic.

Such co-operation among non-Arctic actors could serve several purposes, for instance enabling them to combine their scientific, economic and logistical resources as well as to discuss and address concerns or issues more specific to distant nations. At the same time, any co-operation involving non-Arctic states would need to walk a fine line in order to avoid appearing to challenge the primary role that Arctic states and indigenous peoples legitimately expect to play with regard to any activity occurring in the region. Assessing past co-operation among non-Arctic actors and exploring opportunities to further develop such co-operation could help to evaluate the feasibility and benefits of such co-operation.

Fourthly, the historical evolution of the presence of various non-Arctic states highlights the important role that crises—be they economic or geopolitical—play in shaping the latitude for engagement by external actors. The economic crisis impacting Iceland in 2008–09 ('kreppa') for instance forced the country to reconsider its ties to distant powers. During the crisis and its aftermath, stronger economic ties with China were considered by some actors as a potential solution to support the economy of the country and the finances of the government. Additionally, the country also initiated formal negotiations with the EU towards a potential accession of the nation to the European Union. Both of these discussions were however terminated as soon as the economy of the country began to recover.[27]

Additionally, the ongoing tensions between Russia and the West over the Ukrainian crisis have impacted the nature of the relations between Russia and some of the key external actors, most importantly the EU and China. While Arctic scholars highlighted that, at the time of writing, the political co-operation between Russia and other Arctic states had not yet significantly

[27] See eg E Bergmann, *Iceland and the International Financial Crisis: Boom, Bust and Recovery* (London, Palgrave Macmillan, 2014).

suffered from the Ukrainian crisis, economic relations in the Arctic have undoubtedly taken a major blow due to the sanctions resulting from this crisis. These increased tensions have however led to the strengthening of the ties that Russia maintains with other players interested in greater involvement in the Arctic.

When the Ukrainian crisis bolstered the tensions between Russia and the West, Russia turned to the East with a new enthusiasm. As one symbol of this, Russia and China signed two blockbuster-size framework agreements for the supply of natural gas from Russia to China during the next 30 years. These agreements were important for Moscow; they reduce Russia's reliance on Europe and show that Russia is not isolated by financial sanctions imposed by the EU and United States.

VI. BRIDGING CULTURES, BRIDGING DISCIPLINES

This volume should be seen as a product of the discussions between researchers from the Arctic Centre at University of Lapland and from the Research Institute of Environmental Law, University of Wuhan. The core objectives of these exchanges were not only to examine the gradually growing importance of China in Arctic politics from the perspectives of international law and world politics, but also to represent a diversity of perspectives on this particular issue, reflecting the different disciplines and academic cultures through which the authors considered aspects of this broader theme.

While the methodological differences existing between the approaches pursued by lawyers and political scientists are well known, the present volume might also contribute to identifying differences prevailing in the work undertaken by European and Chinese scholars. While being internally heterogeneous, messy, complex and vast, these academic cultures have some peculiar characteristics that make them recognisable at least remotely.

While many European scholars in the fields of law and international relations are often expected to concentrate on analytical research while leaving most normative choices to politicians, Chinese academics may seek to contribute through research to the identification of legal options and opportunities benefiting the country and are often expected to inform its national government. This demand might guide their work, which often looks at the world explicitly from the perspective of China and of the position of the country in the international plane. While the often Eurocentric work of European academics might be more familiar to the readership of this volume, we hope that some of its content might have also enlightened its reader on the traits of a more Chinese-centric perspective on the subject of our research. Perhaps the key difference is in the way that the objectives and purposes of the research are represented and how much they are tied to the interests of a single nation.

The researchers involved in this research project were offered the opportunity throughout the project to encounter, discuss and learn from colleagues belonging to another discipline and another academic culture. Although this did not lead to immediate changes in their worlds, bonds were created, ideas exchanged and seeds for future co-operation planted. The project confirmed many similarities among our perspectives but also helped us, by highlighting cultural differences, to better understand the perspective of our colleagues.

In our book, texts from both academic backgrounds flourish and communicate on their own terms. They speak with each other and other academic texts simply by means of arguments and references. Additionally, they illustrate their academic backgrounds as described above. The reader thus has a possibility to compare them from both perspectives and decide herself what the texts represent and what they do not. All in all, we hope that our book encourages others to engage in intercultural academic projects and discussions. Science is about seeking the best arguments—and also about creating understanding between people and peoples.

VII. CONCLUDING WORDS

Despite references in the public narrative to the persistence or emergence of conflicts in the high north, international law provides clear responses to most questions related to the legal status of areas of the Arctic, or offers processes to deal with these issues in a co-operative manner. Furthermore, the Arctic states have demonstrated their commitment to this normative framework, guaranteeing that the area serves as a space for co-operation that is relatively insulated from geopolitical crises affecting the relations between these eight nations with respect to other regional issues. Under this framework, the vast majority of resources found in the Arctic Ocean are within the jurisdiction of one of the five Arctic coastal states. The regime however also guarantees some rights for third states, for instance in relation to the freedom of navigation. Additionally, the scale of the investments required in relation to many Arctic economic developments provides an incentive for multilateral co-operation, including potentially with the participation of non-Arctic actors.

In this context, many actors lacking direct access to the Arctic Ocean, including countries that are members of the Arctic Council such as Finland as well as more distant actors including China and the EU, have demonstrated an increasing interest in strengthening their participation in Arctic developments. These actors have adopted different approaches to consolidating their position in the region. In Finland, this interest has been translated into the adoption of Arctic strategies expected to strengthen the importance of the Arctic in the country's internal and foreign policies and an emphasis on the 'Arctic Identity' of the country. China has highlighted its experience in conducting Arctic research and has sought economic partnerships with regional actors.[28] The EU has relied on a complex approach, adopting several policy statements relevant to the region and demonstrating its legitimacy in the region by assessing its own contribution to environmental harms impacting the Arctic.[29]

Among Arctic states and Arctic indigenous peoples' organisations, the response to this growing interest has been mixed, with external actors sometimes being given the cold shoulder.[30] The opposition of some regional actors to the EU ban on the import of seal fur and the implications of this dispute for the EU's observer status at the Arctic Council demonstrated the need for a truly Arctic sensibility among non-Arctic actors when dealing with such issues.[31] Potential investments by China have also raised suspicions and concerns locally. In this context, the assessment of the different approaches and positions adopted by China, Finland and the EU provides valuable insights as it enables the identification of good practices and challenges among the approaches followed by the three entities.

The decision reached at the 2013 Kiruna ministerial meeting to admit new observers to the Arctic Council provided a formal acknowledgement of these developments as major international actors were formally offered the opportunity to contribute to the work of the council. Since this decision, several other members of the international community have expressed interest in contributing as observers to the proceedings of the Arctic Council. With the increasing number of observers, and the growing diversity among these actors, any lessons on effective and responsible involvement in Arctic governance could be useful in order for those relative newcomers to benefit from the lessons gained from the experience of other observers.

[28] See Heininen in this volume, Ch 6.

[29] See eg A Airoldi, *European Union and the Arctic: Main Developments July 2008–July 2010* (Copenhagen, Nordic Council of Ministers, 2010).

[30] See eg K Dodds, 'Environment, Resources, and Sovereignty in the Arctic Region: The Arctic Council as Regional Body' (2013) 14(2) *Georgetown Journal of International Affairs* 29, 32.

[31] See K Hossain, 'The EU Ban on the Import of Seal Products and the WTO Regulations: Neglected Human Rights of the Arctic Indigenous Peoples?' (2013) 49(2) *Polar Record* 154.

Index

Note: Alphabetical arrangement is word-by-word, where a group of letters followed by a space is filed before the same group of letters followed by a letter, eg "fish stocks" will appear before "fisheries". In determining alphabetical arrangement, initial articles and prepositions are ignored.

www.ingramcontent.com/pod-product-compliance
Lightning Source LLC
LaVergne TN
LVHW052252200926
848481LV00002B/350
* 9 7 8 1 5 0 9 9 3 0 0 9 8 *